Intelligent Learning Tools, Enhancing Student Skills, and Career Preparedness

Reda Mohamed Said Abdelaal
https://orcid.org/0000-0001-8806-2115
Helwan University, Egypt

Mustafa Kayyali
https://orcid.org/0000-0003-3300-262X
Maaref University of Applied Sciences, Syria

IGI Global Scientific Publishing
Publishing Tomorrow's Research Today

Vice President of Editorial — Melissa Wagner
Director of Acquisitions — Mikaela Felty
Director of Book Development — Jocelynn Hessler
Production Manager — Mike Brehm
Cover Design — Jose Rosado

Published in the United States of America by
IGI Global Scientific Publishing
701 East Chocolate Avenue
Hershey, PA, 17033, USA
Tel: 717-533-8845 | Fax: 717-533-7115
Website: https://www.igi-global.com E-mail: cust@igi-global.com

Library of Congress Cataloging-in-Publication Data

Names: Abdelaal, Reda Mohamed Said, 1956- editor | Kayyali, Mustafa, 1990- editor
Title: Intelligent learning tools, enhancing student skills, and career preparedness / [edited by] Reda Mohamed Said Abdelaal, Mustafa Kayyali.
Description: Hershey, PA : IGI Global Scientific Publishing, [2026] | Includes bibliographical references and index. | Summary: "This book explores the technological advancements in educational landscapes to help equip students in academic development. It examines the innovation and advancements in academia"-- Provided by publisher.
Identifiers: LCCN 2026004862 (print) | LCCN 2026004863 (ebook) | ISBN 9798337392257 hardcover | ISBN 9798337392264 paperback | ISBN 9798337392271 ebook
Subjects: LCSH: Artificial intelligence--Educational applications | Educational technology
Classification: LCC LB1028.44 .I58 2026 (print) | LCC LB1028.44 (ebook)
LC record available at https://lccn.loc.gov/2026004862
LC ebook record available at https://lccn.loc.gov/2026004863

British Cataloguing in Publication Data
A Cataloguing in Publication record for this book is available from the British Library.

Editorial Advisory Board

Table of Contents

Preface xiv

Acknowledgement xix

Introduction xxii

Chapter 1
Revolutionizing Interdisciplinary Education and Research: What Does Artificial Intelligence Do for Humanity? 1
Wasswa Shafik, Dig Connectivity Research Laboratory (DCRLab), Uganda

Chapter 2
The Evolution of AI in Education: A Historical and Technological Overview ... 31
Mustafa Kayyali, Maaref University of Applied Sciences, Syria

Chapter 3
Intelligent Curricula: Personalizing Learning With Artificial Intelligence and Developing Transformative Skills 53
Abílio Lourenço, University of Minho, Portugal
Sabina Valente, Polytechnic Institute of Portalegre, Portugal

Chapter 4
Using AI to Foster Creativity, Critical Thinking, and Innovation in Students ... 89
Panchalingam Suntharalingam, Birmingham City University, UK

Chapter 5
Revolutionizing Mathematics Education With AI-Based Learning Tools: A Synergistic Approach to Pedagogy and Digital Transformation 125
Mahak Bhatia, Poornima Institute of Engineering and Technology, India
Honey Gocher, Amity University, Jaipur, India
Gunjan Verma, Amity University, Jaipur, India
Yudhveer Singh, Amity University, Jaipur, India
Vishal Sharma, Amity University, Jaipur, India

Chapter 6
AI-Enhanced Collaboration and Teamwork in Virtual Learning Environments 149
Syed Mohd Faisal, Malla Reddy Technical Campus, Malla Reddy Vishwavidyapeeth University, Hyderabad, India
Wasim Khan, Symbiosis Institute of Technology, Symbiosis International University, India
Mohammad Ishrat, VIT Bhopal University, Sehore, India

Chapter 7
Levelling Up Learning: Gamification and LEGO-Based Strategies for Coaching and Peer Teaching in Higher Education in the Global South 177
Aradhana Ramnund-Mansingh, University of Free State, South Africa & MANCOSA, South Africa
Gareth Daniel Paul, MANCOSA, South Africa

Chapter 8
Perceptions of ChatGPT-Assisted Writing in the Stages of the Writing Process: An Exploratory Study 219
Jessica Ruiz Quiñonero, University of Murcia, Spain
Aitor Garcés-Manzanera, University of Murcia, Spain

Chapter 9
Perceived Usability, Usefulness, and Satisfaction of Educational Virtual Assistant Chatbots: Teachers' and Students' Perception Study 251
Anil Kumar Nayak, Christ University, India
Ayushi Zina, Christ University, India
Nilesh Kumar, Amity University, Ranchi, India

Chapter 10
The Rise of the Digital Tutor: AI Chatbots and Virtual Assistants in Education 279
Goh Ying Yingsoon, Universiti Teknologi MARA, Malaysia
Liu Wenpang, Teesside University, UK
Zhang Suyan, Shandong Jianzhu University, China
Nurul Ain Chua Binti Abdullah, University Terengganu Malaysia, Malaysia
Nurul Ajleaa Abdul Rahman, Universiti Teknologi MARA, Malaysia

Chapter 11
The Role of Artificial Intelligence in Bridging the Gap Between Academia and Labor Markets 307
Dania Mohammad Waleed Sagheer, Al-Shahbaa Private University, Syria

Compilation of References 343

About the Contributors 395

Index 401

Detailed Table of Contents

Preface xiv

Acknowledgement xix

Introduction xxii

Chapter 1
Revolutionizing Interdisciplinary Education and Research: What Does Artificial Intelligence Do for Humanity? 1
Wasswa Shafik, Dig Connectivity Research Laboratory (DCRLab), Uganda

The study explores the transformative impact of artificial intelligence (AI) on interdisciplinary education and research, highlighting its potential to revolutionize learning and knowledge integration across diverse fields. AI is reshaping educational landscapes by enhancing personalized learning experiences, enabling adaptive teaching methods, and providing powerful tools for researchers. The study examines how AI-driven technologies, such as intelligent tutoring systems, data analytics, and collaborative platforms, break down traditional barriers between disciplines, fostering cross-disciplinary solutions to complex global challenges. Morestill, by leveraging AI, educational institutions and research organizations can create more efficient, dynamic, and inclusive environments that encourage innovation and accelerate progress. Therefore, the study emphasizes the crucial role of AI in shaping the future of education and research, where interdisciplinary collaboration and technological advancements work together to address societal needs and improve outcomes across various sectors.

Chapter 2
The Evolution of AI in Education: A Historical and Technological Overview... 31
Mustafa Kayyali, Maaref University of Applied Sciences, Syria

This chapter traces the evolution of artificial intelligence in education, mapping its trajectory from early computer-assisted instruction to the sophisticated AI systems reshaping today's learning environments. By contextualizing technological progress within historical shifts in pedagogy, it explores how each phase of innovation responded to specific educational needs and social pressures. The discussion critically examines the milestones that led to current AI applications, such as personalized learning platforms, predictive analytics, and virtual teaching assistants. More than a timeline, the chapter reflects on the changing role of educators and the persistent ethical and equity challenges AI introduces. Ultimately, it offers insights into how a historically grounded understanding of AI's development can inform future-proof curriculum strategies that balance innovation with humanistic values.

Chapter 3
Intelligent Curricula: Personalizing Learning With Artificial Intelligence and Developing Transformative Skills.. 53
Abílio Lourenço, University of Minho, Portugal
Sabina Valente, Polytechnic Institute of Portalegre, Portugal

This chapter explores how artificial intelligence can transform curriculum design by personalising learning and supporting the development of essential 21st-century skills. Integrating artificial intelligence into curricula enables adaptive learning environments that respond to individual student needs, promoting equity and improving educational outcomes. The chapter begins by contextualising the growing role of artificial intelligence in education and examining current opportunities and challenges for educators and institutions. It then discusses personalised learning mechanisms, offering examples of how generative artificial intelligence can enhance the student experience. The second section focuses on developing key skills such as critical thinking, collaboration, and digital literacy, showing how they can be integrated into the curriculum with the support of artificial intelligence. Ethical and inclusion issues are also considered to ensure fair and accessible implementation.

Chapter 4
Using AI to Foster Creativity, Critical Thinking, and Innovation in Students ... 89
Panchalingam Suntharalingam, Birmingham City University, UK

Artificial Intelligence (AI) is reshaping education by fostering creativity, critical thinking, and innovation among students. AI-powered tools support content creation, personalised learning, and collaborative ideation, enabling students to explore novel ideas. In critical thinking development, AI aids in data analysis, argumentation, and gamified learning, sharpening students' reasoning skills. Additionally, AI nurtures innovation through STEM education, entrepreneurship, and research, preparing students for future challenges. However, ethical considerations such as bias, data privacy, and balancing AI with human interaction must be addressed. The future of AI in education promises advancements like virtual tutors, immersive learning, and AI-assisted career guidance. By responsibly integrating AI, educators can enhance student learning experiences and equip them with essential skills for the evolving world.

Chapter 5
Revolutionizing Mathematics Education With AI-Based Learning Tools: A Synergistic Approach to Pedagogy and Digital Transformation 125
Mahak Bhatia, Poornima Institute of Engineering and Technology, India
Honey Gocher, Amity University, Jaipur, India
Gunjan Verma, Amity University, Jaipur, India
Yudhveer Singh, Amity University, Jaipur, India
Vishal Sharma, Amity University, Jaipur, India

Mathematics has always played a pivotal role in education, contributing significantly to the intellectual development of learners by fostering analytical reasoning, logical thinking, and problem-solving abilities. Despite its importance, mathematics is often perceived as one of the most challenging subjects by both students and educators. However, mathematics is undergoing a radical transformation. When paired with advancements in Artificial Intelligence (AI), this ancient system of learning can be revitalized into a powerful learning tool. AI has already transformed many aspects of education, including mathematics. This proposed book chapter explores this convergence, offering a holistic, interdisciplinary perspective on integrating AI and Vedic mathematics into contemporary mathematics education, also presents real-world case studies from Indian and global contexts where such innovations have been applied. It examines how intuitive, mental-math techniques, when coupled with data-driven technologies, transforms the teaching and understanding of mathematics across educational levels.

Chapter 6
AI-Enhanced Collaboration and Teamwork in Virtual Learning Environments 149
Syed Mohd Faisal, Malla Reddy Technical Campus, Malla Reddy Vishwavidyapeeth University, Hyderabad, India
Wasim Khan, Symbiosis Institute of Technology, Symbiosis International University, India
Mohammad Ishrat, VIT Bhopal University, Sehore, India

Artificial Intelligence (AI) offers transformative potential for enhancing collaboration and teamwork in Virtual Learning Environments (VLEs). Leveraging techniques such as Natural Language Processing, Reinforcement Learning, Recommender Systems, and Sentiment Analysis, AI systems facilitate intelligent group formation, dynamic role allocation, adaptive scaffolding, and early conflict detection. Grounded in educational psychology and systems engineering, this work synthesizes theoretical frameworks with empirical applications from platforms like Coursera, IBM Watson Tutor, and Microsoft Teams. Key ethical concerns—algorithmic bias, data privacy, and instructional control are critically examined, with mitigation strategies proposed through Explainable AI and Federated Learning. Emerging directions include immersive metaverse-based collaboration, neuroadaptive feedback systems, and hybrid AI–human facilitation architectures. The findings contribute to the development of equitable, scalable, and pedagogically aligned AI-enhanced collaborative learning ecosystems.

Chapter 7
Levelling Up Learning: Gamification and LEGO-Based Strategies for Coaching and Peer Teaching in Higher Education in the Global South 177
Aradhana Ramnund-Mansingh, University of Free State, South Africa & MANCOSA, South Africa
Gareth Daniel Paul, MANCOSA, South Africa

Coaching and peer teaching are essential student skills that foster collaboration, leadership, and interpersonal communication while enhancing the quality and depth of individual learning and group dynamics. Despite their significance, innovative methods for cultivating these competencies remain underexplored in the Global South, particularly in resource-deficient educational contexts. This study examines gamification and concepts like LEGO Serious Play as engaging, flexible, and bespoke learning tools to foster coaching and peer teaching skills, emphasising their transformative impact on academic performance and personal growth. The research employs a secondary desktop study to analyse existing literature and case studies on experiential learning, gamified education, and hands-on approaches, such as LEGO-based learning. Data was collected using the PRISMA method and systematically appraised using the Critical Appraisal Skills Programme (CASP) framework to ensure methodological rigour and comprehensive evaluation. Findings are synthesised to identify effective strategies, enablers, and barriers to skill development. Results show that gamification, achieved through rewards, leaderboards, and interactive challenges, enhances student motivation, engagement, and collaboration. Similarly, Lego provides a tactile and creative medium for simulating real-world problem-solving and teamwork, enabling students to practice coaching and peer teaching dynamically and experientially. Participants engaging in these methods reported increased confidence, critical thinking, and facilitation skills. However, challenges such as unequal access to resources and initial scepticism towards unconventional methods were observed. This study highlights the importance of incorporating gamified learning and LEGO-based activities into higher education curricula. Institutions can nurture a culture of shared learning and mutual growth by preparing students for academic and professional success. The findings contribute to the growing literature on peer learning, offering practical recommendations for scalable and context-sensitive interventions to effectively cultivate coaching and peer teaching skills in diverse educational environments.

Chapter 8
Perceptions of ChatGPT-Assisted Writing in the Stages of the Writing Process: An Exploratory Study 219
Jessica Ruiz Quiñonero, University of Murcia, Spain
Aitor Garcés-Manzanera, University of Murcia, Spain

Artificial intelligence chatbots have recently drawn considerable attention for their potential to revolutionise education systems in myriad ways. Notwithstanding the growing interest in examining the use of chatbots in Foreign Language Teaching (FLT), research on Chatbot-Assisted Writing remains scarce. This study explores how 16 first-year upper secondary students from a Spanish high school interact with ChatGPT while writing an argumentative essay. Specifically, it gathers perceptions about the impact of this tool on the main stages of the Writing Process, namely Planning, Translating, and Reviewing. For this purpose, data on students' interactions with the tool, written essays, and responses to two different questionnaires were collected. Findings revealed that students predominantly used the chatbot for Planning, particularly when they lacked ideas or arguments. Consequently, their overall perceptions after completing the Chatbot-Assisted Writing Task were remarkably positive, suggesting that learners value their use in education and FLT.

Chapter 9
Perceived Usability, Usefulness, and Satisfaction of Educational Virtual Assistant Chatbots: Teachers' and Students' Perception Study 251
Anil Kumar Nayak, Christ University, India
Ayushi Zina, Christ University, India
Nilesh Kumar, Amity University, Ranchi, India

Artificial Intelligence (AI) is changing education with tools like chatbots and virtual assistants. These tools provide personalized support and make academic tasks easier. This study examines how teachers and students view chatbot usability, usefulness, and satisfaction in different educational settings. The researcher used a quantitative survey design and collected data from 238 participants across various institutions and fields. The results are promising. About 59.2% of participants found chatbots easy to use. Additionally, 78.2% said these tools helped them work more efficiently, and 79% reported having positive experiences. ChatGPT and Grammarly were the most commonly used platforms. While the overall opinions were positive, the study highlights the need for organized integration, ethical guidelines, and training to improve engagement and learning results. These findings indicate that educational chatbots are not just trends; they are becoming vital parts of modern teaching, suggesting ways to create more inclusive and adaptable learning environments.

Chapter 10
The Rise of the Digital Tutor: AI Chatbots and Virtual Assistants in Education 279
Goh Ying Yingsoon, Universiti Teknologi MARA, Malaysia
Liu Wenpang, Teesside University, UK
Zhang Suyan, Shandong Jianzhu University, China
Nurul Ain Chua Binti Abdullah, University Terengganu Malaysia, Malaysia
Nurul Ajleaa Abdul Rahman, Universiti Teknologi MARA, Malaysia

This chapter delves into the burgeoning role of AI chatbots and virtual assistants within the educational landscape. As artificial intelligence continues to advance, these tools are increasingly being integrated into classrooms and online learning environments, promising to revolutionize how students learn and educators teach. This chapter will explore the various applications of AI chatbots and virtual assistants in education, including personalized learning, automated feedback, 24/7 student support, and the creation of immersive learning experiences. It will discuss the benefits and challenges associated with their implementation, such as improved student engagement, accessibility, and efficiency, while also addressing concerns regarding data privacy, algorithmic bias, and the potential impact on human interaction. Finally, it will explore the future trajectory of AI in education, considering the ethical and pedagogical implications of these technologies and their potential to reshape the future of learning.

Chapter 11
The Role of Artificial Intelligence in Bridging the Gap Between Academia and Labor Markets 307
Dania Mohammad Waleed Sagheer, Al-Shahbaa Private University, Syria

This chapter investigates the persistent gap between academic education and labor market demands, using theoretical frameworks and empirical studies to analyze its underlying causes. A conceptual model defines the scope of the mismatch, highlighting structural barriers such as outdated curricula and limited industry engagement. The chapter introduces artificial intelligence (AI) and data science as potential tools to bridge this gap, showcasing applications like predictive analytics and intelligent recommendation systems. International and regional case studies demonstrate how AI technologies can help align educational outcomes with job requirements. A localized example from Syria illustrates a hypothetical data-driven approach to enhance graduate employability. The chapter concludes by outlining implementation challenges and offering policy recommendations. Overall, it advocates for strategic collaboration between academia and industry to develop AI-supported, skill-based learning environments responsive to evolving workforce needs.

Compilation of References 343

About the Contributors 395

Index 401

Preface

Artificial intelligence and intelligent learning tools are reshaping the foundations of education, equipping students with adaptive skills and preparing them for evolving career landscapes. *Intelligent Learning Tools, Enhancing Student Skills, and Career Preparedness* bring together global perspectives that demonstrate how AI-powered platforms, personalized tutoring systems, and data-driven analytics transform pedagogy, curriculum design, and student engagement. The chapters highlight innovations in creativity, critical thinking, collaboration, and workforce readiness, while also addressing ethical concerns, equity, and institutional challenges. By combining case studies, theoretical insights, and practical strategies, this volume serves as both a scholarly reference and a pragmatic guide, showing how intelligent learning tools can empower students to thrive academically and professionally in an AI-driven world.

In the modern world, intelligent learning tools occupy a central position in the transformation of education and workforce development. As economies shift toward automation, data-driven decision-making, and AI-powered industries, schools and universities face the urgent challenge of preparing students with adaptable skills, critical thinking, and career readiness. Intelligent tutoring systems, virtual assistants, and AI-driven analytics are not only reshaping classrooms but also bridge the gap between academic learning and labor market demands. These tools fit into global priorities such as digital equity, lifelong learning, and sustainable employability, ensuring that students are equipped to thrive in rapidly evolving professional environments. By aligning pedagogy with technological innovation, intelligent learning tools have become essential to building inclusive, future-ready societies.

This book is intended for educators, trainers, and curriculum designers who are actively seeking ways to integrate intelligent learning tools into teaching and skill development. It also speaks to higher education leaders and policymakers who are shaping strategies for career preparedness in an AI-driven economy. Researchers and graduate students will find valuable case studies and theoretical insights that connect pedagogy with emerging technologies, while industry partners and workforce development specialists can explore how intelligent tools align academic learning with professional demands. By engaging these audiences, the volume provides both scholarly depth and practical guidance, positioning intelligent learning tools as essential instruments for enhancing student skills and bridging the transition from education to career readiness.

CHAPTER OVERVIEW

Chapter 1: Revolutionizing Interdisciplinary Education and Research: What Does Artificial Intelligence for Humanity?

Wasswa Shafik explores AI's transformative role in interdisciplinary education and research. His chapter highlights how intelligent tutoring systems, analytics, and collaborative platforms break down barriers between disciplines, fostering cross-disciplinary solutions to global challenges. By enabling adaptive teaching and personalized learning, AI creates dynamic, inclusive environments that accelerate innovation and societal progress.

Chapter 2: The Evolution of AI in Education: A Historical and Technological Overview

Mustafa Kayyali charts the evolution of AI in education, from early computer-assisted instruction to today's advanced learning technologies. It links each innovation to shifting pedagogical needs and societal pressures, examining milestones like personalized platforms and predictive analytics. The chapter reflects on the changing role of educators and ongoing ethical and equity concerns. It concludes by advocating for historically informed curriculum strategies that balance technological advancement with humanistic values.

Chapter 3: Intelligent Curricula: Personalizing Learning with Artificial Intelligence and Developing Transformative Skills

Abílio Lourenço examines how AI reshapes curriculum design by personalizing learning and embedding 21st-century skills. His chapter discusses adaptive environments that respond to individual needs, integrating critical thinking, collaboration, and digital literacy. Ethical and inclusion issues are addressed to ensure equitable access, while generative AI examples illustrate how curricula can be transformed to improve outcomes.

Chapter 4: Using AI to Foster Creativity, Critical Thinking, and Innovation in Students

Panchalingam Suntharalingam emphasizes AI's potential to nurture creativity, reasoning, and innovation. His chapter shows how AI supports content creation, gamified learning, and collaborative ideation, sharpening students' problem-solving skills. Applications in STEM, entrepreneurship, and research prepare learners for future challenges, while ethical concerns such as bias and privacy are critically examined.

Chapter 5: Revolutionizing Mathematics Education with AI-Based Learning Tools: A Synergistic Approach to Pedagogy and Digital Transformation

Honey Gocher explores how AI revitalizes mathematics education by combining Vedic math techniques with data-driven technologies. Her chapter presents case studies from India and beyond, showing how AI enhances problem-solving, logical reasoning, and analytical skills. This interdisciplinary approach demonstrates how AI can transform mathematics into a more engaging and accessible subject.

Chapter 6: AI-Enhanced Collaboration and Teamwork in Virtual Learning Environments

Syed Mohd Faisal examines AI's role in strengthening collaboration in virtual learning environments. His chapter discusses NLP, recommender systems, and sentiment analysis for intelligent group formation and conflict detection. Ethical concerns are addressed through explainable AI and federated learning. Emerging directions include metaverse-based collaboration and neuroadaptive feedback systems.

Chapter 7: Levelling Up Learning: Gamification and LEGO-Based Strategies for Coaching and Peer Teaching in Higher Education

Aradhana Ramnund-Mansingh investigates gamification and LEGO Serious Play as tools for coaching and peer teaching. Her chapter shows how these methods enhance motivation, teamwork, and critical thinking. Students reported increased confidence and facilitation skills, though challenges such as resource access and skepticism remain. The study highlights creative methods for student skill development.

Chapter 8: Perceptions of ChatGPT-Assisted Writing in the Stages of the Writing Process: An Exploratory Study

Jessica Ruiz Quiñonero explores how secondary students in Spain used ChatGPT during essay writing. Her study reveals students relied on the chatbot mainly for planning, generating ideas, and arguments. Overall perceptions were positive, suggesting learners value chatbot assistance in foreign language teaching and writing processes, particularly for brainstorming and structuring.

Chapter 9: Perceived Usability, Usefulness & Satisfaction of Educational Virtual Assistant Chatbots: Teachers' and Students' Perception Study

Anil Kumar Nayak presents survey findings from 238 participants on chatbot usability and satisfaction. His chapter shows that most found chatbots are easy to use and beneficial for efficiency. Tools like ChatGPT and Grammarly were widely adopted. While perceptions were positive, he stressed the need for ethical guidelines, structured integration, and training.

Chapter 10: The Rise of the Digital Tutor: AI Chatbots and Virtual Assistants in Education

Goh Ying Yingsoon analyzes the growing role of AI chatbots and virtual assistants in personalized learning and student support. Her chapter highlights benefit such as automated feedback and accessibility, while raising concerns about privacy and human interaction. She projects future trajectories of immersive, ethical AI tutors reshaping educational experiences.

Chapter 11: The Role of Artificial Intelligence in Bridging the Gap Between Academia and Labor Markets

Dania Mohammad Waleed Sagheer investigates how AI can align academic outcomes with labor market needs. Her chapter introduces predictive analytics and recommendation systems to reduce mismatches. Case studies illustrate global and regional applications, including a localized Syrian example. She concludes with policy recommendations for academia-industry collaboration and skill-based learning.

In conclusion, *Intelligent Learning Tools, Enhancing Student Skills, and Career Preparedness* make a significant contribution to the evolving discourse on artificial intelligence in education by demonstrating how intelligent systems can enhance student learning, foster critical skills, and bridge the transition from academia to the workforce. Through its diverse chapters, the book highlights innovations in pedagogy, curriculum design, collaboration, and career readiness, while also addressing ethical concerns and institutional challenges. By combining global case studies with practical strategies, it impacts the field by offering both scholarly depth and actionable guidance. Ultimately, the volume positions intelligent learning tools not merely as technological enhancements but as catalysts for building inclusive, future-ready educational ecosystems that empower students to thrive in an AI-driven world.

Reda M.S. Abdelaal
Former Professor, Helwan University, Egypt

Mustafa Kayyali
Maaref University of Applied Sciences, Syria

Acknowledgement

To be conscious that you are ignorant is a great step to knowledge — Benjamin Disraeli

My enduring appreciation goes to *Helwan University*, the institution where my academic path first took shape and where I learned to approach knowledge with rigor, curiosity, and purpose. The university's culture of perseverance and its commitment to advancing higher education laid the groundwork for my professional values. The formative experiences I gained there continue to influence my thinking, my scholarship, and my dedication to strengthening educational systems.

I am equally grateful to *King Abdulaziz University*, where I served as a Professor of Industrial Engineering and worked closely with senior leadership on strategic initiatives. My time there broadened my understanding of institutional development and exposed me to ambitious, forward-looking projects that enriched my academic and administrative perspectives. The trust extended to me by the university's leadership and the collaborative spirit of its academic community played a significant role in shaping my approach to innovation and educational transformation.

My sincere thanks extend to *AlMaarefa University*, where I had the opportunity to advise the University President and contribute to major developmental efforts across the institution. My participation in the establishment of the Industrial Engineering Department remains a highlight of my engagement there, reflecting the university's commitment to growth and national advancement. The supportive environment and the shared dedication to building strong academic structures made my work both meaningful and impactful.

Above all, I owe my deepest gratitude to my family—*my wife, Fatma Shafik, my daughter, Sarah, and my son, Ahmed*—whose unwavering love, patience, and support sustained me at every stage of this journey. Their belief in my work, their sacrifices, and their constant encouragement have been the anchor that allowed me to pursue ambitious ideas with confidence and purpose. This book is as much theirs as it is mine, a testament to the strength, unity, and inspiration that only family can provide.

Reda M.S. Abdelaal

Former Professor, Helwan University, Egypt

****

This book grew slowly, the way serious work usually does—through discipline, revisions, second thoughts, and the steady insistence that ideas must be refined before they are shared. But behind that process, there was something even more important: support. Not the temporary kind, but the kind that stays consistent across stress, deadlines, and the fatigue that comes when you try to do meaningful work while still carrying the weight of everyday responsibilities. For that reason, I want these acknowledgements to read as a true dedication, not a routine paragraph.

To my colleagues at *Maaref University of Applied Sciences*, I offer my sincere thanks and dedicate this book to you. Your support took many forms—some direct and visible, others quiet and unspoken—but all of them mattered. There were times when the workload was intense and the expectations were high, yet you continued to show professionalism, teamwork, and patience. You made space for progress, you protected the spirit of collaboration, and you reminded me that institutions do not rise because of slogans; they rise because of people who care about quality, about responsibility, and about the reputation of the work they represent. I am grateful not only for what you did, but for the spirit in which you did it. That spirit, for me, is one of the most valuable assets an academic community can have.

I also dedicate this book to the *Board of HE Higher Education Ranking*. Your inspiration has been a guiding force in shaping my thinking about evaluation, performance, and academic impact. You helped me see how measurement can be meaningful when it is built on fairness, transparency, and a genuine commitment to improvement. You also reminded me that higher education needs systems that encourage institutions to become better versions of themselves—not systems that reward visibility at the expense of substance. The board's conversations, standards, and ambition influenced the way I approached this book: pushing me to aim for depth, to treat evidence seriously, and to keep the bigger purpose in view.

To my family, I offer the kind of gratitude that cannot be fully written. To my father, *Abdullah Kayyali*, thank you for your guidance and for the values that shaped my character long before my career took shape. Your example taught me endurance, humility, and the importance of building a name through integrity rather than words. To my wife, *Noura Abduljalil*, thank you for being my anchor. You carried the emotional and practical weight that often comes with a partner's demanding commitments. Your patience was not passive—it was an active kind of support, the kind that allows someone else to keep moving forward without guilt or instability. I am deeply thankful for your love and your presence.

And to my angels—*Abdullah Junior (this first dedication is for you)*—you are my most intimate reason to keep striving. You have made me think about legacy not as a title or recognition, but as the quality of what we leave behind in the minds and hearts of those we love. May this book be a small reflection of that intention: to value knowledge, to share it with responsibility, and to build something that serves others.

Tired of chasing roads that never end, I ask for peace.
Rest feels like a country my feet can't reach anymore.
All I want is a simple life that doesn't demand I bleed.
Even my hope is exhausted, folded thin in my hands.
How long can a heart keep walking without a home?
Year after year, I search for a way that won't break me.
My dreams have grown quiet—like candles in the wind.
Every step I take, I beg the noise to soften.
Voices of the world are loud, but none say "stay."
I am looking for a path that leads to calm, not conquest.
Giving up the fight sounds less like failure, more like mercy.
Down in my chest, the fatigue has learned my name.
Life keeps asking for more, and I have less to offer.
Under all this effort, I only want to breathe.
On my knees in the dark, I trade answers for silence.
Would someone show me a doorway where peace begins?
I would give my heart just to live without war inside.

Mustafa Kayyali

Maaref University of Applied Sciences, Syria

Introduction

Artificial intelligence and intelligent learning tools are reshaping the foundations of education, equipping students with adaptive skills and preparing them for evolving career landscapes. The accelerating pace of technological change has made it clear that traditional models of teaching and learning are no longer sufficient to meet the demands of the twenty-first century. *Intelligent Learning Tools, Enhancing Student Skills, and Career Preparedness* brings together global perspectives that demonstrate how AI-powered platforms, personalized tutoring systems, and data-driven analytics are transforming pedagogy, curriculum design, and student engagement. The chapters highlight innovations in creativity, critical thinking, collaboration, and workforce readiness, while also addressing ethical concerns, equity, and institutional challenges. By combining case studies, theoretical insights, and practical strategies, this volume serves as both a scholarly reference and a pragmatic guide, showing how intelligent learning tools can empower students to thrive academically and professionally in an AI-driven world.

In the modern world, intelligent learning tools occupy a central position in the transformation of education and workforce development. As economies shift toward automation, data-driven decision-making, and AI-powered industries, schools and universities face the urgent challenge of preparing students with adaptable skills, critical thinking, and career readiness. Intelligent tutoring systems, virtual assistants, and AI-driven analytics are not only reshaping classrooms but also bridging the gap between academic learning and labor market demands. These tools fit into global priorities such as digital equity, lifelong learning, and sustainable employability, ensuring that students are equipped to thrive in rapidly evolving professional environments. By aligning pedagogy with technological innovation, intelligent learning tools have become essential to building inclusive, future-ready societies.

The chapters in this book reflect a wide range of scholarly voices, each contributing unique insights into the evolving relationship between AI and education. Together, they highlight the opportunities and challenges that arise when intelligent systems are embedded into teaching, learning, and career preparation. From personalized learning environments and adaptive curricula to faculty development and workforce integration, the book provides a panoramic view of the ways AI is transforming education. At its core, this work emphasizes that intelligent learning tools are not simply technological enhancements but catalysts for rethinking the very foundations of how students acquire skills, how educators design learning experiences, and how institutions prepare graduates for professional success. By integrating AI into these processes, schools and universities can foster more inclusive, adaptive, and future-ready ecosystems. Yet, as the chapters demonstrate, this transformation must be accompanied by careful attention to issues of ethics, equity, and human values, ensuring that technological progress aligns with the broader mission of education.

This book is intended for educators, trainers, and curriculum designers who are actively seeking ways to integrate intelligent learning tools into teaching and skill development. It also speaks to higher education leaders and policymakers who are shaping strategies for career preparedness in an AI-driven economy. Researchers and graduate students will find valuable case studies and theoretical insights that connect pedagogy with emerging technologies, while industry partners and workforce development specialists can explore how intelligent tools align academic learning with professional demands. By engaging these audiences, the volume provides both scholarly depth and practical guidance, positioning intelligent learning tools as essential instruments for enhancing student skills and bridging the transition from education to career readiness.

The contributions span a wide range of disciplines and contexts, from interdisciplinary education and STEM innovation to humanities, management, and workforce integration. They demonstrate how AI can foster creativity, critical thinking, and collaboration, while also raising critical questions about overreliance, ethical governance, and equitable access. By situating intelligent learning tools within diverse educational settings, the book underscores their universal relevance while acknowledging the importance of cultural and institutional specificity. Each chapter offers not only theoretical insights but also practical strategies, ensuring that readers can translate ideas into action within their own contexts.

In conclusion, *Intelligent Learning Tools, Enhancing Student Skills, and Career Preparedness* makes a significant contribution to the evolving discourse on artificial intelligence in education by demonstrating how intelligent systems can enhance student learning, foster critical skills, and bridge the transition from academia to the workforce. Through its diverse chapters, the book highlights innovations in pedagogy, curriculum design, collaboration, and career readiness, while also addressing ethical concerns and institutional challenges. By combining global case studies with practical strategies, it impacts the field by offering both scholarly depth and actionable guidance. Ultimately, the volume positions intelligent learning tools not merely as technological enhancements but as catalysts for building inclusive, future-ready educational ecosystems that empower students to thrive in an AI-driven world.

Reda M.S. Abdelaal
Helwan University, Egypt

Mustafa Kayyali
Maaref University of Applied Sciences, Syria

Chapter 1
Revolutionizing Interdisciplinary Education and Research: What Does Artificial Intelligence Do for Humanity?

Wasswa Shafik
https://orcid.org/0000-0002-9320-3186
Dig Connectivity Research Laboratory (DCRLab), Uganda

ABSTRACT

The study explores the transformative impact of artificial intelligence (AI) on interdisciplinary education and research, highlighting its potential to revolutionize learning and knowledge integration across diverse fields. AI is reshaping educational landscapes by enhancing personalized learning experiences, enabling adaptive teaching methods, and providing powerful tools for researchers. The study examines how AI-driven technologies, such as intelligent tutoring systems, data analytics, and collaborative platforms, break down traditional barriers between disciplines, fostering cross-disciplinary solutions to complex global challenges. Morestill, by leveraging AI, educational institutions and research organizations can create more efficient, dynamic, and inclusive environments that encourage innovation and accelerate progress. Therefore, the study emphasizes the crucial role of AI in shaping the future of education and research, where interdisciplinary collaboration and technological advancements work together to address societal needs and improve outcomes across various sectors.

DOI: 10.4018/979-8-3373-9225-7.ch001

1. INTRODUCTION

Artificial intelligence can, in fact, revolutionize interdisciplinary education and research. As technology continues to become increasingly pervasive in all aspects of human life, learning institutions have also come to realize the necessity of fusing technological artifacts and the powers of technological realms into the fabric of scholastic discourse (Rusydiana, 2024). The traditional canons of pedagogy and curricular developments in universities and colleges need to be reconstructed in order to forge powerful cross-disciplinary platforms for social issues and problem-solving. Responding to those technological demands, this paper importantly starts its exploration of innovative educational and research methodologies by considering the power of AI (O'Brien & Davenport, 2024). The root rationale for this choice is that AI technology represents the current evolution from earlier instruments of human cognition.

Thus, it is the power of the AI universe and its technological artifacts that educational institutions must adapt themselves to in order to head off the criticism that they are divorced from the scholarly requirements of society. The body of the chapter is subdivided into several sections that would illuminate the ways AI technology can impact interdisciplinary education and research (Mohammed & Hossain, 2024). These include the intersection of AI technologies with disciplines, transformative learning and critical thinking, fostering creativity and innovation, an analysis of AI's capabilities and limitations vis-à-vis interdisciplinary education, and recommendations. In each section, our point of departure will be broader contemporary interests, such as critical analytic intelligence, creative adaptation, cross-disciplinary project-based learning, and the innovative capacities that have been redefined in diverse sectors, to illustrate the practical dimensions of philosophical concerns and the concrete relevance of this discussion (Kurti et al., 2024).

A revolution is taking place in the world of work, driven by phenomena such as automation, robotization, artificial intelligence, virtualization, big data, augmented reality, and the Internet of Things. This revolution, often referred to as the Fourth Industrial Revolution, is characterized by the increasing use of machines and systems to replace a multitude of tasks currently being performed by humans. Nonetheless, there is still no consensus on what the future of work will look like. It is expected, however, that the labor skills required by industries in the future will involve the ethical regulation and programming of robots and the establishment of a synergy between human beings and machines (Bull & Kharrufa, 2024). In the field of education, the creation of useful, imaginative, and conscientious human beings who could coexist peacefully and responsibly with other conscious entities on a habitable planet is widely accepted as a priority. Throughout history, educational principles and approaches have always been systemic and here-and-now methodologies, adapted to the moment and subject matter under consideration. Despite their impelling context, educational principles have been gradually accelerated by means of accumulated knowledge. The spread of education is often linked to the extensions of knowledge generation, validation, and storage. Several transformations in education have been influenced by mechanical and digital technological phenomena, such as the industrial machines of the eighteenth and nineteenth centuries, which led to the appearance of new school subjects (Alam & Mohanty, 2024). The evolution of these subjects continues to take place, given the scientific and technological advancements. At present, education is subject to continuing technological mutations leading to increasingly strong curricular integration and interdisciplinary approaches. Ultimately, the irruption of AI is a new and exciting game-changer that raises expectations about its potential impact on both education and society as a whole. Despite encouraging learning environments in educational systems, teachers and other educators work in ordinary classrooms in both formal and informal networks. Interdisciplinary knowledge flows take place throughout scholarship and research, mapping concepts through AI techniques, as categorized in Figure 1 (Shafik, 2024d).

Figure 1. Categories of artificial intelligence

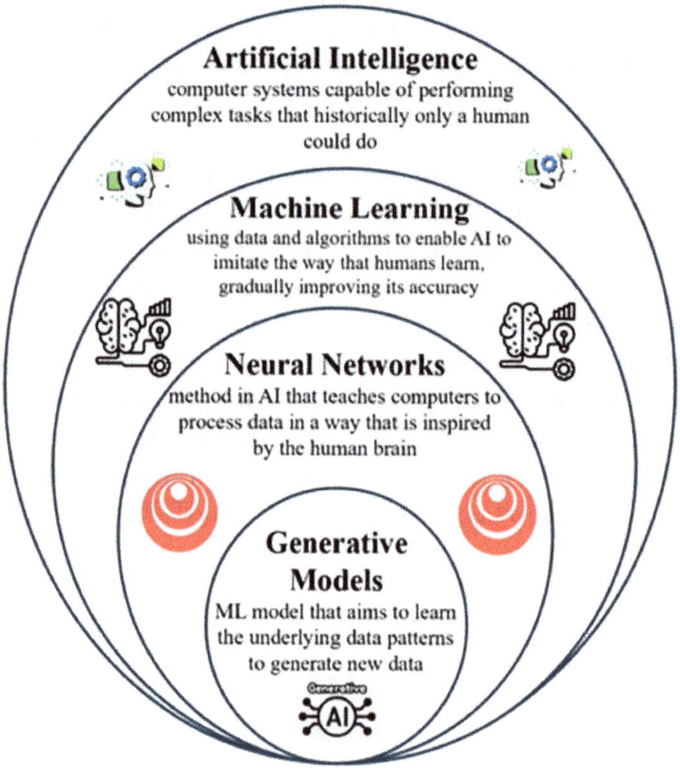

The definitive impact of artificial intelligence (AI) on interdisciplinary education and research will have significant implications not only in India but also in the global arena. The proposed essay concentrates on the extensive investigation of AI's impact on interdisciplinary education. The objective of the chapter is to develop an understanding of how AI can potentially stimulate a revolutionary effect in education. While understanding the influence of AI on interdisciplinary education, it is essential to measure the effectiveness of AI applications for optimizing teaching methodologies, enhancing learning activities, and adopting new and effective research procedures or methodologies (Abubakari et al., 2024b). A prime aim of this paper, thus, is to assess how the application of AI can intensify educational outcomes. The study also aims to examine prospective opportunities and complications that arise as a result of such advancements. A comprehensive exploration of ethical concerns related to AI's application in education and learning has been carried out. Furthermore, this paper presents current scenarios of how AI has contributed to making progress in several educational sectors. This essay's intended audience is both students and researchers who are enthusiastic about exploiting the potential of AI to transform interdisciplinary education. By focusing on their opportunities and potential for realizing them, it intends to establish how AI could revolutionize interdisciplinary education and contribute to the expansion of the perimeter of our thoughts (Abubakari et al., 2024a).

2. FOUNDATIONS OF INTERDISCIPLINARY EDUCATION

The growing importance of interdisciplinary thinking in complex and emergent situations, now joined by interest in meeting societal challenges, has led to an equally growing interest in interdisciplinary methods in education. This interest is seen across a wide range of educational institutions. Interdisciplinary education also challenges current educational systems with their silos. The new generation of students applies for higher education with societal challenges in mind, and they expect to graduate with an integrative perspective on these challenges. As researchers, we apply a part of the collected knowledge to solve societal challenges, and so we need interdisciplinary and transdisciplinary research (Abubakari et al., 2024a). There are a number of terms to describe these new forms of education associated with different histories, which we could, therefore, use to frame our definitions. We could describe a range of forms of learning and research not based on traditional disciplinary divisions. Each of these forms involves the continued existence of disciplines within a whole structure; thus, we could describe them as forms of multi-focus education. Alternatively, each of the forms we are writing about could be a way of dealing with the limitations and biases of disciplines, and we might prefer to use the term 'interdisciplinary practice' to describe these new efforts. Since most of the literature is about interdisciplinary education, we find it most useful to use the word 'interdisciplinary' as a catch-all term (Shafik, 2024a). The growing knowledge economy and information age rely increasingly on new technologies, with an emphasis on artificial intelligence.

2.1. Definition and Conceptual Framework

One easy definition of interdisciplinary is “two scholars talking to each other.” While our summarization will go beyond such a conceptually succinct discussion, this somewhat glib description provides the impetus for employing an interdisciplinary approach, which can offer creativity and thinking from multiple perspectives. Interdisciplinary approaches utilize varying branches of knowledge to provide solutions to complex situations. The combining of disciplines considers and uses different disciplinary perspectives for problem framing and seeks to bring these perspectives together to provide a better understanding of the situation being faced (Shafik, 2024c). Interdisciplinary learning seeks to teach the process of thinking and research using a variety of ways of knowing. Learning based on real-world problem solving, using a variety of expertise tools, is creative and rewards critical thinking skills. Interdisciplinary learning practices should cultivate the cross-pollination of ways of knowing, resources, and theoretical perspectives from all disciplines involved in meaningful projects of overt significance, availing several applications as presented in Figure 2.

Figure 2. Applications of Artificial Intelligence

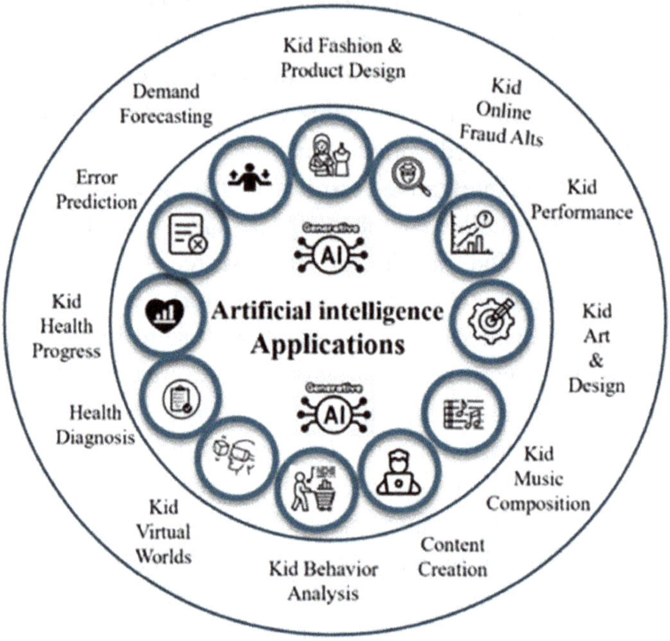

It should be noted that the boundaries of interdisciplinarity are fluid enough to be found in many environmental areas already happening. This allows for project-based courses that connect looping cycles of knowing, doing, and learning. At its most, configuration requires collaboration among team members (in this case, team members can be staff, students, mentors, and project sponsors). These teams, in turn, are connected to a broader system where they are required to integrate and apply knowledge across a range of disciplines or fields of study. Ten process practices, or "ethical principles and supportive practices," that support integrative learning, are important to considering the implementation and implications of integrating AI in the classroom (Rusydiana, 2024). Therefore, "interdisciplinary learning," "multidisciplinary," "cross-disciplinary," or "trans-disciplinary" are similar terms used interchangeably. Interdisciplinary learning seeks to recognize and problem-solve from a variety of viewpoints. This framework situates interdisciplinary education as a way to tackle real-life problems comprehensively. This subsection's definition reaches from educational thought into common practice. As human affairs integrate multiple factors, so can learning through multiple disciplines. Interdisciplinary learning has, at its most fundamental nature, a practical connection to 'real world' issues. Integration and collaboration in learning (Mohammed & Hossain, 2024): Students synthesize their study of biology, business, and ethics to create a project for a pharmaceutical company that desired local biological and business expertise in Latin America. A conceptual framework that provides an encompassing lens through which to understand interdisciplinary education is a growing pedagogical practice that defies any single, easily understood definition. While various definitions suggest the consolidation or combination of a variety of disciplines, the exciting potential for this approach derives from the combination of disciplinary points of view and essentially divergent and unique ways of knowing (Bull & Kharrufa, 2024).

2.2. Historical Evolution

In order to grasp interdisciplinary education as we know it today, it is imperative to set the historical background into which the concept is formed. Some have perceived interdisciplinary education as an innovation in the contemporary world, underpinned by such trends as advanced communication technology. However, interdisciplinary study has evolved deeply rooted in a complex reaction between the acceleration of societal development and technological advancement. History's lessons can remind us that interdisciplinary education has always been aligned with issue-driven initiatives, triggered as responses to pressing societal issues, of which AI is now considered the main driving technology. Significantly, interdisciplinary strategies have a long-lasting integrative dimension that can reconcile structures of alienation, thus linking with efforts of curriculum innovations and life-world connections in education (Sharma, 2024). This section completes its focus on how interdisciplinarity offers the solution to complex societal, economic, technological, and environmental challenges by learning from past lessons. Consequently, breathtaking improvements in information technology raise concerns and create urgent needs for a broad, comprehensive, historicized, integrated, philosophically founded student education that can enable learners to manage the consequences of these great technological strides. Reports, framework documents, case studies, charters, policy papers, qualitative surveys, and annual reviews were authored, published, and archived by educational professionals and organizations in the last decade and beyond (Criollo-C et al., 2024). This section surveys a selection of these artifacts to assess how change can be brought about in interdisciplinary learning and to look for recurring practical, philosophical, and material reasoning that might guide appropriate future directions after the AI revolution. Globally, the emergence of transdisciplinary, interdisciplinary, and cross-disciplinary programs, pedagogy, curriculum, and research is following the trend, east and west, fueled in part by modern forces of globalization, as presented in Table 1 (Gómez Redondo et al., 2024).

Table 1. AI's Influence on Key Aspects of Interdisciplinary Education

Aspect	Traditional Approach	AI-Enhanced Approach	Benefits	Challenges	Reference
Curriculum Design	Fixed, standardized	Adaptive, personalized	Tailored learning experiences	Requires advanced AI models	(Digón-Regueiro et al., 2024)
Teaching Methods	Lecture-based	AI-driven simulations & tutoring	Interactive & engaging	Faculty upskilling needed	(Sezgin & Fırat, 2024)
Research Collaboration	Limited to specific fields	AI-driven cross-disciplinary insights	Expands knowledge frontiers	Data privacy concerns	(Bartlett & Camba, 2024)
Data Analysis	Manual, time-consuming	Automated AI-powered analytics	Faster, more accurate insights	Bias in AI models	(Benítez et al., 2024)
Assessment & Evaluation	Exams & assignments	AI-based continuous assessment	Real-time feedback	Ethical Concerns Over Grading Fairness	(Atkinson et al., 2024)
Student Support	Human advisors	AI-powered chatbots & assistants	24/7 personalized guidance	Lack of human empathy	(Eghrefuvwoma et al., 2024)
Knowledge Discovery	Field-specific research	AI-driven pattern recognition across domains	Unlocks hidden connections	Dependence on AI accuracy	(Boscardin et al., 2024)
Academic Publishing	Manual peer review	AI-assisted review & summarization	Faster publication process	AI bias in research validation	(Yim & Su, 2024)
Experimentation	Traditional labs	AI-powered virtual labs & simulations	Safe, cost-effective trials	High computational demands	(Yan et al., 2024)
Interdisciplinary Integration	Human-led collaborations	AI-driven knowledge synthesis	Faster cross-field innovation	Requires robust AI governance	(Cheung et al., 2024)
Lifelong Learning	Fixed curricula	AI-powered personalized learning paths	Continuous skill enhancement	Digital divide issues	(Alvarez-Icaza & Huerta, 2024)

continued on following page

Table 1. Continued

Aspect	Traditional Approach	AI-Enhanced Approach	Benefits	Challenges	Reference
Student Engagement	Passive learning	AI-driven gamification & adaptive content	Higher motivation & retention	Potential over-reliance on AI	(Madden, 2024)
Ethical Considerations	Instructor-driven policies	AI-monitored compliance & fairness	Ensures integrity in learning	Risk of AI-driven surveillance	(Yi et al., 2024)

3. THE ROLE OF ARTIFICIAL INTELLIGENCE IN EDUCATION

Artificial intelligence (AI) has garnered quite a bit of attention in educational circles. However, the focus on AI in learning environments has predominantly dwelled on the teacher and how AI technologies will revolutionize the teaching side of the educational landscape. Undoubtedly, AI has a role in helping teaching professionals expand their capacities and capabilities in nurturing lifelong learners; however, this text will focus on learning and unconditional education, using AI to cultivate interdisciplinary competencies among students. Interdisciplinary collaborations via AI technologies are shaping critical consciousness while simultaneously inquiring into the best practices for educating and preparing graduates for this AI-driven future (Hand & Ihara, 2024). Scientific scholarship in education, engineering, and information systems is investing in research and development of AI mechanisms used to advance teaching and learning. Major applications currently lead to AI for Education. AI-Ed applications have the potential to transform not just current pedagogical practices and the places where education happens; they also hold the potential for reinventing the metrics used to define what constitutes learning and competence. Its ability to not just support, but to personalize learning experiences across strengths and weaknesses, positions, abilities, prior knowledge, and even different cultures will challenge current approaches to psychometric testing and the premise of one-size-fits-all testing in defined closed environments (Zhang et al., 2024). AI's analytical capacity to process data, examine performance, and predict individuals' and groups' learning journeys holds a great deal of potential in diversifying and validating the legitimate expectations of any given course. Key AI tools that are being employed include adaptive learning systems, intelligent tutoring systems, AI-driven analytics, and augmented and virtual reality technologies, which also lean on AI capacity in small measures. Moreover, AI-driven applications not only offer efficiencies and effectiveness but, in addition, offer deep insights into future directions that are rapidly appearing in our thoughts and hidden societal needs (Liu et al., 2024). The potential practical applications and directions of these emerging technologies in schools is a field still to be explored; it is proposed that they could be integrated into curricular frameworks and senior secondary subjects. Incorporating these technologies offers a range of efficiencies, effectiveness, and opportunities for the school and student, but in doing so, normative, ethical, and pedagogical issues also arise. Moreover, it is argued that before these technologies are incorporated, it is crucial they undergo rigorous research, be evaluated, and be systematically refined. Also, it is proposed that senior education and society will benefit from clear and informed education research on these AI adaptive technologies in schools (Rezigalla, 2024).

3.1. AI Applications in Teaching and Learning

AI has a wide variety of uses in teaching and learning, including creating novel and integrated learning experiences. Virtual assistants, which are computer-based programs explicitly designed to assist students in various tasks, are one such application of AI in university education. These assistants can help answer questions, suggest potential educational materials, and even tailor materials to students' needs or preferences. The system does not replace instructional practices per se, but using it changes the traditional arrangements for how we work with students (Yang, 2024). AI tools can be used to create space for collaboration, providing students with automated feedback on rough drafts or discussion points, discussions that are sometimes underutilized given the time needed to do them. AI tools can be employed to automate administrative tasks, including grading and assessment. Eliminating these duties would, therefore, provide instructors with more time to devote to teaching and developing relationships with students. A small number of case studies exist about AI applications in universities and schools. Virtually all of them agree on the potential of AI to transform teaching and learning in practical settings. Results range from improved student performance to increased levels of creative work and personal interaction. Trials increased student confidence and decreased the likelihood of requiring assistance (Alier et al., 2024).

3.2. Enhancing Personalization and Adaptation

Personalization and adaptation have long been a goal of educational systems worldwide. AI technologies can be employed nowadays to achieve this goal by tailoring learning experiences to fit the precise needs and preferences of individual students. For example, adaptive learning platforms have been designed that make use of AI to tailor educational content and to pace in real-time based on formative assessments, course completion patterns, or other behavioral indicators. Interventions on these platforms include content recommendations, scaffolded exercises, hints and feedback, and motivational messages (Shafik, 2024d). However, there is also some evidence that providing more data and/or recommendations can be confusing or intimidating or simply not useful enough to support decisions to make a difference in student outcomes. Research suggests that the success of personalized learning platforms depends heavily on the algorithms that drive their support recommendations and on the extent to which teachers can access and act on the data that underlie these recommendations. AI can be used to tailor educational content by diagnosing and making predictions about the knowledge, skills, interests, and social or cultural background of individual learners (Wahed & Pitterson, 2024). For example, based on the learning data, the analysis of learner profiles, including lifestyle, learning styles, life goals, social interactions, behaviors, and accomplishments, can support the development of individual learning paths, using AI tools, as presented in Figure 3. Even though a learner's profile may not be dynamic, individual learning trajectory inferencing can facilitate the personalization together with the trajectory update based on graduated updates. Therefore, this type of content personalization leans on content recommendation and a content architecture that allows dynamic paths. It also requires access to learning data, data models of what relevant courses can cover, data model ontologies for visualization, learning pathways in terms of difficulty levels on existing content, and policy, privacy, and security rules (SARI et al., 2024).

Figure 3. Sampled AI-enabled educational tools

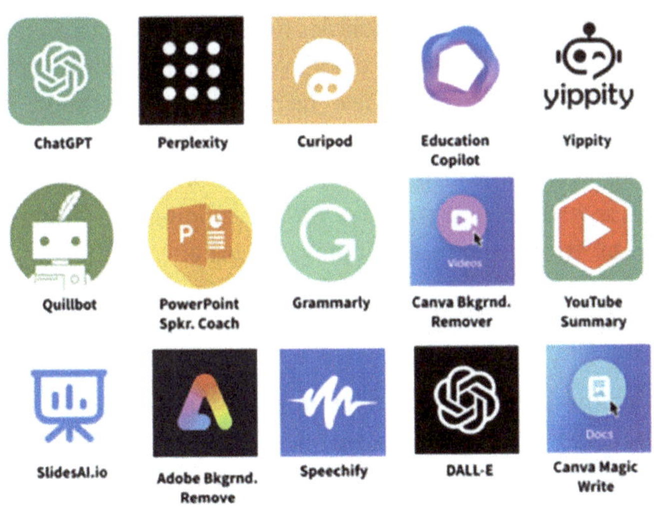

4. CHALLENGES AND OPPORTUNITIES IN INTERDISCIPLINARY RESEARCH

Despite the many calls to overcome disciplinary barriers and the widely identified need for more innovative and systems-based approaches, working across fields is often much easier said than done. Many so-called "interdisciplinary centers or institutes" often consist of faculty who are primarily or only affiliated with that locale or activity — uniqueness in a sea of silos. At the same time, computer scientists are not often recognized for long lists of papers in other areas, and breaking into and being perceived as specialties in those other fields is a challenge for computer scientists. This is true even though one could argue that computer science traditionally has been one of the most inherently interdisciplinary fields, already drawing on foundational work in logic, electrical engineering, psychology, and physics and being transformed by the advent of affordances provided by artificial intelligence (Weidener & Fischer, 2024).

We believe it is imperative to identify the major impediments while at the same time identifying the affordances provided by artificial intelligence technologies that could revolutionize both education and research. There are many challenges to successfully promoting a culture of interdisciplinary collaboration, ranging from libraries needing to have new strategies for cataloging, organizing, and revealing links across fields to biases in hiring, promotion, and tenure practices at universities, not to mention the challenge in aligning reporting mechanisms for cross-disciplinary grants and creating a mechanism to bridge differing approaches to developing processes for "broader impacts" and "societally engaged research." (Wahed & Pitterson, 2024).In addition, despite all of the new opportunities to create, store, manage, analyze, and share data and software tools associated with AI programs, we still have challenges in allowing free and open access and use of resources, including those that facilitate clear communication across fields through guidelines developed by consensus. We provide examples of these challenges with the hope of inspiring others to develop policies, programs, and strategies to assist with developing an artificially intelligent ecosystem for educational and research progress (Alier et al., 2024).

4.1. Barriers to Collaboration

Dynamic multidisciplinary work drives interdisciplinary research and education. In order to progress toward these aims, we must identify and dismantle institutional policies that inject barriers to innovative collaboration. These obstacles are outlined in the following sections. Institutional Silos Disciplinary and methodological siloed cultures have prioritized the use of different terminologies, disciplinary domain membership, and norms between functions. Silos also facilitate gatekeeping and decrease the willingness of contributors to experiment with 'non-traditional' methods of problem-solving (Rusydiana, 2024). Researchers not only face career demands from senior researchers in their fields but also grant review panels. Researchers with little experience in interdisciplinary work may be hesitant to lead or contribute to an interdisciplinary research initiative as they may feel unqualified. Few discretionary resources are available to fund such initiatives in today's decentralized research funding environment. Furthermore, universities that emphasize teaching over research could see few rewards in nurturing dedicated research institutes, including the encouragement of interdisciplinary work. Those in attendance at the conference expressed the belief that, as long as silos persist, interdisciplinary education as a whole will continue to be increasingly difficult. The creation and maintenance of institutional policies that support and value a culture of diversity is critical to successful interdisciplinary education and research (O'Brien & Davenport, 2024). Such a culture frequently requires increased resources, including time, money, autonomy, and an environment that encourages risk-taking and unusual approaches to goods and services. Studies on parallels and contradictions in basic and applied research reveal the importance of investments in basic research to the success of society as a whole. Proper investment in basic research programs is slowing because of pressure from elected officials and private industry. Small-scale project-oriented research will dominate the research trials at academic institutions if these negative trends persist (Alam & Mohanty, 2024).

4.2. Promoting Cross-Disciplinary Communication

Even the most technically excellent work can be thwarted by poor communication. This is certainly as true for interdisciplinary interactions between researchers as it is for any other sphere of human activity. In fact, if anything, successful interdisciplinary research depends even more fundamentally on cross-disciplinary communication than any other activity: differences in basic language, assumptions, worldviews, theories, research methods, and practical skills all conspire to make effective discussion a major challenge. Efforts to promote cross-disciplinary communication, therefore, tend to occupy a central role in most schemes for encouraging successful interdisciplinary research (Sharma, 2024). In order to promote mutual understanding and appreciation of the problems associated with the proposed interdisciplinary collaboration, it is necessary to foster an appreciation of what separates different research cultures from one another. Training schemes aim to foster cross-disciplinary communication and to provide the user with the practical tools and insights necessary to assess or conduct effective interdisciplinary research, usually encompassing appreciation of the key concepts and tensions addressed below (Criollo-C et al., 2024).

One of the greatest challenges facing a multi-skilled team of researchers is finding ways of allowing them to understand each other's concerns and approaches despite major differences in disciplinary training and objectives. Two reasons, then, for why cross-disciplinary communication can break down, whether they be interpersonal or between different academic fields, are the problem of developing a common language and the problem of offering unifying conceptual, theoretical, or methodological frameworks. Developing such commonalities may be more effective by removing individual labels and thereby their associations, rather than just re-baptizing them using new labels that are free of associations (Weidener & Fischer, 2024). The case for teams as the major vehicle for managing and indeed performing interdisciplinary research has already been made. Indeed, an earlier report unequivocally commends teams, writing, large-scale interdisciplinarity, drawing together major disciplinary strengths, is increasingly recognized as a powerful road to effective research for the effective cultivation of inter-disciplinarity, since it is new minds and diverse perspectives working together that transforms interdisciplinary work from a struggle at the margins of existing disciplines into an established and valuable new field of shared understanding, thus encouraging a shared culture of intra-disciplinary collaboration. Furthermore, a strategy concluded that variety is crucial to success (Wahed & Pitterson, 2024). Funding is directed at the creation of e-learning solutions that exploit new technologies at the frontiers of our understanding of disciplines and of pedagogy.

5. ETHICAL AND SOCIAL IMPLICATIONS OF AI IN EDUCATION AND RESEARCH

AI applications, including educational ones, are surrounded by ethical and social implications. In the educational and research guide, where data is a primary fuel, special attention needs to be given to the privacy of the personal information of every student and the organization. Of course, the ethical issues to discuss should not be reduced to security and privacy. We discussed, for instance, some possibilities of social bias or fairness problems in AI systems. Indeed, AI systems are actually black-box algorithms that can make decisions. Therefore, it is a real issue to respect the social acceptability level and to assess the benefits against potential negative impacts of AI development in this context (Alier et al., 2024). Different points of view, pros and cons, appear and should be regarded in any ethical framework drawing. There are several research gaps that require further analysis in approaching responsible AI in the context of multimodal and interdisciplinary dimensions, such as frameworks and guidelines for ethical development inclusive of AI, the potential of development through AI of state-of-the-art for the multimodal/multidisciplinary acquisition and/or serious games and simulation, the storage and sensitive sharing of data, and the potential to propose improvements in policy-making and management. Moreover, the issue of significant changes in policy research, which after the sensationalistic adventures of 'AI power' in the media, we look forward to reinforcing a paper on 'responsibility in the AI education domains and the link to responsible AI' (Shafik, 2024b).'

The professional profile of training educators could be displaced by a new technology of AI, and it is of great importance to debate the real potential of dislocation and transformation in labor profiles, and of what types, as well as the agents of this policy in the transition periods. Our paper should show some possible languages of expectations for this new technology and its impact on policy and technology itself. Also, we should present awareness-proof research and help to illuminate the best ways to adopt this new automated technology for responsible self-contact in educational institutions in each state (Rusydiana, 2024). As attention continues to focus on the ethics and AI theme in the realm of artificial intelligence, multiple studies are beginning to be published on the challenges and reflections on the adoption of AI in education. It is important to clarify that the AI for training field for colleges and universities has its scope of study, research, and community individuals that integrate it, and who are responsible for its development and decision-making. The publication of this paper could also foster concern about the possibly bad practices of integrating AI in education, provide an interesting access to debate the social responsibility of educational institutions, and expand the proposal in the elaboration of guidelines that ensure the acquisition of AI technology and some ingrained ethical issues (O'Brien & Davenport, 2024). It seeks to design a comprehensive approach, and when examining the main thematic axis and ongoing special interest in this publication, encourages the internationalization of public and academic debate, and increases the level of engagement in developing informed public policy and educators in the field of training.

5.1. Privacy and Data Security Concerns

Privacy and Data Security Concerns. One of the major concerns of educators, students, and other stakeholders in the use of artificial intelligence technologies in a wide range of academic, administrative, and research activities in higher education is the safety and security of data about students and the educators who teach them. Student course data may include grades, attendance records, student-instructor communication logs, and a variety of demographic data. Access to student data must be carefully controlled, and educators have an expectation that their intellectual property and data about teaching methods could be kept confidential (Kurti et al., 2024). For these reasons, institutions and faculty members may be hesitant to participate or cooperate in AI initiatives and interoperability of systems. Data Breach. Security risks in academic data abound. Possibilities of data breaches can involve hacked systems, inside jobs, system failures, or stolen devices. Ensuring best and reputable practices, or trusted vendors regardless of the precautions taken could sometimes be circumvented through human influences, employees, or individuals with access to systems. However trustworthy someone might be, there is bound to be specific and unintended exposure of sensitive information. Accidental data exposure is one of the common data breaches in higher education. There's also the possibility of insiders acting maliciously; surely there have been multiple instances of staff, faculty, and student 'insiders' being criminally involved, knowingly engaging in fraud. Data Security Measures (Alam & Mohanty, 2024). Ensuring best practices in the management of various types of interest data and at the same time providing a convenient teaching and learning process, the following are some recommended security measures: Data Governance, usage of secured monitoring, encryption and firewall, regular staff training and stocktaking of information in and out of the systems, effective vetting process, regular assessments, tax management, regular patches and updates, use of two-factor authentication, and regularly reviewing network system confidential data such as student-employee-educator-based data. Providing Trust to Stakeholders. Stakeholders would want to trust that their personal and/or students' teaching data and methods would be secured with confidentiality; this will enable them to engage in AI initiatives and the interoperability of systems. There must be an explicit statement confirming compliance with the relevant laws (Sharma, 2024). Educational institutions must ensure that all stakeholders know what data is collected and what it is being used for; this would contribute to ensuring trust.

5.2. Bias and Fairness Issues

The increasing use of AI for education and research raises concerns about the potential for AI to either perpetuate or exacerbate existing socioeconomic and individual inequalities. In general, machine learning algorithms can inadvertently reproduce and amplify the biases present in the training data, potentially exacerbating existing inequalities. Since no data are unbiased, this raises questions about the appropriateness of using AI in academia for such purposes as student assessment and predictions. Research on fairness is addressing various normative considerations that can guide the development and use of AI systems, with a focus on technical methods for mitigating bias (Gómez Redondo et al., 2024). Proponents of the fairness in AI movement emphasize that AI systems should make decisions that do not systematically disadvantage certain groups of users and provide different prediction contours needed to determine the downstream effects of such decisions. Others extend upon this to argue that fairness encompasses a shift from group-based fairness, which addresses the treatment of members of different protected classes, to fairness of opportunity or equal distribution of incentives. Fairness-aware AI, in the context of higher education, must adhere to the principle that all students have access to equal opportunities. In terms of technical methods, it has been argued that multitudes of considerations can be used to work towards fairness in AI applications, but increasingly, there is a push for co-design with affected communities and for transparency in benchmarks for AI fairness (SARI et al., 2024). A long-term solution to these issues necessarily includes the creation of accurately and genuinely representative datasets and the increase of diverse participation in their creation. Practical strategies to ensure fair AI, in use and development, are to constantly re-evaluate and potentially refine the procedure, as presented in Table 2.

Table 2. AI's Role in Advancing Interdisciplinary Research

Research Aspect	Before AI Integration	After AI Integration	Advantages	Limitations	Reference
Data Processing	Manual, slow	AI-powered automation	Faster insights	Requires high-quality datasets	(Boscardin et al., 2024)
Hypothesis Generation	Human-driven	AI-assisted hypothesis discovery	Identifies novel patterns	Risk of misleading correlations	(Bartlett & Camba, 2024; Eghrefuvwoma et al., 2024)
Literature Review	Time-consuming	AI-driven automated synthesis	Saves researchers' time	Potential bias in source selection	(Frizell et al., 2024)
Experiment Design	Traditional, iterative	AI-driven simulations & optimizations	More efficient resource use	AI's assumptions may be flawed	(Abubakari et al., 2024b)
Collaboration Across Fields	Requires human networking	AI-driven research matchmaking	Enhances interdisciplinary synergy	Data security concerns	(Vartanian, 2024)
Research Methodologies	Fixed frameworks	AI-driven adaptive approaches	More flexible and scalable	Ethical concerns in AI decision-making	(Digón-Regueiro et al., 2024)
Publication & Citation	Manual search	AI-recommended citations & summaries	Speeds up literature tracking	AI-generated errors in citations	(Rusydiana, 2024)
Funding & Grant Allocation	Human-reviewed proposals	AI-assisted grant evaluations	Reduces bias, improves allocation	Transparency & fairness concerns	(Mohammed & Hossain, 2024)

continued on following page

Table 2. Continued

Research Aspect	Before AI Integration	After AI Integration	Advantages	Limitations	Reference
Predictive Modeling	Limited by human analysis	AI-driven predictive analytics	More accurate forecasting	AI models need validation	(Alam & Mohanty, 2024)
Knowledge Integration	Slow knowledge synthesis	AI-powered cross-domain insights	Accelerates discovery	Risk of misinformation	(Sharma, 2024)
Open-Access Research	Human-curated databases	AI-enabled knowledge dissemination	Democratizes access	Data ownership issues	(Gómez Redondo et al., 2024)
Research Ethics & Compliance	Manual monitoring	AI-driven ethical compliance tools	Ensures research integrity	AI biases may affect fairness	(Weidener & Fischer, 2024)
Sustainability & Resource Efficiency	High resource usage	AI-optimized research processes	Reduces costs & waste	Energy-intensive AI models	(Alier et al., 2024)

6. INNOVATIVE PEDAGOGICAL APPROACHES

The complementarity of AI tools and innovative pedagogical approaches is anticipated to transform the realm of education by immersing students in knowledge generation and idea sharing. Project-based learning undoubtedly becomes a well-suited approach to strengthen students' abilities for problem-solving and critical thinking, as well as to develop cooperation and teamwork (Yang, 2024). The capability of gamification, when appropriately applied and combined with project-based learning, excites students, enhances their motivation, and sense of learning. The simplicity reminiscent of certain games drew expert attention during conceptualization, revealing its potential for use in low-cost e-learning contests. With AI tools, an augmented resource of interesting gamification-related learning paths can be developed, providing students with a more immersive experience. Moreover, gamification must add a fun component for the students, not to make it dull; therefore, students tend to develop impressively long-lasting involvement throughout the initiative (Liu et al., 2024).

Guiding principles and methodologies in AI allow for adaptable, flexible, learner-centered pedagogical strategies, beneficial to educators in their pursuit of future innovation. Educators in a rapidly advancing technical field should guide industry with innovative ideas that evolve rapidly while maintaining a significant grounding in pedagogical principles to bring out a professional with the optimal combination of digital graphical interaction, intelligent software, and human interaction (Hand & Ihara, 2024). Group collaboration and interdisciplinary projects are fundamentally changing the student mindset in the learning environment. Programming through video games has been implemented as having an attractive effect for active teaching, though AI has demonstrated limitations when it comes to people living with disabilities, as sampled in Figure 4. The only significant investment, besides funding, is time for talent in producing software-based video games to carry out this initiative. Hence, the winner would be rewarded for an extension of their work with the potential for implementing a larger computer-based virtual learning environment; thus, the competition winners' material will not only be a fun game but additionally a useful learning resource. Educators are encouraged to use this as a model to encourage and foster innovative methods of computer science education in classroom projects (Alvarez-Icaza & Huerta, 2024).

Figure 4. Limitations of AI in the lenses of People living with Disabilities

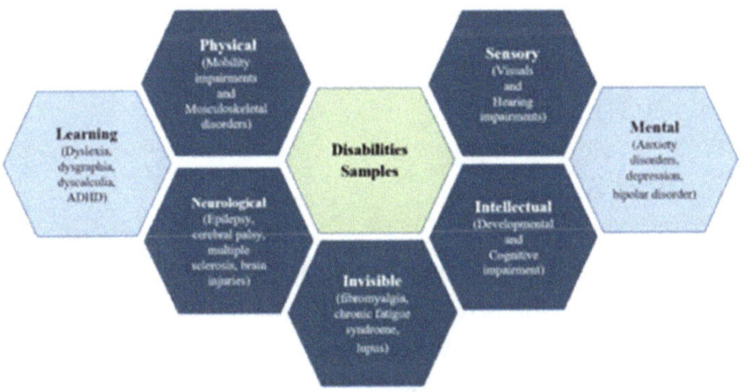

6.1. Project-Based Learning

Project-based learning (PBL) is an instructional approach that is dynamic, engaging, and grounded in what we know about how people learn. PBL emphasizes real-world challenges and connects students with issues that are central to the concerns of society. To address these challenges, students must master and use a number of higher-order skills linked to problem-solving, critical thinking, analysis, creativity, synthesis, evaluation, problem-solving, and decision-making. PBL offers a means for students to develop the essential "21st century" skills that are needed for high-level research and have been identified as one of the most important skills for future careers. All Project-Based Learning Academy projects involve students in doing real work that addresses real needs (Yan et al., 2024). To do this, students' work as individuals and in teams utilizes AI, data, computer vision, machine learning, and natural language tools to make human work more effective. By using live and real-time data, these students are able to see the product of their decisions and the application of the course theory. AI is embedded into every project phase: exploration and research, project design and prototype, and background case research on current practices. Projects and project schedules are designed to resemble real-time project execution with real-world clients and, when possible, real industry support. Student teams present and document their work in project management logs (Yim & Su, 2024). This Academy course is framed by accredited project management and communication workshops that form part of their project. Work-based learning is a common form of applied learning in higher education and can take several forms. PBL extends the strategy of work-based learning by offering the chance for further theoretical understanding. The reflective cycle is reinforced through individual feedback at the end of the project summary and student evaluations of the process. PBL is now fundamental to the education of all programs at RMIT Vietnam due to the value attributed to it in a work-based education. It is a growing movement in international higher education and is a key feature of several universities overseas (Boscardin et al., 2024).

6.2. Gamification Strategies

One way to increase student engagement is to implement gamification strategies in the classroom. Gamification is when game design techniques are applied to non-game contexts, such as education. When using game principles, the students can become engrossed in the learning experience without realizing how much they are actually learning. Besides increasing student motivation, implementing gamification can also result in competitions that can develop or maintain a good relationship with the students while also keeping them interested in the material. Students will have the motivation to actively participate in order to gain the recognition of not only their instructor but also of their peers (Atkinson et al., 2024). To successfully implement gamification, one must first understand the psychological principles used in the theory behind it. The use of game mechanics engages the students and increases their motivation. Turning learning into a game can result in a higher willingness for students to be involved in and succeed in the activities. When considering the need to know learners individually, it is important to mention AI as an enabler, making gamification mainly adaptive to the participants' personal situations. For example, with AI-based support, the learning analytics solution actively tracks employees' learning outcomes and adapts them to the learners' profiles (Benítez et al., 2024). By analyzing the habits and patterns of individual employees, it can not only provide personalized content for employees and managers using AI, but can also make the gamification experience more interesting and relevant. This brings it in line with our framework. Overall, this paper aims to foster a better understanding of the forms of AI-based adaptive gamification possible across different scenarios and to explore the current practice in this field. However, in order to implement AI-based adaptive gamification, we argue that first the two main elements of gamification (independent of the level of personalization) should be considered (Digón-Regueiro et al., 2024). These include building an emotional connection with the participants and nudging them closer to intended learning outcomes.

7. EMERGING TRENDS AND FUTURE DIRECTIONS

With the growing interest in and application of AI in education and learning, several significant trends can be expected in the not-too-distant future that will likely redefine what and how teaching and learning are conducted: - Curriculum design will be increasingly conducted with AI's help. An ever-evolving workforce and skills retraining demands will be the main drivers for this shift. - More content in courses and specific competencies will be taught by AI as opposed to human instructors. This will continue with a trend toward AI being used more for instruction in theory and practice, providing a personalized learning path and curriculum (Abubakari et al., 2024b). This will be cheaper, better, and faster and will allow organizations to develop new programming based on the skills those industries need. - Interdisciplinary learning will shift from a focus on job-based skills to "skills of the mind" that will be desired in educational environments. Real-time oversight of compliance and root cause investigation by physically sampling educational events "happening" at partner institutions and determining which events resulted in individuals who were "workforce ready" versus those that were not will be the norm. This will be based on real-time assessments—and employing AI to dynamically measure, adjust, and assess learning outcomes will be a growing industry (Frizell et al., 2024).

It will be critical that we are ahead of the trend curve and cross-trained to understand and apply AI and technologically infused instructions, workshops, and/or curricula. As very few colleges are currently equipping students to be prepared for AI's learning environments, these will be in high demand. We will also need to prepare institutions to help non-digital natives and future students to cross digital divides created by a new wave of technology-driven instruction. Also, if machine ethics and value alignment are not well resolved, it will be critical to create core AI, human-centered AI, and AI ethics as minors that are not just a mix of programmatic learning artifacts and requirements from their stand-alone major or discipline. AI education will become an interactive and AI hybrid between human and artificial minds that will mutually inform and shape how students and researchers/consumers learn together in a resurgent interdisciplinary moment (Seibert et al., 2024). If present, this will also be a key topic in ethics, responsibility, policy, and governance.

7.1. AI-Driven Curriculum Design

Another approach that has the potential to revolutionize teaching and learning is using data analytics for customizing educational programs based on the actions of the students. There needs to be a divide between using AI for enabling adaptive learning systems and using it to aid basic curricular and resource planning, but such a distinction isn't obvious. Personalizing the type of content shown to students based on their actions and learning styles can help increase the effectiveness of learning management systems. AI-driven curriculum design allows educators to move from the notion of scheduling and putting topics in the real world to orchestrating how students learn (Bjørnerås et al., 2024). The system can track how students are performing in courses, the material that is causing them issues, and the kinds of changes that are made on an assignment-by-assignment basis. Because of this, the course can adapt to student performance. There are many examples of how adaptive learning systems can be helpful in collecting, analyzing, and acting upon user interactions, which range from the world of games to learning management systems. In games, what determines the system's behavior is the player's history within it, and designers innovate the level of adaptability that the system has to achieve the desired impact. AI-driven curriculum design is an even more challenging project because, in an educational context, one must create a collaboration of educators and technologists that can decide the meaning of learning, learning loss, and learning gain, and to decide the ultimate outcome of the whole course (Hay et al., 2024). When using comprehensive data collected about student interactions within a VLE, a broader consideration concerning data recall makes the system's biggest challenge: what is legitimate and what is not legitimate to recall about students. In addition, there is a growing interest in the ethical implications of using data about students to make pedagogic and learning design interventions or to inform the design of interventions. The examples provided showed the cultural values and privacy concerns addressed (Corte & Amrein-Beardsley, 2024).

7.2. Integrating AI Ethics into Educational Programs

This chapter has outlined a vision for transformative AI-powered multidisciplinarity. Accompanying the vision is the need to address ethical issues in AI. Educational programs for future learning environments must consider AI ethics as part of the foundational aspects, given the potentially severe consequences arising from the misuse of AI. Strategies to address AI ethics in education highlight the importance of fostering awareness of ethics in AI among educators and students. When ethical considerations are an integral element of decision-making linked to the design and application of systems such as AI, we promote a more responsible use of these systems (Vartanian, 2024). Ethical dangers and warnings are less effective than matching ethical solutions. Consequently, part of educational reform is the development of curricula that address the ethical side of AI technologies for students to work in a world where the use of such technologies will be 'business as usual.' This reformative process requires an intergenerational and trans-professional approach, which is the best and provides the greatest hope for meaningful, impactful, and ethically congruent AI. Stakeholders from educational institutions, government, and private industry will need to create comprehensive Ethical Artificial Reasoning frameworks and collaborate on the best ways to teach EAR (Shafik, 2025). While ethics in science is acknowledged as an essential consideration, acceptance of the idea that intercollegiate and interdisciplinary ethics in science demand interdisciplinary and trans-professional cooperation has sadly proven difficult for many STEM professionals. In addition, joint efforts are required between all of us actually involved in this work, not only those who lead or guide it. As an example of successful ethics integration, explicit attention to developing the 'habits of mind and heart' supportive of AI is possible. We hope that future ethical approaches reflect the idea of widely applicable good values that are a force for positive social change (O'Brien & Davenport, 2024; Shafik, 2023).

8. CONCLUSION

AI, particularly embodied AI, stands to revolutionize how we educate future interdisciplinary researchers, especially how we help them learn to think interdisciplinarity and how we assess their interdisciplinary capabilities. Further, AI will enable important new interdisciplinary research about how we improve the practice of interdisciplinary education and assessment. Given these developments, future educational institutions must be very different from today's, yet today's educational institutions are usually the ones that must define the future. In the AI era, educational organizations should not act as gatekeepers against AI or try to control the impact of new technologies. Like it or not, AI is rapidly evolving, as is its impact on society. The more responsible approach for those in educational leadership positions, including policymakers, educators, and researchers, is to structure responsibility and to adapt to emerging trends. For policymakers, this will include developing overarching principles for AI use with strong recommendations for the ethical use of data. Collaboration will be key, especially with industry and within institutions to provide practical and relevant learning experiences that are responsibly implemented. Policymakers must also not be afraid of regulating data and AI use as part of a much wider partnership to ensure the responsible use of these enabling technologies currently impacting all of society. Therefore, we advocate that future AI policy in education should be rational and evidence-based, actively searching for the research that helps guide ethical, data-driven AI decisions. The ethical considerations of AI must extend to those actively developing and using AI in education, with raised awareness around data and inclusive digital practices. As early adopters and pioneers of new educational practices, we study and research these innovations, particularly where they intersect with technology, data, and society. Aligned to this, it is right to support an approach that advocates the future and encourages open collaboration with like minds and technology in new interdisciplinary ways. The advice to organizations retains clarity even when assessed retrospectively, aligning with the interdisciplinary principles and approaches that are argued for. Managing transitions and the heightened ethics surrounding AI in society remains ongoing, often long-term, areas of emerging research. Therefore, we conclude our piece with a look toward the future, future practices underpinned by AI, and the characteristics that AI is and could be likened to. After all, it seems evident to us that with or without AI, an interdisciplinary approach grounded in evidence looks toward the future to effectively shape society.

REFERENCES

Abubakari, M. S., Shafik, W., & Hidayatullah, A. F. (2024a). Evaluating the Potential of Artificial Intelligence in Islamic Religious Education. In *AI-Enhanced Teaching Methods* (pp. 216–239). IGI Global., DOI: 10.4018/979-8-3693-2728-9.ch010

Abubakari, M. S., Shafik, W., & Hidayatullah, A. F. (2024b). Evaluating the Potential of Artificial Intelligence in Islamic Religious Education: A SWOT Analysis Overview. In *AI-Enhanced Teaching Methods* (pp. 216–239). IGI Global.

Alam, A., & Mohanty, A. (2024). Integrated constructive robotics in education (ICRE) model: A paradigmatic framework for transformative learning in educational ecosystem. *Cogent Education, 11*(1). Advance online publication. DOI: 10.1080/2331186X.2024.2324487

Alier, M., García-Peñalvo, F. J., & Camba, J. D. (2024). Generative Artificial Intelligence in Education: From Deceptive to Disruptive. *International Journal of Interactive Multimedia and Artificial Intelligence*, *8*(5). Advance online publication. DOI: 10.9781/ijimai.2024.02.011

Alvarez-Icaza, I., & Huerta, O. (2024). Augmented intelligence for open education: Bridging the digital gap with inclusive design methods. *Frontiers in Education, 9*. Advance online publication. DOI: 10.3389/feduc.2024.1337932

Atkinson, A. R., Abbott, C., Oswald, A., Boucher, A., Cavalcanti, R. B., Frank, J. R., & Snell, L. S. (2024). Strategies to Enable Transformation in Medical Education: Faculty and Trainee Development in Competence By Design. *Perspectives on Medical Education, 13*(1). Advance online publication. DOI: 10.5334/pme.960

Bartlett, K. A., & Camba, J. D. (2024). Generative Artificial Intelligence in Product Design Education: Navigating Concerns of Originality and Ethics. *International Journal of Interactive Multimedia and Artificial Intelligence*, *8*(5). Advance online publication. DOI: 10.9781/ijimai.2024.02.006

Benítez, T. M., Xu, Y., Boudreau, J. D., Kow, A. W. C., Bello, F., Van Phuoc, L., Wang, X., Sun, X., Leung, G. K. K., Lan, Y., Wang, Y., Cheng, D., Tham, Y. C., Wong, T. Y., & Chung, K. C. (2024). Harnessing the potential of large language models in medical education: Promise and pitfalls. *Journal of the American Medical Informatics Association : JAMIA*, *31*(3). Advance online publication. DOI: 10.1093/jamia/ocad252

Bjørnerås, A. B., Witsø, A. E., Kvam, L., Eide, A. H., Jahren, L., & Horghagen, S. (2024). Identifying Key Concepts in Ambassador Interventions for Students with Disabilities in Higher Education: A Scoping Review. *International Journal of Disability Development and Education*, *71*(3). Advance online publication. DOI: 10.1080/1034912X.2022.2095558

Boscardin, C. K., Gin, B., Golde, P. B., & Hauer, K. E. (2024). ChatGPT and Generative Artificial Intelligence for Medical Education: Potential Impact and Opportunity. *Academic Medicine*, *99*(1). Advance online publication. DOI: 10.1097/ACM.0000000000005439

Bull, C., & Kharrufa, A. (2024). Generative Artificial Intelligence Assistants in Software Development Education: A Vision for Integrating Generative Artificial Intelligence into Educational Practice, Not Instinctively Defending Against It. *IEEE Software*, *41*(2). Advance online publication. DOI: 10.1109/MS.2023.3300574

Cheung, K. K. C., Long, Y., Liu, Q., & Chan, H. Y. (2024). Unpacking Epistemic Insights of Artificial Intelligence (AI) in Science Education: A Systematic Review. *Science and Education*. Advance online publication. DOI: 10.1007/s11191-024-00511-5

Corte, C., & Amrein-Beardsley, A. (2024). Faculty/Staff Training to Examine Racial Implicit Bias: Findings and Implications for Creating Inclusive Educational Spaces. *Innovative Higher Education*, *49*(1). Advance online publication. DOI: 10.1007/s10755-023-09673-6

Criollo-C, S., Guerrero-Arias, A., Guaña-Moya, J., Samala, A. D., & Luján-Mora, S. (2024). Towards Sustainable Education with the Use of Mobile Augmented Reality in Early Childhood and Primary Education: A Systematic Mapping. In *Sustainability (Switzerland)* (Vol. 16, Issue 3). https://doi.org/DOI: 10.3390/su16031192

Digón-Regueiro, P., Méndez-García, R. M., Romero-Rodrigo, M. M., & Becerra-Brito, C. V. (2024). Questioning the role of technology in Early Childhood Education: Divides and false views. *Pixel-Bit. Revista de Medios y Educacion*, *69*. Advance online publication. DOI: 10.12795/pixelbit.98498

Eghrefuvwoma, O. G., Agada, S. A., Ighodaro, I. H., & Olasupo, S. F. (2024). ICT in Higher Education: A Tool for Sustainable Development in West Africa. *International Journal of Research and Innovation in Applied Science*, *IX*(I). Advance online publication. DOI: 10.51584/ijrias.2024.90122

Frizell, C. A., Graham, D., DuVentre, A., & Brown, S. D. (2024). Embracing Neuro-Inclusivity Within Physician Assistant/Associate Education: Challenging Organizational Cultural Norms and Navigating Communication Challenges. *The Journal of Physician Assistant Education : the Official Journal of the Physician Assistant Education Association*. Advance online publication. DOI: 10.1097/jpa.0000000000000575

Gómez Redondo, S., Rodríguez Higuera, C. J., Coca, J. R., & Olteanu, A. (2024). Transhumanism, Society and Education: An Edusemiotic Approach. *Studies in Philosophy and Education*, *43*(2). Advance online publication. DOI: 10.1007/s11217-024-09927-6

Hand, M. D., & Ihara, E. S. (2024). Ageism, Racism, Sexism, and Work With Older Healthcare Clients: Why an Intersectional Approach Is Needed in Practice, Policy, Education, and Research. *International Journal of Aging & Human Development*, *98*(1). Advance online publication. DOI: 10.1177/00914150231171843

Hay, A., Stanley-Clarke, N., Maris, R., Winder, L., & Knook, J. (2024). Building connections in health and wellbeing education: Qualitative findings of a study with New Zealand agricultural students. *Health Education Journal*, *83*(2). Advance online publication. DOI: 10.1177/00178969231225089

Kurti, E., Ferati, M., & Kalonaityte, V. (2024). Closing the gender gap in ICT higher education: Exploring women's motivations in pursuing ICT education. *Frontiers in Education*, *9*. Advance online publication. DOI: 10.3389/feduc.2024.1352029

Liu, J., Wang, C., Liu, Z., Gao, M., Xu, Y., Chen, J., & Cheng, Y. (2024). A bibliometric analysis of generative AI in education: Current status and development. *Asia Pacific Journal of Education*, *44*(1). Advance online publication. DOI: 10.1080/02188791.2024.2305170

Madden, V. J. (2024). Vocal Awareness and K-12 Education: A Qualitative Research Study. *Voice & Speech Review*, *18*(1). Advance online publication. DOI: 10.1080/23268263.2022.2062851

Mohammed, S. P., & Hossain, G. (2024). ChatGPT in Education, Healthcare, and Cybersecurity: Opportunities and Challenges. *2024 IEEE 14th Annual Computing and Communication Workshop and Conference, CCWC 2024*. https://doi.org/DOI: 10.1109/CCWC60891.2024.10427923

O'Brien, S., & Davenport, C. (2024). Embedding the service user voice to co-produce UK mental health nurse education—A lived experience narrative. *Journal of Psychiatric and Mental Health Nursing*, *31*(5). Advance online publication. DOI: 10.1111/jpm.13031

Rezigalla, A. A. (2024). AI in medical education: Uses of AI in construction type A MCQs. *BMC Medical Education, 24*(1). Advance online publication. DOI: 10.1186/s12909-024-05250-3

Rusydiana, A. S. (2024). Alternative Waqf Model for SDG-4 (Quality Education). *The Economic Review of Pesantren, 2*(2). Advance online publication. DOI: 10.58968/erp.v2i2.370

SARI, T., NAYİR, F., & BOZKURT, A. (2024). Reimagining education: Bridging artificial intelligence, transhumanism, and critical pedagogy. *Journal of Educational Technology and Online Learning, 7*(1). Advance online publication. DOI: 10.31681/jetol.1308022

Seibert, A., Aldave de las Heras, L., Boboridis, K., Colineau, E., Eloirdi, R., Fontana, C. L., Hult, M., Jenet, A., Michailidou, E., Nilsson, K. F., Paradela, C., Raison, P., Schillebeeckx, P., & Taucer, F. (2024). The nuclear research infrastructures open access scheme of the Joint Research Centre (JRC) at the European Commission – Contributions to education, training, mobility and scientific excellence. *Nuclear Engineering and Design, 420*. Advance online publication. DOI: 10.1016/j.nucengdes.2024.113000

Sezgin, S., & Fırat, M. (2024). Exploring the Digital Divide in Open Education: A Comparative Analysis of Undergraduate Students. *International Review of Research in Open and Distance Learning, 25*(1). Advance online publication. DOI: 10.19173/irrodl.v25i1.7236

Shafik, W. (2023). Introduction to ChatGPT. In *Advanced Applications of Generative AI and Natural Language Processing Models*. https://doi.org/DOI: 10.4018/9798369305027.ch001

Shafik, W. (2024a). Enhancing AI-Enabled Education Through Mobile Learning and Bring Your Own Device (BYOD) Integration. In *Exploring Youth Studies in the Age of AI* (pp. 140–173). IGI Global.

Shafik, W. (2024b). Generative AI for Social Good and Sustainable Development. In *Generative AI: Current Trends and Applications* (pp. 185–217). Springer.

Shafik, W. (2024c). Mobile Learning and Bring Your Own Device (BYOD): Enhancing Education in the Digital Age. In *Integrating Cutting-Edge Technology Into the Classroom* (pp. 240–267). IGI Global.

Shafik, W. (2024d). *Towards Trustworthy and Explainable AI Educational Systems.*, DOI: 10.1007/978-3-031-72410-7_2

Shafik, W. (2025). Human-Computer Interaction (HCI) Technologies in Socially-Enabled Artificial Intelligence. In *Future of Digital Technology and AI in Social Sectors* (pp. 121–150). IGI Global.

Sharma, P. (2024). Faculty competences development components: An integrated model for the development of educational leaders in technical education institutes. *International Journal of Educational Management, 38*(2). Advance online publication. DOI: 10.1108/IJEM-07-2023-0363

Vartanian, A. M. (2024). Fostering Environmental Responsibility in U.S. K-12 Education: A Comparative Study of Strategies Integrating STEM. *Journal of Advanced Research in Education, 3*(1). Advance online publication. DOI: 10.56397/jare.2024.01.05

Wahed, S., & Pitterson, N. (2024). Empowering Diverse Learners: Embracing Culturally Relevant Pedagogy (CRP) in Engineering, Higher Education, and K-12 Settings. *Lecture Notes in Networks and Systems, 901 LNNS*. https://doi.org/DOI: 10.1007/978-3-031-53022-7_20

Weidener, L., & Fischer, M. (2024). Artificial Intelligence in Medicine: Cross-Sectional Study Among Medical Students on Application, Education, and Ethical Aspects. *JMIR Medical Education, 10*(1). Advance online publication. DOI: 10.2196/51247

Yan, L., Sha, L., Zhao, L., Li, Y., Martinez-Maldonado, R., Chen, G., Li, X., Jin, Y., & Gašević, D. (2024). Practical and ethical challenges of large language models in education: A systematic scoping review. In *British Journal of Educational Technology* (Vol. 55, Issue 1). https://doi.org/DOI: 10.1111/bjet.13370

Yang, Z. (2024). Revisiting Educational Issues in the Age of Generative Artificial Intelligence. *Journal of Contemporary Educational Research, 8*(1). Advance online publication. DOI: 10.26689/jcer.v8i1.5810

Yi, H., Liu, T., & Lan, G. (2024). The key artificial intelligence technologies in early childhood education: A review. *Artificial Intelligence Review, 57*(1). Advance online publication. DOI: 10.1007/s10462-023-10637-7

Yim, I. H. Y., & Su, J. (2024). Artificial intelligence (AI) learning tools in K-12 education: A scoping review. *Journal of Computers in Education*. Advance online publication. DOI: 10.1007/s40692-023-00304-9

Zhang, Y., Adams, D., & Lee, K. C. S. (2024). Assessing academic staff's ICT integration in higher education: Instrument development and validation. *Journal of Computers in Education*, *11*(1). Advance online publication. DOI: 10.1007/s40692-022-00248-6

Chapter 2
The Evolution of AI in Education: A Historical and Technological Overview

Mustafa Kayyali
https://orcid.org/0000-0003-3300-262X
Maaref University of Applied Sciences, Syria

ABSTRACT

This chapter traces the evolution of artificial intelligence in education, mapping its trajectory from early computer-assisted instruction to the sophisticated AI systems reshaping today's learning environments. By contextualizing technological progress within historical shifts in pedagogy, it explores how each phase of innovation responded to specific educational needs and social pressures. The discussion critically examines the milestones that led to current AI applications, such as personalized learning platforms, predictive analytics, and virtual teaching assistants. More than a timeline, the chapter reflects on the changing role of educators and the persistent ethical and equity challenges AI introduces. Ultimately, it offers insights into how a historically grounded understanding of AI's development can inform future-proof curriculum strategies that balance innovation with humanistic values.

INTRODUCTION

Education, as both a human endeavor and a social institution, has always evolved in response to the changing needs of societies and the tools available to meet them. From oral traditions and handwritten manuscripts to printed textbooks and digital platforms, each era has introduced new technologies that have gradually reshaped the

DOI: 10.4018/979-8-3373-9225-7.ch002

way knowledge is delivered, acquired, and assessed. Yet, no transformation has been as rapid, far-reaching, or controversial as the integration of artificial intelligence (AI) into educational systems (Williamson & Eynon, 2020). While the idea of intelligent machines has existed for centuries in philosophical musings and speculative fiction, its real-world application to education only began to materialize in the latter half of the 20th century—and has since accelerated with astonishing speed.

This chapter embarks on a journey through the layered history of educational technologies, focusing specifically on the rise of AI and its shifting role in learning ecosystems. To understand where we are today—and where we might be headed—it is essential to explore how AI has moved from the periphery of experimental edtech initiatives to the very center of curriculum reform and policy discourse. The term "AI in education" today encompasses a wide array of applications: intelligent tutoring systems, adaptive learning platforms, automated assessment tools, learning analytics dashboards, natural language processing chatbots, and even emotionally responsive virtual mentors. But these innovations did not appear overnight. They emerged from decades of research, trial and error, cross-disciplinary collaboration, and, importantly, reflection on what it means to teach and to learn.

In the 1960s and 70s, early computer-assisted instruction (CAI) programs like PLATO and LOGO hinted at the potential of machines to support learning, but they were limited by the hardware and programming constraints of the time (Kelkar, 2022). The AI revolution in education has been more evolutionary than revolutionary—a process of cumulative breakthroughs in fields such as machine learning, data science, neuroscience, and education theory. As algorithms became more sophisticated, and as data collection became more pervasive and granular, AI systems began to demonstrate capabilities that were once thought to be uniquely human: recognizing patterns, making predictions, offering personalized feedback, and even simulating human conversation. However, the narrative of progress is incomplete without acknowledging the tensions and contradictions that accompany it. AI has introduced both promise and peril. It offers unprecedented opportunities for scalability, personalization, and inclusivity, but also raises concerns about bias, surveillance, and the dehumanization of education (Costa, 2023). These dualities have fueled debates across academic, policy, and practitioner communities. Is AI a tool for liberation or for control? Does it support the democratization of education or reinforce existing inequities under a more technical guise?

This chapter does not seek to answer these questions definitively, but rather to provide a grounded historical and technological context in which such questions can be meaningfully explored. By tracing the evolution of AI in education—from its conceptual foundations to its current implementations—we hope to equip educators, curriculum designers, researchers, and policymakers with the perspective needed to make informed, ethical, and strategic decisions about the future (Ejjami, 2024). In doing so, we also aim to highlight the enduring role of human judgment, creativity, and care in a landscape increasingly mediated by algorithms. As we stand on the cusp of what some call the Fourth Industrial Revolution, the stakes for education could not be higher. Understanding the historical path of AI's integration into education is not merely an academic exercise—it is a necessary foundation for designing curricula that are both technologically informed and philosophically anchored in the principles of equity, critical thinking, and lifelong learning.

From Chalkboards to Chatbots: A Historical Timeline of Educational Technologies

It's easy to forget, in a world buzzing with virtual classrooms, AI tutors, and intelligent dashboards, that for much of human history, learning was entirely analog—tactile, auditory, communal. The earliest classrooms had no electricity, no projectors, not even books as we know them. Just a teacher, a group of learners, and a shared space where ideas were passed down like heirlooms—fragile and sacred. And yet, each age has found ways to imprint its character onto education through the tools it created. From the grainy dust of chalk to the seamless digital whispers of chatbots, the story of educational technology is less about gadgets and more about the evolving relationship between people, knowledge, and the world they hope to understand.

There's something oddly poetic about the chalkboard—a slab of black or green slate, cold and unforgiving, yet infinitely reusable. Introduced into classrooms in the early 19th century, it offered what felt like a minor revolution: a way to scale instruction. One teacher could now write once, and many students could see the same thing, at the same time (Whitaker, 2020). No longer limited to speaking or scribbling on individual slates, educators could orchestrate a collective experience. It's curious to think how this simple invention foreshadowed many of today's ambitions—accessibility, efficiency, scalability. And yet, back then, it was just chalk and slate. Messy. Dusty. But strangely powerful.

Then came the textbook, an artifact that seemed to promise permanence. Standardization of knowledge. A portable curriculum. The industrial era's love affair with mass production found a willing partner in the printing press, and education, too, became standardized—some might say sterilized. The textbook era brought with it a new rhythm: read, memorize, regurgitate. It cemented the notion that knowledge was something to be consumed, not negotiated. And while that had its utility, it also silenced the unpredictable magic of the classroom—the improvisation, the curiosity, the organic spirals of thought that rarely fit neatly into bullet points.

Fast forward to the mid-20th century, and the classroom started to buzz—literally. The overhead projector, a contraption that hummed and glowed, made its way into lecture halls and elementary schools alike. It marked a shift toward visual learning, toward the performative aspect of teaching. Educators were no longer just facilitators; they became presenters, narrators of information displayed in light. It was still analog, sure, but the idea of augmenting teaching with media had taken root.

The 1960s and 70s introduced something more experimental—almost utopian in its aspirations. Early computer-based instruction systems like PLATO (Programmed Logic for Automated Teaching Operations) emerged from university labs (Cope & Kalantzis, 2023). They were clunky, expensive, and limited, but they shimmered with promise. With pixelated screens and rudimentary interfaces, these machines tried to mimic tutors. The idea that a machine could *teach* was as intoxicating as it was absurd. But there they were—proto-lessons, branching logic, feedback loops. They weren't intelligent, not by today's standards, but they were persistent. PLATO, in particular, hinted at the future: social forums, online testing, even digital art and games. It was the seed of what would later become the edtech forest.

In the decades that followed, computers crept into schools like curious guests—first a novelty, then a necessity. The 1980s and 90s witnessed a surge in educational software, often wrapped in cheerful packaging and animated characters. Remember *Reader Rabbit* or *Math Blaster*? These programs weren't just tools; they were experiences. For many children, they offered a kind of learning that textbooks couldn't touch—interactive, rewarding, playful. And yet, beneath the play, there lingered a question: were these tools *teaching*, or merely *entertaining*?

Around the turn of the millennium, the internet cracked things wide open. No longer was technology confined to the classroom or the home computer. Suddenly, knowledge was everywhere—floating in the cloud, scattered across forums, videos, articles, simulations. Platforms like Khan Academy, Coursera, and Edmodo reimagined what learning could look like outside the physical classroom. Education became disembodied, asynchronous, borderless. It was liberating, and disorienting. The teacher's role began to shift again—not as the sole source of truth, but as a guide through an overwhelming sea of content.

This was also the era when data began to matter. Learning Management Systems (LMS) weren't just about posting homework or tracking grades—they became quiet observers of student behavior (Winstone et al, 2021). Clicks, timestamps, page views—every interaction was logged, analyzed, repurposed. The classroom had eyes now, and they were watching silently, building models, predicting outcomes. This invisible architecture of surveillance was sold as personalization. And in many ways, it was. But it also introduced a strange tension: learning became both more intimate and more monitored. And then came artificial intelligence—not suddenly, not with a bang, but gradually, like a fog rolling in. Chatbots, recommendation engines, predictive analytics, automated grading—they started to populate the educational landscape not as flashy disruptors, but as silent assistants. They answered questions, flagged struggling students, suggested next steps. They didn't lecture; they whispered. And students, often unknowingly, began to learn in partnership with algorithms.

This evolution—from chalkboards to chatbots—is not merely technological. It's philosophical. It reflects shifting assumptions about what it means to know, to teach, to be a learner. The chalkboard emphasized collective witnessing—everyone saw the same thing at the same time. AI emphasizes individual experience—each learner receives a tailored path, a private narrative (Sundari et al, 2024). Is something lost in that solitude? Perhaps. Or perhaps it's a necessary response to the diversity of modern learners, each with their own context, needs, constraints.

Still, amid all this change, the human core of education resists extinction. Technologies come and go, but the classroom remains—physical or virtual—as a space of connection, conflict, questioning. Even the most sophisticated chatbot cannot replicate the subtle nuance of a teacher's gaze when a student is lost, or the thrill of a spontaneous debate erupting from a tangential question. AI may process faster, recall perfectly, and adapt in milliseconds, but it does not *care*. At least, not yet. And perhaps that's the final boundary—emotion, empathy, the messiness of being human. And let's not pretend the journey has been smooth or equitable. The digital divide is real and persistent. Many schools, particularly in the Global South or underserved urban areas, struggle to access even basic digital infrastructure, let alone AI-powered tutors (Ahmed, 2024). Meanwhile, elite institutions are piloting virtual reality labs and biometric feedback systems. The gap widens, not just in access but in imagination—what students believe is possible for their future is shaped by the tools they are given today. Educational technology, then, is not just about *how* we learn, but *who* gets to learn what, and under what conditions.

Looking back, it's astonishing how many of today's educational debates mirror those of the past, albeit in new guises. Should we prioritize skills or content? Can machines replace teachers? Does personalization improve outcomes or isolate learners? Each generation grapples with its own version of these questions, using the tools of its time as both mirrors and hammers—reflecting values, reshaping practices. And perhaps that's the point. Technology in education is not a straight line but a spiral—each turn echoing the last, but with a twist. The chalkboard wasn't just a tool; it was a worldview (Rennie et al, 2019). So is the chatbot. Each carries with it assumptions about power, knowledge, agency. What's written, what's spoken, what's computed—these aren't neutral acts. They shape how we think, how we relate to others, how we make sense of the world. So, as we sit here now, surrounded by intelligent machines and endless data, it's worth pausing. Not to romanticize the past or demonize the future, but to remember that every educational technology, no matter how advanced, is just a tool—amplifying some human intention, muting another. The chalkboard amplified the teacher's voice; the chatbot amplifies data-driven responsiveness. But the question remains: whose voice is missing, and who decides what gets amplified next? Because in the end, learning is still—perhaps always will be—an act of shared meaning-making. No algorithm can automate that.

The Rise of Artificial Intelligence in Pedagogical Practice

One doesn't quite notice the quiet arrival of a revolution until it's everywhere—woven into daily routines, embedded in tools we take for granted, murmuring softly behind the scenes of what once required only human hands. Artificial intelligence in education didn't roar its way into classrooms. It crept in. A whisper here. A shortcut there. A suggestion box that seemed just a bit too precise. And before long, teachers weren't just instructors—they were interacting with something else entirely. Something that didn't sleep, didn't forget, didn't guess. Something that *learned.*

The infusion of AI into pedagogy is not, as some headlines suggest, a sudden rupture from tradition (Selwyn, 2019). It's more like sediment layered over time—complex, subtle, and, at points, unsettling. What began as basic automation—grading multiple-choice questions or organizing class schedules—has evolved into something far more sophisticated: algorithms that monitor engagement levels, systems that predict student performance before even the students themselves suspect trouble, and chatbots that simulate a tutor's voice with eerie fluency.

The question isn't whether AI is present in pedagogical practice. It is. The question is how deeply it's shaping the underlying structures of how teaching happens—and what that means for the nature of learning itself. For decades, pedagogy was built around scarcity: one teacher, many students; limited time, infinite needs. AI, at least in theory, flips that equation. Suddenly, there's no reason every student should receive the same worksheet, hear the same explanation, or wait until they fail to receive support. Adaptive learning platforms—like Knewton, Squirrel AI, or Content Technologies Inc.—promise real-time personalization (Rizvi et al, 2025). Not personalization as a euphemism, but literal path branching: each click, pause, mistake, and success folding into a profile that guides what the learner sees next. The dream? A curriculum that molds itself to the learner like clay around a hand. But dreams have shadows. There's a quiet unease in handing over pedagogical judgment to a machine, however "intelligent" it may appear. Educators are trained to read nuance, to sense hesitation behind a raised hand, to catch the flicker of confusion that doesn't register in test scores. AI, for all its predictive prowess, lacks that deeply human radar. A student may complete every task the algorithm serves and still feel unseen. Still feel lost. Still feel like education is something happening to them, not with them.

That said, AI has filled certain voids with impressive competence. Take intelligent tutoring systems (ITS) for example—programs designed not just to deliver content but to respond, adapt, and scaffold (Phillips et al, 2020). Systems like Carnegie

Learning or ALEKS don't just hand out problems; they analyze patterns, break down errors, and offer hints calibrated to just the right level of difficulty (Sonmez Unal et al, 2025). Not too hard. Not too easy. Just enough friction to move learning forward. For subjects like math or coding, where structure and logic rule, these tools can be transformative. They offer students a safe space to fail, to iterate, to receive feedback untethered from judgment or social pressure. But is pedagogical practice merely a sequence of optimizations? Is teaching just a matter of feeding the right input to get the desired output? If so, AI excels. If not, something else is at stake. Somewhere in the pedagogical field, there's always been an emotional charge—an unspoken current that flows between teacher and learner. It's in the stories that make a concept stick. In the unexpected laughter. In the moment a teacher pauses mid-lesson because someone asked a question that veers off-script but opens a door no algorithm saw coming. Can AI do that? Should it?

One of the more fascinating shifts AI has brought is how it reframes the role of the educator (Luckin, 2025). No longer just a knowledge-giver, the teacher becomes a facilitator, an interpreter, a curator of machine-generated insights. It's a role that demands fluency not just in subject matter, but in *data literacy*. Educators are now expected to understand dashboards that spit out heatmaps and predictive models. To adjust instruction based on metrics. To trust, or question, what the algorithm says about their students. It's a new literacy—a kind of pedagogical numeracy—that not every teacher feels prepared for. And yet, there's a kind of beauty in watching how some educators are integrating AI not as a threat, but as a partner. Teachers using AI-driven platforms to identify which students might need a nudge, not a lecture (Ray & Sikdar, 2024). Instructors leveraging automated essay scoring not to replace their feedback, but to amplify it—freeing them to focus on content, voice, originality. In these moments, AI becomes less about replacing the human element and more about re-centering it—liberating teachers from the grind so they can spend more time *teaching*.

Still, caution remains warranted. Not all AI tools are created equal, and many carry embedded assumptions, biases, or blind spots that reflect the data on which they were trained (Scatiggio, 2020). A system trained primarily on Western English-language materials might misinterpret or penalize students whose linguistic or cultural backgrounds differ. Predictive models, while useful, can sometimes become self-fulfilling prophecies. Label a student "at risk" too early or too often, and eventually, the label sticks—regardless of actual capacity or potential. The danger lies not in the prediction, but in how educators respond to it. And here lies one of the thorniest dilemmas: when AI speaks, do we listen more than we should? There's a seduction to data-driven certainty. To believe that numbers know best. But teaching has always involved a degree of mystery, of trusting instincts, of making decisions based not only on evidence, but on care. A teacher might know, deep down, that a student is capable of more than their grades suggest. Will that conviction stand in a room where the algorithm says otherwise?

There's also a moral dimension to AI in pedagogy that can't be swept aside. Questions of surveillance—how much data should we collect? Who owns it? What happens if it's misused?—loom large. When AI tools track every keystroke, every pause, every click, the classroom becomes a panopticon (Kayyali, 2025 D). And while transparency can improve learning, it can also chill risk-taking. Will students experiment, play, fail, if they know the system is always watching, always logging?

The rise of AI also intersects uneasily with the commercialization of education (ADENIYI & AKINSUROJU, 2024). Tech companies often pitch their AI tools with the sleek language of disruption and scalability. But education is not a startup. It's a public good. When profit motives seep into pedagogical tools, priorities can shift in troubling ways. Optimization becomes more important than transformation. Engagement becomes a metric, not a relationship. And teachers, once central figures, risk becoming mere implementers of pre-packaged "solutions."

Yet despite all this, there is something undeniably hopeful in the potential AI brings. Not in replacing teachers, but in augmenting their reach. Not in standardizing learning, but in personalizing it. Imagine a rural classroom with no full-time science teacher, where an AI platform fills the gap—not perfectly, but better than nothing. Imagine a shy student who never speaks in class but blossoms in an AI-mediated writing program that gives them space to experiment without fear of embarrassment. These are not science fiction. They're happening. Still, it's crucial to remember that AI doesn't operate in a vacuum. Its impact depends on how it's designed, deployed, interpreted, and, above all, questioned. Pedagogical practice is not a plug-and-play system—it's a living, breathing negotiation between people, contexts, cultures. AI may enhance that dance, but it cannot choreograph it entirely.

In the end, the rise of AI in pedagogy is not a conclusion. It's a beginning. A new chapter in an age-old story of how humans teach and learn, stumble and adapt (Muthuswamy, 2022). It demands humility—acknowledging that even our smartest machines reflect our own limitations, our values, our blind spots. But it also demands imagination. Because maybe, just maybe, with care and caution and creativity, AI can help us build learning spaces that are more just, more responsive, and more deeply human than we've dared to dream.

Milestones in AI-Driven Learning Tools and Systems

Tracing the lineage of AI-driven learning tools is like walking through a gallery of ambition—each artifact a testament to what we once thought machines might be capable of, each innovation a brushstroke shaped by the era's pedagogical hunger, technological constraints, and often, a pinch of naivety. Some tools flared briefly, flickered out. Others quietly endured, evolved, and became embedded in the educational DNA of millions of learners worldwide. And between the lines of this history, one can read something more profound than technological progress: the slow but unrelenting redefinition of what it means to "teach" and "learn" in a world co-constructed with algorithms.

The earliest milestones were never really about "intelligence" in the contemporary sense. They were about structure—about carving out a sequence, a logic, a pathway through which content could be delivered systematically, repetitively, predictably. Take the case of PLATO (Programmed Logic for Automated Teaching Operations), developed in the 1960s at the University of Illinois (Cope & Kalantzis, 2021). It was massive, clunky, and constrained by hardware that, by today's standards, would struggle to power a smartwatch. Yet PLATO was a marvel in its time. It didn't merely display content; it engaged. It tracked. It adjusted. It even supported early forms of social interaction—message boards, real-time chat—long before such features became pedagogical fashion. PLATO wasn't intelligent in the modern machine learning sense, but it was radically aware of its learner. And that, for the time, was enough to turn heads.

Then came the 1980s and 90s, when the world fell in love with "edutainment." Tools like *Reader Rabbit*, *Math Blaster*, and *Carmen Sandiego* blurred the lines between learning and play (Brooks, 2022). While not technically AI in the formal sense, these tools hinted at a new philosophy: that engagement might be the doorway to comprehension, and that learning needn't feel like drudgery. They weren't responsive in the algorithmic sense, but they were immersive—and that immersion laid the emotional groundwork for what AI systems would later capitalize on: the promise of tailored, intuitive, even delightful education.

True AI in education, though—the kind that learns from learners—began to bloom in earnest at the turn of the century. This was the age of Intelligent Tutoring Systems (ITS), such as AutoTutor, Cognitive Tutor, and ALEKS (Ali, 2022). These platforms weren't just repositories of content. They *watched*. They made inferences. They probed. Based on a learner's input, timing, errors, and progress, they adapted their responses—nudging, scaffolding, recalibrating the difficulty of tasks in real time. They mimicked the behavior of expert tutors, albeit in a limited domain, and they did so with a kind of relentless patience only machines can muster.

Take Cognitive Tutor, developed by Carnegie Mellon researchers—it was built on cognitive models of how students learn algebra (Park, 2020). When a student made an error, the system didn't simply flag it as wrong; it tried to understand *why* the error occurred. Was it a conceptual misunderstanding? A calculation slip? A procedural misstep? Then, based on that diagnosis, it offered targeted feedback. Not just correction—*correction with care*. The kind that, in the hands of a human, might be considered "good teaching." This was AI stepping into the pedagogical arena not as a gimmick but as a serious participant. And yet, despite the sophistication of these tools, their reach remained narrow. They worked best in domains with clean rules—math, physics, grammar. Messier fields—like literature, ethics, or creative writing—resisted their structure. AI could parse syntax, sure, but could it understand tone? Could it respond meaningfully to ambiguity, metaphor, subtext? Not really. Still can't, at least not reliably. But progress didn't wait for perfection.

As the 2010s rolled in, so did the tidal wave of Learning Analytics and Educational Data Mining. Platforms like Khan Academy, Duolingo, and Coursera began embedding machine learning into their scaffolding (Ip, 2024). Not just to deliver content, but to *learn* from learners. Every click, pause, rewind, and response became data—data that fed algorithms designed to predict success, flag risk, and personalize paths. Suddenly, learning was no longer linear. One learner might jump ahead based on performance, while another looped back for reinforcement, all orchestrated by an invisible conductor made of code.

Duolingo, in particular, deserves mention—not because it's perfect (far from it), but because it exemplifies the modern fusion of gamification, spaced repetition, and AI-driven adaptability. Its algorithms adjust the frequency and difficulty of vocabulary and grammar exercises based on your historical performance. Struggle with past participles? You'll see them more often. Breeze through colors and numbers? You'll get less of them. It's an elegant dance, and while critics rightly point out the limitations of its approach (it won't make you fluent), it reflects a milestone in scale: AI that not only adapts, but adapts for millions, simultaneously.

Another inflection point came with automated essay scoring systems—a controversial yet inevitable development. Systems like E-rater (used by ETS) or Project Essay Grade (PEG) promised to reduce the burden of grading by evaluating essays for structure, grammar, vocabulary richness, and coherence (Nikhil et al, 2025). To some, this was a blessing—a liberation from hours of red ink and rubrics. To others, it felt like an affront to the art of writing. Can an algorithm grasp voice, argument, nuance? Can it reward originality? The jury's still out. What's clear is that these tools, flawed though they are, have carved out a role—not as final arbiters, but as co-assessors, assistants that help educators manage scale while preserving judgment.

More recent years have seen an explosion of AI-powered chatbots and virtual teaching assistants. Tools like Jill Watson, developed at Georgia Tech, famously passed as a human teaching assistant in an online course, answering student queries with such accuracy and empathy that most students had no idea they were interacting with a machine. This milestone was not just technical—it was philosophical. It blurred the boundaries between human and machine in pedagogy. If a student feels heard, guided, supported—does it matter who, or what, is doing the guiding? And then, of course, came the neural networks. Transformer-based models like GPT-3 and beyond—now ubiquitous across platforms—ushered in a new era of linguistic sophistication (Veeramachaneni, 2025). No longer constrained by rule-based parsing or templated responses, these models could generate essays, solve math problems, translate languages, simulate historical conversations, and even write code. Their integration into educational tools has been both exhilarating and deeply disorienting. On one hand, they offer unprecedented support: instant explanations, flexible tutoring, on-demand content generation. On the other, they raise a barrage of questions. Are students learning, or are they just outsourcing thought? Are educators assessing understanding, or merely evaluating the output of a machine?

It's hard to pinpoint one final milestone, because the terrain is shifting too rapidly. AI-based proctoring systems—capable of tracking eye movement, facial expressions, background noise—have surged in response to remote learning, sparking heated debates around surveillance and equity. Emotion recognition tools claim to assess student engagement or frustration through facial cues, though their validity remains hotly contested. And adaptive learning environments like Squirrel AI in China use multi-modal data—keystrokes, timing, biometric cues—to customize instruction in real time. It's impressive. It's also, frankly, a bit uncanny. And yet, amid all this technological fanfare, the deeper question persists: are these tools *advancing* learning, or merely *accelerating* it? Are we deepening understanding or just shaving minutes off the process? Is education becoming more humane, or more mechanical?

Perhaps the most significant milestone is not a single tool or system, but a shift in posture—a growing willingness among educators to view AI not as a gimmick or a threat, but as a collaborator. A messy, imperfect, often opaque collaborator—but one that, when used thoughtfully, can extend human capacity rather than replace it. It's a milestone of mindset, not machinery.

Looking ahead, the next frontier may be less about new tools and more about integration—about building ecosystems where AI, teachers, learners, and communities co-create educational experiences that are not only efficient but meaningful. Where machines do the heavy lifting, yes, but where humans still drive the vision. Because if history teaches anything, it's that the most enduring educational technologies are not those that dazzle, but those that serve—quietly, consistently, and with respect for the messy, marvelous business of learning.

The Shifting Role of Educators in the Age of Intelligent Machines

Something is changing. Slowly, subtly, and sometimes with a disquieting elegance, the figure of the teacher—long revered as the anchor of the classroom—has begun to shift. Not disappear, not diminish exactly, but morph into something different. In an age where algorithms can simulate explanations, grade essays in seconds, predict which students are likely to struggle, and even offer encouragement in strangely fluent prose, one begins to wonder: what remains distinctively human in the act of teaching? What is the role of the educator when intelligent machines seem to know so much?

It's tempting to take a defensive stance, to draw thick lines in the sand between machine and mind, to insist that teachers are irreplaceable—and many have, with just cause. But knee-jerk reactions rarely yield clarity. Better, perhaps, to sit with the discomfort, to let the unease speak. Because buried in that discomfort is something revealing, something vital: a sense that teaching has never been about information alone. It has always been about presence. Judgement. Care. The slow and messy business of helping someone become more than they were.

Still, the world is changing fast. Digital tutors don't need sleep. They don't get distracted. They don't forget names or misplace assignments. And yet, in all their efficiency, they lack something that isn't easy to measure—something tactile, ineffable (Kayyali, 2024). Call it intuition, maybe. Or empathy. Or the subtle art of knowing when to push and when to pull back. A good teacher doesn't simply transmit knowledge. They listen between the lines. They read a room. They notice the student who looks away whenever math is mentioned, or the one whose questions hide a hunger for recognition. These are not things AI does well—not yet, at least.

Still, machines are encroaching on pedagogical ground that once seemed uniquely human (FABER, 2021). And that's forced educators to rethink who they are in this new landscape. For some, the shift feels like liberation. Freed from the tyranny of grading stacks of quizzes or crafting dozens of differentiated worksheets, they can focus on mentorship, on dialogue, on fostering critical inquiry. For others, it feels like displacement—a slow erosion of their authority, their centrality, their craft. And for many, it's both at once: an opening and a loss.

There was a time, not too long ago, when being a teacher meant being the primary source of knowledge in the room. The encyclopedia. The oracle. That era is gone. Students can now fact-check in real time, summon definitions with a flick of the wrist, watch world-class lectures from their phones on the way to school. The authority of expertise has been diluted by the immediacy of information. But maybe that's not the tragedy it first appears to be. Maybe the teacher's role was never meant to be about hoarding knowledge, but about helping others navigate it. Interpret it. Wrestle with it. And so, the teacher of today—and perhaps more so, of tomorrow—is becoming less a fountain of facts and more a guide through the noise. A curator. A facilitator. A bridge. They orchestrate experiences rather than deliver monologues. They ask better questions instead of just giving better answers. They help students learn how to think, not just what to think. In a world overflowing with content, discernment becomes the most precious skill—and that's something no machine can quite instill. Not in the same way. Not with the same resonance.

Yet, let's not romanticize. The integration of AI into educational environments hasn't been seamless or uniformly empowering (Qutieshat, 2025). In many cases, teachers are handed tools they didn't choose, trained in workshops that feel rushed and superficial, then expected to adopt systems that monitor their every move. Teaching has become data-rich, but also increasingly surveilled. Dashboards track not just student performance, but teacher compliance. Metrics become mandates. And somewhere along the way, the space to improvise, to wander, to be human—it shrinks. What happens when the artistry of teaching is flattened into checkboxes and key performance indicators?

There's also a generational tension at play. Younger educators, raised with digital fluency, may embrace AI with curiosity, even enthusiasm. But for others—veterans of chalkboards and overhead projectors—the shift feels alien. Like something essential is being lost. Something soulful. And they're not wrong to worry. When the language of education becomes saturated with terms like "optimization," "efficiency," and "personalized delivery," one has to ask: where is the space for wonder? For slow thinking? For serendipity? And yet, for all the hand-wringing, something quietly hopeful is emerging. In classrooms where AI is used thoughtfully, not as a replacement but as an enhancement, something powerful happens. A teacher sees that a student who rarely speaks is suddenly excelling on an adaptive writing platform. A shy learner blossoms under the patient, nonjudgmental guidance of a chatbot tutor (Choi & Chang, 2025). Time once spent on repetitive administrative tasks is redirected toward conversations that matter. The machine doesn't teach—it *frees* the teacher to do the things machines still can't. But this balance is delicate. Because while AI can assist, it can also subtly dictate. When teachers rely too heavily on algorithmic suggestions—on predictive analytics, automated feedback, or "recommended" interventions—they risk outsourcing their judgment. And judgment is the heart of pedagogy. It's not just about knowing what works—it's about knowing *when* it works, for *whom*, and *why*. No dashboard knows a student's home life. No chatbot sees the tear in someone's eye. No algorithm grasps the full context of a human story. And education, when done well, is always deeply personal.

There's also the question of emotional labor. As machines take over cognitive tasks, teachers are increasingly expected to serve as emotional anchors. Counselors. Motivators. Social workers. The pandemic only intensified this shift. As students returned to classrooms bearing grief, anxiety, and disconnection, teachers were asked to do more than teach. They were asked to *heal*. But who supports the teachers? Who holds space for their exhaustion, their burnout, their own disorientation in a world that keeps reinventing itself faster than anyone can catch up?

Perhaps the role of the educator now is not to resist AI, nor to surrender to it, but to dance with it—clumsily at first, perhaps, but with growing rhythm. To use it as a mirror and a tool, not a master. To reimagine pedagogy as a collaboration between the analytical strengths of machines and the emotional, ethical, and relational strengths of human beings (Sarı et al, 2024). That collaboration requires trust. It requires agency. And it requires a seat at the table where decisions about technology's role in education are being made. Because here's the truth: AI will not stop advancing. It will grow more nuanced, more persuasive, more ubiquitous. It will write lessons, answer questions, even offer feedback that feels eerily thoughtful. But it will not care. It will not celebrate a student's growth, mourn their setbacks, or change its mind because of a moment of empathy. And perhaps that is where the teacher's role now lives—in those messy, liminal spaces where machines cannot follow. In the hesitations. The jokes. The digressions. The silence after a tough question. The knowing glance. The leap of faith.

The educator in the age of intelligent machines is not obsolete. Far from it. They are more necessary than ever—not as clerks of information, but as architects of meaning. Not as content deliverers, but as cultural translators, ethical stewards, mentors in a world awash with synthetic certainty. The future of education is not about choosing between humans and machines (Kayyali, 2025 A). It's about choosing *how* humans and machines learn to coexist, and who gets to shape that relationship. So yes, the role is shifting. It's uncertain. It's evolving faster than most can track. But maybe that's the point. Maybe education was never meant to be static. Maybe teaching, like learning itself, is a process of becoming. And if educators are to remain at the heart of that process, they must be allowed the same grace we afford to students: the space to adapt, to experiment, to get it wrong, and to grow.

Lessons from the Past, Roadmaps for the Future: Toward a Resilient AI-Integrated Curriculum

If education has always been a mirror of society—its hopes, its anxieties, its shifting values—then curriculum, in all its scripted rigidity and whispered improvisations, is the reflection that lingers longest. It's both a container and a compass. A slow-moving river that absorbs every new current and yet, somehow, never loses the shape of its banks. And in this moment—this messy, humming moment of AI-infused everything—we find ourselves staring at that reflection, squinting for clarity. What should a future-ready curriculum actually *look* like? Not the blueprint drawn in sleek slides and policy memos, but the real one: flawed, lived-in, resilient enough to survive the tremors of rapid change.

The thing about history—if you listen closely enough—is that it rarely whispers the same lesson twice in the same language. It mutates. The overconfidence of one era becomes the cautionary tale of the next. And nowhere is this clearer than in our uneasy dance with educational technology (Levine & Van Pelt, 2021). We've been here before, haven't we? The hype cycles. The silver-bullet solutions. The promises of transformation wrapped in the seductive language of disruption. Radio was going to democratize knowledge. So was television. Then computers. Then the internet. Each time, the world tilted slightly, yet the core questions—What does it mean to learn? Who decides what matters? How do we build a just and inclusive education system?—remained, like a heartbeat under the noise. So, what can be salvaged from the clutter of past reforms? What patterns, if any, are worth keeping close?

First, perhaps, is the reminder that no technology, however advanced, can fix what is fundamentally a human issue. Inequity, disengagement, curriculum irrelevance—these are not software problems. They are design problems, cultural problems, political problems (Kayyali, 2025 B). AI may accelerate certain capabilities, but it cannot resolve the deeper contradictions baked into many of our educational systems. A curriculum built for compliance will not suddenly become critical because it's delivered by a machine. Personalization algorithms won't matter if the foundational content lacks meaning. The medium may evolve, but the message needs more than a technical upgrade—it needs a soul-searching rewrite.

Second, there's the lesson of adaptability—not as a buzzword, but as an ethos. Curricula that endure tend to be those that breathe. That allow for surprise. That leave room for the unexpected. During the COVID-19 pandemic, the systems that bent survived; the ones that clung rigidly to pre-packaged content crumbled (Sutcliffe, 2024). Teachers improvised. Students adapted. And amid the chaos, many discovered that flexibility is not the enemy of rigor—it's often its companion. If we're to integrate AI into curricula without ossifying the process, we need structures that accommodate change without losing coherence. Think modular, iterative, dialogic. Think curriculum not as a script, but as a scaffolding that evolves with both technology and learners.

And yet, it's not enough to tinker. If AI is truly going to be more than a tacked-on novelty—if it's to shape the core of what and how we learn—then we need to ask harder questions about design. A resilient AI-integrated curriculum cannot be built around content alone. It must also reckon with process. With ethics. With the deepening entanglement between cognition, emotion, and machine mediation. It has to teach students not just how to use AI tools, but how to *understand* them—where they come from, how they're trained, what assumptions they carry, and what biases lurk inside their code.

That means embedding *AI literacy* at multiple levels. Not just coding or prompt engineering, though those are part of it. But also philosophical literacy. Ethical reasoning. Historical understanding. Why does an algorithm recommend what it recommends? Who benefits when a predictive model shapes university admissions or hiring practices? What happens when a language model misrepresents a marginalized voice? These are not technical questions. They are civic ones. And the curriculum must prepare learners to face them with clarity and conscience.

To do this well, interdisciplinary design becomes non-negotiable. The days of siloed subjects—math here, history there, technology over in its own digital corner—feel increasingly archaic in a world where data, narrative, and systems thinking collide at every turn. A resilient curriculum needs to dissolve some of those boundaries (Brogden et al, 2022). Imagine literature classes where students analyze not just the themes of a dystopian novel, but the predictive algorithms that echo its warnings. Science classes that don't just teach the principles of machine learning, but explore its environmental impact. Social studies that interrogate how surveillance tools reshape public space, identity, and resistance. These are not add-ons. They are the curriculum. But even the most visionary curriculum risks irrelevance without the right pedagogical approach. AI does many things well—but it does not nurture. It does not provoke. It does not wonder. The human teacher, then, remains central—not as a content dispenser, but as a facilitator of inquiry, a co-learner, a translator between machine output and human meaning. A resilient curriculum must empower educators, not sideline them. It must build in spaces for teacher agency, professional judgment, and localized adaptation. Because what works in a rural Syrian village may not land in a New York charter school. Context matters. Culture matters. And AI, brilliant though it may be, often forgets that.

One of the more subtle dangers of AI integration is the drift toward what could be called *algorithmic determinism*—the quiet assumption that data-driven insights are inherently neutral, superior, or final (Elliott, 2021). A curriculum shaped too heavily by analytics may begin to chase outcomes at the expense of questions. It may prioritize efficiency over exploration. Worse, it may narrow the horizon of what counts as success. If predictive systems suggest that a student is unlikely to thrive in a particular path, will the curriculum steer them elsewhere? Will it limit ambition in the name of optimization?

Resilience, then, is not just about technical robustness. It's about epistemic humility. A willingness to let mystery persist. To leave room for failure, contradiction, serendipity. In designing AI-integrated curricula, we need to protect the soft edges of education—the spaces where students linger, meander, change their minds. Where learning isn't always linear, and outcomes aren't always quantifiable. Because those are often the moments that shape a life. And what about assessment? In a world where machines can write essays, solve equations, and simulate dialogue with eerie competence, traditional forms of evaluation begin to wobble. If students can generate flawless answers with a prompt, what are we really measuring? Knowledge? Effort? Strategy? The resilient curriculum will need to shift toward performance, process, reflection. Assessments that value *how* a student arrives at an insight, not just whether they reached the destination. Portfolios, peer critique, creative synthesis—these may become more central than ever, not out of nostalgia, but out of necessity.

Of course, none of this happens in a vacuum. Policy frameworks, infrastructure investment, teacher training, and community engagement all play a role. But curriculum—if designed with intention—can act as a lever. A kind of quiet revolution. A blueprint not just for what students learn, but for the kind of society we want to build. And in that sense, the integration of AI into curriculum isn't just a technical challenge—it's a moral one. Who decides what is taught, and by extension, what is not? Which histories are centered? Which futures are imagined?

There's no final roadmap—no one-size-fits-all schematic to follow. But there are principles. Rooted in experience, shaded by failure, shaped by listening. The resilient AI-integrated curriculum will likely be messy. Incomplete. Always evolving. But it will be anchored in something enduring: the belief that education is not a transaction but a transformation. That learners are not data points but stories in motion. That the future is not something to be optimized, but something to be co-authored. And maybe that's the real lesson. That even in the age of intelligent machines, the work of teaching and learning remains, at its heart, a profoundly human endeavor—fragile, flawed, and utterly irreplaceable.

CONCLUSION

The integration of artificial intelligence into education is not an isolated phenomenon, nor is it merely a matter of technological substitution. It represents a profound shift in how we conceptualize knowledge, the learner, and the very purpose of education. As we reflect on the historical trajectory of AI in education—from the rudimentary teaching machines of the mid-twentieth century to today's data-rich, adaptive learning environments—we begin to see a pattern of increasing complexity, personalization, and automation. But this evolution has not been linear, nor has it been universally embraced. At each stage, the promises of AI have been accompanied by skepticism, resistance, and a critical reevaluation of educational values.

One of the most striking realizations from this historical overview is the extent to which each new generation of AI tools has reflected the pedagogical priorities and societal anxieties of its time. In the early days, AI was seen primarily as a means of delivering information more efficiently—aligned with behaviorist models of learning that emphasized repetition and reinforcement. Later, as constructivist theories gained traction, AI tools evolved to support exploration, creativity, and learner agency. Today, amid growing concerns about global competitiveness, mental health, and the ethics of data collection, AI in education is being positioned as both a solution and a source of new dilemmas.

This duality cannot be ignored. AI can foster deeper engagement through personalized content and real-time feedback, yet it can also contribute to learner isolation if it replaces rather than complements human interaction. It can democratize access to high-quality instruction, yet it can also entrench existing inequalities when deployed in resource-poor settings or when biased algorithms go unchecked. It can streamline administrative burdens, freeing educators to focus on teaching, yet it can also pressure them to conform to data-driven performance metrics that reduce education to a series of quantifiable outputs.

Therefore, as we look toward the future of curriculum design, the question is not whether we should adopt AI, but *how* we can do so in ways that preserve the humanistic core of education. Future-proofing the curriculum means more than embedding the latest tools or anticipating labor market trends—it means cultivating a generation of learners who can think critically about the tools they use, who understand the ethical dimensions of AI, and who are prepared not just to *use* intelligent systems, but to *question*, *shape*, and *co-govern* them.

Educators and policymakers must be wary of the allure of technical determinism—the belief that technology alone can solve deeply human problems. While AI can offer powerful new capabilities, the values that guide its use must come from us. The historical and technological overview presented in this chapter is a reminder that every technological turn in education has been shaped not only by what machines can do, but by what humans decide they *should* do.

In closing, the story of AI in education is still being written. It is a narrative in which educators, learners, technologists, ethicists, and communities all have a voice. If we are to ensure that the integration of AI serves to deepen rather than diminish the human experience of learning, we must remain critically engaged, historically informed, and ethically grounded. Only then can we design educational futures that are both innovative and just.

REFERENCES

Adeniyi, F. B., & Akinsuroju, O. E. (2024). Harnessing artificial intelligence (AI) for strategic human resource planning, educational commercialization, and navigating marketization dynamics. FUOYE Journal of Educational Management, 1(2).

Ahmed, F. (2024). The digital divide and AI in education: Addressing equity and accessibility. *Journal of AI Integration in Education*, *1*(2), 12–23.

Ali, U. (2022). Cognitive computing and intelligent tutoring systems in education technology. *Multidisciplinary Research in Computing Information Systems*, *2*(2), 77–99.

Brogden, L., Bernie, D., Boston, M., Forster, A. M., Galbrun, L., Hepburn, L. A., & Morkel, J. (2022). A learning design framework for community resilience: International and transdisciplinary perspectives on a boundary object. *International Journal of Educational Research Open*, *3*, 100200.

Brooks, C. D. (2022). Prodigy Game and Third-Grade Mathematics Achievement in an Urban Setting (Doctoral dissertation, Walden University).

Choi, W. C., & Chang, C. I. (2025). *A Survey of Techniques*. Design, Applications, Challenges, and Student Perspective of Chatbot-Based Learning Tutoring System Supporting Students to Learn in Education.

Cope, B., & Kalantzis, M. (2021). A Little History of e-Learning.

Cope, B., & Kalantzis, M. (2023). A little history of e-learning: Finding new ways to learn in the PLATO computer education system, 1959–1976. *History of Education*, *52*(6), 905–936.

Costa, S. (2023). Artificial intelligence in education: Challenges and opportunities in learning.

Ejjami, R. (2024). The future of learning: AI-based curriculum development. *International Journal for Multidisciplinary Research*, *6*(4), 1–31.

Elliott, A. (2021). *Making sense of AI: Our algorithmic world*. John Wiley & Sons.

FABER, L. (2021). Augmenting Human Pedagogy: A Cultural History of Automation in Teaching. *Popular Culture Studies Journal*, *9*(1), 44.

Ip, K. (2024). The rise of EdTech: Transforming education through entrepreneurial ventures. Advances in Online Education: A Peer-Reviewed Journal, 3(2), 177-193.

Kayyali, M. (2024). Future possibilities and challenges of AI in education. In *Transforming education with generative AI: Prompt engineering and synthetic content creation* (pp. 118–137). IGI Global Scientific Publishing.

Kayyali, M. (2025a). The Future of AI in Education: Predictions and Emerging Trends. Next-Generation AI Methodologies in Education, 367-406.

Kayyali, M. (2025b). AI in Higher Education: Revolutionizing Curriculum and Administration. In AI Adoption and Diffusion in Education (pp. 31-62). IGI Global Scientific Publishing.

Kayyali, M. (2025c). Generative AI and Education: Transforming Teaching and Learning Through Collaborative Intelligence. In Humans and Generative AI Tools for Collaborative Intelligence (pp. 25-52). IGI Global Scientific Publishing.

Kelkar, S. (2022). Between AI and learning science: The evolution and commercialization of intelligent tutoring systems. *IEEE Annals of the History of Computing*, *44*(1), 20–30.

Levine, A., & Van Pelt, S. (2021). *The great upheaval: Higher education's past, present, and uncertain future*. JHU Press.

Luckin, R. (2025). Nurturing human intelligence in the age of AI: Rethinking education for the future. *Development and Learning in Organizations*, *39*(1), 1–4.

Muthuswamy, P. R. (2022). *New age education models: Innovation and reform in the 21st century*. Notion Press.

Nikhil, V., Annamalai, R., & Jayapal, S. (2025). NLP-Driven Approaches to Automated Essay Grading and Feedback. In Adopting Artificial Intelligence Tools in Higher Education (pp. 99-117). CRC Press.

Park, S. (2020). The Effects of a Web-Based Tool with Reading and Cognitive Procedural Scaffolds on Algebra Learning Among Low-And-High-Achieving Readers and its Evaluation from Teachers' Perspectives (Doctoral dissertation).

Phillips, A., Pane, J. F., Reumann-Moore, R., & Shenbanjo, O. (2020). Implementing an adaptive intelligent tutoring system as an instructional supplement. *Educational Technology Research and Development*, *68*(3), 1409–1437.

Qutieshat, A. (2025). *Artificial Intelligence in Higher Education: A Contemporary Examination of Illich's Theories*. Springer Nature.

Ray, S., & Sikdar, D. P. (2024). AI-Driven flipped classroom: Revolutionizing education through digital pedagogy. *Psychology (Irvine, Calif.)*, *7*(2), 169–179.

Rennie, L. J., Stocklmayer, S., & Gilbert, J. K. (2019). *Supporting self-directed learning in science and technology beyond the school years*. Taylor & Francis.

Rizvi, I., Bose, C., & Tripathi, N. (2025). Transforming Education: Adaptive Learning, AI, and Online Platforms for Personalization. In *Technology for Societal Transformation: Exploring the Intersection of Information Technology and Societal Development* (pp. 45–62). Springer Nature Singapore.

Sarı, T., Nayir, F., & Bozkurt, A. (2024). Reimagining education: Bridging artificial intelligence, transhumanism, and critical pedagogy. *Journal of Educational Technology and Online Learning*, *7*(1), 102–115.

Scatiggio, V. (2020). Tackling the issue of bias in artificial intelligence to design ai-driven fair and inclusive service systems. How human biases are breaching into ai algorithms, with severe impacts on individuals and societies, and what designers can do to face this phenomenon and change for the better.

Selwyn, N. (2019). *Should robots replace teachers?: AI and the future of education*. John Wiley & Sons.

Sonmez Unal, D., Solovey, E., Arrington, C. M., & Walker, E. (2025). Modeling the phases of rule learning during problem solving with an interactive learning environment. *User Modeling and User-Adapted Interaction*, *35*(1), 7.

Sundari, M. S., Penthala, H. R., & Nayyar, A. (2024). Transforming education through AI-enhanced content creation and personalized learning experiences. In *Impact of artificial intelligence on society* (pp. 98–118). Chapman and Hall/CRC.

Sutcliffe, R. (2024). *The Fourth Civilization, Volume Two: Technology, Ethics, and Society*. Wipf and Stock Publishers.

Veeramachaneni, V. (2025). Large language models: A comprehensive survey on architectures, applications, and challenges. *Advanced Innovations in Computer Programming Languages*, *7*(1), 20–39.

Whitaker, T. (2020). *What great teachers do differently: Nineteen things that matter most*. Routledge.

Williamson, B., & Eynon, R. (2020). Historical threads, missing links, and future directions in AI in education. *Learning, Media and Technology*, *45*(3), 223–235.

Winstone, N., Bourne, J., Medland, E., Niculescu, I., & Rees, R. (2021). "Check the grade, log out": Students' engagement with feedback in learning management systems. *Assessment & Evaluation in Higher Education*, *46*(4), 631–643.

Chapter 3
Intelligent Curricula: Personalizing Learning With Artificial Intelligence and Developing Transformative Skills

Abílio Lourenço
https://orcid.org/0000-0001-6920-0412
University of Minho, Portugal

Sabina Valente
https://orcid.org/0000-0003-2314-3744
Polytechnic Institute of Portalegre, Portugal

ABSTRACT

This chapter explores how artificial intelligence can transform curriculum design by personalising learning and supporting the development of essential 21st-century skills. Integrating artificial intelligence into curricula enables adaptive learning environments that respond to individual student needs, promoting equity and improving educational outcomes. The chapter begins by contextualising the growing role of artificial intelligence in education and examining current opportunities and challenges for educators and institutions. It then discusses personalised learning mechanisms, offering examples of how generative artificial intelligence can enhance the student experience. The second section focuses on developing key skills such as critical thinking, collaboration, and digital literacy, showing how they can be integrated into the curriculum with the support of artificial intelligence. Ethical and inclusion issues are also considered to ensure fair and accessible implementation.

DOI: 10.4018/979-8-3373-9225-7.ch003

1. INTRODUCTION

Digital transformation has decisively shaped all sectors of contemporary society, and education is no exception. Among emerging technologies, artificial intelligence (AI) stands out as one of the most promising and disruptive in the educational context. Its potential to analyze large volumes of data, identify patterns, and make automated or assisted decisions opens new possibilities for more effective, personalized, and equitable teaching and learning (Holmes et al., 2019).

Moreover, project-based pedagogical approaches have demonstrated proven effectiveness in the development of complex skills, with AI serving as a catalytic agent that enhances these practices by providing personalized and adaptive resources capable of meeting students' individual needs, promoting more meaningful and contextualized learning (Lourenço & Paiva, 2024).

In recent years, AI has been progressively integrated into educational systems on multiple fronts, including adaptive learning platforms, virtual assistants, intelligent tutoring systems, predictive analytics of student performance, and support for school management (Chen et al., 2020). This trend, also driven by advances in machine learning and natural language processing, is redefining how teachers teach, students learn, and educational institutions design their curricula.

However, the mere introduction of AI technologies into the school environment does not guarantee an automatic improvement in teaching and learning processes. On the contrary, without intentional, critical, and well-structured curriculum design, there is a risk of reinforcing inequalities, algorithmic biases, and outdated pedagogical practices (Williamson & Eynon, 2020). In this sense, it becomes urgent to rethink curricula in light of the potential and challenges brought by generative AI (GenAI), giving rise to the concept of "smart curricula."

1.1. Smart Curricula: Definition and Purpose

In the context of this chapter, "smart curricula" are understood as educational structures that incorporate AI technologies in a critical, ethical manner, oriented toward the holistic development of students. They are characterized by being dynamic, adaptive, and student-centered, promoting personalized learning based on data, without compromising fundamental pedagogical principles, social justice, and the active role of teachers (Holmes et al., 2019; Luckin et al., 2016).

Although the term *smart curricula* do not yet have a single, consolidated definition in the literature, its conception aligns with contemporary pedagogical approaches that value personalization, responsible technological mediation, and educational intentionality. Authors emphasize the importance of critically integrating GenAI in education, highlighting the need to maintain a focus on human development and equity (e.g., Selwyn, 2019; Williamson & Eynon, 2020). These curricula, therefore, are not limited to automating processes but propose an intentional redesign of teaching, in which GenAI acts as an ally to the teacher, expanding the possibilities for student-centered learning.

Unlike traditional approaches, smart curricula do not follow a linear or uniform logic for all students. On the contrary, they aim to offer personalized pathways that take into account individual pace, interests, difficulties, and learning styles. In this process, Holmes and Tuomi (2022) address the concept of AI-mediated personalized learning and discuss the teacher's role in this context. The authors emphasize that although GenAI can offer personalized learning paths, it should be used as a tool to enhance learning, not to replace the teacher or homogenize instruction.

The discussion focuses more on the application of GenAI in the educational system and the associated pedagogical implications.

Beyond personalization, smart curricula assume as a central goal the development of transformative skills, those necessary not only for the constantly evolving job market but also for critical citizenship in a digitized, uncertain, and interdependent world. This includes skills such as critical thinking, creativity, collaboration, digital literacy, complex problem-solving, and ethical awareness (OECD, 2018).

1.2. Generative AI as a Vector of Transformation in Education

GenAI can serve as a catalyst for curriculum renewal through three main avenues (Zawacki-Richter et al., 2019): improving pedagogical efficiency by automating repetitive tasks and providing real-time feedback; personalizing instruction by adjusting content and strategies to student needs; and supporting the development of 21st-century skills by facilitating collaborative, exploratory, and data-driven learning environments.

However, this transformation does not occur without challenges. Issues such as unequal access to technology, lack of teacher training, risks of educational surveillance, and biases in AI algorithms raise legitimate concerns that must be addressed with seriousness and responsibility (Dignum, 2019; Selwyn, 2019).

1.3. Chapter Objectives

Based on this framework, the main objectives of this chapter are:

1. To analyze the opportunities and challenges of integrating generative AI into educational curricula;
2. To explore mechanisms for personalized learning supported by GenAI, with practical examples and empirical evidence;

3. To identify and discuss essential transformative skills in the digital age and strategies to integrate them into the curriculum;
4. To reflect on the ethical, social, and institutional dilemmas of using GenAI in education;
5. To propose future directions for the research and practice of smart curricula, with a focus on inclusion, equity, and pedagogical innovation.

Throughout the following sections, the chapter seeks to offer a comprehensive and critical perspective on the role of GenAI in building more responsive, personalized, and transformative learning environments, respecting the principles of humanistic and future-oriented education.

2. THE GENERATIVE AI REVOLUTION IN EDUCATION: OPPORTUNITIES AND CHALLENGES

GenAI has established itself as one of the driving forces of educational innovation in the 21st century. By offering tools that enable automation, personalization, and predictive analysis, GenAI is reshaping teaching practices, learning methods, and even the principles that govern curriculum design. This section of the chapter explores current applications of GenAI in teaching and learning, reviews the most recent literature on the subject, and discusses the main technical, pedagogical, and cultural challenges associated with its implementation.

2.1 Current Applications of Generative AI in Teaching and Learning

The applications of AI in the educational context are broad and diverse, ranging from institutional management to the classroom. Among the most recurring uses are:

Adaptive Learning Systems

GenAI has been widely applied in adaptive learning systems (Holmes & Tuomi, 2022). The authors explore how Intelligent Tutoring Systems use GenAI to provide automated, adaptive, and individualized instruction, adjusting content and teaching methods based on student performance. They highlight that many of these systems are based on cognitive architectures, reflecting a view of learning centered on information processing and problem-solving. Examples such as Knewton and

DreamBox have been utilized to implement adaptive learning practices, adjusting content according to students' progress.

The use of adaptive learning systems is not limited to content personalization but also extends to data analysis to predict which students may face difficulties in the future. These tools enable the creation of more dynamic and responsive curricula that not only react to student performance but also anticipate their needs, creating a more predictive and preventive approach (Chen et al., 2024).

Information and Communication Technologies

Information and Communication Technologies play a fundamental role in ensuring that AI-based solutions are effective in education. The digital infrastructure, including online learning platforms, communication networks, and mobile devices, enables AI to be used to personalize learning, optimize student interaction, and analyze data in real time. The interactivity and connectivity provided by Information and Communication Technologies are essential for collecting data on student performance and adapting teaching approaches (Luckin, 2016). Without a solid technological foundation, the effectiveness of AI tools in education would be significantly limited. As discussed by Lourenço and Paiva (2024), the globalization of education requires the integration of digital skills to ensure that both teachers and students can take advantage of emerging and adaptive technologies.

These systems, when supported by a robust technological infrastructure, provide teachers with the ability to monitor student progress, offer real-time feedback, and personalize instruction according to each student's specific needs, creating more inclusive and efficient learning environments.

Intelligent Tutoring

The use of GenAI in personalized teaching is transforming education. These systems employ AI to interact with students individually, effectively simulating the role of a human tutor. The technology can answer questions, provide real-time feedback, and help reinforce concepts taught in the classroom (Gomes et al., 2024). For example, Google's Socratic allows students to receive immediate support in math and science questions, while platforms like Carnegie Learning offer real-time tutoring across various subjects.

These systems not only help students understand content more deeply but also provide teachers with valuable insights into areas where students may be facing difficulties. Therefore, they do not replace the teacher but complement them, offering a more focused and effective approach to learning (Reyes & Torres, 2024).

Predictive Analytics

Another significant advancement of AI in the education sector is predictive analytics. Using behavioral data, such as frequency of access to learning platforms or assessment results, predictive analytics tools are able to identify students at risk of dropping out or experiencing learning difficulties (Bo, 2024). This allows teachers to intervene early, taking corrective measures to improve academic performance and reduce dropout rates. Organizations like Knewton have worked with platforms that help predict student performance in real time and suggest the best approaches for intervention (OECD, 2023).

Virtual Assistants and Educational Chatbots

Virtual assistants and educational chatbots have gained popularity in recent years. These systems are based on generative language models, such as OpenAI's GPT-4, and are used to answer questions, support text writing, and even foster critical thinking in educational contexts. Vast databases power these systems and are capable of providing contextually accurate responses to a wide range of academic questions. A practical example is the use of chatbots in universities, such as Georgia State University, which implemented a virtual assistant to help with enrollment and clarify students' administrative questions (Allman et al., 2023).

Automated Feedback Tools

Automation is also present in feedback tools, which can efficiently assess and comment on students' work. Platforms such as Turnitin and Grammarly utilize GenAI to detect plagiarism, suggest improvements in texts, and provide immediate feedback on students' writing (Mayo et al., 2024). Additionally, systems like Gradescope help teachers grade and evaluate exams quickly and accurately, using GenAI to identify patterns in students' errors and suggest areas for improvement.

These tools provide constant feedback, allowing students to adjust their study approaches and continuously improve their academic performance, while also relieving teachers' workload, enabling them more availability for pedagogical mediation and for developing their students' social and emotional skills (Narváez et al., 2025).

Detection of Emotions and Engagement

The detection of emotions and engagement is also being explored in education using GenAI. The analysis of digital behavior, including facial recognition, allows educational systems to adjust teaching in real time to better respond to students' emotional and cognitive needs. Tools like EmoReact have been used to assess students' emotional engagement on learning platforms, adjusting the pace of the lesson or offering pedagogical interventions as needed (Ravenor, 2023). These tools help create more empathetic and receptive learning environments, making teaching more inclusive.

ChatGPT

ChatGPT has been used in both formal and informal contexts for the co-creation of texts, problem-solving, and support for metacognitive reflection (Ruiz-Rojas et al., 2024). The ability to produce complete and coherent responses to a wide range of questions makes ChatGPT a powerful tool to support the development of writing skills, critical reasoning, and creative problem-solving. In this sequence, students can utilize ChatGPT to explore different perspectives on a topic, generate ideas for projects, and even learn to structure arguments logically and convincingly (Suh et al., 2025). Tools like ChatGPT have been increasingly integrated into the teaching and learning process since 2022, providing teachers with new ways to facilitate active learning and the development of critical thinking (Ali et al., 2025).

2.2 Literature Review

In recent years, scientific literature has shown growing interest in the intersection between GenAI and education. The systematic review by Zawacki-Richter et al. (2019) identified significant gaps in teacher involvement in the development and implementation processes of AI technologies. This critique remains valid, but new studies show important advances.

Luckin et al. (2024) advocate a human-centered approach in which AI complements, rather than replaces, teachers' intelligence and roles. AI should enhance human capacities such as empathy and critical thinking. The authors emphasize the importance of integrating technology ethically and consciously. The focus is on empowering educational relationships and personalizing learning. Meanwhile, UNESCO (2023) warns about the ethical risks and global inequalities associated with the adoption of GenAI, reinforcing the need for public policies that ensure access, teacher training, and ethical development of these technologies. Additionally, the OECD (2023) published updated frameworks for integrating digital and GenAI skills into school curricula, underlining the importance of aligning technological innovation with clear pedagogical goals.

The study by Li et al. (2023) analyzes the use of devices with integrated AI to monitor students' behavior in real time in face-to-face classrooms, allowing teaching to be adapted according to their emotional responses. Although it does not directly address virtual or hybrid environments, the principles presented can be adapted to these contexts, provided that pedagogical mediation accompanies them. Behavioral analysis with GenAI can support collaborative practices by improving student interaction and engagement, contributing to more effective learning.

Another emerging theme in the literature is the relationship between AI and equity. Studies highlight the need to develop inclusive technological solutions that consider the cultural, socioeconomic, and cognitive diversity of students (Holmes et al., 2019; Selwyn, 2019; Williamson & Eynon, 2020). The authors warn that without a robust ethical approach, GenAI may perpetuate or exacerbate existing inequalities, such as reproducing biases through biased algorithms or excluding students with limited access to technology. They argue that the development and implementation of AI in education must be guided by solid ethical principles, ensuring inclusion and equity for all students.

The literature has also emphasized the role of GenAI in promoting metacognition and self-regulation of learning, as well as valuing data-driven pedagogical practices, provided they are critically interpreted. The study by D'Mello & Graesser (2023) explores how intelligent tutoring systems can support students in developing metacognitive skills, such as monitoring and regulating their learning, through adaptive interactions and real-time feedback.

The authors discuss how these systems, by incorporating natural dialogue models and data analysis techniques, can provide personalized support that encourages students to reflect on their thinking processes and adjust their learning strategies as needed. Furthermore, they emphasize the importance of critically interpreting data collected by these systems to ensure that pedagogical interventions are effective and ethically sound.

2.3 Technical, Pedagogical, and Cultural Challenges

Despite the enthusiasm, the integration of AI in education presents substantial challenges. They can be grouped into three main categories:

1. *Technical:* The first set of challenges concerns technical issues. Infrastructure limitations, including a lack of connectivity and inadequate equipment, remain a significant obstacle, particularly in developing countries. The quality of data used by GenAI systems is also a concern, as the effectiveness of the tools depends on the accuracy and diversity of the data collected. Additionally, interoperability between educational platforms and GenAI systems is a constant challenge. Often, platforms fail to share data efficiently, which limits teachers' ability to make data-based interventions in real-time (UNESCO, 2023).

2. *Pedagogical:* Pedagogical challenges are mainly related to inadequate teacher training, resistance to new methodologies, and the depersonalization of education. Many teachers still feel uncomfortable about adopting new technologies, especially when these tools are perceived as substitutes for traditional teaching methods. Furthermore, the lack of pedagogical training focused on the use of AI makes it challenging for teachers to effectively integrate these tools into their daily practices. Authors such as Williamson et al. (2023) advocate for strengthening teacher agency as a means to mitigate the risks associated with excessive automation in education. They argue that GenAI should be integrated in a way that complements and strengthens teachers' work without replacing their critical and human mediation. They criticize the growing dependence on automated solutions and the influence of large tech companies, which can reduce teacher autonomy and standardize pedagogical practices. They propose an ethical and critical approach to AI, aiming to strengthen the role of teachers and promote more personalized and inclusive teaching.
3. *Cultural and Ethical:* The cultural and ethical impact of GenAI in education is one of the most debated aspects in current literature. GenAI can perpetuate algorithmic biases, as shown by studies on the use of GenAI in admission and educational assessment systems, which often favor more privileged social groups and discriminate against marginalized groups. Facial recognition and surveillance in classrooms, for example, raise questions about student privacy and the act of observing or excessively controlling something in educational environments. Mohamed et al. (2020) warn of the risk of "digital colonialism," in which AI technologies developed from Eurocentric perspectives are indiscriminately applied in distinct cultural contexts, perpetuating inequalities and historical forms of domination. The authors advocate using a critical approach that challenges the legacies of colonialism, especially in forms of knowledge and power, as a tool for anticipating and critically analyzing sociotechnical futures, enabling the anticipation and mitigation of asymmetric impacts. They highlight, therefore, the importance of developing culturally sensitive, ethical, and politically aware GenAI systems, rejecting universal technological approaches that ignore local specificities.

Furthermore, the role of international guidelines in shaping educational policies related to AI is notable. A relevant example is the UNESCO report on AI and Education (2019), which presents recommendations for the design, development, and implementation of AI technologies in educational systems, emphasizing the inevitability of their presence in the sector. Although the document proposes a roadmap for the inclusive adoption of these technologies, it does not address the hidden costs of AI, which could be revealed by a critical approach to colonial legacies. From this perspective, there is a need for deeper cultural and ethical reflection in the design and application of GenAI in education.

3. PERSONALIZATION OF LEARNING WITH AI

Personalization of learning has become one of the most central concepts in modern education, especially with the growing adoption of GenAI technologies. The use of these tools enables the development of adaptive curricula that can be shaped to the needs and learning pace of each student, resulting in a more effective and engaging educational experience. This chapter explores how GenAI enables personalization of learning, offers practical examples of implementation, and discusses the potentialities and limitations of this approach.

3.1 Personalization of Learning: The Role of AI

Personalization of learning, with the use of AI, allows educational processes to be adapted to the individual needs of students, optimizing their learning experiences. By analyzing student performance, GenAI can adjust the pace, content, and teaching methodologies, promoting a more student-centered approach (Santos & Franqueira, 2020). This has a positive impact on motivation, autonomy, and academic performance by demonstrating how adapting teaching favors learning more effectively (Campos et al., 2025).

Personalization also strengthens self-regulated learning, as it offers the student control over their learning process, allowing them to adjust their strategies as needed (Ferreira & Pedrosa, 2024). However, implementing this personalization requires accurate data and ethical care in the use of such information (Luckin et al., 2016). Furthermore, the role of the teacher remains essential, as technology should not replace human interaction but be used as a complementary tool in the teaching process (Williamson et al., 2023). Thus, personalization through GenAI offers great opportunities but also challenges that must be addressed with caution.

Intelligent tutoring systems are a classic example of how GenAI can personalize learning. These systems utilize AI algorithms to monitor student progress in real-time and provide adaptive feedback. According to Nascimento-Fragoso & Coutinho (2025), intelligent tutoring systems are designed to imitate the behavior of a human tutor, adjusting the difficulty level of questions and pedagogical approach based on student responses. The system analyzes student interactions, identifies areas of difficulty, and offers specific support to improve performance. Studies, such as those by VanLehn (2011), show that the use of these systems has produced positive results, with students demonstrating significant improvements in their learning.

The author discusses how intelligent tutoring systems can adapt question difficulty, adjust pedagogical approaches, and provide specific feedback based on student interactions. The author emphasizes that these systems are designed to diagnose student difficulties and provide personalized support, attempting to simulate the effectiveness of a human tutor in the teaching and learning process.

For example, the Cognitive Tutor Algebra I intelligent tutoring system, developed by Carnegie Learning, has been widely used for teaching mathematics. The platform adapts content according to student performance, providing specific materials and exercises for areas where students have more difficulty (Sales & Pane, 2021). The system's design assumes students follow a predefined order of material, moving from one section to the next only after mastering the skills of the previous section. However, the software offers teachers the flexibility to override this structure, allowing them to reassign students to different sections of the curriculum. These systems have proven effective in helping students overcome specific obstacles in the learning process and progress at their own pace, resulting in improved educational outcomes.

3.2 Adaptive and Student-Centered Curricula

With the incorporation of GenAI, school curricula can be continuously adjusted to the individual needs of students. Instead of adopting a uniform curricular model, GenAI allows dynamic adaptation of content and pedagogical methodologies as the profile and progress of students evolve. AI-based adaptive learning platforms represent a clear example of this transformative potential, promoting personalized learning pathways with a direct impact on student engagement and academic performance. Solutions like Carnegie Learning, DreamBox Learning, Smart Sparrow, and Knewton demonstrate how these technologies can shape curricula based on each student's preferences, pace, and difficulties, optimizing the educational experience (Dutta et al., 2024).

The Carnegie Learning Cognitive Tutor programs stand out for offering personalized learning adapted to the pace and needs of each student. Through the integration of educational technology, applied curriculum, and principles of cognitive science, these programs promote a more effective and student-centered teaching experience. According to Giraffa and Kohls-Santos (2023), one of the main differentiators is the use of intelligent software that continuously assesses the student's knowledge level and adjusts, in real time, the proposed content and exercises, ensuring an individualized learning path. The theoretical robustness and proven results in school environments position the Cognitive Tutor programs as an innovative and effective educational solution with great potential to improve academic performance and student autonomy.

DreamBox Learning, for example, offers a math teaching platform that adapts not only to the student's skill level but also to their learning style. The system continuously analyzes student responses and dynamically adjusts the learning pace. According to Dutta et al. (2024), students who used DreamBox Learning showed significant performance gains compared to those using traditional teaching methods.

Smart Sparrow is an adaptive learning platform designed to create personalized and interactive educational experiences centered on the student. This platform allows teachers to create dynamic digital content that adjusts to each student's performance (Sikora et al., 2021). Through intuitive authoring tools, teachers can develop personalized learning paths, offering immediate feedback and adapting content according to individual student responses and needs. One of its distinctive features is the ability to provide detailed analytical data on student progress and behavior, enabling more effective pedagogical interventions.

Knewton, in turn, is an adaptive learning platform that uses student interaction data to adjust content in real time, aiming to maximize learning effectiveness (Navarro, 2024). When a student encounters difficulties with a specific concept, the system adjusts the content, providing support material to reinforce that concept before moving on to new concepts. This is possible because the system collects and analyzes a large amount of data on student performance, which allows curriculum personalization.

These examples are just a few of many that demonstrate how GenAI can be used to create a learning experience that is not only more personalized but also more efficient, as it allows each student to learn at their own pace without the pressure of keeping up with peers who progress at different rates.

3.3 Practical Cases and Empirical Evidence

Several empirical studies have investigated the impact of AI systems on the personalization of learning. The study by García et al. (2023) examines the application of artificial intelligence algorithms in virtual learning environments, aiming to adapt teaching to the needs of students in Digital Systems courses. The research proposes a hybrid learning model (b-learning) that integrates face-to-face classes and online activities, utilizing virtual, in-person, and remote laboratories equipped with reconfigurable technology, such as Field-Programmable Gate Arrays. Based on connectivism theory, the model applies AI algorithms to personalize learning, adjusting content and practices according to student performance data, aiming to optimize academic outcomes. Furthermore, the research suggests the use of libraries for developing data science and machine learning algorithms, emphasizing the personalization of the educational experience to improve teaching effectiveness and respond to individual student needs.

Another empirical example comes from Luckin et al. (2016), which explores how AI-based intelligent tutoring systems can offer personalized learning experiences. These systems simulate individualized tutoring, adapting to students' cognitive needs and providing targeted and timely feedback without the need for a teacher to be present. Additionally, the study emphasizes that AI can enhance student engagement by allowing them to feel more involved in the learning process. The use of open learning models can also motivate students by enabling them to track their progress and reflect on their learning.

López's (2022) research analyzes how AI and computer vision techniques can be applied to the educational context to monitor, in real time, indicators such as facial expressions, body posture, and student attention levels. Based on this data, systems are capable of dynamically adapting content and pedagogical strategies, promoting a more student-centered experience. The author further highlights that this type of technology can be particularly useful in hybrid or remote environments, where direct teacher monitoring is more limited, reinforcing GenAI's capacity to offer personalized and responsive support tailored to each student's learning profile.

3.4 The Potential of Personalization: Advantages for Students and Teachers

The use of AI in learning personalization presents a series of advantages for both students and teachers. For students, personalization allows a learning experience more centered on their needs, helping them learn more effectively and with less frustration (Nascimento-Fragoso & Coutinho, 2025). The ability to learn at one's own pace can be especially beneficial for students with learning difficulties, as it allows them to receive the necessary support without the pressure of keeping up with their peers.

The Bo (2024) study, inspired by the OECD report (2023), examines how AI-based technologies can be integrated into digital educational ecosystems, placing special emphasis on learning personalization.

The research highlights the potential of AI as an ally to teachers, offering advanced tools to monitor student progress and early identify those who need additional support. Among these tools, educational information management systems and digital assessment platforms stand out, as they utilize predictive analysis algorithms to anticipate risk situations, such as learning difficulties or school dropout. By enabling more effective and targeted pedagogical interventions, these technologies contribute to a more personalized and proactive approach in teaching. The study also emphasizes the importance of establishing guidelines and safeguards that ensure the ethical and equitable use of AI in education, promoting trust and transparency among all involved in the educational process.

3.5 Limitations and Challenges of Learning Personalization with AI

Despite the great potential of GenAI to personalize learning and improve educational outcomes, the UNESCO report (2023) warns of significant challenges, especially regarding unequal access to digital technologies. In many regions, particularly in developing countries, the lack of adequate technological infrastructure hinders the effective implementation of these solutions, widening the digital divide between students from more privileged backgrounds and those in vulnerable situations. The report reveals that only 40% of primary schools have internet access, and less than 10% of institutions have internal policies on AI use, highlighting the urgent need for investments in connectivity, infrastructure, and training to ensure equitable and sustainable adoption of GenAI in education.

Another challenge is the issue of privacy and ethics in data usage. The study by Williamson and Eynon (2020) critically examines the ethical and political challenges associated with the use of AI in education, including concerns over student data privacy. The authors warn about the growth of an increasingly data-driven educational ecosystem, in which algorithms are used to monitor, predict, and even shape student behavior. In this context, the massive collection of personal data raises serious concerns regarding transparency, consent, and information security. Williamson and Eynon (2020) argue that without robust governance and clear ethical principles, the use of AI can reinforce opaque surveillance and control practices, compromising the autonomy of teachers and students. Furthermore, they emphasize the need for public policies regulating the use of educational technologies based on GenAI, ensuring respect for fundamental rights in the school environment.

In this sense, Williamson et al. (2023) adopt a critical perspective on the use of GenAI in education, drawing attention to the risks associated with excessive automation, especially concerning the depersonalization of teaching and the reduction of meaningful human interactions. The authors argue that by prioritizing data- and algorithm-based solutions, there is a risk of neglecting fundamental aspects of the educational process, such as empathy, pedagogical supervision, and the bond between teachers and students. They also warn about the trend of commercialization in education, where technological platforms seek to replace or standardize educational practices based on logics of algorithmic efficiency. This can compromise the richness of learning experiences and deepen inequalities by imposing automated models that ignore students' cultural, social, and emotional contexts. The study reinforces that

GenAI should complement, not replace, the teacher's role, preserving the human and relational nature of teaching.

In summary, the discussion across the previous points highlights that AI-mediated learning personalization represents one of the most promising advances in the transformation of contemporary education. The ability these technologies offer to adapt curricula, content, and pedagogical strategies to the individual needs of students can result in more effective, engaging, and student-centered learning experiences (Holmes et al., 2019). According to Chen et al. (2020), AI systems applied to education have proven effective in personalized adaptation, providing real-time educational interventions that respect each student's learning pace and style. However, this innovative potential is not without significant challenges. Issues such as equity in access to technology, data privacy, and risks of depersonalizing education need to be carefully addressed. UNESCO (2023) warns of the growing digital inequality, highlighting that the implementation of AI may exacerbate disparities between students with and without access to adequate technological infrastructure. At the same time, Dignum (2019) emphasizes the importance of developing and applying AI systems responsibly, particularly in terms of algorithmic transparency and the protection of students' personal data.

Furthermore, there is a legitimate concern that the indiscriminate adoption of GenAI could lead to the undue replacement of the teacher's role by automated systems. In this sense, Giraffa and Kohls-Santos (2023) emphasize the importance of teacher mediation in the pedagogical application of AI, warning of the risks of excessive automation that compromise the essential human bond in the educational process. This concern is shared by Holmes et al. (2019), who emphasize that, although AI can support learning personalization, it should not replace teachers' pedagogical judgment but rather complement and expand their role.

The risk of depersonalizing teaching and the ethical use of technology are also emphasized by Williamson et al. (2023), who discuss the political, economic, and social impacts of GenAI in education. They highlight the dangers of excessive commercialization and algorithmic discrimination, evidencing the need for educational measures that ensure the fair and equitable use of these tools. Nascimento-Fragoso and Coutinho (2025), in turn, specifically analyze learning personalization with GenAI, highlighting both its potential and the technical, ethical, and pedagogical challenges involved in its implementation.

Given this scenario, it becomes evident that the success of AI-based learning personalization depends not only on technological advancement but also on commitment to ethics, equity, and active teacher supervision. As the analyzed authors suggest, these technologies must be implemented responsibly, always aiming to meet students' needs and to strengthen, not weaken, the human dimension of education.

4. TRANSFORMATIVE SKILLS AND CURRICULUM DESIGN

The emergence of AI as a structuring force in social, economic, and cultural dynamics in the 21st century demands a profound revision of the purposes of education. The growing presence of GenAI in productive processes, social interactions, and political decision-making mechanisms reconfigures the concept of competence, expanding it beyond technical and cognitive skills. Transformative skills, such as critical thinking, collaboration, creativity, empathy, and digital literacy, become essential for preparing students not only for the world of work but also for life in an increasingly complex and hyper-connected society. In this context, curriculum design must be rethought based on a broad, critical, and technology-sensitive formative perspective.

4.1 Essential Skills in the Generative AI Era

Critical Thinking and Algorithmic Ethics

The complexity of digital societies requires critical thinking to transcend logical analysis and involve an ethical and political dimension. It is not enough to identify fallacies or inconsistencies: it is necessary to understand how algorithmic systems shape reality, reproduce inequalities, and operate with biases (Eubanks, 2018).

According to Christen et al. (2020), information ethics and algorithmic ethics must be integrated into contemporary education as fundamental elements. For the authors, it is essential to prepare students to question automated decisions, understand the limits of GenAI, and act responsibly in technology-mediated environments. When addressing the moral dilemmas associated with automation and algorithmic decision-making, they highlight the need to develop, also in the school context, a critical awareness of the social impacts of these technologies. The construction of a technologically ethically oriented society, according to the authors, requires continuous and interdisciplinary training. Such a perspective underscores the importance of incorporating topics like algorithmic justice and digital ethics into school curricula, thereby fostering education that promotes critical and transformative citizenship.

Critical thinking, therefore, is not a neutral skill: it is deeply related to the construction of an active and vigilant digital citizenship. Students need to develop skills to identify informational manipulation, disinformation, and political uses of AI (Selwyn, 2019). This type of critical thinking is a practice of freedom, as it enables a critical reading of the world and engagement to transform it.

Collaboration, Empathy, and Emotional Intelligence

Although automation is transforming the labor market, human skills such as collaboration, empathy, and emotional intelligence remain irreplaceable. Schleicher (2018) highlights that, in the future of work, socioemotional skills such as collaboration, empathy, and emotional intelligence will be the most valued. In AI-mediated educational contexts, these skills become increasingly important because students must interact with peers, teachers, and virtual assistants, necessitating the development of communication, negotiation, leadership, and cooperation skills in hybrid environments.

The author argues that as automation replaces traditional cognitive skills like memorization and mechanical problem-solving, human skills become irreplaceable. Thus, education should emphasize the development of these socioemotional skills, preparing students for an unpredictable and interconnected future. He further stresses the need to rethink school curricula, incorporating these skills as central components of student training, creating environments that promote collaboration, empathy, and emotional intelligence, and preparing students to interact effectively with new technologies.

Lourenço et al. (2024) highlight the relevance of emotional intelligence in the organizational context, analyzing its impact on the culture and climate of Higher Education institutions. The authors consider emotional intelligence essential for promoting healthy interpersonal relationships and collaborative environments, which are fundamental aspects in the development of socioemotional skills, including those in technology-mediated educational contexts. The study suggests that this competency can be stimulated through pedagogical practices such as simulations and social interactions, making it particularly relevant when associated with technological tools like immersive environments, serious games, and emotional feedback platforms. Thus, it is argued that emotional intelligence can be cultivated in the educational context with the support of innovative digital resources.

Creativity, Problem Solving, and Computational Thinking

Creativity, often seen as an artistic skill, is increasingly valued as a transversal competency across all fields of knowledge. In times of AI, creativity means thinking outside the box, producing innovative solutions, exploring new languages, and combining interdisciplinary knowledge. Trevallion and Nischang (2021) argue that traditional school models inhibit creativity by punishing mistakes and valuing only correct answers. They advocate, in contrast, for a curriculum centered on transformative skills that promote experimentation and recognize error as part of the creative process. They emphasize creativity as an essential transversal competency in the

21st century and propose innovative pedagogical practices, such as project-based learning and interdisciplinary approaches, to prepare students for the challenges of a world marked by innovation and technology.

Problem solving, especially in digital environments, is closely linked to computational thinking, which involves understanding structured logic, breaking down complex problems, and modeling solutions. In this context, AI can play an important role, as argued by Luckin et al. (2016), by personalizing learning and promoting skills such as problem solving and critical thinking. AI enables content adaptation and real-time feedback, stimulating the development of these skills.

The application of explainable AI is particularly relevant, as it makes AI systems more transparent and understandable to users. In educational settings, explainable AI can strengthen the trust of students and teachers by clearly explaining how decisions are made by the systems. This aligns with Holzinger's (2021) discussion regarding the importance of explainable AI, which not only improves interaction but also enhances learning and the critical use of technologies.

Data and AI Digital Literacy

In an increasingly data-driven world, digital literacy must be understood broadly, including skills such as the critical and creative use of digital tools, understanding the influence of algorithms on information access, critical reading of data, and a basic understanding of how AI works (Long & Magerko, 2020).

The authors define AI literacy as the ability to critically evaluate these technologies, interact with them effectively, and utilize them in various contexts, ranging from virtual environments to everyday situations. They also emphasize that this literacy is interconnected with digital and data literacy, with the former being a prerequisite to understanding AI, and the latter especially relevant in areas like machine learning, where there is an overlap of skills.

When discussing AI literacy, Luckin et al. (2016) propose that educators and students develop a functional and ethical understanding of GenAI, including its potentials and limits. This is essential to ensure the digital agency of individuals, that is, their ability to act autonomously and critically in technological contexts.

4.2 Challenges and Possibilities in the Curricular Integration of these Skills

The curricular integration of transformative skills faces considerable challenges, ranging from structural to epistemological issues. Below are some of them, along with their potential solutions for overcoming.

Curricular rigidity and traditional assessment culture

Many school curricula are still organized into isolated subjects, focusing on compartmentalized content and standardized assessments. This structure hinders the transversal and interdisciplinary approach required by complex skills. Additionally, the emphasis on measurable results and school rankings can hinder pedagogical practices focused on the socio-emotional and critical development of students. (Wiliam et al., 2024).

To break this paradigm, it is necessary to adopt a competency-based integrated curriculum approach. In this perspective, content does not disappear but is mobilized as a means to solve significant problems linked to real contexts and mediated by digital technologies. As discussed by Third et al. (2025), these technologies play a fundamental role in promoting critical and digital skills in authentic contexts. This highlights the importance of digital education and the conscious use of technology in developing essential skills for contemporary life, such as digital citizenship, critical thinking, and problem-solving in digital environments.

Role of AI as pedagogical support

AI can be a powerful ally in building personalized learning pathways that respect each student's pace and learning styles. Holmes et al. (2019) highlight that the use of GenAI-based technologies in the educational context, such as intelligent tutors, writing assistants, sentiment analysis systems, and adaptive feedback mechanisms, has great potential to enrich teaching and learning processes. Such tools allow the personalization of learning trajectories, respecting each student's pace and learning styles by providing real-time feedback and adaptive support.

According to Sajja et al. (2023), intelligent tutors, for example, monitor the individual student's progress and adjust content based on their performance. Writing assistants contribute to the development of written expression by offering contextually relevant suggestions. Sentiment analysis enables the inference of a student's emotional state from their interactions with the platform, allowing for more sensitive pedagogical responses. Meanwhile, adaptive feedback dynamically adjusts to the needs manifested throughout the learning experience.

However, the use of these technologies must be subordinated to clearly defined pedagogical purposes and grounded in ethical principles, such as ensuring privacy, promoting equity, and ensuring algorithmic transparency. Even in the face of GenAI's growing presence in education, the central role of the teacher and respect for students' differences must remain essential foundations of the educational process.

Some authors warn that uncritical use of AI can reduce education to technical training, deepen inequalities, introduce algorithmic biases, and weaken the relational and humanizing dimension of teaching (Selwyn, 2019; Williamson et al., 2023). Thus, they emphasize the need for an interdisciplinary approach involving social sciences, philosophy, and critical theory to evaluate its implications. They further argue that curriculum design should go beyond the use of AI as a pedagogical tool, promoting its critical analysis as an object of study, in line with ethical values and well-defined educational objectives.

Continuous and critical teacher training

The teacher is a central agent in mediating between curriculum, technologies, and students. Without critical training, the AI use tends to be instrumental, superficial, or even harmful. Therefore, teacher preparation must go beyond technical mastery, incorporating pedagogical, epistemological, and ethical foundations. Zawacki-Richter et al. (2019) highlight the scarcity of critical reflections and the weak connection with pedagogical perspectives in AI studies, warning that this gap compromises the relational dimension of teaching. Thus, they advocate for the critical and ethical integration of GenAI into the curriculum, reinforcing the need for broader teacher training.

Similarly, Giraffa et al. (2023) and UNESCO (2019) emphasize the importance of an interdisciplinary approach to empower teachers to understand the ethical and educational implications of GenAI, ensuring its meaningful use aligned with educational objectives.

Furthermore, it is essential to foster communities of practice among teachers to share experiences, collaboratively develop projects, and jointly design innovative curricula. Continuing education programs focused on digital and pedagogical skills are indispensable for the successful integration of GenAI in school environments.

4.3 Pedagogical Strategies for the Skill Curriculum Supported by AI

Next, a set of pedagogical strategies is proposed to guide the effective integration of transformative skills with the use of AI, assisting in learning personalization, critical thinking development, promotion of collaboration, and ethical training of students, aligning with contemporary educational goals.

Project-Based Learning

Project-Based Learning is configured as an effective pedagogical approach for the development of multidimensional skills, as it promotes the investigation of real problems, stimulates the proposal of creative solutions, and favors collaborative work among students. The integration of GenAI in this context enhances these processes by offering advanced tools for research, data analysis, scenario simulation, and creativity support. For example, generative models like ChatGPT can be used to explore different writing styles, conduct discourse analysis, simulate historical dialogues, or create digital prototypes, expanding the possibilities for student engagement and deepening (Holmes et al.,2019). Furthermore, project-centered pedagogical approaches show proven effectiveness in developing complex skills, with AI acting as a catalyst that enhances these practices by offering personalized and adaptive resources capable of meeting individual student needs, promoting more meaningful and contextualized learning. The incorporation of AI in Project-Based Learning also contributes to the development of critical digital skills, considered essential in the contemporary educational context. Thus, Project-Based Learning stands as a robust methodology for competency development, while AI represents a valuable tool to enrich these educational processes. However, studies address AI from a broader perspective, highlighting its transformative potential in teaching and learning in general, encompassing strategies such as Project-Based Learning (Dutta et al., 2024; Ruiz-Rojas et al., 2024). In this sense, Gomes et al. (2024) emphasize that Project-Based Learning favors the integration of cognitive, social, and ethical skills, aligning with the principles of transformative education.

Data and Digital Ethics Labs

Another relevant strategy is the creation of pedagogical labs focused on data and digital ethics. These spaces can be interdisciplinary and involve activities such as analysis of recommendation algorithms, construction of simple GenAI systems (using tools like Scratch or Teachable Machine), and discussion of cases about algorithmic decisions in areas such as justice, health, and security (Long & Magerko, 2020; Nemorin, 2024; Williamson et al., 2023).

These labs help develop data literacy, computational thinking, and civic responsibility. These skills should be cultivated from early education to prepare students for an increasingly automated society.

Zhou (2025) proposes the creation of pedagogical labs that promote children's practical and critical interaction with data, algorithms, and ethical issues related to GenAI. These educational spaces are conceived as interdisciplinary environments where students participate in activities such as analysis of recommendation algorithms, construction of simple AI systems using accessible tools like Scratch and Teachable Machine, as well as discussions of real cases involving algorithmic decisions in social contexts, including justice, health, and security.

The central goal of these labs is to develop data literacy, computational thinking, and civic responsibility from the earliest school years, preparing students to act consciously and critically in an increasingly automated society mediated by intelligent technologies.

Multimodal Assessment and Digital Portfolios

When guided by humanistic values, AI can become a strategic ally in building more just, participatory, and empowering educational practices. For this, its implementation must align not only with technical skills but also with the development of emotional intelligence, a fundamental basis for promoting school environments that are more humane, critical, and aware of their social role. The school of the future will not only be digital but also a space where empathy, collaboration, and ethics walk together with critical thinking and digital literacy. Thus, skills such as critical thinking, collaboration, digital literacy, ethics, and emotional intelligence cease to be merely instruments of adaptation and become fundamental tools of emancipation, capable of forming citizens prepared to understand, question, and transform the world they live in (Lourenço et al., 2024).

Andrade and Brookhart (2020) conceive classroom assessment, especially multimodal assessment, as a co-regulation process of learning, in which teachers and students share responsibility for goal-setting, use of formative rubrics, and metacognitive reflection on their progress. As Shepard (2000) suggests, assessing complex skills such as critical thinking and self-regulation requires strategies beyond traditional tests, including portfolios and self-assessments. Digital portfolios, which aggregate multiple forms of learning evidence, become powerful tools when combined with AI, which can analyze and offer personalized feedback. Additionally, authors like Luckin et al. (2016) and Holmes et al. (2019) highlight AI's potential to support these practices by organizing evidence, analyzing patterns, and offering personalized recommendations, always subordinate to the teacher's pedagogical judgment. Thus, AI acts as diagnostic support, expanding formative feedback and strengthening student engagement in the assessment process. By providing real-time data on performance, it contributes to more effective pedagogical decisions, promoting personalized and reflective learning, in line with the principles of co-regulation.

The construction of a curriculum oriented by transformative skills with the support of GenAI should be seen not only as a technical initiative but as a political and pedagogical decision deeply linked to promoting critical, ethical, and inclusive education. The use of GenAI in this context demands a commitment to the holistic education of students, making it essential that its application be guided by humanistic and democratic principles, ensuring that technology strengthens equity and social justice in the school environment (Dignum, 2019; Williamson et al., 2023).

5. ETHICS, INCLUSION, AND THE ROLE OF TEACHERS

The increasing incorporation of GenAI technologies in education necessitates a thorough examination of their ethical, social, and institutional implications. Although AI represents enormous potential for personalizing learning, educational management, and supporting skills development, its use also raises concerns about equity, privacy, teacher autonomy, and social justice. This topic discusses three fundamental dimensions of this process: the ethical and social implications of GenAI in education, ensuring equity and access, and teacher training and the institutional changes necessary for responsible integration of GenAI.

5.1. Ethical and Social Implications of Generative AI in Education

Ethics in the use of GenAI in education goes beyond technical issues. It involves understanding the consequences of algorithmic decisions on the lives of students, teachers, and institutions. The Williamson et al. (2023) study indicates that, algorithmic systems in education are not merely technical tools but sociotechnical products that incorporate normative values and reproduce dominant conceptions of learning and performance. Ignoring these aspects can lead to subtle forms of discrimination, exclusion, and loss of pedagogical autonomy.

As Eubanks (2018) highlights, algorithmic systems used in social contexts often operate as surveillance and punishment mechanisms targeted at the most vulnerable populations and reinforcing stigmas and historical inequalities. Transposed to the educational field, these systems can manifest as recommendations or automated feedback forms that limit learning trajectories based on past data. Selwyn (2019) reinforces this concern by emphasizing that the adoption of intelligent technologies in education often operates opaquely and technocratic, legitimizing pedagogical decisions based on logics of efficiency and performance, to the detriment of social justice principles.

A central aspect of the ethical debate on AI in education is the need for transparency and interpretability of systems. Explainable AI aims to address this challenge by making algorithmic processes more transparent and understandable to teachers and students. As Holzinger (2021) and Christen et al. (2020) state, the lack of explainability compromises institutional accountability and hinders transparency in pedagogical decisions. Explainable AI contributes to strengthening trust and facilitating scrutiny by justifying recommendations and predictions in a manner accessible to users.

Educational AI ethics also involve considerations of power and coloniality, raising questions about the dominance of Eurocentric perspectives and values in algorithmic models. Building fairer systems requires questioning this hegemony and including multiple voices, cultural contexts, and forms of knowledge, especially those from historically marginalized regions (Mohamed et al., 2020; Nemorin, 2024). Decolonizing AI thus means recognizing and integrating diverse epistemologies in the design and application of these technologies.

5.2. Guarantee of Equity and Access

One of the greatest risks of widespread AI adoption in education is the deepening of existing structural inequalities. Unequal access to devices, connectivity, and digital literacy can exclude certain groups from fully benefiting from AI-based solutions. UNESCO (2019; 2023) and OECD (2023) emphasize the importance of public policies and institutional strategies that ensure equity in access to and use of these technologies.

Equity, in this context, should be understood not only as the fair distribution of technological resources but also as the active inclusion of diverse student profiles in decision-making processes and solution building. As Third et al. (2025) argue, it is essential to recognize students' rights, especially younger ones, in the digital environment, ensuring their active participation, protection, and ability to make informed decisions, act autonomously, and influence processes that affect their online experience. Digital policies and practices must be grounded in evidence that reflects the experiences and perspectives of students themselves, thereby promoting their effective inclusion in decision-making and solution-building processes. In this sense, equity extends beyond the simple distribution of technological resources, encompassing the inclusion of diverse student profiles as active agents, rather than mere passive recipients, of educational technologies.

In this regard, GenAI can be both part of the problem and the solution. Studies such as those by Nascimento-Fragoso and Coutinho (2025) show that GenAI-mediated personalized teaching can benefit students with specific difficulties by promoting real-time adaptations. However, this personalization is only effective if based on representative data and inclusive mechanisms.

Inclusion also involves accessibility. AI technologies can support students with visual, auditory, or cognitive disabilities by offering multimodal interfaces and adaptive resources (Dutta et al., 2024; Suh et al., 2025). However, this requires user-centered design that considers diverse ways of interacting with learning systems.

Another fundamental aspect is data privacy. The intensive collection of information about students, their interactions, and outcomes raises concerns about the protection of personal data and the ethical use of such information. According to García et al. (2023), clear standards for consent, anonymization, and the purpose of educational data use must be established.

Finally, ensuring equity also involves empowering all educational stakeholders to understand and critique how AI works. So-called "AI literacy" (Long & Magerko, 2020; Zhou, 2025) should be a cross-cutting competency, not only for programmers but for everyone involved in education.

5.3. Teacher Training and Institutional Changes

The role of teachers is central in the ethical and inclusive mediation of AI in education. However, many teachers still feel disoriented or even threatened by these technologies, revealing a gap between technological advances and daily pedagogical practice. As noted by Zawacki-Richter et al. (2019) and Giraffa and Kohls-Santos (2023), a significant disconnect exists between technological developments and everyday teaching practices. This gap demands a profound reconfiguration of initial and ongoing teacher training. The integration of AI into training curricula must go beyond technical mastery. It is necessary to develop critical, ethical, and pedagogical skills so that teachers can use AI reflectively, adapted to their contexts and educational objectives.

Authors such as Holmes and Tuomi (2022) and Luckin et al. (2016; 2024) argue that AI can act as an ally of teachers, automating repetitive tasks and providing data for more precise diagnostics. However, this potential is only realized if teachers have the autonomy and knowledge to interpret and act upon this information.

Teacher training should include: understanding the fundamentals of AI and its algorithmic models; the ability to critically evaluate educational tools based on GenAI; knowledge about data protection, privacy, and digital ethics; skills to adapt pedagogical practices with AI support without dehumanizing teaching; and training to promote a culture of responsible innovation in schools and universities.

Furthermore, higher education institutions must promote structural changes to support this transformation. So, assessment and curriculum need to be rethought in light of the new possibilities and challenges of AI (Andrade & Brookhart, 2020; Sales & Pane, 2021). This includes redesigning assessment strategies focused on self-regulation of learning (Ferreira & Pedrosa, 2024) and valuing socio-emotional skills (Lourenço et al., 2024).

From an institutional standpoint, it is essential to promote collaborative experimental environments where teachers, students, technicians, and researchers can jointly develop AI-based solutions. As Williamson et al. (2023) emphasize, teacher involvement in the development and regulation of AI is a necessary condition for its ethical and effective adoption.

Ultimately, it is essential to develop and implement public policies and institutional guidelines that promote the responsible use of GenAI. Teacher training cannot be dissociated from clear legal and regulatory frameworks that ensure ethical standards, effective control mechanisms, and the protection of the rights of all parties involved.

Thus, the integration of GenAI in teacher training is a transformative opportunity, but one that requires prudence, critical thinking, and ethical action. The risk of reproducing and amplifying inequalities, compromising rights, and emptying the role of teachers is real if measures are not implemented to guarantee equity, transparency, and critical training of teachers.

In this scenario, teachers cease to be mere users of technologies to become active agents in their ethical and pedagogical configuration. They must be empowered to play their role as mediators of knowledge, promoters of inclusion, and defenders of genuinely human-centered education.

6. CONCLUSION

The GenAI incorporation in education represents an emerging paradigm with transformative potential, but also with complex and multifaceted challenges. Throughout this chapter, it has been highlighted how GenAI can act both as a powerful tool to personalize teaching and promote inclusion, as well as a vector that can perpetuate inequalities and vulnerabilities if not implemented with an ethical and critical vision. A deep understanding of the technical, social, cultural, and ethical aspects is essential to ensure that smart curricula evolve toward a truly human-centered education.

Main insights from the chapter

First, it was shown that AI-mediated educational personalization has the potential to meet the specific needs of students with diverse difficulties, adapting content in real time and favoring more effective learning (Nascimento-Fragoso & Coutinho, 2025). However, this efficacy depends on the quality and representativeness of the data used, as well as the inclusion of mechanisms that guarantee equity and justice in access and outcomes. The active inclusion of multiple student profiles, especially those facing barriers, must be a priority, aligning with proposals for technological accessibility and digital equity (Dutta et al., 2024; Suh et al., 2025).

Another fundamental insight is the ethical dimension of GenAI serving education, which transcends technical issues to encompass debates about power, coloniality, and values implicit in algorithms (Mohamed et al., 2020; Nemorin, 2024). The hegemony of Eurocentric data and epistemologies can marginalize knowledge from the Global South, making the "decolonization" of GenAI models essential—that is, the inclusion of multiple voices and cultural contexts in the development of these technologies. Ethics in digital education therefore requires a commitment to epistemological diversity and social justice.

Additionally, transparency and explainability of AI systems are central issues for institutional accountability and for building trust between teachers and students. The absence of clear explanations about algorithmic decision-making processes can generate opacity and technological dependence, harming pedagogical autonomy (Holzinger, 2021; Christen et al., 2020). In this sense, the development of Explainable AI emerges as a promising path to ensure that automated decisions are understandable and contestable, reinforcing transparency and ethics in educational environments.

Finally, the empowerment of educational agents—teachers, students, and technicians—is a crucial pillar for the ethical and effective use of GenAI in education. GenAI literacy, understood as a transversal competence, allows all involved to understand and critique the functioning of these technologies, promoting more active and conscious participation in educational processes (Long & Magerko, 2020; Zhou, 2025). The role of teachers, in particular, is crucial in mediating the impacts of AI; yet many still feel disoriented before rapid technological innovations, revealing a gap between technical development and daily pedagogical practice (Giraffa & Kohls-Santos, 2023; Zawacki-Richter et al., 2019).

Practical recommendations

Based on these insights, some practical recommendations can guide the responsible and inclusive implementation of smart curricula:

- Ensure representativeness and diversity in educational data and algorithms: it is fundamental to collect and use data that reflect the diversity of students, avoiding biases that may reinforce inequalities. Development teams should include specialists in cultural diversity and ethics to continuously review the models and data used.
- Develop and implement explainable AI systems: GenAI educational platforms should provide clear and accessible mechanisms that explain their decisions and recommendations to teachers and students. This strengthens transparency, trust, and the possibility of contestation, all of which are essential to democratic pedagogical practice.
- Promote AI literacy as a transversal competence: continuous training for teachers and students should include content addressing the functioning, limitations, and ethical impacts of GenAI. This empowers users to be critical and informed mediators, avoiding uncritical acceptance of automated results.
- Foster collaborative environments for the development of GenAI solutions in education: Educational institutions should encourage joint participation of

teachers, students, technicians, and researchers in the creation and evaluation of GenAI-based tools. This collaborative process ensures that solutions reflect real needs and shared values.

- Respect and protect students' digital rights, with special attention to children: clear policies should ensure privacy protection, informed consent, and students' agency in the use of educational technologies. Active participation of students in the design and implementation of systems should be prioritized to avoid their mere submission to technologies.

Critical and open vision for the evolution of smart curricula

When designing the future of smart curricula, it is essential to maintain a critical and open vision, recognizing that AI is a constantly evolving tool embedded in dynamic and challenging social contexts. Although technological advances offer unprecedented opportunities for personalization and democratization of learning, they also increase risks related to inequalities, excessive surveillance, and pedagogical alienation (Eubanks, 2018; Williamson et al., 2023).

Study's emphasize that smart curricula must avoid reproducing colonialist and exclusionary patterns, adopting a pluriversal perspective that values diverse epistemologies and the active participation of involved subjects (e.g., Mohamed et al. 2020; Third et al. 2025). This plurality necessitates curricular flexibility, allowing for multiple learning pathways and accommodating varied cultural contexts.

On the other hand, increasing dependence on automated systems can generate opacity and reduce the autonomy of teachers and students, as pointed out by Holzinger (2021) and Christen et al. (2020). Investment in explainable AI is a necessary response but insufficient without continuous ethical reflection and participatory management that includes all educational agents.

Moreover, technological and critical empowerment of educational agents is a challenge that requires ongoing investments and integrated public policies. The gap between technical innovation and daily teaching practice, observed by Giraffa & Kohls-Santos (2023) and Zawacki-Richter et al. (2019), shows the need to bring these two worlds closer so that technology truly enhances the educational process.

Therefore, the smart curricula of the future must be built based on human values, social justice, and transparency, incorporating diverse knowledge and promoting real inclusion. Technology, in this context, is a means, not an end in itself, for an education that respects the dignity, autonomy, and rights of all its participants.

REFERENCES

Ali, H. ul Mustafa, A., & Aysan, A. F. (2025). Global adoption of generative AI: What matters most? *Journal of Economy and Technology, 3*, 166-176. https://www.sciencedirect.com/science/article/pii/S2949948824000520

Allman, B., Kimmons, R., Rosenberg, J., & Dash, M. (2023). Trends and topics in educational technology. *TechTrends, 67*(3), 583–591. https://link.springer.com/content/pdf/10.1007/s11528-023-00840-2.pdf PMID: 37216141

Andrade, H. L., & Brookhart, S. M. (2020). Classroom assessment as the co-regulation of learning. *Assessment in Education: Principles, Policy & Practice, 27*(4), 350–372. https://www.tandfonline.com/doi/abs/10.1080/0969594X.2019.1571992

Bo, N. S. W. (2024). *OECD digital education outlook 2023: Towards an effective education ecosystem.* Hungarian Educational Research Journal., DOI: 10.1556/063.2024.00340

Campos, K. E., Rigo, S. J., & Barbosa, J. L. V. (2025). Detecção da autoeficácia em ambientes computacionais de aprendizagem. *RECIMA21-Revista Científica Multidisciplinar, 6*(1). e616174-e616174. https://recima21.com.br/index.php/recima21/article/view/6174

Chen, L., Chen, P., & Lin, Z. (2020). Artificial intelligence in education: A review. *IEEE Access : Practical Innovations, Open Solutions, 8*, 75264–75278. https://ieeexplore.ieee.org/stamp/stamp.jsp?arnumber=9069875

Chen, L., Ifenthaler, D., Yau, J. Y. K., & Sun, W. (2024). Artificial intelligence in entrepreneurship education: A scoping review. *Education + Training, 66*(6), 589–608. https://www.emerald.com/insight/content/doi/10.1108/et-05-2023-0169/full/html

Christen, M., Gordijn, B., & Loi, M. (2020). *The ethics of cybersecurity.* Springer Nature. https://library.oapen.org/handle/20.500.12657/47324

D'Mello, S. K., & Graesser, A. (2023). Intelligent tutoring systems: How computers achieve learning gains that rival human tutors. In Schutz, P. A., & Muis, K. R. (Eds.), *Handbook of educational psychology* (pp. 603–629). Routledge., https://www.taylorfrancis.com/chapters/edit/10.4324/9780429433726-31/intelligent-tutoring-systems-sidney-mello-art-graesser

Dignum, V. (2019). *Responsible artificial intelligence: how to develop and use AI in a responsible way.* Springer.

Dutta, S., Ranjan, S., Mishra, S., Sharma, V., Hewage, P., & Iwendi, C. (2024). *Enhancing educational adaptability: A review and analysis of AI-driven adaptive learning platforms*. In 2024 4th International Conference on Innovative Practices in Technology and Management (ICIPTM) (pp. 1-5). IEEE. https://ieeexplore.ieee.org/abstract/document/10563448

Eubanks, V. (2018). *Automating inequality: How high-tech tools profile, police, and punish the poor*. St. Martin's Press.

Ferreira, A., & Pedrosa, D. (2024). Uso da inteligência artificial para apoiar a autorregulação de aprendizagem: Uma revisão de literatura. *PRATICA-Revista Multimédia de Investigação em Inovação Pedagógica e Práticas de e-Learning, 7*(2), 101-111. https://parc.ipp.pt/index.php/elearning/article/view/5823

García, V., Kemper, N., Bárcenas, J., & Ruiz-Velasco, E. (2023). La Inteligencia Artificial en tecnologías digitales LMS para cursos de Sistemas Digitales. In E. R. V. Sánchez & J. B. López (Coords.), *Inteligencia Artificial para la transformación de la Educación* (pp. 36-46). SMCE. https://books.google.pt/books?hl=pt-PT&lr=&id=G2LoEAAAQBAJ&oi=fnd&pg=PA36&dq=

Giraffa, L., & Kohls-Santos, P. (2023). Inteligência artificial e educação: conceitos, aplicações e implicações no fazer docente. *Educação em Análise, 8*(1), 116-134. https://ojs.uel.br/revistas/uel/index.php/educanalise/article/view/48127

Gomes, A. J. F., Verçosa, B. F. M., Pinto, C. R. S., de Moura, C. C., dos Santos Silva, C., & dos Reis, O. B. (2024). Potencializando a aprendizagem ativa com tecnologia de IA. *Revista Ibero-Americana de Humanidades. Ciência & Educação (Bauru), 10*(8), 3625–3631. https://periodicorease.pro.br/rease/article/view/15451

Holmes, W., Bialik, M., & Fadel, C. (2019). *Artificial Intelligence in Education Promises and Implications for Teaching and Learning* (1st ed.). Center for Curriculum Redesign., https://discovery.ucl.ac.uk/id/eprint/10139722/

Holmes, W., & Tuomi, I. (2022). State of the art and practice in AI in education. *European Journal of Education, 57*(4), 542–570. https://onlinelibrary.wiley.com/doi/10.1111/ejed.12533

Holzinger, A. (2021). Explainable AI and multi-modal causability in medicine. *i-com, 19*(3), 171-179. https://www.degruyterbrill.com/document/doi/10.1515/icom-2020-0024/html

Li, L., Chen, C. P., Wang, L., Liang, K., & Bao, W. (2023). Exploring artificial intelligence in smart education: Real-time classroom behavior analysis with embedded devices. *Sustainability, 15*(10), 7940. https://www.mdpi.com/2071-1050/15/10/7940

Long, D., & Magerko, B. (2020). What is AI Literacy? Competencies and Design Considerations. In *Proceedings of the 2020 CHI conference on human factors in computing systems* (pp. 1–16). ACM., https://dl.acm.org/doi/abs/10.1145/3313831.3376727

López, L. A. S. (2022). Inteligencia artificial y visión por computadora aplicada a la educación. *Revista Odigos, 3*(2), 61-73. https://revista.uisrael.edu.ec/index.php/ro/article/view/587

Lourenço, A., Paiva, M. O., & Valente, S. (2024). Emotional Intelligence: A Catalyst for Organizational Culture and Climate in Higher Education. In Kayyali, M. (Ed.), *Building Organizational Capacity and Strategic Management in Academia* (pp. 183–212). IGI Global., DOI: 10.4018/979-8-3693-6967-8.ch007

Lourenço, A. A., & Paiva, M. O. A. (2024). Globalization of Higher Education: The Internationalization from a Multifactorial Perspective. In Kayyali, M. (Ed.), *Building Resiliency in Higher Education: Globalization, Digital Skills, and Student Wellness* (pp. 285–305). IGI Global., DOI: 10.4018/979-8-3693-5483-4

Luckin, R., Holmes, W., Griffiths, M., & Forcier, L. B. (2016). *Intelligence Unleashed. An argument for AI in Education.* Pearson. https://discovery.ucl.ac.uk/id/eprint/1475756/

Luckin, R., Rudolph, J., Grünert, M., & Tan, S. (2024). Exploring the future of learning and the relationship between human intelligence and AI. An interview with Professor Rose Luckin. *Journal of Applied Learning and Teaching, 7*(1). https://journals.sfu.ca/jalt/index.php/jalt/article/view/1659

Mayo, E. G. M., Sarmiento, E. X. B., Ayo, M. R. S., & Llivicota, A. S. M. (2024). Implementação de inteligência artificial como estratégia de ensino para o desenvolvimento da escrita em estudantes do ensino superior: uma sequência de ensino inovadora. *Pólo do Conhecimento, 9*(10), 1649-1665. https://polodelconocimiento.com/ojs/index.php/es/article/view/8199/html

Mohamed, S., Png, M. T., & Isaac, W. (2020). Decolonial AI: Decolonial theory as sociotechnical foresight in artificial intelligence. *Philosophy & Technology, 33*, 659–684. https://link.springer.com/article/10.1007/s13347-020-00405-8

Narváez, P. A. H., Herrera, M. G. M., Herrera, M. R. M., & Cruz, M. E. C. (2025). Didáctica inteligente: aplicaciones de la inteligencia artificial en la enseñanza y evaluación educativa. *Polo del Conocimiento, 10*(3), 187-208. https://polodelconocimiento.com/ojs/index.php/es/article/view/9048

Nascimento-Fragoso, M. D. J., & Coutinho, D. J. G. (2025). Inteligência artificial no apoio à educação personalizada: Potencialidades e desafios. *Revista Ibero-Americana de Humanidades. Ciência & Educação (Bauru), 11*(4), 2509–2523. https://periodicorease.pro.br/rease/article/view/18748

Navarro, J. Á. M. (2024). Optimizando el aprendizaje: examinando el impacto de la inteligencia artificial en DreamBox Learning y Knewton. *Revista Electrónica Investigamos, 1*(2), 100-117. https://revistainvestigamos.com/ojs/index.php/home/article/view/16

Nemorin, S. (2024). Towards decolonising the ethics of AI in education. *Globalisation, Societies and Education*, •••, 1–13. DOI: 10.1080/14767724.2024.2333821

OECD. (2018). *The future of education and skills: Education 2030 framework.* OECD Publishing. https://www.oecd.org/education/2030-project/

OECD. (2023). *OECD digital education outlook 2023: Towards an effective education ecosystem* [White paper]. OECD Publishing. https://doi.org/DOI: 10.1787/c74f03de-en

Ravenor, R. Y. (2023). AI-Based Facial Emotion Recognition Solutions for Education: A Study of Teacher-User and Other Categories. arXiv preprint arXiv:2308.15119. https://www.oajaiml.com/uploads/archivepdf/827742122.pdf?utm_source=chatgpt.com

Reyes, R. S., & Torres, S. C. S. (2024). Socratic method in the use of web tools. *American Journal of Management Science and Engineering, 9*(4), 75–83. http://ajmgtse.org/article/10.11648/j.ajmse.20240904.11

Ruiz-Rojas, L. I., Salvador-Ullauri, L., & Acosta-Vargas, P. (2024). Collaborative working and critical thinking: Adoption of generative artificial intelligence tools in higher education. *Sustainability, 16*(13), 5367. https://www.mdpi.com/2071-1050/16/13/5367

Sajja, R., Sermet, Y., Cikmaz, M., Cwiertny, D., & Demir, I. (2023). Artificial intelligence-enabled intelligent assistant for personalized and adaptive learning in higher education. *Information (Basel), 15*, 596. DOI: 10.3390/info15100596

Sales, A. C., & Pane, J. F. (2021). Student log-data from a randomized evaluation of educational technology: A causal case study. *Journal of Research on Educational Effectiveness, 14*(1), 241–269. https://www.tandfonline.com/doi/abs/10.1080/19345747.2020.1823538

Schleicher, A. (2018). Educating learners for their future, not our past. *ECNU Review of Education, 1*(1), 58-75. https://journals.sagepub.com/doi/full/10.30926/ecnuroe2018010104

Selwyn, N. (2019). *Should robots replace teachers? AI and the future of education.* John Wiley & Son.

Shepard, L. A. (2000). The role of assessment in a learning culture. *Educational Researcher, 29*(7), 4–14. https://journals.sagepub.com/doi/abs/10.3102/0013189x029007004

Sikora, Y. B., Usata, O. Y., Mosiiuk, O. O., Verbivskyi, D. S., & Shmeltser, E. O. (2021). Approaches to the choice of tools for adaptive learning based on highlighted selection criteria. *CTE Workshop Proceedings, 8*, 398–410. https://doi.org/DOI: 10.55056/cte.296

Suh, S., Bang, J., & Han, J. W. (2025). Developing Critical Thinking in Second Language Learners: Exploring Generative AI like ChatGPT as a tool for Argumentative Essay Writing. arXiv preprint arXiv:2503.17013. https://arxiv.org/pdf/2503.17013

Third, A., Livingstone, S., & Lansdown, G. (2025). Recognizing children's rights in relation to the digital environment: challenges of voice and evidence, principle and practice. In B. Wagner, M. C. Kettemann, K. Vieth-Ditlmann & S. Montgomery (Eds.), *Research Handbook on Human Rights and Digital Technology* (pp. 325-360). Edward Elgar Publishing.

Trevallion, D., & Nischang, L. C. (2021). The creativity revolution and 21 st century learning. International Journal of Innovation, Creativity and Change, 15(8), 1-25. https://www.ijicc.net/images/Vol_15/Iss_8/15800_Trevallion_2021_E_R.pdf

UNESCO. (2019). Beijing consensus on artificial intelligence and education. In International Conference on Artificial Intelligence and Education, Planning Education in the AI Era: Lead the Leap. https://scholar.google.com/scholar_lookup?title=Beijing+Consensus+on+Artificial+Intelligence+and+Education&author=UNESCO&publication_year=2019

UNESCO. (2023). SDG Resources for Educators: Quality Education. https://en.unesco.org/themes/education/sdgs/material/04

VanLehn, K. (2011). The relative effectiveness of human tutoring, intelligent tutoring systems, and other tutoring systems. *Educational Psychologist, 46*(4), 197–221. https://www.tandfonline.com/doi/abs/10.1080/00461520.2011.611369

Wiliam, D., Fisher, D., & Frey, N. (2024). *Student assessment: Better evidence, better decisions, better learning*. Corwin Press.

Williamson, B., & Eynon, R. (2020). Historical threads, missing links, and future directions in AI in education. *Learning, Media and Technology*, *45*(3), 223–235. https://www.tandfonline.com/doi/pdf/10.1080/17439884.2020.1798995

Williamson, B., Eynon, R., Knox, J., & Davies, H. (2023). Critical perspectives on AI in education: Political economy, discrimination, commercialization, governance and ethics. In du Boulay, B., Mitrovic, A., & Yacef, K. (Eds.), *Handbook of artificial intelligence in education* (pp. 553–570). Edward Elgar Publishing., https://www.elgaronline.com/edcollchap/book/9781800375413/book-part-9781800375413-37.xml

Zawacki-Richter, O., Marín, V. I., Bond, M., & Gouverneur, F. (2019). Systematic review of research on artificial intelligence applications in higher education – where are the educators? *International Journal of Educational Technology in Higher Education*, *16*(1), 1–27. https://link.springer.com/content/pdf/10.1186/s41239-019-0171-0.pdf

Zhou, X. (2025). *Embodied interactions with data, algorithms, and ethics in AI learning experiences for children* [Doctoral thesis, University of Rochester]. ProQuest Dissertations Publishing. https://www.proquest.com/openview/2a66cf8379f5e4a17d25221a13f67714/1?cbl=18750&diss=y&pq-origsite=gscholar

KEY TERMS AND DEFINITIONS

Algorithmic Ethics: field dedicated to the critical analysis of automated decisions made by algorithms, addressing issues such as transparency, fairness, inclusion, and the social and political impacts of these decisions in education.

Artificial Intelligence Literacy: The ability of students and teachers to understand, use, and critically assess AI-based systems, promoting ethical, informed, and conscious use of these technologies.

Competency-Based Curriculum: An educational model organized around the development of relevant and applicable skills, rather than solely on content, favoring meaningful and contextualized learning.

Digital Equity: A principle that ensures fair and inclusive access to digital technologies in education, guaranteeing that all students, regardless of background or condition, can benefit from AI-driven learning opportunities.

Generative Artificial Intelligence: A branch of artificial intelligence capable of creating new content: such as texts, images, or code, based on large volumes of data, and which can be used in education to personalize instruction and support skill development.

Intelligent Tutoring Systems: Educational technologies that simulate the actions of a human tutor, offering adaptive feedback and personalized support based on student performance.

Multimodal Assessment: An evaluation approach that uses multiple forms of learning evidence (such a digital portfolio, self-assessments, and automated feedback), promoting a more comprehensive and personalized view of student progress.

Personalized Learning: An educational process that adapts content, pace, and teaching methods to students' individual needs, supported by technology and the pedagogical mediation of the teacher.

Smart Curriculum: A curricular structure that integrates artificial intelligence technologies in a critical and ethical way, promoting personalized, adaptive, and student-centered learning, while respecting pedagogical principles and social justice.

Transformative Skills: A set of essential 21st-century abilities such as critical thinking, creativity, collaboration, digital literacy, and ethics that empower students to act consciously and responsibly in a complex, digitalized world.

Chapter 4
Using AI to Foster Creativity, Critical Thinking, and Innovation in Students

Panchalingam Suntharalingam
https://orcid.org/0000-0002-0125-9634
Birmingham City University, UK

ABSTRACT

Artificial Intelligence (AI) is reshaping education by fostering creativity, critical thinking, and innovation among students. AI-powered tools support content creation, personalised learning, and collaborative ideation, enabling students to explore novel ideas. In critical thinking development, AI aids in data analysis, argumentation, and gamified learning, sharpening students' reasoning skills. Additionally, AI nurtures innovation through STEM education, entrepreneurship, and research, preparing students for future challenges. However, ethical considerations such as bias, data privacy, and balancing AI with human interaction must be addressed. The future of AI in education promises advancements like virtual tutors, immersive learning, and AI-assisted career guidance. By responsibly integrating AI, educators can enhance student learning experiences and equip them with essential skills for the evolving world.

INTRODUCTION

The 21st century heralds an era of rapid technological advancement, with artificial intelligence (AI) at the forefront of this transformation. Within the realms

DOI: 10.4018/979-8-3373-9225-7.ch004

of education, AI presents a unique opportunity to significantly enhance creativity, critical thinking, and innovation among students. While it brings several benefits, the adoption of AI in education also introduces challenges and concerns that need to be addressed. This chapter explores the mission of integrating AI into education to foster these essential skills, while also addressing the potential concerns associated with its use.

BACKGROUND

The integration of artificial intelligence (AI) in education has created significant attention in recent years, with a growing body of research exploring its potential to enhance creativity, critical thinking, and innovation among students. This section explores the key findings and theoretical underpinnings of this emerging field.

1. Theoretical Foundations

The application of AI in education is grounded in several educational theories, which emphasises the importance of active learning and knowledge construction. AI tools can facilitate personalised learning experiences, enabling students to engage with content in ways that align with their individual learning styles and preferences (Jackson, 2024).

2. Enhancing Creativity

AI has the potential to foster creativity by providing students with new tools and resources for creative expression. Generative AI technologies, such as those used in digital storytelling and game development, allow students to experiment with different ideas and approaches, thereby enhancing their creative thinking skills. Research has shown that AI-supported co-regulated learning can significantly improve students' project design performance and learning motivation (Fu et al., 2024).

3. Promoting Critical Thinking

AI-powered intelligent tutoring systems and virtual labs offer opportunities for students to develop critical thinking skills. These systems can pose challenging questions, provide instant feedback, and encourage students to approach problems from multiple perspectives. Studies have demonstrated that AI-generated content can positively influence students' critical thinking and learning attitudes (Bura & Myakala, 2024).

4. Encouraging Innovation

AI can serve as a catalyst for innovation by enabling students to explore interdisciplinary connections and apply knowledge in novel ways. AI-driven tools can support the development of innovative solutions in fields such as design, engineering, and healthcare. Additionally, AI-generated content has been shown to foster students' innovation and entrepreneurship abilities (Bura & Myakala, 2024).

5. Ethical and Pedagogical Considerations

The integration of AI in education also raises important ethical and pedagogical considerations. Researchers emphasise the need for institutions to develop clear AI policies, uphold academic integrity, and promote equitable access to AI technologies. Ensuring that AI complements traditional learning methods and supports diverse learners is crucial for maximising its benefits while mitigating potential risks (Fu et al., 2024).

The use of AI in education holds great promise for fostering creativity, critical thinking, and innovation among students. By using AI technologies, educators can create more engaging and personalised learning experiences that prepare students for the complexities of the modern world.

THE ROLE OF AI IN EDUCATION

AI encompasses various technologies, including machine learning, natural language processing, and computer vision, which can be harnessed to transform the value of the educational opportunity. The integration of AI into education aims to supplement traditional teaching methods, making learning more personalised, engaging, and effective. By using AI, educators can create a dynamic and adaptive learning environment that caters to individual students' needs, preferences, and learning styles (Holmes et al., 2019).

1. **Fostering Creativity:** Creativity is an essential skill in the modern knowledge-based economy, allowing individuals to generate novel ideas, solutions, and innovations that drive progress in various subject fields. As the world rapidly evolves with technological advancements, creativity is no longer just a desirable trait but a necessity for success in personal, academic, and professional domains. One of the most significant developments in recent years is the integration of Artificial Intelligence (AI) into education, which has proven to be a valuable tool in fostering creativity among students. AI enhances creativity

through personalised learning, inspiring imagination, facilitating collaboration and innovation, and supporting creative problem-solving. These elements help students develop their creative thinking abilities, enabling them to navigate an increasingly competitive world.

2. **Personalised Learning:** Personalised learning is a revolutionary approach that tailors educational experiences to individual students' needs, preferences, and learning styles. AI-powered platforms can analyse students' strengths, weaknesses, and interests to develop customised learning paths. By offering tailored content and activities, AI encourages students to explore their creativity in areas they are passionate about (Luckin et al., 2016).

One of the key benefits of AI-driven personalised learning is its ability to cater to diverse learning styles. Some students may prefer visual learning, while others thrive with auditory or kinaesthetic methods. AI algorithms can assess students' learning habits and adjust instructional methods accordingly, providing engaging content that stimulates creative thinking. For instance, a student interested in storytelling may receive AI-generated writing prompts and narrative-building exercises, while another student passionate about design may be introduced to AI-powered digital art tools.

Personalised learning helps students move beyond rote memorisation and encourages exploration. Traditional education methods often focus on standardised curricula, limiting opportunities for creative expression. AI disrupts this model by allowing students to progress at their own pace and delve into ideas that spark their curiosity. As a result, students are more likely to experiment with new ideas, take intellectual risks, and develop original solutions to problems.

AI-powered platforms like adaptive learning software and intelligent tutoring systems also provide instant feedback, helping students refine their creative skills. When students receive real-time insights into their work, they can iterate on their ideas, improve their artistic or problem-solving approaches, and develop a growth mindset. This continuous cycle of feedback and improvement fosters resilience, a crucial trait for creative individuals who can then navigate failures and setbacks as part of the creative process.

3. **Inspiring Imagination:** AI tools can play a crucial role in inspiring students' imagination and expanding their creative potential. Advanced AI-driven technologies, such as generative art algorithms, music composition software, and creative writing assistants, provide students with novel ways to experiment with different forms of expression. These tools open new avenues for creativity by allowing students to explore ideas they may not have considered otherwise (Miller, 2020). For example, AI-powered generative design tools can assist students in visual arts by generating unique patterns, colour combinations, and

abstract compositions. Programs like Deep Dream by Google and AI-based painting applications allow students to experiment with artistic styles they may not have encountered before. By interacting with these tools, students can refine their artistic skills and develop a deeper appreciation for different artistic movements.

In the field of creative writing, AI-driven writing assistants can help students overcome writer's block by suggesting plot ideas, character development techniques, and stylistic improvements. AI can generate prompts based on students' writing preferences, guiding them to explore new genres and storytelling techniques. This exposure to diverse perspectives and writing styles enriches students' creative abilities and broadens their literary horizons.

Similarly, AI in music composition can introduce students to different musical styles, chord progressions, and rhythmic patterns. Applications like OpenAI's MuseNet, Mureka and Google's Magenta use machine learning to compose original pieces of music, allowing students to collaborate with AI as co-creators. By experimenting with AI-generated compositions, students can push the boundaries of their musical creativity and develop their unique artistic voices.

AI-driven tools also promote interdisciplinary creativity by encouraging students to integrate concepts from multiple domains. For example, a student interested in both technology and storytelling may use AI-powered game design software to create interactive narratives. This cross-disciplinary approach enhances creativity by fostering a deeper understanding of how different fields intersect and influence one another.

4. **Collaboration and Innovation:** Creativity thrives in environments that encourage collaboration and the exchange of ideas. AI-powered collaborative platforms enable students to work together on projects, share insights, and receive instant feedback from peers and instructors. These platforms foster innovation by creating a dynamic space where students can brainstorm, refine ideas, and build upon each other's creativity (Ferguson et al., 2019).

AI-driven collaborative tools, such as shared digital whiteboards, virtual brainstorming applications, and AI-assisted project management software, make teamwork more efficient and productive. Students can collaborate in real time, regardless of geographical location, breaking down barriers to creative exchange. These tools also facilitate interdisciplinary collaboration, allowing students from different academic backgrounds to combine their expertise and generate innovative solutions.

AI-powered discussion forums and idea-generation platforms use natural language processing to analyse students' contributions and suggest relevant resources or discussion topics. By providing intelligent recommendations, AI enhances the depth and quality of collaborative discussions, ensuring that students engage in meaningful exchanges that stimulate creative thinking.

Another critical aspect of AI-driven collaboration is the ability to receive constructive feedback. Traditional peer review processes can be time-consuming and subjective, but AI-powered assessment tools provide instant and objective evaluations. These tools can analyse written work, artistic compositions, and design projects, offering valuable insights that help students refine their creative output. By incorporating AI-generated feedback into their work, students can iteratively improve their projects and develop a mindset of continuous innovation.

5. **Creative Problem-Solving:** Creative problem-solving is a fundamental aspect of innovation, enabling individuals to approach challenges from multiple perspectives and develop original solutions. AI-driven simulations, serious games, and problem-solving applications present students with real-world challenges that require creative thinking. By engaging in these activities, students enhance their ability to analyse complex issues, generate innovative solutions, and adapt to changing circumstances (Woolf et al., 2013).

AI-powered educational games immerse students in interactive scenarios where they must think critically and creatively to overcome obstacles. For example, AI-driven escape room simulations challenge students to solve puzzles using logic, reasoning, and lateral thinking. These activities encourage students to experiment with different problem-solving approaches and develop resilience in the face of uncertainty.

AI can also enhance design thinking methodologies by guiding students through ideation, prototyping, and testing phases. AI-powered design platforms assist students in visualising concepts, simulating potential outcomes, and refining their ideas based on data-driven insights. This iterative process strengthens students' ability to innovate and adapt their creative approaches.

Additionally, AI in STEM education fosters creativity by allowing students to explore scientific concepts through hands-on experimentation. AI-driven virtual laboratories and coding platforms provide students with opportunities to develop and test hypotheses, analyse data, and create innovative solutions to scientific and engineering challenges. By integrating AI into STEM learning, educators can cultivate a generation of creative thinkers who can tackle global challenges with ingenuity.

AI is revolutionising education by fostering creativity in ways that were previously unimaginable. Through personalised learning, AI tailors educational experiences to individual students' strengths and interests, enabling them to explore their creativity in meaningful ways. AI-powered tools inspire imagination by offering new forms of artistic and literary expression, while collaborative platforms facilitate innovation through teamwork and knowledge-sharing. Additionally, AI-driven simulations and problem-solving activities enhance students' ability to think creatively and develop original solutions to complex challenges.

As AI continues to evolve, its role in fostering creativity will only expand, providing students with even more opportunities to explore, innovate, and excel. By integrating AI into education, we can nurture a generation of creative thinkers who are equipped to navigate an ever-changing world and contribute to society in profound and meaningful ways.

ENHANCING CRITICAL THINKING

Critical thinking is the ability to analyse information, evaluate evidence, and make informed decisions. It is a foundational skill that underpins academic success and informed educational experiences and can enhance critical thinking skills in several ways such as:

1. **Data Analysis and Interpretation:** AI-powered tools can help students analyse and interpret large datasets, identifying patterns and drawing meaningful conclusions. This process encourages students to think critically about the information they encounter and develop evidence-based reasoning (Sarker, 2021).
2. **Interactive Learning Environments:** AI-driven interactive platforms can present students with complex scenarios and case studies, requiring them to analyse information, weigh evidence, and make decisions. These activities help students develop critical thinking skills by challenging them to think deeply and critically (Goldie, 2016).
3. **Adaptive Assessments:** AI-powered assessment tools can provide instant feedback on students' performance, highlighting areas for improvement and guiding them towards more critical thinking. These assessments can adapt to students' progress, presenting increasingly challenging tasks that require higher-order thinking (Baker & Siemens, 2014).
4. **Debate and Discussion:** AI-powered discussion forums and debate platforms can facilitate meaningful conversations among students on various topics. By engaging in debates and discussions, students learn to articulate their arguments, consider different perspectives, and think critically about complex issues (Laurillard, 2013).

PROMOTING INNOVATION

Innovation is the ability to develop new ideas, products, or processes that create value. In an increasingly competitive global economy, fostering innovation is essential for students' future success. The ability to think creatively, solve complex problems, and develop novel solutions is a crucial skill set in the modern world. As technological advancements continue to shape industries, integrating artificial intelligence (AI) into the learning process can significantly enhance students' capacity for innovation. AI can promote innovation in several ways, including idea generation, prototype development, and entrepreneurial skill-building. By using AI tools and technologies, students can harness their creativity and drive meaningful change in various fields such as:

1. **Idea Generation:** A critical component of innovation is generating new ideas. AI-powered brainstorming tools can help students develop creative solutions by providing prompts, suggestions, and inspiration. These tools can expand students' thinking and encourage them to explore unconventional solutions (Akinwalere & Ivanov, 2022). By analysing large datasets and identifying emerging trends, AI can help students uncover insights that may not be immediately apparent through traditional brainstorming methods.

AI-powered tools such as natural language processing (NLP) algorithms can analyse students' inputs and suggest relevant concepts, helping them refine their ideas. For example, AI-driven platforms like OpenAI's ChatGPT or IBM Watson can generate unique problem-solving approaches based on previous successful innovations. This capability allows students to explore various perspectives and refine their ideas before committing to a particular concept.

AI can facilitate collaboration among students by connecting individuals with similar interests and complementary skills. Virtual brainstorming sessions powered by AI can bring together diverse viewpoints, leading to richer discussions and more innovative ideas. AI-enhanced collaboration tools can analyse conversation patterns, suggest relevant resources, and highlight potential areas of improvement in real-time. These benefits make AI an invaluable asset in fast tracking the creative process, ensuring that students develop well-rounded, innovative solutions to real-world problems.

2. **Prototype Development:** Once an idea is conceived, the next step is to develop a prototype that brings the concept to life. AI-driven design and engineering tools can assist students in developing prototypes and testing their ideas. By

providing instant feedback and iterative improvements, AI helps students refine their concepts and innovate more effectively (George, 2023).

For instance, AI-driven design software, such as Autodesk's Fusion 360, allows students to create 3D models of their concepts with precision. These tools can automate complex design processes, optimise structural integrity, and simulate real-world performance. This functionality enables students to test multiple iterations quickly, identify design flaws, and make necessary modifications without extensive manual calculations or physical testing verification processes.

AI can also streamline the prototyping process by integrating with 3D printing technologies. AI algorithms can optimise designs for manufacturability, reducing material waste and improving efficiency. Students can experiment with different materials, shapes, and functionalities, gaining hands-on experience in rapid product development.

AI-powered simulation tools can help students evaluate their prototypes in virtual environments before physical production. This capability is particularly valuable in fields such as robotics, automotive engineering, and aerospace, where prototyping can be expensive and time-consuming. By using AI-driven simulations, students can test the feasibility of their innovations and refine them to achieve optimal performance.

3. **Entrepreneurial Skills:** Turning innovative ideas into viable businesses requires a solid foundation in entrepreneurship. AI-powered platforms can offer students resources and guidance on entrepreneurship, helping them develop the skills needed to bring their ideas to market. These platforms can connect students with mentors, investors, and potential customers, fostering a culture of innovation and entrepreneurship (Bell & Bell, 2023).

AI-driven market analysis tools can provide students with valuable insights into consumer preferences, industry trends, and competitive landscapes. By analysing social media data, customer reviews, and online discussions, AI can help students identify gaps in the market and tailor their products or services accordingly. This data-driven approach enhances decision-making and increases the likelihood of a successful business venture.

AI-powered business planning tools can guide students through the process of creating business models, financial projections, and marketing strategies. Platforms like Bizplan and LivePlan use AI to generate business plans based on industry benchmarks and best practices. These tools simplify complex business concepts, making entrepreneurship more accessible to students with limited experience.

AI chatbots and virtual assistants can also play a crucial role in supporting student entrepreneurs. By handling customer inquiries, processing transactions, and managing administrative tasks, AI-driven virtual assistants allow students to focus on refining their products and expanding their businesses. These tools can automate repetitive tasks, enabling young entrepreneurs to operate efficiently with limited resources.

AI matchmaking systems such as MeetingHand can facilitate networking opportunities by matching students with industry experts, mentors, and investors. AI-driven mentorship platforms analyse students' interests and expertise to connect them with relevant professionals who can provide guidance and support. This exposure to real-world business experiences helps students develop critical entrepreneurial skills and build confidence in their directional goals.

4. **Cross-Disciplinary Collaboration:** Cross-disciplinary collaboration is an essential component of modern education and innovation. AI-powered collaborative platforms serve as a bridge, enabling students from diverse academic backgrounds to come together and work on interdisciplinary projects. These platforms provide a structured yet flexible environment where students can share their expertise, exchange ideas, and collectively develop solutions to complex problems that transcend individual disciplines.

By facilitating interaction among students from various fields such as engineering, medicine, business, and the arts, AI-powered platforms promote a holistic approach to problem-solving. For instance, a project focused on sustainable urban development may involve landscape architecture students designing infrastructure, environmental science students assessing ecological impact, and economics students analysing financial feasibility. Such collaboration enables participants to move beyond their disciplinary silos, fostering creative problem-solving that integrates multiple perspectives.

AI-powered collaboration tools enhance efficiency and organisation in interdisciplinary teamwork. Features such as intelligent matchmaking, which pairs students based on complementary skills, automated knowledge-sharing, and real-time communication, streamline the collaborative process. This can also assist in managing workflows, providing data-driven insights, and offering personalised recommendations to enhance project outcomes.

The benefits of cross-disciplinary collaboration extend beyond academic learning. Students develop essential 21st-century skills such as adaptability, critical thinking, and effective communication. Exposure to diverse viewpoints broadens their intellectual horizons, preparing them for real-world challenges where interdisciplinary cooperation is crucial. Companies and research institutions increasingly seek professionals who can integrate knowledge from multiple domains, making this experience highly valuable for career development.

THE ROLE OF EDUCATORS IN AI-DRIVEN INNOVATION

While AI offers numerous benefits in promoting innovation, educators play a crucial role in guiding students to use these technologies effectively. Teachers must integrate AI tools into the curriculum in a way that encourages creativity and problem-solving. Providing students with hands-on experience in AI-powered innovation processes can help them develop confidence in using these technologies for real-world applications.

Educators should also emphasise ethical considerations when using AI for innovation. Students must understand the implications of AI-driven decision-making, data privacy concerns, and the ethical responsibilities of developing new technologies. Encouraging discussions on these topics ensures that students use AI responsibly and consider the societal impact of their innovations.

Schools and universities should invest in AI literacy programs that equip students with the technical skills needed to harness AI for innovation. Providing training in machine learning, data analysis, and AI programming can empower students to develop AI-driven solutions independently. By fostering an AI literate generation, educational institutions can contribute to a more innovative and competitive workforce.

Promoting innovation is essential for preparing students to succeed in a rapidly evolving world. AI serves as a powerful catalyst for innovation by enhancing idea generation, facilitating prototype development, and fostering entrepreneurial skills. By using AI-powered tools, students can expand their creative thinking, refine their concepts, and transform their ideas into viable business ventures.

The integration of AI into education not only enhances students' problem-solving abilities but also equips them with the skills necessary to succeed in technology-driven industries. Educators, policymakers, and industry leaders must collaborate to create an ecosystem that supports AI-driven innovation. By embracing AI as a tool for creativity and problem-solving, educators can empower the next generation of innovators to make meaningful contributions to society.

As AI continues to evolve, its role in innovation will only become more significant by fostering a culture of experimentation, learning an ensure that students develop the skills and confidence needed to push the boundaries of innovation. With the right resources and guidance, AI can be a transformative force in shaping the future of education and entrepreneurship.

CHALLENGES IN INTEGRATING AI INTO EDUCATION

While the integration of AI into education offers considerable benefits, it also presents several challenges that need to be addressed. These challenges include ethical considerations, pedagogical concerns, and issues related to equity and accessibility.

One of the primary ethical considerations in AI-driven education is data privacy. AI systems require vast amounts of data to function effectively, and this includes sensitive student information. Protecting this data from breaches, unauthorised access, and misuse is a significant concern. There is the question of consent, whether students and parents are fully informed about how their data is being collected, stored, and used. Educational institutions must implement strict data protection policies and ensure compliance with regulations such as the General Data Protection Regulation (GDPR) and the Family Educational Rights and Privacy Act (FERPA).

Another ethical concern is bias in AI algorithms. AI systems are only as objective as the data they are trained on. If the training data includes biases, AI tools may reinforce and perpetuate these biases in educational settings. This can lead to unfair treatment of students from underrepresented backgrounds, affecting their learning opportunities and assessments. Therefore, AI developers and educators must work together to ensure that these systems are designed to be fair and unbiased.

Pedagogically, the integration of AI in education raises concerns about the role of human teachers. While AI can enhance learning through personalised instruction, there is a risk that it may diminish the importance of human interaction in the classroom. Learning is not just about acquiring knowledge but also about developing critical thinking, creativity, and emotional intelligence, areas where human teachers excel. Over-reliance on AI tools could lead to a depersonalised learning experience, making it essential for educators to strike a balance between AI-driven instruction and human mentorship.

AI-based learning tools may not always align with traditional educational methods. As an example, existing curricula and assessment methods are designed with conventional classroom teaching in mind. The introduction of AI requires significant adjustments, including training teachers to effectively use AI tools and redesigning assessment strategies to measure students' learning outcomes accurately. Resistance to change among educators and institutions may slow down the adoption of AI in classrooms.

Equity and accessibility also pose significant challenges as AI has the potential to provide personalised learning experiences, but not all students have equal access to the technology required to benefit from these advancements. Socioeconomic disparities can limit students' access to AI-driven educational tools, further widening the digital divide. Schools in underprivileged areas may struggle with inadequate funding for AI infrastructure, putting their students at a disadvantage compared to those in well-funded institutions.

AI-based learning tools must be designed to accommodate students with disabilities. This includes ensuring compatibility with assistive technologies such as screen readers, speech-to-text software, and other accessibility features. If not designed inclusively, AI-powered education systems may inadvertently exclude students with disabilities, reinforcing barriers rather than removing them.

While AI has the potential to revolutionise education, it is essential to address these challenges proactively. Ethical considerations, pedagogical concerns, and equity issues must be carefully managed to ensure that AI enhances learning without compromising fairness, inclusivity, and human engagement in education.

ETHICAL CONSIDERATIONS

1. **Bias and Fairness:** AI algorithms can perpetuate and amplify existing biases present in the data they are trained on. This can lead to unfair treatment of certain groups of students and reinforce existing inequalities. Ensuring fairness and mitigating bias in AI systems is a critical ethical consideration (Noble, 2018).
2. **Privacy and Security:** The use of AI in education often involves the collection and analysis of students' personal data. Ensuring the privacy and security of this data is essential to protect students' rights and maintain trust in AI systems (Crawford & Calo, 2016).
3. **Transparency and Accountability:** AI algorithms can be complex and opaque, making it difficult for educators and students to understand how decisions are made. Ensuring transparency and accountability in AI systems is crucial to maintain trust and ensure that these systems are used responsibly (Binns, 2017).

PEDAGOGICAL CONCERNS

1. **Teacher Roles and Responsibilities:** The integration of artificial intelligence (AI) into education is transforming traditional pedagogical structures, necessitating a redefinition of teacher roles and responsibilities. While AI has the potential to assist educators in various capacities, including personalised learning, grading, and administrative tasks, it is crucial to ensure that teachers remain central to the educational process. AI can automate routine tasks, such as grading assignments and managing student data, thereby allowing teachers to dedicate more time to instructional activities and student engagement (Williamson, 2015). However, this shift also demands that teachers acquire new digital com-

petencies and adapt to evolving educational technologies. One of the critical concerns associated with AI integration is the potential for teachers to become overly reliant on technological tools, leading to a diminished emphasis on their traditional pedagogical roles. Educators must be empowered with continuous professional development to effectively integrate AI into their teaching strategies while maintaining their unique human-centred approach to education. This includes understanding how AI functions, recognising its limitations, and using it responsibly to enhance student learning outcomes without compromising the teacher-student relationship. It is important that teachers play a crucial role in fostering critical thinking, creativity, and emotional intelligence skills that AI cannot effectively replicate. Ensuring that educators are equipped to navigate this evolving landscape requires systemic support, including policy development, resource allocation, and training programs designed to enhance their ability to incorporate AI responsibly. Ethical considerations must be addressed, particularly regarding data privacy, bias in AI algorithms, and the implications of automated decision-making on students' educational experiences. Ultimately, AI should be viewed as a complementary tool rather than a replacement for teachers. The success of AI-driven education depends on striking a balance where technology supports and enhances traditional pedagogical practices rather than diminishing the essential role of educators in shaping students' intellectual and social development.

2. **Overreliance on Technology:** The growing presence of AI and digital technologies in education brings both opportunities and challenges. One significant concern is the potential for overreliance on technology, which may lead to a reduced emphasis on critical pedagogical practices and human interaction. While AI can streamline administrative processes and offer personalised learning experiences, it cannot fully replicate the nuances of human engagement, mentorship, and the social aspects of education (Teräs, 2022). An overreliance on AI-driven learning systems may contribute to a decline in traditional classroom interactions, where students develop interpersonal skills, emotional intelligence, and collaborative problem-solving abilities. Education is not solely about knowledge acquisition; it is also about fostering relationships, building character, and developing the capacity for empathy and ethical reasoning. If AI-based learning platforms become the primary mode of instruction, students may miss out on essential social experiences that are critical for their personal and professional growth. AI algorithms, while powerful, are not infallible. They may reinforce biases present in the data they are trained on, leading to disparities in educational outcomes. An excessive dependence on AI for assessment and learning recommendations could inadvertently perpetuate inequalities, particularly for marginalised or underrepresented student groups. It is essential to ensure that

AI systems are transparent, equitable, and continuously monitored to prevent unintended consequences. To mitigate these risks, educators and policymakers must adopt a balanced approach that integrates AI as a supplementary tool rather than a primary instructional medium. Hybrid models that combine traditional teaching methods with AI-driven enhancements can help maintain the integrity of the educational experience while leveraging the benefits of technology. Schools and institutions should establish clear guidelines on the appropriate use of AI, emphasising the importance of teacher involvement and human oversight in all aspects of learning. Students must be educated on the responsible use of technology, including digital literacy, ethical considerations, and critical thinking skills. Encouraging students to engage critically with AI tools rather than passively consuming algorithm-driven content can foster a more thoughtful and informed approach to technology integration in education.

3. **Skill Development:** A well-rounded student educational experience should aim to develop a diverse set of skills that prepare students for the complexities of the modern world. While AI has the potential to enhance creativity, critical thinking, and innovation, it is crucial to ensure that foundational skills, such as literacy, numeracy, and social-emotional competencies, are not neglected (Livingstone, 2011).

AI-driven learning platforms can provide personalised instruction, adapting to students' individual needs and pacing. This capability can be particularly beneficial for addressing learning gaps and reinforcing subject-specific knowledge. However, the reliance on AI-generated content and automated assessment tools should not come at the expense of essential cognitive and interpersonal skills that require human interaction and experiential learning. For instance, literacy and numeracy skills form the foundation of academic success and lifelong learning. While AI can assist in tutoring and practice exercises, students must also engage in active reading, writing, and problem-solving exercises that promote deeper comprehension and critical analysis. Similarly, social-emotional skills, including teamwork, communication, and resilience, are best cultivated through meaningful human interactions, discussions, and real-world experiences.

The increasing prevalence of AI in education raises concerns about students' ability to develop metacognitive skills. These skills enable students to reflect on their own learning processes and adapt their strategies accordingly. AI-driven personalised learning environments may reduce students' opportunities to struggle, make mistakes, and develop perseverance, which are essential components of intellectual growth.

SOLVING THE CHALLENGES

To address these challenges, educational institutions should adopt a holistic approach that integrates AI while maintaining a strong emphasis on fundamental skills and social-emotional development. The implementation of AI in education must be balanced, ensuring that students develop essential cognitive abilities, emotional intelligence, and ethical reasoning alongside their technical proficiency. This comprehensive strategy may involve the following components:

1. **Blended Learning Approaches:** Blended learning combines AI-driven instruction with traditional teaching methods, ensuring that students benefit from both technological advancements and human guidance. AI-powered tools, such as personalised learning platforms, adaptive assessments, and intelligent tutoring systems, can provide students with tailored educational experiences that cater to their individual needs and learning paces. These technologies can analyse student performance data in real-time, identifying areas where they struggle and offering customised resources to help them improve.

The role of teachers remains crucial in this approach. Educators serve as facilitators, providing context, encouragement, and deeper insights that AI cannot replicate. They help students develop higher-order thinking skills, such as analysis, evaluation, and synthesis, which are essential for meaningful learning. Furthermore, the human aspect of teaching fosters emotional connections and motivation, elements that AI-driven instruction alone cannot fully provide.

Blended learning also supports diverse learning styles by incorporating various instructional formats, such as video lectures, interactive simulations, and face-to-face discussions. For instance, students who prefer visual learning can benefit from AI-generated visualisations, while those who learn best through discussion can engage in teacher-led debates and collaborative activities. By leveraging the strengths of both AI and traditional teaching, blended learning ensures a well-rounded educational experience.

2. **Project-Based and Experiential Learning:** Encouraging students to engage in hands-on, real-world projects is essential for fostering critical thinking, creativity, and collaboration. Project-based learning (PBL) shifts the focus from rote memorisation to active problem-solving and innovation. In a technology-driven world, students must learn how to apply knowledge in practical scenarios, work effectively in teams, and think critically about complex issues.

AI can enhance PBL by providing data-driven insights, automating routine tasks, and offering intelligent feedback. For example, AI-powered coding platforms can help students debug their programs, while AI-driven design tools can assist in creating prototypes for engineering projects. Additionally, AI can facilitate virtual and augmented reality experiences, enabling students to explore concepts in immersive environments. For instance, a history class could use virtual reality to tour ancient civilisations, or a biology class could interact with 3D models of human anatomy.

Despite these advancements, the role of educators in project-based learning remains irreplaceable. Teachers guide students in developing research skills, posing meaningful questions, and reflecting on their learning experiences. They also help students navigate challenges, fostering resilience and adaptability, qualities essential for success in the modern workforce.

Experiential learning opportunities, such as internships, service-learning projects, and entrepreneurship initiatives, allow students to apply their skills in real-world contexts. Schools can collaborate with industry partners to provide students with hands-on experience in various fields, from technology and healthcare to business and the arts. By integrating AI into these experiences, students can gain insights into how technology is shaping different industries and develop the ability to work alongside AI systems effectively.

3. **Ethical and Digital Literacy Education:** As AI becomes increasingly integrated into education and daily life, teaching students ethical and digital literacy is imperative. Students must learn how to critically evaluate AI-generated content, understand algorithmic biases, and develop responsible technology usage habits.

One major concern with AI-driven content is the potential for misinformation and bias. AI models are trained on vast datasets, which may contain inaccuracies or reflect societal biases. Without proper critical thinking skills, students may take AI-generated information at face value, leading to misunderstandings and misinformation spread. Educators must teach students how to question the credibility of sources, recognise biases in AI algorithms, and cross-reference information with reliable sources.

Ethical education should focus on the societal implications of AI, including privacy concerns, data security, and the impact of automation on employment. Students should engage in discussions about the ethical dilemmas posed by AI, such as facial recognition technology, autonomous weapons, and deepfake videos. By exploring these issues, students can develop a sense of responsibility and awareness regarding the ethical use of technology.

Digital literacy education should include lessons on online safety, cybersecurity, and responsible social media usage. Many students today interact with AI-driven algorithms on social media platforms without understanding how their data is collected and used. Teaching students about digital footprints, data privacy, and the potential consequences of online behaviour can help them navigate the digital world more safely and responsibly.

4. **Teacher-Led Interventions:** While AI can enhance learning experiences, it should not replace the human element of education. Teachers play an essential role in guiding students' learning experiences, providing feedback, and fostering a growth mindset. AI-driven tools can assist educators by automating administrative tasks, such as grading and attendance tracking, allowing teachers to focus more on instruction and student engagement.

One of the most significant advantages of teacher-led interventions is the ability to provide personalised support. While AI can identify learning gaps, teachers can offer nuanced explanations, address misconceptions, and adapt their teaching strategies based on students' unique needs. Human interaction is particularly crucial in subjects that require discussion, debate, and ethical reasoning, such as literature, philosophy, and social studies.

Teachers serve as mentors and role models, helping students develop soft skills such as communication, empathy, and resilience. In an era where AI is automating many technical tasks, these human-centred skills are becoming increasingly valuable in the workforce. By emphasising mentorship, educators can inspire students to become lifelong learners who approach challenges with curiosity and determination.

Another essential aspect of teacher-led interventions is fostering a growth mindset, the belief that intelligence and abilities can be developed through effort and perseverance. AI-driven assessments can provide instant feedback, but teachers play a crucial role in encouraging students to view mistakes as learning opportunities rather than failures. By promoting a positive learning environment, educators can help students build confidence and resilience in the face of challenges.

The integration of AI in education presents both opportunities and challenges. By adopting a holistic approach that balances AI-driven instruction with fundamental skills and social-emotional development, educational institutions can prepare students for the future while preserving the essential human aspects of learning. Blended learning approaches ensure that students benefit from AI-powered personalisation while maintaining the invaluable guidance of teachers. Project-based and experiential learning fosters creativity, critical thinking, and real-world problem-solving skills. Ethical and digital literacy education equips students with the ability to navigate AI-driven information responsibly and understand the broader societal implications of technology. Finally, teacher-led interventions ensure that students receive personalised support, mentorship, and encouragement to develop a growth mindset.

Ultimately, the goal of integrating AI in education should not be to replace traditional teaching methods but to enhance them. By leveraging AI as a tool rather than a substitute, educators can create a dynamic, engaging, and effective learning environment that empowers students to thrive in an increasingly AI-driven world. The role of AI in education should be designed to enhance, rather than replace, traditional skill development. This requires careful curriculum planning, where AI tools are integrated in a way that complements rather than dominates instructional practices. Additionally, policymakers and educators must work together to develop assessment models that evaluate not only students' academic progress but also their critical thinking, creativity, and interpersonal abilities.

The integration of AI in education presents both opportunities and challenges that must be carefully navigated. While AI has the potential to enhance personalised learning, streamline administrative tasks, and support skill development, it is essential to ensure that teachers remain central to the educational process. Overreliance on technology should be avoided, as it may lead to a reduction in human interactions and critical pedagogical practices. Additionally, a balanced approach to skill development is necessary to ensure that students acquire both foundational competencies and advanced cognitive abilities.

By adopting a thoughtful and strategic approach to AI integration, educational institutions can leverage technological advancements while preserving the core values of human centred education. Ongoing research, policy development, and professional training will be crucial in shaping an educational landscape where AI serves as an empowering tool rather than a replacement for the invaluable role of teachers and traditional learning methodologies.

EQUITY AND ACCESSIBILITY

1. **Digital Divide:** The integration of AI in education has the potential to widen the digital divide, particularly for students from disadvantaged backgrounds who may lack access to AI-powered tools and resources. Economic disparities can lead to unequal access to devices, reliable internet connectivity, and advanced educational technologies, putting some students at a significant disadvantage (Robinson et al., 2015). If AI-driven learning tools become a standard feature of education, students from low-income families or underfunded schools may struggle to keep up with their more privileged peers.

Bridging this digital divide requires strategic investments in infrastructure, such as expanding broadband access to rural and underserved communities, providing affordable or subsidised devices, and ensuring that all students can benefit from

AI-enhanced learning experiences. Policymakers and educators must work together to implement initiatives that make AI resources accessible to all students, regardless of socioeconomic status.

Digital literacy training should be integrated into curricula to ensure that students can effectively use AI tools. Merely providing access to technology is insufficient; students must also develop the skills needed to navigate and critically engage with AI-powered educational resources.

2. **Inclusivity:** AI technologies in education must be designed with inclusivity in mind to accommodate students with disabilities and special educational needs (Shelton, 2024). AI-driven tools, such as speech-to-text applications, screen readers, and adaptive learning platforms, have the potential to enhance learning experiences for students with diverse needs. However, if inclusivity is not a priority in AI development, these technologies may inadvertently exclude certain student demographics.

Ensuring that AI-powered educational tools are accessible involves incorporating universal design principles and compliance with accessibility standards. Developers must actively seek input from educators, students, and disability advocates to create AI solutions that address a wide range of learning needs. Teachers should be trained to utilise AI tools effectively to support diverse learners and provide personalised learning experiences that cater to individual strengths and challenges.

Ultimately, achieving equity and accessibility in AI-driven education requires a commitment to bridging gaps in digital access and ensuring that technological advancements benefit all students. By prioritising inclusivity and proactive policy interventions, educational institutions can create a more equitable learning environment where AI serves as a tool for empowerment rather than exclusion.

IMPLEMENTATION STRATEGIES FOR AI IN EDUCATION

Successfully integrating Artificial Intelligence (AI) into education requires a thoughtful and strategic approach. AI has the potential to revolutionise the learning experience by personalising education, automating administrative tasks, and providing real-time feedback. However, to maximise its benefits and mitigate potential challenges, educators and institutions must adopt structured strategies. Several key strategies can help ensure that AI is used effectively to foster creativity, critical thinking, and innovation among students. These include training programs for educators, promoting collaborative learning, and providing ongoing support and resources.

1. **Training Programs for Educators:** A critical first step in implementing AI in education is equipping educators with the knowledge and skills required to effectively use AI tools in their teaching. Many educators may lack familiarity with AI technologies, making it essential to introduce comprehensive training programs. These training programs should focus on various aspects:

    Understanding AI Basics: Educators need to understand fundamental AI concepts, including machine learning, natural language processing, and adaptive learning systems. A foundational knowledge of AI will help teachers make informed decisions about selecting and implementing AI tools in their classrooms.

    Hands-on Experience with AI Tools: Providing teachers with hands-on experience with AI-powered educational tools is crucial. Platforms such as adaptive learning systems, intelligent tutoring systems, and AI-driven grading tools can significantly enhance the learning process. By actively engaging with these tools, educators can gain confidence in their use.

    Pedagogical Integration: Training should emphasise how AI can be integrated into various subjects and learning activities. AI should not replace traditional teaching methods but rather complement and enhance them. Educators should learn how to use AI to personalise learning experiences, identify students' strengths and weaknesses, and provide tailored support.

    Ethical Considerations and Bias Awareness: AI systems are not immune to biases, and it is essential for educators to be aware of ethical concerns associated with AI use in education. Training programs should include discussions on data privacy, algorithmic bias, and responsible AI usage to ensure that AI is applied in an ethical and inclusive manner.

2. **Promoting Collaborative Learning:** Collaboration among educators is another essential strategy for successfully implementing AI in education. AI is a rapidly evolving field, and teachers can benefit significantly from shared knowledge and collective problem-solving. Schools and institutions should encourage collaborative learning in the following ways:

    Professional Learning Communities (PLCs): Professional Learning Communities (PLCs) provide a platform for educators to collaborate, share insights, and discuss best practices for integrating AI into teaching. Regular meetings, workshops, and discussion forums can help educators stay updated on new AI tools and methodologies.

    Peer Mentorship Programs: More experienced educators who have successfully integrated AI into their teaching can mentor their colleagues. Peer mentorship programs foster a supportive learning environment where educators can seek guidance, ask questions, and gain practical insights from their peers.

Interdisciplinary Collaboration: AI is a versatile tool that can be used across various subjects, from STEM to the humanities. Encouraging interdisciplinary collaboration allows educators from different fields to work together and explore innovative ways to incorporate AI into their respective subjects. For example, language teachers can use AI-powered translation tools, while science teachers can use AI-driven simulations to enhance experiments.

International and Cross-Institutional Partnerships: Engaging in collaborations with international educational institutions and AI research organisations can provide educators with access to global best practices and new AI developments. Virtual conferences, online workshops, and collaborative research projects can help educators expand their understanding of AI in education.

3. **Providing Ongoing Support and Resources:** Implementing AI in education is not a one-time effort but an ongoing process. Schools and institutions must ensure that educators have continuous access to support and resources to effectively use AI in their teaching practices. This can be achieved through various means:

Access to AI Experts and Technical Support: Educators may encounter technical challenges when using AI tools. Providing access to AI experts and technical support teams can help teachers resolve issues quickly and ensure smooth integration of AI into classrooms. AI specialists can also offer guidance on selecting the most appropriate tools for specific educational needs.

Online Resource Hubs: Creating online resource hubs that compile AI-related teaching materials, tutorials, and case studies can be beneficial for educators. These hubs should include:

- Instructional videos on how to use AI tools
- Lesson plans incorporating AI applications
- Research articles on AI in education
- Discussion forums for educators to exchange ideas

Regular Professional Development Opportunities: Education institutions should organise regular professional development sessions, workshops, and webinars focused on AI in education. These events should be tailored to different skill levels, ensuring that both beginners and advanced users can benefit from them.

Encouraging Experimentation and Innovation: Educators should be encouraged to experiment with AI tools and explore innovative ways to use them in their teaching. Schools can allocate time for teachers to pilot new AI-driven teaching methods, gather feedback from students, and refine their approaches accordingly.

Policy and Framework Development: To ensure consistency and effectiveness in AI implementation, educational institutions should develop policies and frameworks outlining best practices for AI usage. These policies should address:

- Guidelines for selecting and evaluating AI tools
- Data privacy and security measures
- Ethical considerations in AI-driven education

4. **Challenges and Considerations:** While AI has the potential to transform education, there are several challenges that educators and institutions must address:

   Equity and Accessibility: Not all schools have equal access to AI resources, which can widen the digital divide. Institutions must work towards ensuring that AI-powered education is accessible to all students, regardless of their socioeconomic background.

   Data Privacy and Security: AI systems collect and analyse vast amounts of student data. It is crucial to implement strong data protection policies to safeguard student information and prevent unauthorised access or misuse.

   Over-Reliance on AI: While AI can enhance learning, it should not replace human interaction and critical thinking skills. Educators must strike a balance between AI-driven and traditional teaching methods to provide a well-rounded educational experience.

The successful implementation of AI in education requires a well-structured strategy encompassing educator training, collaborative learning, and continuous support. By equipping teachers with the necessary knowledge and skills, fostering a culture of collaboration, and providing ongoing resources, educational institutions can maximise the benefits of AI. Addressing challenges such as equity, privacy, and ethical concerns is also crucial to ensure AI is used responsibly. With careful planning and execution, AI can be a powerful tool that enhances education, empowers teachers, and provides students with personalised and engaging learning experiences.

CURRICULUM INTEGRATION

1. **Embedding AI in the Curriculum:** Integrating AI concepts and tools into the curriculum is essential for preparing students for the rapidly evolving digital

world. AI is transforming industries, and students need to understand both its fundamental concepts and real-world applications. By embedding AI into various subjects, educational institutions can ensure that students develop a strong foundational knowledge that is relevant to their future careers.

One approach to integrating AI into the curriculum is by incorporating AI-related topics into existing subjects. For example, in mathematics, students can explore how algorithms work, delve into probability and statistics, and study optimisation techniques, all of which are fundamental to AI. In computer science classes, AI can be taught through programming exercises that involve machine learning models, natural language processing, and robotics. Social sciences can also integrate AI by discussing its ethical implications, policy considerations, and societal impact.

Another strategy is to create dedicated AI courses that cover both theoretical and practical aspects of AI. These courses can range from introductory AI literacy courses for all students to advanced machine learning and neural network courses for those specialising in technology fields. AI-focused courses should emphasise hands-on activities, such as coding AI models, analysing large datasets, and understanding AI biases. This approach helps students become proficient in using AI tools while also fostering critical thinking about AI's role in society.

Embedding AI in the curriculum should also include discussions on the ethical considerations and biases inherent in AI systems. Students should learn about responsible AI development, transparency, and accountability. They should be encouraged to think critically about the implications of AI technologies in areas such as privacy, employment, and decision-making. By systematically embedding AI concepts across various subjects and levels of education, institutions can equip students with essential AI literacy, ensuring they are prepared to engage with and contribute to the AI-driven future.

2. **Project-Based Learning:** Project-based learning (PBL) is a powerful pedagogical approach that allows students to engage with AI in a hands-on manner. By working on real-world projects, students not only gain technical expertise but also develop essential soft skills such as problem-solving, teamwork, and innovation. Encouraging project-based learning can make AI education more engaging and practical.

One effective way to implement PBL in AI education is by designing projects that require students to apply AI tools to solve real-world problems. For example, students can develop AI-powered chatbots to assist in customer service, build predictive models for climate change analysis, or create image recognition systems for medical diagnostics. These projects allow students to explore different AI techniques while working on meaningful applications that have social and economic implications.

Collaborative projects can also enhance learning by promoting teamwork and interdisciplinary collaboration. AI is not confined to computer science alone; it intersects with fields such as healthcare, finance, agriculture, and the arts. Encouraging students from different disciplines to work together on AI projects fosters a richer understanding of how AI can be applied across various domains. For instance, a team comprising computer science students and biology students could work together on an AI-driven disease prediction model.

Project-based learning can be structured to involve mentorship from industry professionals. Schools and universities can partner with tech companies, research institutions, and government agencies to provide students with real-world exposure. Industry professionals can offer insights, share best practices, and guide students through the challenges of AI development.

Another key aspect of PBL is encouraging students to document and present their work. By writing reports, creating presentations, and demonstrating their AI projects, students enhance their communication skills and gain confidence in explaining complex concepts. Competitions and hackathons can also serve as platforms for students to showcase their AI projects, receive feedback, and further refine their skills.

By incorporating project-based learning into AI education, students not only develop technical expertise but also gain practical experience in applying AI concepts to solve real-world challenges. This approach fosters creativity, critical thinking, and innovation—skills that are crucial in an AI-driven world.

3. **Interdisciplinary Approaches:** AI is a multidisciplinary field, and promoting interdisciplinary approaches to AI education can help students see the broader implications and applications of AI technology. By integrating AI with various disciplines, educators can provide students with a more holistic understanding of AI and its transformative potential.

One way to implement an interdisciplinary approach is by blending AI with subjects such as business, healthcare, engineering, and the arts. For example, business students can explore how AI is used in data analytics, marketing automation, and financial forecasting. Healthcare students can learn about AI applications in medical imaging, personalised treatment plans, and drug discovery. Engineering students can explore AI-driven automation in manufacturing, robotics, and smart infrastructure. In the arts, students can experiment with AI-generated music, digital painting, and creative storytelling.

Interdisciplinary learning also fosters a deeper appreciation of AI's ethical, social, and economic implications. By incorporating discussions on AI ethics, bias, and fairness in social science courses, students can critically analyse how AI technologies impact society. This approach can be particularly valuable in courses related to law, philosophy, and public policy, where students examine the legal and moral dimensions of AI deployment. Interdisciplinary approaches can be enhanced through collaborative projects that bring together students from different academic backgrounds. For instance, a team of psychology and computer science students could develop an AI system that detects mental health issues through speech and text analysis. Similarly, journalism and AI students could collaborate to explore how AI can be used in fact-checking and combating misinformation.

To facilitate interdisciplinary AI learning, institutions can design specialised programs that combine AI education with other disciplines. For example, a "Computational Social Sciences" program can teach students how AI is used in sociology and political science, while a "Digital Humanities" program can explore the intersection of AI and literature, history, and philosophy.

Interdisciplinary learning can be supported by guest lectures, workshops, and seminars led by experts from various fields. These events can expose students to diverse perspectives and inspire them to explore AI applications beyond traditional tech domains. By promoting interdisciplinary approaches, educators can help students understand AI's broad applications and equip them with the skills to work in diverse fields. AI is not just a technological tool; it is a transformative force that impacts every aspect of society. Encouraging interdisciplinary learning ensures that students are well-prepared to use AI in innovative and responsible ways.

The integration of AI into the curriculum is essential for preparing students for the future. By embedding AI concepts and tools into existing subjects, students can develop a deeper understanding of AI and its applications. Project-based learning provides hands-on experiences that allow students to apply AI tools in practical ways, fostering creativity and problem-solving skills. Interdisciplinary approaches help students see the connections between AI and various fields, promoting a more comprehensive understanding of AI's impact on society.

By implementing these strategies, educational institutions can ensure that students are not just passive consumers of AI technology but active contributors to its development and ethical use. AI literacy is becoming as fundamental as traditional literacy and numeracy, and a well-integrated AI curriculum will empower students to navigate and shape the AI-driven world effectively.

COLLABORATION WITH INDUSTRY AND RESEARCH INSTITUTIONS

Integrating AI into education is not a venture that can be accomplished in isolation. Collaboration with industry and research institutions is crucial to successfully fostering creativity, critical thinking, and innovation among students. Such partnerships bring a wealth of resources, expertise, and practical experiences that can greatly enrich the educational process.

PARTNERSHIPS

1. **Access to Cutting-Edge Technology:** By collaborating with industry leaders and research institutions, educational institutions can gain access to the latest AI technologies and tools. This exposure allows students to work with state-of-the-art resources, enhancing their learning experience and preparing them for the evolving job market (Wang et al., 2011).
2. **Expert Guidance:** Industry experts and researchers can provide valuable insights and mentorship to students. Their expertise can help bridge the gap between theoretical knowledge and practical application, guiding students in their projects and research endeavours. This mentorship can also inspire students to pursue careers in AI and related fields (Nguyen,2025).
3. **Internships and Real-World Experience:** Partnerships with industry can offer students opportunities for internships and hands-on experiences. By working on real-world projects, students can apply their classroom knowledge to practical challenges, developing their creativity, critical thinking, and innovation skills. These experiences can also help students build a professional network and enhance their employability (Hodges et al., 2020).
4. **Collaborative Research Projects:** Joint research projects between educational institutions and industry or research organisations can lead to ground-breaking discoveries and innovations. Students can actively participate in these projects, contributing their ideas and learning from seasoned researchers. Such collaborations can foster a culture of innovation and drive advancements in AI and education (Mishra & Koehler, 2006).

GUEST LECTURES AND WORKSHOPS

1. **Exposure to Industry Practices:** One of the key benefits of guest lectures and workshops is the exposure they provide to industry practices. Inviting

professionals from the industry and researchers to share their knowledge and experiences allows students to gain first-hand insights into current industry trends, challenges, and innovations. Unlike textbooks and traditional classroom instruction, which often focus on theoretical aspects, guest lectures provide real-world perspectives that help bridge the gap between academic knowledge and professional applications.

For instance, in the field of Artificial Intelligence (AI), industry professionals can discuss the latest advancements in machine learning, natural language processing, and robotics. These sessions enable students to understand how AI technologies are being applied across various sectors, including healthcare, finance, automotive, and cybersecurity. They can also learn about ethical considerations, biases in AI models, and responsible AI development practices. This exposure helps students develop a more comprehensive understanding of the field and prepares them for careers in AI and related domains.

Industry experts can share insights into emerging trends such as explainable AI, federated learning, and AI-driven automation. By understanding these trends, students can anticipate future developments and align their learning accordingly. This knowledge not only enhances their academic performance but also provides them with a competitive edge in the job market. Moreover, industry professionals can discuss the skills and competencies required to succeed in AI-related careers, offering valuable guidance on career planning and skill development (Hodges et al., 2020).

2. **Hands-On Learning Opportunities:** Workshops conducted by industry experts provide invaluable hands-on learning experiences that complement theoretical instruction. These workshops often involve practical exercises, interactive sessions, and real-world case studies, allowing students to apply theoretical concepts in a practical setting. Hands-on learning is essential in technical fields like AI, as it enables students to experiment with various tools and technologies, reinforcing their understanding and fostering creativity. For example, a workshop on machine learning might involve coding exercises using Python, TensorFlow, or PyTorch. Students may engage in activities such as training machine learning models, evaluating their performance, and fine-tuning hyperparameters. These exercises help students grasp the intricacies of AI algorithms and encourage them to think critically about model optimisation and interpretability.

Similarly, workshops on natural language processing (NLP) could include tasks such as sentiment analysis, chatbot development, or text summarisation. By working on these projects, students can gain hands-on experience in implementing NLP techniques and understanding their real-world applications. Workshops may also introduce students to AI-driven tools for data visualisation, predictive analytics, and automation, further broadening their skill set (Holmes et al., 2019).

Hands-on learning encourages collaboration and teamwork, as students often work in groups to solve problems and complete projects. This collaborative approach not only enhances their technical skills but also improves their communication and problem-solving abilities. Engaging in workshops led by industry professionals also exposes students to industry-standard methodologies and best practices, making them better prepared for internships and full-time roles in the AI industry.

3. **Inspiration and Motivation:** Guest lectures and workshops play a crucial role in inspiring and motivating students. Learning from professionals who have made significant contributions to the field can spark curiosity and enthusiasm among students. These sessions showcase the achievements of leading experts and highlight the impact of AI on society, encouraging students to pursue their own innovative projects and research initiatives.

Hearing success stories from AI pioneers can be particularly motivating. For example, guest speakers who have developed ground-breaking AI applications, founded start-ups, or contributed to major research breakthroughs can share their journeys, challenges, and key learnings. Understanding how these professionals overcame obstacles and achieved success can instil a sense of determination and perseverance in students.

Guest lectures provide an opportunity for students to interact with professionals, ask questions, and seek mentorship. Direct engagement with industry leaders can be highly beneficial, as students can receive personalised advice on their academic and career aspirations. This interaction can also help students build professional networks, opening doors to internship and job opportunities in the AI field. Guest lectures and workshops are invaluable components of AI education, providing students with exposure to industry practices, hands-on learning opportunities, and inspiration from leading professionals.

By engaging with experts, students gain practical insights into the field, develop critical technical skills, and receive motivation to pursue innovative projects and research initiatives. These sessions not only enhance academic learning but also prepare students for successful careers in AI and related domains. Institutions should actively incorporate guest lectures and workshops into their curricula to ensure students remain at the forefront of AI advancements and industry trends.

Another aspect of inspiration comes from discussions on the ethical and societal implications of AI. Guest speakers can address topics such as bias in AI models, data privacy concerns, and the role of AI in social good initiatives. Understanding these broader issues helps students develop a sense of responsibility and purpose in their AI careers. They may be inspired to work on projects that address societal challenges, such as AI-driven solutions for healthcare, climate change, or accessibility for individuals with disabilities (Treve, 2024).

Exposure to cutting-edge research and innovations can ignite students' curiosity and drive them to explore new ideas. For instance, learning about advancements in generative AI, reinforcement learning, or AI-powered creativity tools can encourage students to experiment with novel concepts and contribute to the field through their own research and projects.

RESEARCH OPPORTUNITIES

1. **Collaborative Research Initiatives:** Partnering with research institutions provides students with opportunities to engage in collaborative research initiatives that address real-world challenges and contribute to advancements in AI and education. These projects allow students to gain valuable research experience, develop critical thinking skills, and enhance their problem-solving abilities (Ferguson et al., 2019). Collaborative research fosters an interdisciplinary approach, encouraging students to work alongside experts from various fields to develop innovative solutions.

Such initiatives provide exposure to cutting-edge methodologies and technologies, equipping students with the skills required to conduct meaningful research. Through hands-on involvement in research projects, students can learn about data collection, analysis, and ethical considerations in research, which are crucial competencies in academia and industry.

2. **Access to Research Resources:** Collaboration with research institutions grants students access to extensive resources, including large datasets, computational infrastructure, and specialised laboratories. These resources enable students to explore innovative solutions to complex problems, advancing both their technical skills and theoretical understanding (Alqahtani & Wafula, 2024).

Having access to well-equipped research facilities allows students to conduct experiments, test hypotheses, and validate AI models under professional supervision. Additionally, access to academic databases and journals provides students with the latest insights into their research areas, fostering a culture of continuous learning and discovery.

3. **Publication and Presentation Opportunities:** Engaging in collaborative research projects can lead to opportunities for students to publish their findings in academic journals and present their work at conferences. Publishing research not only enhances students' critical thinking and communication skills but also establishes their credibility as emerging researchers (Hodges et al., 2020).

Presenting at conferences allows students to engage with scholars and industry professionals, receive feedback on their work, and build professional networks. These experiences contribute to academic growth and can open doors to scholarships, research grants, and career opportunities in both academia and industry.

Encouraging students to participate in research publication and presentation fosters a culture of inquiry, innovation, and academic excellence, preparing them for leadership roles in research and development fields.

ENTREPRENEURIAL SKILLS DEVELOPMENT

1. **Support for Start-ups and Innovation:** Industry partnerships can provide students with substantial support in developing start-ups and innovative ventures. These collaborations can offer guidance on business development, access to funding sources, and opportunities to pitch ideas to investors. With the right support, students can transform their creative ideas into viable products or services (Laurillard, 2013).

Many universities and institutions are forming incubators and accelerators that help students refine their business strategies, access mentorship, and secure investment. These environments foster innovation and provide essential resources such as co-working spaces, prototyping tools, and legal advice on intellectual property rights. Encouraging students to engage with real-world business challenges enhances their entrepreneurial mindset and prepares them for future success.

2. **Mentorship and Networking:** Collaborating with industry connects students with experienced entrepreneurs and innovators who provide valuable guidance and insights. These mentors help students navigate the complexities of launching and scaling a start-up, offering advice on overcoming challenges and seizing opportunities (Bell & Bell, 2023). Networking with industry professionals opens doors to collaborations and potential partnerships. Engaging in networking events, workshops, and conferences enables students to build relationships that may lead to investment, job opportunities, or business ventures. Such connections

are instrumental in bridging the gap between academic learning and practical application, giving students a competitive edge in entrepreneurial opportunities.

3. **Entrepreneurship Programs and Competitions:** Industry partnerships can facilitate the creation of entrepreneurship programs and innovation competitions that encourage students to develop critical entrepreneurial skills such as ideation, prototyping, and pitching (Luckin et al., 2016). These initiatives provide students with platforms to showcase their innovative solutions, receive feedback from industry leaders, and gain recognition for their contribution to new knowledge.

Competitions, such as start-up pitch events and hackathons, not only provide funding opportunities but also simulate real-world entrepreneurial challenges, helping students refine their business acumen and problem-solving abilities. Many institutions integrate these programs into their curricula, ensuring that students acquire hands-on experience in entrepreneurship while still in an educational learning environment.

Collaboration with industry and research institutions creates a pivotal role in using AI to foster creativity, critical thinking, and innovation in students. These partnerships provide access to cutting-edge technologies, expert guidance, real-world experiences, and research opportunities, all of which enrich the educational experience. By leveraging the strengths of industry and academia, educational institutions can create a dynamic and supportive environment that nurtures students' entrepreneurial abilities and prepares them for the challenges and opportunities of the future.

CONCLUSION

The integration of AI into education represents a transformative opportunity to enhance creativity, critical thinking, and innovation among students. By using AI technologies, educators can create personalised and engaging learning environments that cater to individual students' needs and promote the development of essential skills. AI can inspire students to think creatively, analyse information critically, and develop innovative solutions to complex problems.

The successful integration of AI into education requires careful consideration of ethical, pedagogical, and equity-related challenges. Ensuring fairness, transparency, privacy, and inclusivity in AI systems is crucial to maintain trust and provide equal learning opportunities for all students. Additionally, collaboration with industry and research institutions can provide valuable resources, expertise, and real-world experiences that enrich the educational process.

The goal is to create a balanced and holistic approach to education that integrates AI as a supplement to traditional teaching methods. By addressing the challenges and harnessing the potential of AI, we can create a future where technology enhances the learning experience and prepares students for the challenges and opportunities of the 21st century. This vision of education not only equips students with the skills they need to thrive in a rapidly changing world but also empowers them to become innovative thinkers and problem solvers who can contribute positively to society.

REFERENCES

Akinwalere, S. N., & Ivanov, V. (2022). Artificial intelligence in higher Education: Challenges and opportunities. *BORDER CROSSING*, *12*(1), 1–15. DOI: 10.33182/bc.v12i1.2015

Alqahtani, N., & Wafula, Z. (2024). Artificial intelligence Integration: Pedagogical strategies and policies at leading universities. *Innovative Higher Education*. Advance online publication. DOI: 10.1007/s10755-024-09749-x

Baker, R., & Siemens, G. (2014). Educational Data Mining and Learning Analytics. In R. K. Sawyer (Ed.), *The Cambridge Handbook of the Learning Sciences* (pp. 253–272). chapter, Cambridge: Cambridge University Press.

Bell, R., & Bell, H. (2023). Entrepreneurship education in the era of generative artificial intelligence. *Entrepreneurship Education*, *6*(3), 229–244. DOI: 10.1007/s41959-023-00099-x

Binns, R. (2017). Fairness in Machine Learning: Lessons from Political Philosophy. *arXiv (Cornell University)*. https://doi.org//arxiv.1712.03586DOI: 10.48550

Bura, C., & Myakala, P. K. (2024). Advancing Transformative Education: Generative AI as a Catalyst for equity and innovation. *arXiv (Cornell University)*. https://doi.org//arxiv.2411.15971DOI: 10.48550

Ferguson, R., Coughlan, T., Egelandsdal, K., Gaved, M., Herodotou, C., Hillaire, G., Jones, D., Jowers, I., Kukulska-Hulme, A., McAndrew, P., Misiejuk, K., Ness, I. J., Rienties, B., Scanlon, E., Sharples, M., Wasson, B., Weller, M., Whitelock, D., & Open University. (2019). *Innovating Pedagogy 2019*. The Open University. https://iet.open.ac.uk/files/innovating-pedagogy-2019.pdf

Fu, Y., Bin, H., Zhou, T., Wang, M., Chen, Y., Da Costa Lai, Z. G., Wobbrock, J. O., & Hiniker, A. (2024). Creativity in the Age of AI: Evaluating the impact of generative AI on design outputs and designers' creative thinking. *arXiv (Cornell University)*. https://doi.org//arxiv.2411.00168DOI: 10.48550

George, A. S. (2023). Preparing students for an AI-driven world: Rethinking curriculum and pedagogy in the age of artificial intelligence. *Partners Universal Innovative Research Publication*, *1*(2), 112–136.

Goldie, J. G. S. (2016). Connectivism: A knowledge learning theory for the digital age? *Medical Teacher*, *38*(10), 1064–1069. DOI: 10.3109/0142159x.2016.1173661

Hodges, C. B., Moore, S., Lockee, B. B., Trust, T., & Bond, M. A. (2020, March 27). *The difference between emergency remote teaching and online learning*. http://hdl.handle.net/10919/104648

Holmes, W., Bialik, M., & Fadel, C. (2019). *Artificial intelligence in education: Promises and Implications for Teaching and Learning*. Centre for Curriculum Redesign.

Jackson, E. A. (2024). *The Evolution of Artificial Intelligence: A Theoretical Review of its Impact on Teaching and Learning in the Digital Age*. https://hdl.handle.net/10419/280893

Laurillard, D. (2013). Teaching as a design science. In *Routledge eBooks*. https://doi.org/DOI: 10.4324/9780203125083

Livingstone, S. (2011). Critical reflections on the benefits of ICT in education. *Oxford Review of Education*, *38*(1), 9–24. DOI: 10.1080/03054985.2011.577938

Luckin, R., Holmes, W., Griffiths, M., & Forcier, L. B. (2016). *Intelligence Unleashed: An argument for AI in Education*. Open Ideas; Pearson Education, London.

Miller, A. I. (2020). *The artist in the machine: The World of AI-Powered Creativity*. MIT Press.

Mishra, P., & Koehler, M. J. (2006). Technological Pedagogical Content Knowledge: A Framework for Teacher Knowledge. *Teachers College Record*, *108*(6), 1017–1054. DOI: 10.1111/j.1467-9620.2006.00684.x

Nguyen, K. V. (2025). The Use of Generative AI Tools in Higher Education: Ethical and Pedagogical Principles. *Journal of Academic Ethics*. Advance online publication. DOI: 10.1007/s10805-025-09607-1

Noble, S. U. (2018). *Algorithms of oppression: How Search Engines Reinforce Racism*. NYU Press.

Robinson, L., Cotten, S. R., Ono, H., Quan-Haase, A., Mesch, G., Chen, W., & Stern, M. J. (2015). Digital inequalities and why they matter. *Information Communication and Society*, *18*(5), 569–582. DOI: 10.1080/1369118X.2015.1012532

Sarker, I. H. (2021). Data Science and Analytics: An Overview from Data-Driven Smart Computing, Decision-Making and Applications Perspective. *SN Computer Science*, *2*(5). Advance online publication. DOI: 10.1007/s42979-021-00765-8

Shelton, K., & Lanier, D. (2024). The promises and perils of AI in education: Ethics and Equity Have Entered the Chat. *Lanier Learning*, 2024. ISBN 9798990840508

Teräs, M. (2022). Education and technology: Key issues and debates. *International Review of Education, 68*(4), 635–636. DOI: 10.1007/s11159-022-09971-9

Treve, M. (2024). Integrating Artificial Intelligence in Education: Impacts on student learning and innovation. *International Journal of Vocational Education and Training Research, 10*(2), 61–69. DOI: 10.11648/j.ijvetr.20241002.14

Wang, Q., Woo, H. L., Quek, C. L., Yang, Y., & Liu, M. (2011). Using the Facebook group as a learning management system: An exploratory study. *British Journal of Educational Technology, 43*(3), 428–438. DOI: 10.1111/j.1467-8535.2011.01195.x

Williamson, B. (2015). Political computational thinking: Policy networks, digital governance and 'learning to code'. *Critical Policy Studies, 10*(1), 39–58. DOI: 10.1080/19460171.2015.1052003

Woolf, B. P., Lane, H. C., Chaudhri, V. K., & Kolodner, J. L. (2013). AI grand challenges for education. *AI Magazine, 34*(4), 66–84. DOI: 10.1609/aimag.v34i4.2490

Chapter 5
Revolutionizing Mathematics Education With AI-Based Learning Tools:
A Synergistic Approach to Pedagogy and Digital Transformation

Mahak Bhatia
Poornima Institute of Engineering and Technology, India

Honey Gocher
https://orcid.org/0000-0002-6924-1764
Amity University, Jaipur, India

Gunjan Verma
https://orcid.org/0009-0004-4995-3707
Amity University, Jaipur, India

Yudhveer Singh
Amity University, Jaipur, India

Vishal Sharma
https://orcid.org/0009-0007-1219-1317
Amity University, Jaipur, India

DOI: 10.4018/979-8-3373-9225-7.ch005

ABSTRACT

Mathematics has always played a pivotal role in education, contributing significantly to the intellectual development of learners by fostering analytical reasoning, logical thinking, and problem-solving abilities. Despite its importance, mathematics is often perceived as one of the most challenging subjects by both students and educators. However, mathematics is undergoing a radical transformation. When paired with advancements in Artificial Intelligence (AI), this ancient system of learning can be revitalized into a powerful learning tool. AI has already transformed many aspects of education, including mathematics. This proposed book chapter explores this convergence, offering a holistic, interdisciplinary perspective on integrating AI and Vedic mathematics into contemporary mathematics education, also presents real-world case studies from Indian and global contexts where such innovations have been applied. It examines how intuitive, mental-math techniques, when coupled with data-driven technologies, transforms the teaching and understanding of mathematics across educational levels.

1. INTRODUCTION

Mathematics serves as the foundation for logical reasoning, problem-solving, and analytical thinking. It plays a critical role in shaping students' intellect, to enhance their lifelong learning capabilities. Despite its importance, mathematics is often perceived as abstract, rigid, and intimidating. The overreliance on rote memorization and procedural teaching has led to widespread math anxiety and disengagement among the students (Ashcraft & Krause, 2007). In an era, where technology is rapidly reshaping educational practices, it is imperative to explore innovative pedagogical models that make mathematics more engaging, accessible, and applicable to real-world contexts. (Cobb et al., 1991, 1992) analyse the impact of classroom environment on learning mathematics education. Since we carry with us the culture of learning from generations, there is growing recognition of the value of integrating traditional systems of knowledge into modern education to enrich learners' experiences. One such system; Vedic mathematics, originating from ancient Indian scriptures (Fig.1); offers efficient mental computation techniques that enhance number sense, pattern recognition, and intuitive understanding. These methods simplify complex calculations and promote creativity, aligning well with modern cognitive theories.

Despite its potential, Vedic mathematics remains underutilized in formal education. Through personalized learning, adaptive assessments, and real-time feedback, AI can identify learning gaps, customize instruction, and support educators in making data-informed decisions. Virtual tutors, intelligent classroom assistants, and predictive analytics are redefining the teacher-learner dynamic by enabling individual support and deeper conceptual understanding. By moving beyond one-size-fits-all instruction, AI tools help to make mathematics more engaging, contextual, and relevant to real-world applications making it student-centric. Additionally, AI fosters innovative teaching pedagogies, such as flipped classrooms, problem-based learning, and gamification, all of which enhance student cognitive skills and participation. Combining the strengths of Vedic mathematics with AI-driven tools offers a unique opportunity to create a blended framework that promotes conceptual clarity, computational speed, creativity, and critical thinking. Such a framework bridges tradition and innovation while addressing many pedagogical and psychological barriers in mathematics learning.

Figure 1. Conceptualization and analogy of AI (Hassani et al., 2020), learning environment (Harden, 2001) and Vedic Mathematics (Tirtha et al., 1992)

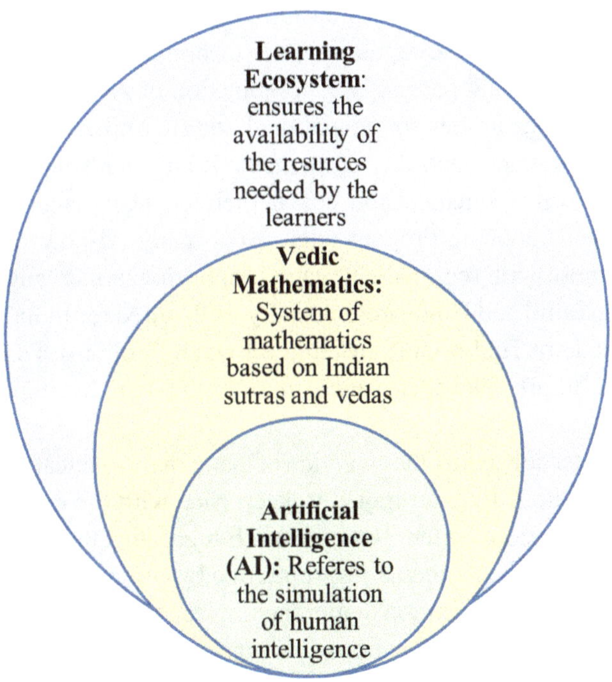

Approach to mathematics education by integrating the ancient system of Vedic mathematics aims to highlight how the fusion of AI and Vedic mathematics transforms learning experiences, foster deeper conceptual understanding, and align mathematical instruction with the evolving needs of the 21st-century learner. There are many stories piled up in the lap of current scenario that describes how parents and students leave the traditional school education and pursue their passion and became one of the leading pioneers setting up an example to excel if you really want to achieve it. People around the world are getting educated choosing their own content what they need to be learnt and develop a skill. These stories (Wadsworth et al., 2007) challenge our traditional education system of learning in a classroom. The new learning platforms, niches use of technology enables people of all ages to pursue their learnings on their own terms. At the same time there is a demand of the curriculum that will upgrade the skills of the student to meet the industrial skill set. (Hassani et al., 2020)

With the advancement in digital era, students no longer want to hear the classroom lectures or filling up the worksheets. Besides this there are only few teachers left who really dedicate their time with the students to prepare the students for the standardized tests. All these compiled together henceforth, pushed the school to follow the practice that will meet the basic requirement of the learners with the limited learning choices providing the space to technology to widens the options.

In addition to enhancing pedagogy, a combination of AI and Vedic mathematics provides new opportunities for educational equity. Multilingual AI interfaces together with the language neutrality of mathematics make it simple for students to understand complex mathematical concepts in their local languages thus improving comprehension and reducing dropout rates. Now many AI-powered educational tools including those with regional language support for Indian languages such as Bengali, Telugu, Tamil and Hindi are especially well-suited for India's multilingual environment. Students find it more meaningful when Vedic math's inherent logic combines with culturally relevant learning opportunities which is important in terms of motivation and retention.

Hence the chapter delves into the evolution of mathematics education, highlighting how traditional methods have struggled to keep pace with the cognitive demands and industrial expectations of the 21st century. It highlights the philosophy, structure, and benefits of Vedic mathematics, supported by comparative insights into its effectiveness relative to conventional approaches. The discussion further analyses the role of AI in mathematics education, drawing from current research, classroom practices, and emerging technologies that are reshaping instruction. Central to the chapter is the presentation of a blended pedagogical model that integrates Vedic mathematics with AI-based platforms, including strategies for curriculum alignment, teacher training, tool selection, and implementation. To validate this integrated framework, it also discusses critical challenges such as the digital divide, resistance to change, teacher preparedness, and curriculum standardization.

It further discusses the need for professional development, cross-disciplinary collaboration, and policy-level support to scale the integration of AI and traditional knowledge systems like Vedic mathematics. In its final section, the chapter offers recommendations for educators, curriculum designers, and policymakers on creating inclusive, responsive, and culturally rooted mathematics learning environments. It advocates for a shift from content-heavy instruction to context-driven, skill-oriented pedagogy that prepares learners not only for academic success but also for real-world problem-solving and innovation. Educational leaders are envisioned as key facilitators of this shift, supporting institutional readiness and strategic implementation. By balancing past perception with the tools of the future, the chapter aims to inspire a renewed approach to mathematics education; one that transforms student learning, empowers teachers, and shapes the next generation of thinkers, innovators, and problem-solvers. Exploring Vedic mathematics through the lens of AI not only preserves a rich cultural tradition but also offers a forward-looking strategy to overcome persistent challenges in mathematics education. This proposal presents a timely and necessary contribution to the ongoing efforts to reimagine education in a digital and globalized world, serving as a valuable resource for academics, practitioners, and education leaders committed to driving innovation in teaching and learning.

1.1 A Language of Mathematics

Mathematics is often considered as a universal language due to its ability to convey abstract concepts with precision and clarity (Barwell, 2005; SFARD et al., 1998) across different cultures and disciplines. Just like other spoken and written languages, mathematics has its own language of symbols (Ganesalingam, 2013; Setati, 2005), syntax, and grammar, which allow it to effectively communicate ideas without the ambiguity inherent in natural languages (Devlin, 2000).

Mathematics as a language is always an issue of concern for the learners; (Morgan, 1996; Ní Ríordáin & O'Donoghue, 2009) (Morgan, 1996) with its own characters and patterns to represent. The conceptualization and contextualization of language (Hall-Partee, 1979) varies depending on the reader's sense of mathematical characters and patterns. However, the approach of learning (Barton et al., 2005) mathematics supports to consider the understanding towards the traditional mathematics that further comprehend the modern and advanced mathematical courses. In teaching pedagogy, the use of mathematical language must be at the utmost importance for the educators so that the same understanding can be developed among students. The meaning of mathematical texts differs in the ways it is related or communicates (Planas, 2014) with the authors and readers. The meta functions in mathematics are essential, as they encompass ideational, interpersonal, and textual elements that influence comprehension and interpretation.

We as a instructors want our class to read the textbooks (Dialogue and Learning in Mathematics Education, 2003) to develop their mathematical skills. However, the explanation provided in text is meaningful for us but students often profess that they fail to understand it. This apparent difficulty in reading books often question the student-book relationship (Weinberg & Wiesner, 2011) Most often the students of all the grades, experience low grades in mathematics as they are constrained with the knowledge of "mathematical language".

Once the learners know HOW and WHAT is being said only then they will get WHY it is said. Unlikely, many people see mathematics merely as a collection of some rules, (Austin & Howson, 1979) formulas and axioms. The features that differ mathematics from other languages is its precision. Paradoxically, it's not wrong to highlight that the clarity of the subject makes it more complicated. For this there are two alternatives either to leave the students in the anxiety and fear of mathematics or to tell them the game of rules. The latter involve providing the experience and explanation of assumption upon which the mathematical community has its base. Thus, it has become an important part of all my introductory courses, both at the undergraduate and graduate level. Hence, in the development of mathematical proficiency, mathematics as a language gains an importance and emphasis has been led on teaching mathematical vocabulary.

Over the course of history of education, we as a learner by stepping into kindergarten, to high school to college follow an imprint for a successful educational journey. The pervasiveness of schooling overlooks the fact of being upgrading it with the evolution in technology and according to current era of sustainability; SDG Goal -4 (Quality education) too adds up to this. We are not predicting the collapse of the education system; but a reformation to meet the needs of the prevailing technology. Home schooling, online learning, workplace learning, web communities, are the learning spaces (Collins & Halverson, 2022) with more interactive platform to upgrade the skills. These alternatives make us to think over our classroom teaching pedagogy.

1.2 Rethinking Mathematics Education in the 21st Century

Traditional mathematics education has often been criticized for its inability to adapt to the demands of modern learners and industries. The focus on repetitive calculations and rigid instruction has stifled creativity and problem-solving skills that are increasingly valued in today's digital and data-driven world (National Research Council, 2012). As educational paradigms shift towards active, (Fig. 2) learner-centred methodologies, there is a growing need for teaching models that cultivate adaptive, computational, and critical thinking skills (Boaler, 2016).

Figure 2. Conceptual Comparison of the pedagogy

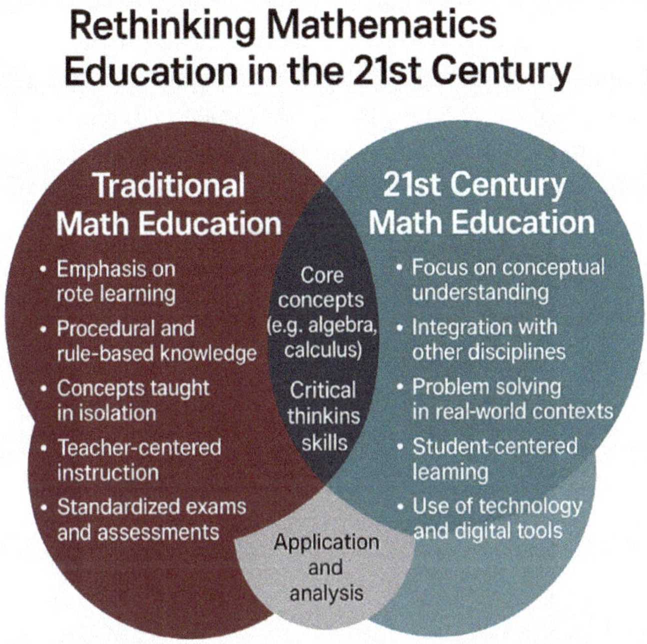

Modern learners must not only perform calculations but also interpret the data, recognize patterns, and devise algorithms. With mathematics expanding into domains such as machine learning, big data analytics, and optimization, instruction must keep pace with these shifts to ensure students are not just consumers of mathematical knowledge but also innovators.

(Cleary & Zimmerman, 2001; Paris & Newman, 1990; Zimmerman, 2002) believes that the self-regulated learning advocates metacognition, self-perceptions, attributions that supports the learners to understand, value and engage in learning that are fundamentally different from their peers.

Parents now-a-days realized that their child is not getting anything that adds up to their skills in school so they decided to take their child out (Cleary & Zimmerman, 2001; Cullingford, 1984; De Boer et al., 2010). A retired engineer tute his child by introducing him to the world of software where child push his limit of mathematical knowledge. This seems to be a clash between the school training and escalated technology. The revolution that the technology brought in; is been observed how job has been changed over a period of time. For example, the farmer job of ploughing and harvesting fields is now expanded to operating machineries and marketing agricultural goods. The technological breakthrough needs a skills of accessing, evaluating, and synthesizing information (Collins & Halverson, 2018).

Consequently, there is a difference in the payroll offered to college and non-college graduates. This further is being stamped by Fig. 3 showing how educational system is being drifted to be digitalised Markin a significant shift in learning.

Meanwhile the school education become more focus towards mathematics and technological courses by introducing the STEM (Science, Technology, Engineering and Mathematics) to the curriculum. Apart from the school lot of changes has taken place in the online learning platforms. So many platforms are being introduced that provides different learning experience to learners.

Figure 3. Shift in educational practices toward Digital and Intelligent Systems

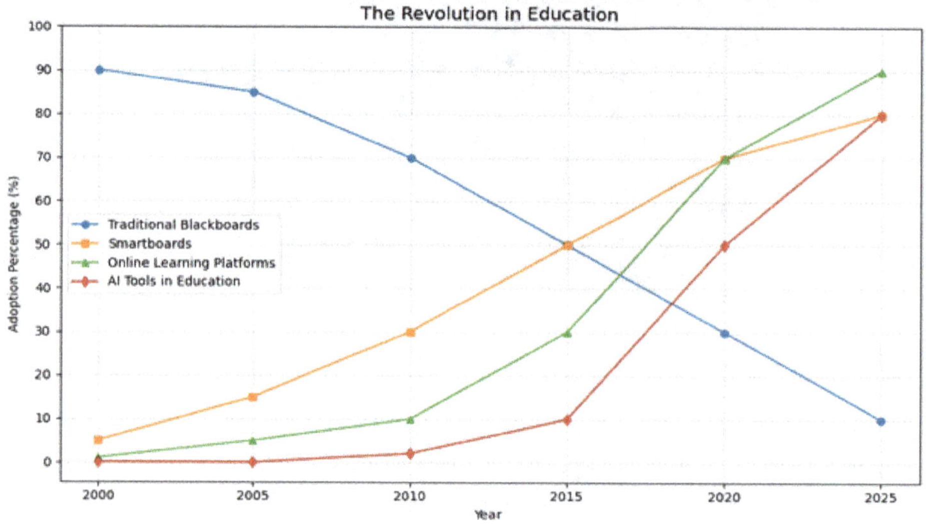

(Pandey & Sharma, 2025)

As the students enter into the world of job, webbed by the computerization and technology their training is guided by different facets of the job. Technology is transforming education (Sfard & Kieran, 2001; Yeo et al., 2024) beyond the limits of classroom learning and workplace. However, the schooling system felt incompatible in balancing a trend between traditional and technological teaching pedagogy. Technology makes difficult for the teachers to cope up with the existing curricula and the use of technology. Self-regulated learners understand, value, and engage academic learning in ways that are fundamentally different than their peers who have difficulty in school.

1.3 Vedic Mathematics: Philosophy, Structure, and Benefits

Vedic mathematics, derived from ancient Indian scriptures known as the Vedas-presents a holistic and intuitive approach to mathematical computation. It is based on 16 sutras (aphorisms) and 13 sub-sutras, which provide simple, elegant methods for arithmetic, algebra, geometry, and calculus operations (Tirthaji, 1965). Unlike conventional methods that rely on step-by-step algorithms, Vedic mathematics (Fig. 4) emphasizes mental agility, number sense, and pattern recognition. For instance, the "Vertically and Crosswise" method simplifies multiplication, while the "All from 9 and the Last from 10" technique aids in rapid subtraction. These methods not only accelerate calculation but also stimulate creative thinking and cognitive flexibility (Sharma, 2011).

Research has shown that students who learn through Vedic mathematics often demonstrate improved performance, confidence, and interest in the subject (Singh & Jain, 2017). However, its use remains largely informal, restricted to coaching centres or extracurricular settings, and not fully integrated into mainstream education. Many school systems simply overlook Vedic maths, leaving students unaware of its shortcuts and rhythms. Vedic principles sit in a corner, interesting but boxed away in niche workshops. If teachers and policy-makers tap digital media, the method could spill quietly onto everyone else's desks.

Figure 4. Evaluation of Contributions of Vedic Mathematical Concepts in Optimization Contexts

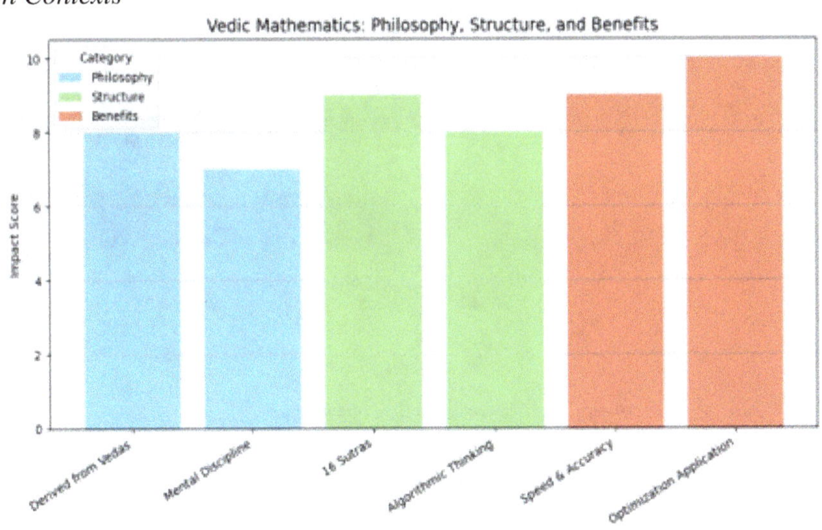

1.4 Optimization and Vedic Mathematics

In the quest for developing intelligent machines, modern science has often looked toward Western paradigms of logic, computation, and cognitive science. However, ancient Indian knowledge systems—particularly Vedic Mathematics—offer an untapped and profound framework that mirrors many modern principles underlying Artificial Intelligence (AI). Far from being just a set of arithmetic tricks, Vedic Mathematics is a philosophy of structured cognition, intuitive reasoning, and efficient computation. Its principles provide fertile ground for rethinking how AI can be constructed and understood from a culturally inclusive and ethically rooted perspective.

In early era, Indian mathematics is being evolved in geometric, arithmetical and algebraic whereas pre-Greek civilization laid an emphasis on computational area. (Roy, 2021) investigates the roots of AI in a mythological manuscript. Barbarik, Kumkaran an epic warrior were all AI robots. (Chaturvedi et al., 2024) use Vedalytics (Ved Analytics) approach to retrieve Scripture Rules and concepts from ancient-words. In 21st century the education system faces a revolution in terms of technology. The higher education learners use different leaning pedagogy for enhancing their knowledge (Guilherme, 2019). As a result of this AI comes up with the solution. Faculty of Educational Studies, Universiti Putra Malaysia focusses on student-centered teaching methodology. The approach contributes the mathematical understanding easy for students.

Figure 5. Inter-aspect Relationship Heatmap of Vedic Mathematics Dimensions

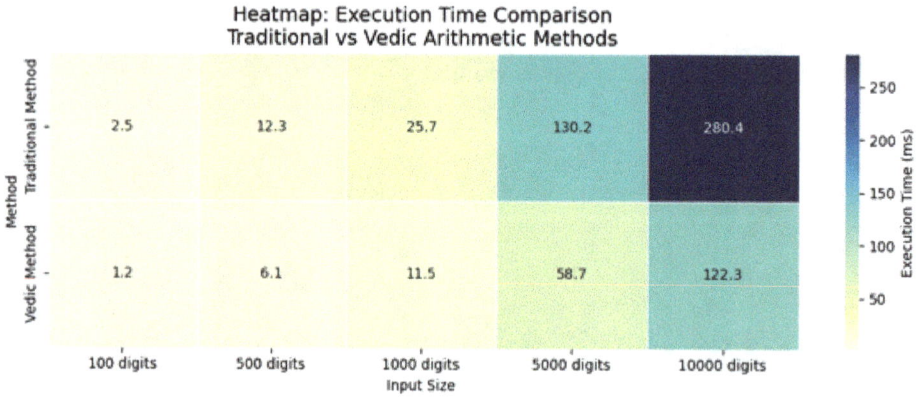

The heatmap (Fig. 5) has been incorporated into this research to visually demonstrate the performance difference between traditional arithmetic computation methods and those based on Vedic Mathematics, particularly in terms of execution time for large numerical inputs. The purpose is to support the hypothesis that Vedic techniques can optimize computational efficiency, making them suitable for modern optimization problems where speed and performance are critical.

1.6 Artificial Intelligence in Mathematics Education

AI has emerged as a transformative force in education (Fig.6), offering tools that personalize learning, enhance engagement, and provide timely feedback. In mathematics, AI applications include intelligent tutoring systems, adaptive assessments, gamified learning platforms, and data-driven curriculum development (Luckin et al., 2016)AI tools can analyze student behaviour, detect misconceptions, and dynamically adjust instructional content to meet individual needs. Systems like Carnegie Learning and ALEKS exemplify AI-powered platforms that tailor learning pathways, allowing students to progress at their own pace (VanLEHN, 2011).

Figure 6. Frequency of AI technology usage in math education

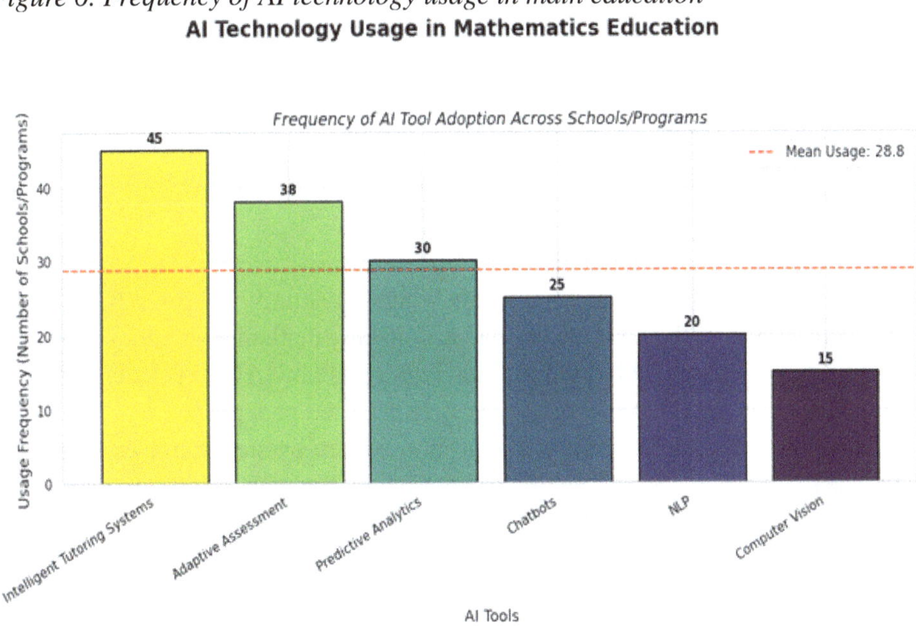

(Delello et al., 2025; Kochmar et al., 2020)

Furthermore, AI facilitates flipped classrooms (Diwanji et al., 2018), problem-based learning, and virtual simulations, which make mathematics more interactive and contextual. By addressing diverse learning styles and enabling precision teaching,

AI not only supports differentiated instruction but also empowers educators with insights for informed decision-making.

Figure 7. Effectiveness of Generative AI Applications in Enhancing Student Academic Performance

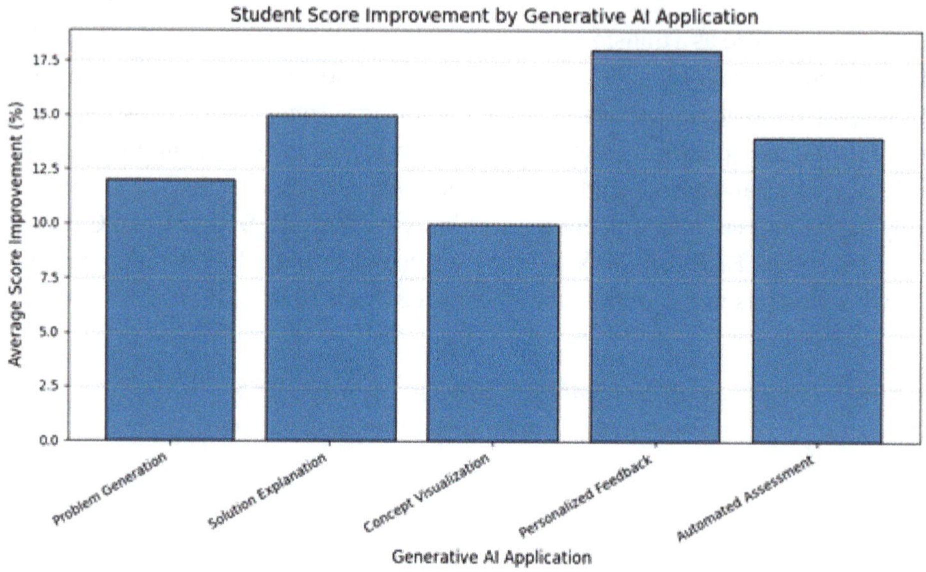

(Jaboob et al., 2024; Qian et al., 2024)

These categories represent core pillars where Generative AI directly supports and enhances (Fig.7) the learning experience, making mathematics education more dynamic, personalized, and scalable. This highlights how AI shifts teaching from static, uniform methods to interactive, learner-centered pedagogy.

Math has always been a discipline of proofs and step-by-step exercises, but lately the scene has cracked open. Generative artificial intelligence walks onto that stage, carrying a bag of tricks that lets numbers breathe and play. One minute a student is staring at a dry textbook; the next, an AI sketching out ten different roads to the same solution nudges the learner to shout What if? out loud. Curiosity clicks on, almost without permission.

Studies reveal that the AI tools does not provide an accurate output for all the mathematical problems. ChatGPT does not provide an overview of geometry. The accuracy of the tool depends on the input and the complexity of the data provided. The tool is expected to be more competent to solve the complex mathematical equations. The advancement in technology has undergone a significant change in educational landscape. The educational landscape in the 21st century has undergone significant changes as a result of advancements in technology, particularly AI (Wardat et al., 2023). The recent progress in machine learning has resulted in the creation of sophisticated and innovative digital content generation technology, such as generative artificial intelligence (GAI) (Snekha & Ayyanathan, 2023).

2. CONVERGING AI AND VEDIC MATHEMATICS: A BLENDED PEDAGOGICAL FRAMEWORK

Bringing together the computational elegance of Vedic mathematics and the adaptability of AI presents a compelling framework for reimagining mathematics education.

Figure 8. A Blended Pedagogical Framework of converging AI Error challenges

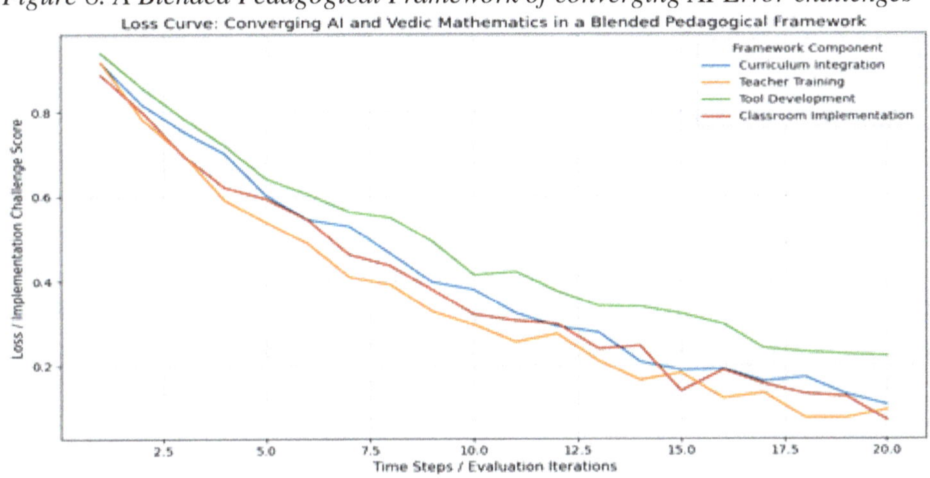

(Alam & Mohanty, 2023)

Fig. 8 illustrates a synthetic loss curve representing the challenges encountered in the blended pedagogical framework that integrates AI and Vedic Mathematics. The curve model four key components - curriculum integration, teacher training, tool development, and classroom implementation over a series of evaluation iterations. Each component initially shows a high level of challenge (loss), which gradually reduces as the framework matures and adaptations are made. This visual metaphor effectively highlights the learning curve and progressive refinement needed in each area, suggesting that with sustained effort and feedback, the pedagogical integration becomes more efficient and impactful over time (Alam & Mohanty, 2023).

The integration of Vedic mathematics into contemporary educational curricula, particularly when supported by artificial intelligence (AI), presents a transformative opportunity for foundational mathematical education. Vedic mathematics, rooted in ancient Indian scripts, is characterized by its simplicity, mental ability, and structured approach to problem-solving. By embedding these time-tested methods into modern learning systems, students metacognitive skills, computational thinking, numeracy understanding can be improved. Artificial Intelligence has revolutionized instructional design, enabling personalized learning experiences that adapt to individual students' needs. When combined with Vedic math principles, introduce a paradigm shift in the teaching and learning of mathematics. Curricula infused with Vedic methods, supported by AI-driven tools, can target both cognitive and metacognitive skills (Tasdelen & Bodemer, 2025) .

AI platforms like intelligent tutoring systems (ITS), adaptive assessments, and gamified content delivery mechanisms can be employed to introduce these concepts in engaging formats. AI-powered diagnostic tools can help identify areas of weakness and personalize the content delivery to match the learner's pace and proficiency. Simulation-based learning environments can allow students to visualize abstract Vedic methods in action, enabling better retention and comprehension. For instance, an AI-driven module may animate the "Vertically and Crosswise" technique in multiplication, allowing learners to experiment with varying inputs and receive instant feedback.

Inclusion of these modules into standard school curricula should be accompanied by formative assessment tools, designed using AI models that track learning progress, suggest remedial content, and adapt to learner behavior. This data-driven approach ensures that every student has the opportunity to master foundational math using both traditional wisdom and modern technology.

Incorporating ethical AI principles such as data privacy, explainability, and inclusivity in tool development is crucial. Tools should comply with educational data protection regulations and be user-friendly for both students and teachers.

It is important that as AI tools become more advanced, they should help in enhancing human interaction in learning while at the same time automating training. Creating AI agents that can serve as mentors, provide individualized support, detect hesitations and encourage self-reflection is one effective approach. This humanized AI interaction method can greatly enhance student involvement especially in mathematics which thrives on confidence. For instance, an AI chatbot may guide a learner through Vedic sutra reasoning, stopping at each step for input and help students articulate their thoughts. Additionally, AI avatars can mimic real teachers by asking Socrates-like questions such as "Why did you choose this method?" or "What if you used another sutra?". Such interactive models of teaching go beyond automation required for deep mathematical thinking.

3. MODERNIZING MATHEMATICS EDUCATION THROUGH THE SYNERGY OF VEDIC TECHNIQUES AND ARTIFICIAL INTELLIGENCE

The integration of Vedic mathematics into the modern education system, particularly when paired with the advancements in artificial intelligence, presents a transformative opportunity to redefine how mathematics is taught and learned. Vedic mathematics, rooted in ancient Indian wisdom, is a system of mental calculation based on a collection of concise formulas known as sutras. These sutras provide systematic methods for solving complex arithmetic problems with speed and accuracy. When these traditional methods are carefully blended with AI technologies, they can offer a unique pedagogical approach that enhances computational thinking, supports differentiated learning, and nurtures mathematical confidence among students from diverse backgrounds.

Bringing Vedic maths into existing curricula is not merely a question of adding more content; rather, it is about embedding an alternative perspective on problem-solving that encourages mental ability and pattern recognition. In many current educational frameworks, mathematics is taught through memorization and repetitive drilling, often leading to math anxiety and disengagement. Vedic mathematics, with its elegant techniques and logical shortcuts, allows learners to grasp numerical relationships quickly, thereby deepening their conceptual understanding. When combined with AI-based platforms, these techniques can be introduced through interactive digital modules, real-time simulations, and adaptive feedback systems. This modern delivery of ancient methods can align seamlessly with learning standards, thereby making the curriculum not only more accessible but also more effective.

Curriculum designers can harness AI to personalize the delivery of Vedic mathematical content. Intelligent tutoring systems can diagnose learners' strengths and weaknesses and adapt lesson content accordingly. For instance, if a student is struggling with division, the AI module could introduce Vedic division techniques like the "Nikhilam Sutra" in a simplified, visual format. These systems can further evaluate learner responses in real-time, offering guidance, corrections, and scaffolding tailored to each student's learning pace. Moreover, AI can provide detailed analytics to educators, highlighting trends in class performance and suggesting targeted interventions. The inclusion of gamified modules, where students solve mathematical puzzles using Vedic strategies to earn rewards, adds an element of motivation that can sustain learner engagement over longer periods.

As the integration of Vedic math and AI into curricula gains traction, there arises a critical need to prepare teachers for this pedagogical shift. Teachers, who play a central role in facilitating learning, must be empowered with both the conceptual understanding of Vedic techniques and the digital literacy required to operate

AI-driven educational tools. This calls for the development of comprehensive professional development programs that address both domains. These programs should begin with foundational training in Vedic mathematical principles, helping educators appreciate the rationale and beauty behind each sutra. This is particularly important as many teachers may not have had formal exposure to Vedic math during their academic careers.

Following this, educators must be introduced to the practical aspects of AI integration. This includes training on how to use AI-powered learning management systems, interpret student performance data, and design lessons that blend traditional instruction with digital interactivity. Workshops, hands-on demonstrations, and certification programs can serve as effective means of skill development. Furthermore, creating collaborative learning communities—both online and offline—can provide teachers with platforms to share experiences, discuss challenges, and co-create lesson plans. These communities can serve as living ecosystems of practice, continually evolving as new tools and methodologies emerge.

Teacher training must also focus on changing mindsets. Many educators may perceive Vedic mathematics as archaic or irrelevant in the context of modern education. Therefore, professional development programs must underscore the cognitive and pedagogical benefits of these techniques, backed by empirical studies and classroom case examples. Demonstrating how Vedic methods align with 21st-century skills such as critical thinking, problem-solving, and mental flexibility can help teachers internalize their value. As teachers become more confident in these dual domains, they are better positioned to create enriched learning environments where traditional and modern methods coexist harmoniously.

An essential component of this integration process lies in the development and selection of appropriate digital tools. These tools must not only be technologically advanced but also pedagogically sound, ensuring that they reflect the logical structure of Vedic mathematics while catering to the diverse needs of learners. The development of such tools necessitates collaboration among software developers, subject matter experts, data scientists, and educators. These interdisciplinary teams can work together to embed Vedic algorithms into AI systems, ensuring that the core logic of the techniques is preserved in the digital environment.

AI-powered educational tools should be designed to provide an engaging and immersive learning experience. Multilingual support is essential to reach students across different linguistic backgrounds, making the content accessible in regional languages alongside English. The use of gamified elements, such as interactive quizzes, mathematical challenges, and timed problem-solving contests, can further increase student motivation and participation. These tools can also offer students immediate feedback, identify patterns of error, and suggest remedial content—functions that are central to effective learning.

Moreover, the tools should allow for adaptive learning paths, meaning the content dynamically adjusts based on a learner's progress and preferences. For example, a student showing mastery in Vedic multiplication techniques may be introduced to more complex algebraic applications using similar logic, while another student may receive additional practice sessions with guided hints. The integration of performance analytics is another critical feature. Teachers and administrators can use these insights to make data-informed decisions, track classroom trends, and identify areas where curriculum adjustments may be necessary.

Importantly, these tools must be designed with user experience in mind. The interface should be intuitive, visually appealing, and responsive across devices such as tablets, smartphones, and laptops. Accessibility features, including audio support, screen readers, and offline functionality, should be incorporated to ensure inclusivity. Furthermore, ethical considerations around data privacy, algorithmic transparency, and bias mitigation must be central to the tool development process. Educational tools should comply with national and international regulations around student data protection, and developers should ensure that AI models are explainable and fair.

Once the tools are developed and educators are trained, the final step involves effective classroom implementation. This is where theory meets practice and where the success of the entire integration effort is ultimately determined. Implementing a hybrid learning model that includes both face-to-face instruction and AI-supported digital learning can significantly enhance the learning experience. Blended classrooms allow students to explore Vedic mathematics through physical manipulatives, oral recitation, and teacher guidance, while also engaging with AI tools that offer personalized practice and instant feedback.

Another strategy involves the use of inquiry-based learning. Here, students are encouraged to explore mathematical patterns, pose questions, and discover Vedic techniques through guided exploration. AI simulations can facilitate this process by allowing students to test hypotheses and receive real-time visualizations of mathematical principles in action. For example, an AI module might allow students to experiment with different multiplication techniques and compare the efficiency and logic behind each method. This fosters a deeper understanding and nurtures a spirit of curiosity and investigation.

The classroom environment must also support differentiated instruction. Students have varied learning styles, speeds, and interests. AI tools can accommodate this diversity by offering multiple pathways to learning the same concept. While one student might prefer visual animations, another might benefit from auditory explanations or textual descriptions. The teacher's role in this environment becomes that of a facilitator who guides students along their personalized learning journeys, supported by the insights and recommendations provided by AI systems.

Infrastructure plays a crucial role in successful implementation. Schools need to invest in reliable hardware, robust internet connectivity, and technical support systems. Teachers must be given sufficient time for lesson planning and tool familiarization. In addition, parental engagement should be considered as part of the implementation strategy. Parents must be informed about the benefits of the Vedic-AI model and how they can support their child's learning at home. Orientation sessions, informational materials, and access to the learning platforms can help bridge the home-school learning divide.

Assessment practices must evolve in tandem with instructional strategies. Traditional tests may not fully capture the depth of learning facilitated by AI-enhanced Vedic instruction. Therefore, schools can adopt a combination of formative and summative assessment methods. AI-generated performance reports, digital portfolios, and project-based evaluations can offer a holistic view of student progress. Peer assessment and reflective journals can also provide valuable insights into students' learning experiences and self-perceptions.

Ultimately, the successful integration of Vedic mathematics and artificial intelligence in education requires a systemic approach involving curriculum reform, teacher empowerment, tool development, and classroom transformation. This integration is not simply a technological upgrade but a philosophical shift toward holistic, student-centered, and culturally grounded education. Vedic mathematics, with its intuitive structure and cognitive appeal, complements AI's capacity for personalization and scalability, offering a powerful solution to some of the most persistent challenges in mathematics education.

Such a framework also holds immense potential for democratizing quality education. By leveraging AI tools, students in remote or underserved regions can access expert-guided Vedic math instruction that was previously unavailable. The scalability of digital platforms ensures that the benefits of this hybrid model can be extended across socio-economic and geographical boundaries. Moreover, the cultural relevance of Vedic mathematics, when taught through modern interfaces, fosters a sense of identity and pride among learners, helping to preserve and promote indigenous knowledge systems in a globalized world.

In conclusion, the fusion of Vedic mathematics with artificial intelligence represents a visionary approach to mathematics education—one that bridges ancient insights with futuristic technologies. It empowers learners with cognitive flexibility, enhances teaching with data-driven precision, and expands educational equity through scalable innovation. As educators, technologists, and policymakers work together to bring this vision to life, we stand at the cusp of a new era in learning—one where tradition and technology coalesce to build a smarter, stronger, and more culturally conscious generation.

To illustrate the comparison between the computational time to calculate the product of two numbers by sing Nikhilam Sutra algorithm and AI we get the following results:

The multiplication result using AI is:

$125 \times 326 = 40{,}750$

Time taken for the calculation: **4.42 X 10^{-8}** seconds

Using the Nikhilam Sutra method:

$125 \times 326 = 40{,}750$

Average time per operation (over 1,000,000 runs):

7.88×10^{-7} seconds

Due to many intermediate steps involve in the process it takes more time to evaluate the (Pradhan & Panda, 2014) solution.

CONCLUSION

As we navigate an era defined by rapid technological advancement, the future of mathematics education must be both innovative and inclusive. The integration of Vedic mathematics with AI represents a powerful synergy honouring the cognitive wisdom of ancient traditions while leveraging the precision and personalization of modern technology. This blended pedagogical model fosters not only numerical competence but also creativity, adaptability, and confidence. By bridging the gap between tradition and innovation, it creates a more holistic, engaging, and future-ready approach to teaching mathematics. Through thoughtful implementation, supportive policies, and sustained collaboration, this vision can transform classrooms, empower educators, and inspire a new generation of mathematical thinkers.

Mathematics education stands at a transformative crossroads, where the confluence of ancient wisdom and cutting-edge technology presents unprecedented opportunities for meaningful reform. As this chapter has explored, integrating Vedic mathematics with Artificial Intelligence offers a compelling pathway to address long-standing pedagogical challenges while enhancing the cognitive, computational, and creative capabilities of learners. Vedic mathematics, with its intuitive and efficient techniques, can demystify complex mathematical processes and foster a deeper number sense. When combined with AI's adaptive, personalized, and data-driven tools, it can support diverse learners, making mathematics more accessible, engaging, and applicable to real-world contexts. The proposed blended pedagogical framework not only bridges tradition and innovation but also redefines the role of educators and learners in the 21st-century classroom. It promotes a shift from rote-based, exam-centric instruction to an experience-rich, student-centered approach that values problem-solving, critical thinking, and interdisciplinary connections. Conclusively, the synergy of AI and Vedic mathematics promotes the SDG 4 making student centric learning space.

REFERENCES

Alam, A., & Mohanty, A. (2023). Educational technology: Exploring the convergence of technology and pedagogy through mobility, interactivity, AI, and learning tools. *Cogent Engineering, 10*(2), 2283282. DOI: 10.1080/23311916.2023.2283282

Austin, J. L., & Howson, A. G. (1979). Language and mathematical education. *Educational Studies in Mathematics, 10*(2), 161–197. DOI: 10.1007/BF00230986

Barton, B., Chan, R., King, C., Neville-Barton, P., & Sneddon, J. (2005). EAL undergraduates learning mathematics. *International Journal of Mathematical Education in Science and Technology, 36*(7), 721–729. DOI: 10.1080/00207390500270950

Barwell, R. (2005). Ambiguity in the Mathematics Classroom. *Language and Education, 19*(2), 117–125. DOI: 10.1080/09500780508668667

Cleary, T. J., & Zimmerman, B. J. (2001). Self-Regulation Differences during Athletic Practice by Experts, Non-Experts, and Novices. *Journal of Applied Sport Psychology, 13*(2), 185–206. DOI: 10.1080/104132001753149883

Cobb, P., Nicholls, J., Wheatley, G., Trigattl, B., & Perlwitz, M. (1991). *Assessment of a problem-centered second-grade mathematics project. 22*(1), 3–29.

Cobb, P., Wood, T., Yackel, E., & Perlwitz, M. (1992). A follow-up assessment of a second-grade problem-centered mathematics project. *Educational Studies in Mathematics, 23*(5), 483–504. DOI: 10.1007/BF00571469

Collins, A., & Halverson, R. (2018). *Rethinking Education in the Age of Technology: The Digital Revolution and Schooling in America*. Teachers College Press.

Collins, A., & Halverson, R. (2022). *Rethinking Education in the Age of Technology: The Digital Revolution and the Schools*. 1–10.

Cullingford, C. (1984). The Battle for the Schools: Attitudes of parents and teachers towards education. *Educational Studies, 10*(2), 113–119. DOI: 10.1080/0305569840100204

De Boer, A., Pijl, S. J., & Minnaert, A. (2010). Attitudes of parents towards inclusive education: A review of the literature. *European Journal of Special Needs Education, 25*(2), 165–181. DOI: 10.1080/08856251003658694

Delello, J. A., Sung, W., Mokhtari, K., Hebert, J., Bronson, A., & De Giuseppe, T. (2025). AI in the Classroom: Insights from Educators on Usage, Challenges, and Mental Health. *Education Sciences, 15*(2), 2. Advance online publication. DOI: 10.3390/educsci15020113

Dialogue and Learning in Mathematics Education (Vol. 29). (2003). Kluwer Academic Publishers. https://doi.org/DOI: 10.1007/0-306-48016-6

Diwanji, P., Hinkelmann, K., & Witschel, H. (2018). Enhance Classroom Preparation for Flipped Classroom using AI and Analytics: *Proceedings of the 20th International Conference on Enterprise Information Systems*, 477–483. https://doi.org/DOI: 10.5220/0006807604770483

Ganesalingam, M. (2013). The Language of Mathematics. In D. Hutchison, T. Kanade, J. Kittler, J. M. Kleinberg, F. Mattern, J. C. Mitchell, M. Naor, O. Nierstrasz, C. Pandu Rangan, B. Steffen, M. Sudan, D. Terzopoulos, D. Tygar, M. Y. Vardi, & G. Weikum (Eds.), *The Language of Mathematics* (Vol. 7805, pp. 17–38). Springer Berlin Heidelberg. https://doi.org/DOI: 10.1007/978-3-642-37012-0_2

Guilherme, A. (2019). AI and education: The importance of teacher and student relations. *AI & Society*, *34*(1), 47–54. DOI: 10.1007/s00146-017-0693-8

Hall-Partee, B. (1979). Semantics—Mathematics or Psychology? In Bäuerle, R., Egli, U., & Von Stechow, A. (Eds.), *Semantics from Different Points of View* (Vol. 6, pp. 1–14). Springer Berlin Heidelberg., DOI: 10.1007/978-3-642-67458-7_1

Harden, R. M. (2001). The learning environment and the curriculum. *Medical Teacher*, *23*(4), 335–336. DOI: 10.1080/01421590120063321

Hassani, H., Silva, E. S., & Unger, S., TajMazinani, M., & Mac Feely, S. (2020). Artificial Intelligence (AI) or Intelligence Augmentation (IA): What Is the Future? *AI*, *1*(2), 143–155. DOI: 10.3390/ai1020008

Jaboob, M., Hazaimeh, M., & Al-Ansi, A. (2024). Integration of Generative AI Techniques and Applications in Student Behavior and Cognitive Achievement in Arab Higher Education. *International Journal of Human-Computer Interaction*, *41*, 1–14. DOI: 10.1080/10447318.2023.2300016

Kochmar, E., Vu, D. D., Belfer, R., Gupta, V., Serban, I. V., & Pineau, J. (2020). Automated Personalized Feedback Improves Learning Gains in An Intelligent Tutoring System. *Artificial Intelligence in Education*, *12164*, 140–146. DOI: 10.1007/978-3-030-52240-7_26

Luckin, R., Holmes, W., & Forcier, L. B. (2016). *An argument for AI in Education.*

Morgan, D. L. (1996). Focus Groups. *Annual Review of Sociology*, *22*(1), 129–152. DOI: 10.1146/annurev.soc.22.1.129

Ní Ríordáin, M., & O'Donoghue, J. (2009). The relationship between performance on mathematical word problems and language proficiency for students learning through the medium of Irish. *Educational Studies in Mathematics, 71*(1), 43–64. DOI: 10.1007/s10649-008-9158-9

Pandey, R., & Sharma, P. (2025). *The Effectiveness of Vedic Mathematics on Problem Solving Ability of Students at Middle Level.* https://doi.org/DOI: 10.51584/IJRIAS.2025.100600146

Paris, S. G., & Newman, R. S. (1990). Development Aspects of Self-Regulated Learning. *Educational Psychologist, 25*(1), 87–102. DOI: 10.1207/s15326985ep2501_7

Planas, N. (2014). One speaker, two languages: Learning opportunities in the mathematics classroom. *Educational Studies in Mathematics, 87*(1), 51–66. DOI: 10.1007/s10649-014-9553-3

Pradhan, M., & Panda, R. (2014). High speed multiplier using Nikhilam Sutra algorithm of Vedic mathematics. *International Journal of Electronics, 101*(3), 300–307. DOI: 10.1080/00207217.2013.780298

Qian, L., Li, W., Feng, Q., & Li, L. (2024). The Effect of Generative Artificial Intelligence on Students' Academic Achievement: A Meta-analysis. *2024 International Conference on Intelligent Education and Intelligent Research (IEIR)*, 1–5. https://doi.org/DOI: 10.1109/IEIR62538.2024.10960226

Setati, M. (2005). Teaching Mathematics in a Primary Multilingual Classroom. *Journal for Research in Mathematics Education, 36*(5), 447–466.

Sfard, A., Nesher, P., Streefland, L., Cobb, P., & Mason, J. (1998). Learning Mathematics through Conversation: Is It as Good as They Say? *FLM Publishing Association, 18*(1), 41–51.

Sfard, A., & Kieran, C. (2001). Cognition as Communication: Rethinking Learning-by-Talking Through Multi-Faceted Analysis of Students' Mathematical Interactions. *Mind, Culture, and Activity, 8*(1), 42–76. DOI: 10.1207/S15327884MCA0801_04

Snekha, S., & Ayyanathan, N. (2023). An Educational CRM Chatbot for Learning Management System. *Shanlax International Journal of Education, 11*(4), 58–62. DOI: 10.34293/education.v11i4.6360

Tasdelen, O., & Bodemer, D. (2025). Generative AI in the Classroom: Effects of Context-Personalized Learning Material and Tasks on Motivation and Performance. *International Journal of Artificial Intelligence in Education*. Advance online publication. DOI: 10.1007/s40593-025-00491-9

Tirtha, S. B. K. Bhāratīkṛsh atīrtha, & Agrawala, V. S. (1992). *Vedic Mathematics*. Motilal Banarsidass Publishing House.

VanLEHN, K. (2011). The Relative Effectiveness of Human Tutoring, Intelligent Tutoring Systems, and Other Tutoring Systems. *Educational Psychologist, 46*(4), 197–221. DOI: 10.1080/00461520.2011.611369

Wadsworth, L. M., Husman, J., Duggan, M. A., & Pennington, M. N. (2007). Online Mathematics Achievement: Effects of Learning Strategies and Self-Efficacy. *Journal of Developmental Education, 30*(3), 6–14.

Wardat, Y., Tashtoush, M. A., AlAli, R., & Jarrah, A. M. (2023). ChatGPT: A revolutionary tool for teaching and learning mathematics. *Eurasia Journal of Mathematics, Science and Technology Education, 19*(7), em2286. Advance online publication. DOI: 10.29333/ejmste/13272

Weinberg, A., & Wiesner, E. (2011). Understanding mathematics textbooks through reader-oriented theory. *Educational Studies in Mathematics, 76*(1), 49–63. DOI: 10.1007/s10649-010-9264-3

Yeo, S., Moon, J., & Kim, D.-J. (2024). Editorial: Transforming mathematics education with AI: Innovations, implementations, and insights. *The Mathematics Educator, 63*, 387–392. DOI: 10.7468/mathedu.2024.63.2.387

Zimmerman, B. J. (2002). Becoming a Self-Regulated Learner: An Overview. *Theory into Practice, 41*(2), 64–70. DOI: 10.1207/s15430421tip4102_2

Chapter 6
AI-Enhanced Collaboration and Teamwork in Virtual Learning Environments

Syed Mohd Faisal
https://orcid.org/0000-0003-2422-3535
Malla Reddy Technical Campus, Malla Reddy Vishwavidyapeeth University, Hyderabad, India

Wasim Khan
https://orcid.org/0000-0003-2311-1451
Symbiosis Institute of Technology, Symbiosis International University, India

Mohammad Ishrat
https://orcid.org/0000-0002-9699-4454
VIT Bhopal University, Sehore, India

ABSTRACT

Artificial Intelligence (AI) offers transformative potential for enhancing collaboration and teamwork in Virtual Learning Environments (VLEs). Leveraging techniques such as Natural Language Processing, Reinforcement Learning, Recommender Systems, and Sentiment Analysis, AI systems facilitate intelligent group formation, dynamic role allocation, adaptive scaffolding, and early conflict detection. Grounded in educational psychology and systems engineering, this work synthesizes theoretical frameworks with empirical applications from platforms like Coursera, IBM Watson Tutor, and Microsoft Teams. Key ethical concerns—algorithmic bias, data privacy, and instructional control are critically examined, with mitigation strategies pro-

DOI: 10.4018/979-8-3373-9225-7.ch006

posed through Explainable AI and Federated Learning. Emerging directions include immersive metaverse-based collaboration, neuroadaptive feedback systems, and hybrid AI–human facilitation architectures. The findings contribute to the development of equitable, scalable, and pedagogically aligned AI-enhanced collaborative learning ecosystems.

1. INTRODUCTION

The proliferation of Virtual Learning Environments (VLEs) has significantly reshaped the paradigms of educational delivery, particularly in response to the global digitization of academic institutions. VLEs such as Moodle, Blackboard, Microsoft Teams, and Canvas provide scalable, asynchronous, and geographically agnostic platforms for instruction, assessment, and learner engagement. However, despite their operational advantages, VLEs often lack the socio-cognitive richness inherent to traditional classroom settings—particularly in facilitating effective collaboration and teamwork among learners. Team-based learning is widely acknowledged in engineering education and cognitive science as a critical pedagogical strategy that promotes higher-order thinking, collective problem-solving, distributed cognition, and knowledge co-construction. These competencies are indispensable in professional engineering practice, where multidisciplinary teams routinely engage in design, development, and system optimization. In VLEs, however, replicating such interactions is non-trivial due to limitations in synchronous communication, lack of affective feedback, and heterogeneity in learner participation. The consequence is a dilution of collaborative efficacy, often reflected in imbalanced contributions, disengagement, and suboptimal learning outcomes (Ryan & Poole, 2019).

Artificial Intelligence (AI), with its data-driven decision-making capabilities and autonomous reasoning mechanisms, offers a robust computational framework for augmenting collaborative learning processes in digital environments. Techniques such as Natural Language Processing (NLP), Machine Learning (ML), Sentiment Analysis, and Reinforcement Learning (RL) can be employed to intelligently facilitate group formation, monitor interaction quality, detect social or cognitive disengagement, and optimize role distribution within learner cohorts (Mueller & Strohmeier, 2011). Furthermore, AI-driven agents can perform real-time analytics on discourse patterns, knowledge contribution indices, and affective states, thereby enabling dynamic instructional adaptation and feedback dissemination without continuous human oversight.

Recent advancements in Explainable AI (XAI) further enhance the transparency and pedagogical validity of these systems by making model decisions interpretable to instructors and learners alike. Additionally, the integration of federated learning models ensures privacy-preserving collaboration analytics across distributed learning systems, which is critical in compliance-driven educational frameworks. Consequently, AI not only addresses operational deficiencies in VLEs but also transforms collaborative learning into a more adaptive, inclusive, and data-optimized pedagogical construct (Faisal & Zaidi, 2020).

This chapter presents a comprehensive exploration of AI-enhanced collaboration in VLEs, bridging theoretical constructions with engineering applications. It systematically examines the role of intelligent systems in augmenting cooperative learning frameworks, elucidates algorithmic mechanisms for team optimization, and investigates real-world implementations across educational platforms. The discussion extends to the benefits, technical limitations, and ethical challenges associated with AI deployment in collaborative contexts. The overarching objective is to delineate an evidence-based roadmap for embedding AI-driven collaboration strategies within future-proof curriculum designs.

The remainder of this chapter is organized to provide a coherent and systematic exposition of AI-enhanced collaboration in virtual learning environments. Following this introduction, Section 2 establishes the theoretical and pedagogical foundations underlying collaborative learning in virtual contexts, drawing from educational psychology and instructional design models. Section 3 explores the landscape of advanced AI techniques—including NLP, recommender systems, and real-time analytics—that are instrumental in supporting and enhancing teamwork among learners. Section 4 delves into intelligent mechanisms for group formation, role allocation, and conflict mediation using ML and optimization algorithms. Section 5 presents empirical evidence and case studies highlighting the deployment of AI-powered collaborative tools in real-world educational platforms. Section 6 provides a critical analysis of the systemic benefits, technical constraints, and ethical considerations associated with the integration of AI into collaborative learning systems. Section 7 projects future directions in the domain, including the emergence of immersive environments, cognitive sensing technologies, and culturally adaptive AI agents. Finally, Section 8 offers concluding insights and practical recommendations for the strategic incorporation of AI-enhanced collaboration into curriculum design, aimed at fostering more resilient and future-ready educational ecosystems.

2. THEORETICAL FOUNDATIONS OF COLLABORATION IN VIRTUAL LEARNING ENVIRONMENTS

Effective collaboration in VLEs is underpinned by well-established educational theories and structured pedagogical strategies. These theoretical foundations not only explain how collaboration fosters deep learning but also provide the basis for designing instructional interventions, including those enhanced by AI. This section explores the psychological and pedagogical principles behind collaborative learning, the structural dimensions of teamwork in digital settings, key instructional models for fostering collaboration, and the challenges inherent in deploying these models online.

2.1. Educational Psychology of Collaboration

2.1.1. Vygotsky's Zone of Proximal Development (ZPD)

Vygotsky's ZPD provides a critical lens for understanding how learners can achieve higher cognitive outcomes when guided by more knowledgeable peers or tools. Within the context of VLEs, this guidance may be delivered through structured peer interaction, tutor facilitation, or AI-driven scaffolding. The presence of an intelligent agent that nudges students toward relevant content, detects learning stagnation, and provides timely assistance can be viewed as an operationalization of Vygotsky's ZPD in a digital context (Shabani et al., 2010).

2.1.2. Social Constructivism and Connectivism

Social constructivism views knowledge as co-constructed through interaction, negotiation, and shared context. In virtual settings, these interactions occur through forums, collaborative documents, and synchronous video sessions. Connectivism, a more recent theory, extends this perspective by incorporating digital tools and networked structures as central to the learning process. It emphasizes that learning is no longer an individualistic endeavor but is distributed across people and intelligent systems, making it highly relevant in AI-enhanced VLEs.

2.2. Dimensions of Teamwork in Digital Learning

2.2.1. Cognitive, Social, and Teaching Presence

The Community of Inquiry (CoI) framework offers a robust lens through which collaborative learning in VLEs can be evaluated. Cognitive presence reflects the extent to which learners construct meaning through critical discourse. Social presence is the degree to which learners project themselves as real participants, an essential factor in promoting group cohesion and emotional engagement. Teaching presence involves instructional design and facilitation strategies that guide learning and foster interaction. These three dimensions must be explicitly cultivated in digital environments, and increasingly, AI systems are being used to scaffold and balance these presences dynamically (Nami et al., 2018).

2.2.2. Characteristics of Effective Online Teams

Effective online collaboration hinges on clearly defined goals, mutual accountability, equitable task distribution, and psychological safety. In VLEs, these characteristics can be compromised due to lack of physical proximity and visual cues. AI systems can address these issues by monitoring communication patterns, flagging non-participation, and recommending interventions to maintain group dynamics. Algorithms may also analyze dialogue contributions to identify dominant voices or marginalized perspectives, thus supporting equity and inclusion (Nami et al., 2018).

2.3. Pedagogical Models for Team-Based Learning

2.3.1. Jigsaw Technique

The Jigsaw model promotes positive interdependence by assigning learners individual components of a topic, which they then teach to their peers. This structure encourages accountability and ensures that each member's input is vital to group success. In VLEs, AI can automate role assignments, track progress, and recommend pacing strategies based on group interactions(Safkolam et al., 2023).

2.3.2. Problem-Based Learning (PBL)

PBL is a constructivist approach where learners collaboratively solve open-ended, real-world problems. It promotes critical thinking, inquiry, and reflective dialogue. AI-driven collaboration systems can support PBL by offering resources dynamically, identifying when a group is stuck, and providing scaffolds to stimulate idea generation.

2.3.3. Think–Pair–Share

This technique, though traditionally used in physical classrooms, adapts well to digital environments. Students think individually, then pair in breakout sessions, and finally share with the entire class through discussion boards or synchronous conferencing. AI agents can support each phase by prompting responses, summarizing discussions, and ensuring balanced participation.

Figure 1. Conceptual Model of Digital Collaboration Layers

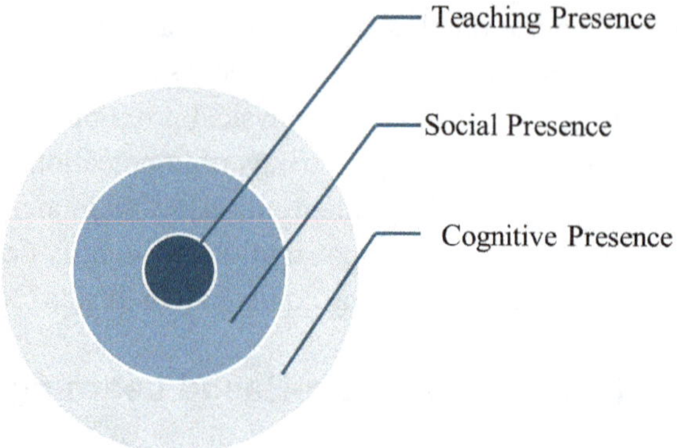

Table 1. Pedagogical Models for Online Teamwork

Model	Collaboration Type	Task Complexity	AI Facilitation Potential	Assessment Strategy
Jigsaw	Structured Interdependence	Moderate	High (role assignment, progress tracking)	Peer Teaching & Contribution Logs
Problem-Based Learning (PBL)	Open-ended, Inquiry-based	High	High (supporting research, nudging)	Rubric-Based Group Assessment
Think Pair Share	Phased Interaction	Low to Moderate	Moderate (prompting, summarizing)	Self and Peer Reflection

2.4. Challenges in Virtual Collaboration

Despite the theoretical robustness and pedagogical promise of collaborative learning frameworks, the transition from physical to VLE presents a unique set of challenges that can significantly hinder the effectiveness of team-based activities. These challenges stem from limitations in communication modalities, technological infrastructure, learner diversity, and the absence of real-time social cues. In VLEs, collaboration is often mediated through text-based tools and asynchronous forums, which, while offering flexibility, may dilute the immediacy and emotional richness of face-to-face interactions. Additionally, virtual teams often suffer from reduced visibility of effort, making it difficult for instructors and peers to accurately evaluate individual contributions. Such limitations necessitate a deeper understanding of the systemic barriers that impede collaborative engagement in digital contexts, especially when designing AI-enhanced support systems (Swart et al., 2022). The subsections below delineate the most prominent of these challenges, drawing on empirical studies and instructional design research.

2.4.1. Asynchronous Misalignment and Communication Gaps

One of the most frequently encountered limitations in VLEs is the temporal disjunction that arises from asynchronous interaction models. While asynchronous systems offer learners the flexibility to engage at their convenience, this same flexibility often results in fragmented discourse, misaligned task progression, and extended feedback latency. Learners may contribute to discussions or collaborative documents without access to the complete historical context, causing redundancy, misinterpretation, or conceptual discontinuity. These issues are further exacerbated in globally distributed learning cohorts where time zone differences prevent real-time dialogue. Moreover, asynchronous misalignment hinders the development of group cohesion and shared momentum, both of which are crucial for sustained engagement and mutual accountability in collaborative settings. AI-enabled systems can mitigate some of these communication gaps by implementing discourse summarization algorithms, thread clustering, and intelligent tagging to reconstruct conversation flow. NLP models may also be leveraged to identify unanswered queries or isolate key discussion points, thereby enabling timely interventions and promoting thread continuity (Nagel et al., 2024).

2.4.2. Social Loafing and Imbalanced Participation

Social loafing—defined as the reduction in individual effort when working in a group context—is an empirically validated phenomenon in both traditional and online collaborative learning environments. In VLEs, this effect is magnified by the inherent lack of visibility and reduced social accountability, where some group members may fail to contribute equitably, relying on others to carry the cognitive and procedural workload. This not only undermines the collective learning experience but also distorts peer assessment mechanisms and degrades team morale. AI-based analytics platforms can help address this issue by quantitatively tracking user activity within collaborative tasks. By measuring interaction frequency, contribution length, semantic relevance, and temporal patterns, AI systems can detect anomalies indicative of social loafing(Faisal et al., 2022). Once detected, these systems may autonomously notify instructors or initiate low-stakes nudges—such as personalized prompts or progress dashboards—to encourage balanced participation. Additionally, XAI techniques can render these insights transparent and interpretable, thus fostering trust among stakeholders.

2.4.3. Equity Gaps and Digital Disparities

Virtual collaboration is inherently mediated by technology, which introduces new layers of inequality that stem from disparities in hardware availability, internet connectivity, digital literacy, and linguistic proficiency. Learners from marginalized socioeconomic backgrounds may experience systemic disadvantages that limit their ability to contribute meaningfully in collaborative online settings. These equity gaps are particularly concerning in group-based learning models, where underperformance by one member can impact the collective output and team dynamics. From a systems engineering perspective, it becomes imperative to design AI solutions that are both adaptive and inclusive. For instance, intelligent systems should be capable of detecting signs of constrained access or low interaction bandwidth and respond by offering simplified user interfaces, low-data modes, or multilingual support. However, the design and deployment of such systems must adhere to fairness-aware ML principles, ensuring that algorithmic decisions do not inadvertently reinforce existing biases. Transparent audits, representative training datasets, and inclusive interface design are essential components of AI frameworks intended to bridge, rather than widen digital divides (Raihan et al., 2024).

2.4.4. Affective Disengagement

In traditional classroom settings, instructors rely on a combination of verbal and non-verbal cues to detect disengagement, such as lack of eye contact, body posture, or silence. These cues are largely absent or attenuated in VLEs, making affective disengagement—defined as the withdrawal of emotional and motivational investment, difficult to detect and address. Learners may appear active by logging into platforms or submitting assignments while remaining psychologically disconnected from collaborative processes. This latent disengagement compromises both individual learning outcomes and the overall cohesion of the team. AI technologies offer emerging capabilities to address this challenge through sentiment analysis, engagement modeling, and, where ethically permissible, multimodal emotion recognition using video, audio, and behavioral data. Sentiment-aware chatbots, for example, can monitor learner language in discussion forums and issue reflective prompts when negativity or apathy is detected. Similarly, time-series analysis of participation patterns can reveal declining engagement trends, triggering early interventions by instructors or AI agents. However, the deployment of affective computing technologies must be carefully governed by privacy regulations, informed consent protocols, and data minimization principles to ensure ethical integrity.

3. AI TECHNOLOGIES FOR SUPPORTING COLLABORATIVE LEARNING

AI has emerged as a transformative enabler in the domain of educational technology, offering data-driven, scalable, and adaptive solutions to complex pedagogical challenges. In the context of collaborative learning within VLEs, AI systems serve multifaceted roles: as facilitators, monitors, adaptors, and evaluators of group interactions. These technologies leverage computational models to infer learner states, guide interaction patterns, allocate resources, and provide real-time feedback, capabilities that are otherwise difficult to scale through human facilitation alone (Ouyang & Zhang, 2024). This section explores the spectrum of AI technologies that are actively reshaping collaborative dynamics in digital education systems.

3.1. Overview of AI Techniques in Education

A wide array of AI methodologies underpins the functionalities deployed in intelligent tutoring and collaborative systems. Among the most used techniques are NLP, Recommender Systems, RL, and Emotion Recognition. NLP facilitates machine understanding and generation of human language. In collaborative settings, NLP models analyze discussion threads, extract key concepts, detect sentiment polarity, and even summarize or rephrase learner contributions to maintain conversational coherence. It also underpins chatbots and virtual agents that respond contextually to learner queries (Bhise et al., 2022).

Recommender systems in education personalize content delivery and team formation based on individual learner profiles, past behavior, and performance metrics. These systems enhance group compatibility and reduce interpersonal friction by assigning team members with complementary skills or learning styles. RL is applied in adaptive environments where AI agents learn to optimize interactions through feedback. In collaborative learning, RL algorithms can dynamically adjust group task difficulty, recommend interventions, or allocate peer mentors by modeling team performance as a reward-based optimization problem. Emotion recognition technologies, often implemented using facial analysis or linguistic cues, aim to detect affective states such as frustration, boredom, or confusion. When integrated with collaborative tools, these systems provide instructors or AI agents with indicators of emotional disengagement or conflict, thereby enabling timely and targeted responses.

3.2. AI as a Facilitator of Collaboration

AI not only supports but actively facilitates collaborative learning processes. Chatbots and conversational agents, designed using dialogue systems and NLP, act as virtual teaching assistants capable of managing discussions, prompting critical thinking, and clarifying misunderstandings during peer interactions. These agents can moderate forums, direct learners to relevant resources, and maintain the thematic focus of group dialogues. Additionally, AI-driven recommender systems can automate the formation of optimal learner groups. These systems analyze learner attributes—such as domain knowledge, engagement patterns, preferred learning modalities, and even personality dimensions—to assign team roles or match learners with high collaboration potential. Such intelligent grouping mitigates common issues like skill mismatches or social isolation within teams and enhances both group efficiency and learner satisfaction (Sheikh et al., 2023).

3.3. Adaptive and Personalized Support

AI technologies offer unprecedented capabilities for providing adaptive scaffolding and personalized nudging in real-time. Adaptive scaffolding refers to dynamic support structures that evolve based on the learner's immediate context, performance, and role within a team. For instance, AI systems can detect when a student is struggling with a subtask and automatically suggest step-by-step guides, examples, or peer assistance. Nudging mechanisms are subtle prompts or cues delivered by AI agents to guide learner behavior without coercion. These include time management alerts, participation reminders, or even goal-refocusing messages that encourage task alignment. AI can also model group-level behavior using probabilistic or reinforcement-based models to forecast potential collaboration breakdowns and take preemptive actions to maintain engagement and cohesion.

Furthermore, behavioral prediction models, trained on longitudinal data, enable systems to anticipate learner dropout, motivational decline, or interpersonal conflict. These predictive insights allow for just-in-time support interventions, enhancing the robustness of the collaborative learning experience.

3.4. Sentiment and Interaction Analysis

Understanding the quality of interactions is pivotal to fostering effective collaboration. AI systems are increasingly equipped with real-time sentiment analysis engines that examine textual and vocal inputs to infer learner emotions. Sentiment polarity (positive, neutral, or negative) provides a proxy for engagement levels, cognitive load, and team dynamics. Additionally, interaction analytics harness data from Learning Management Systems (LMS), collaboration tools, and discussion forums to track variables such as frequency of contributions, message sentiment, timing of responses, and turn-taking patterns (Bradley, 2021). These metrics enable AI systems to construct multidimensional dashboards for instructors and learners, highlighting issues like dominance imbalance, conversational bottlenecks, or passive participation(Faisal, Jadhav, et al., 2025).

AI can also flag emerging conflicts within teams by detecting spikes in disagreement indicators (e.g., negative sentiment, abrupt message tone, or repeated contradictions). Once flagged, the system can either alert a human facilitator or trigger a dialogue re-mediation protocol via the chatbot agent. Equally important is the ability to assess contribution equality, ensuring that each team member's voice is proportionately represented in the discourse.

Table 2. AI Techniques Mapped to Collaborative Learning Functions

AI Technique	Collaborative Function	Application Scenario
Natural Language Processing (NLP)	Analyzing discussions, summarizing threads, identifying key ideas	Forum moderation and reflective journaling
Recommender Systems	Forming balanced teams, matching learners with similar goals	Group project setup in LMS or MOOC platforms
Reinforcement Learning (RL)	Adaptive scaffolding, role allocation, workload balancing	Real-time task adjustment during group activities
Sentiment Analysis	Detecting emotional tone in messages, identifying conflict potential	Monitoring learner sentiment in discussions
Conversational Agents / Chatbots	Facilitating peer discussions, maintaining thematic focus	AI tutor-led collaborative writing sessions
Emotion Recognition	Identifying disengagement through facial/ textual cues	Adaptive support in high-stress team tasks
Behavioral Prediction Models	Predicting dropout, disengagement, or role conflicts	Preemptive instructor alerts failing groups

Figure 2. AI-Augmented Collaboration Loop

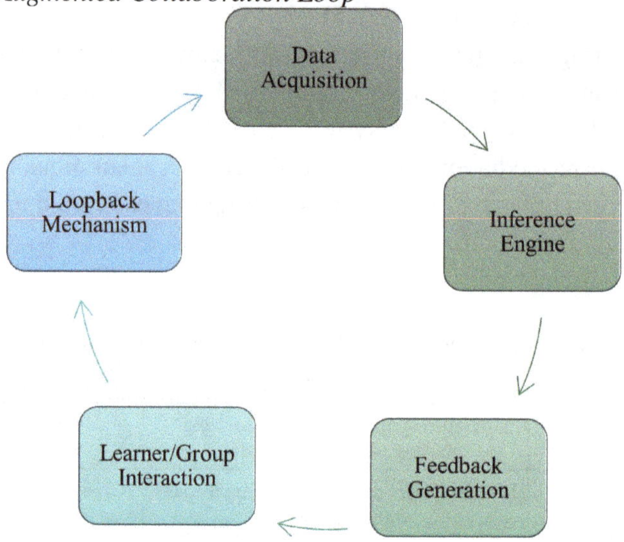

4. INTELLIGENT GROUP FORMATION AND ROLE ASSIGNMENT

The formation of learner groups and assignment of collaborative roles are foundational elements in the design of effective team-based learning experiences. In traditional settings, such tasks are typically managed by instructors using heuristic judgments or randomization methods. However, in VLEs, the increasing complexity of learner profiles, along with the need for equity and scalability, necessitates a more systematic and data-driven approach. AI offers robust tools to support intelligent group formation and role distribution by leveraging ML algorithms, optimization models, and learner analytics (Ishrat, Khan, & Faisal, 2025). This section explores three critical dimensions of AI-enhanced group design: intelligent grouping mechanisms, equitable role assignment, and conflict resolution strategies.

4.1. AI-Based Grouping Mechanisms

AI-based grouping leverages clustering algorithms and predictive analytics to assign learners to optimal collaborative configurations. Traditional methods such as random grouping or self-selection often result in heterogeneous teams with skewed participation and cognitive imbalance. In contrast, AI systems utilize learner data—

including performance metrics, domain knowledge, communication style, learning preferences, and personality traits—to generate balanced teams. Clustering algorithms such as K-Means, Hierarchical Clustering, and DBSCAN can identify subgroups of learners with similar feature vectors, optimizing intra-group cohesion and inter-group diversity. Additionally, Multi-Agent Systems can simulate group interactions to predict collaboration success prior to assignment. These systems analyze historical collaboration patterns to anticipate compatibility and suggest group configurations that minimize conflict and maximize synergy (Varlamov, 2021).

AI-based grouping also accommodates dynamic reconfiguration, allowing teams to evolve as learners' performance or engagement changes over time. RL models can be trained to maximize a global reward function based on team productivity, fairness indices, or learner satisfaction scores. This results in a responsive, adaptive grouping strategy that continuously improves over the course of the learning experience.

Figure 3. Workflow for AI-Based Group Formation and Monitoring

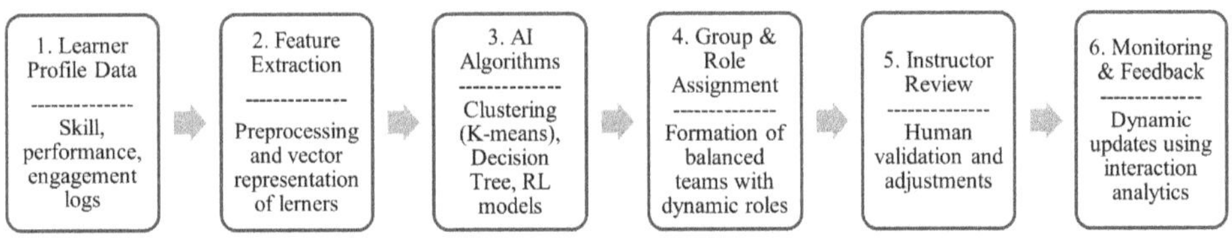

4.2. Fair and Equitable Role Distribution

Effective collaboration requires not only the right team composition but also appropriate and equitable role assignment within the team. Roles such as facilitator, researcher, presenter, and scribe provide structure, promote accountability, and enhance the functional efficiency of the group. However, static or instructor-assigned roles may inadvertently reinforce power dynamics or disengage certain learners. AI systems can introduce dynamic role allocation based on individual strengths, learning objectives, and prior role history(Faisal, Ishrat, et al., 2025). For instance, a learner who consistently excels in research may be rotated to the presenter role to diversify their skillset, fostering a more holistic learning experience. Decision tree classifiers or Bayesian networks can be trained to assign roles based on input variables such as leadership potential, confidence in subject matter, or verbal engagement history. Moreover, equity-aware AI models incorporate fairness constraints to prevent systematic exclusion of certain learners from critical roles. These models track historical role distributions and enforce balanced opportunities across learners, aligning with diversity and inclusion goals in educational policy(Islam & Ivy, 2022).

4.3. Conflict Resolution Models

Group-based tasks are susceptible to interpersonal conflict arising from communication breakdowns, dominance imbalance, or incompatible working styles. In virtual contexts, these conflicts may remain undetected until they significantly impair team performance. AI-driven systems address this challenge through emotion-aware conflict detection and mediation models. Sentiment analysis and emotion recognition technologies can be applied to communication logs—such as chat transcripts, forum posts, or voice interactions—to detect early signs of frustration, disagreement, or withdrawal. ML models trained on annotated conflict datasets can classify interaction types and flag critical incidents in real time.

Once a conflict is identified, AI agents can initiate resolution protocols, such as facilitating anonymous feedback exchanges, recommending communication workshops, or even reassigning roles. In more advanced applications, dialogue systems powered by large language models can mediate group discussions by rephrasing inflammatory language, promoting consensus, and maintaining a constructive tone.

Table 3. Algorithm Comparison for Group Formation and Role Assignment

Algorithm	Primary Use	Strengths	Limitations	Example Application
K-Means Clustering	Grouping learners based on similarity (e.g., skill level, behavior)	Efficient with large datasets, easy to implement	Assumes spherical clusters; may misgroup outliers	Grouping students by performance in a MOOC
Decision Trees	Role assignment based on decision rules from learner attributes	Transparent and interpretable decision-making process	Prone to overfitting; sensitive to biased training data	Assigning leadership roles based on engagement logs
Multi-Agent Simulations	Predicting team compatibility and dynamics through simulation	Models complex group behavior before actual formation	Computationally intensive; requires simulation design	Predicting conflicts before collaborative assignments
Reinforcement Learning (RL)	Optimizing group configurations or role distributions over time	Learns from interaction feedback; adapts dynamically	Needs large amounts of interaction data for training	Dynamically rotating roles to balance team skills

5. CASE STUDIES AND APPLICATIONS

The theoretical underpinnings and algorithmic frameworks explored in prior sections manifest in a diverse array of real-world applications across educational platforms. As institutions and technology providers adopt AI to enhance collaborative learning, case studies provide critical insight into how these systems function at scale, the challenges they address, and the outcomes they produce. This section presents illustrative examples of AI-enhanced collaboration, ranging from Massive Open Online Courses (MOOCs) to gamified environments and enterprise-level educational platforms. The applications reveal both the technical sophistication and pedagogical utility of AI in virtual teamwork contexts.

5.1. Case Study: AI-Powered Peer Feedback in MOOCs

MOOCs, such as those offered by Coursera, face inherent challenges in managing scalable, meaningful peer interactions across thousands of learners. To address this, platforms have integrated NLP models to automate the evaluation and synthesis of peer reviews. Coursera employs AI systems that analyze written peer assessments, extract key themes, and provide summarized feedback to learners. This NLP engine identifies sentiment, content depth, and the presence of constructive critique, thereby maintaining the quality of collaborative evaluation despite high enrollments. These systems also detect superficial or plagiarized feedback and issue prompts encouraging more reflective contributions. As a result, learners receive timely, actionable insights from peer reviewers while instructors are relieved from manually moderating thousands of exchanges. This case illustrates the critical role of AI in maintaining pedagogical rigor in peer-based collaboration at scale (Rahim, 2023).

5.2. Case Study: Intelligent Tutoring Systems Supporting Team Tasks

AI has also found applications in Intelligent Tutoring Systems (ITS) that support collaborative problem-solving tasks. A notable example is the IBM Watson Tutor, deployed in business and management simulations where students work in virtual teams to address case-based challenges. The system leverages a combination of ML models, domain knowledge bases, and real-time analytics to monitor group discourse and intervene when collaboration efficacy drops. Watson can provide hints, rephrase problematic language, recommend relevant resources, and even redistribute tasks among team members to maintain workflow balance. Furthermore, it tracks individual contributions to enable fair grading and feedback. By serving as an AI facilitator embedded in team activities, the ITS reduces instructor workload while ensuring that pedagogical objectives—such as decision-making under constraints and role interdependence—are met (Alrakhawi et al., 2023)(Ishrat, Khan, Faisal, et al., 2025).

5.3. Case Study: AI in Gamified Team Environments

Gamified learning environments are particularly effective in fostering engagement and motivation. In collaborative gamification settings, AI is increasingly used to personalize game dynamics and feedback. A compelling example is the integration of GPT-based feedback systems with platforms like Kahoot, where teams of learners participate in timed challenges, debates, or simulations. Using Natural Language Generation (NLG), the AI system can instantly provide elaborate feedback based on team responses—highlighting strengths, offering corrections, or posing follow-up questions. Moreover, sentiment-aware models monitor emotional tone during gameplay to adapt difficulty or groupings in real time. Such dynamic AI augmentation transforms static quiz formats into adaptive, collaborative learning experiences that respond to both cognitive and affective states (Bezzina & Dingli, 2023).

5.4. Real-World Applications

Several commercial virtual learning platforms have integrated AI to enhance collaborative workflows in practical educational settings:

- Microsoft Teams with Copilot AI provides real-time writing assistance, meeting summaries, task delegation, and collaborative document generation during group assignments (Ahmed, 2025).
- Google Workspace's Duet AI supports brainstorming, auto-formatting, and summarization across Docs and Slides, enabling smoother group document production (Gan et al., n.d.).
- Edmodo's AI Bot assists in managing discussion forums by identifying unanswered questions, recommending student groupings, and flagging off-topic content (Saqr et al., 2024).

These tools collectively demonstrate how AI is no longer peripheral but central to the orchestration and monitoring of collaborative learning processes. Their integration into mainstream platforms signals a shift towards ubiquitous AI mediation in educational teamwork.

Table 4. Summary of AI Applications for Collaborative Learning

Platform / System	AI Feature	Pedagogical Impact
Coursera NLP Engine	Automated peer review analysis and summarization	Improves feedback quality and scalability in large cohorts
IBM Watson Tutor	Real-time tutoring, team discourse monitoring, task reallocation	Supports decision-making, maintains group balance
Kahoot with GPT-based Feedback	Dynamic feedback generation and sentiment-aware adaptation	Enhances engagement and responsiveness in gamified tasks
Microsoft Teams with Copilot	Collaborative writing assistance, task tracking, summarization	Streamlines team collaboration and communication
Google Workspace (Duet AI)	AI-driven content formatting, brainstorming support	Facilitates co-creation of content and idea development
Edmodo AI Bot	Forum moderation, question clustering, team recommendations	Improves group task coordination and forum relevance

6. BENEFITS AND CHALLENGES OF AI-DRIVEN COLLABORATION

The integration of AI into collaborative learning frameworks within VLEs presents a dual-edged paradigm. On one hand, AI enables unprecedented levels of personalization, automation, and real-time responsiveness. On the other hand, it raises significant concerns related to ethical transparency, pedagogical control, and learner agency (Ahmed, 2025). This section delineates the primary benefits and systemic challenges associated with AI-driven collaboration, providing a balanced view of its educational potential and limitations.

6.1. Enhanced Participation, Retention, and Satisfaction

AI systems can significantly improve learner engagement by fostering inclusive participation and maintaining sustained involvement in team activities. Intelligent agents can monitor contribution metrics, identify passive learners, and deliver timely prompts or incentives to re-engage. Gamified AI feedback mechanisms also contribute to improved learner motivation and satisfaction, as tasks become adaptive and dynamically relevant to the learner's current state(Zaidi & Faisal, 2018). Sentiment analysis and activity monitoring enable early detection of disengagement, allowing interventions before attrition occurs. Moreover, personalized nudging based on learner behaviors such as recommending a simpler subtask, offering motivational feedback, or alerting the team about task imbalances, promotes fairness and reduces cognitive overload. Empirical studies have shown that AI-enhanced teamwork yields higher retention rates and deeper learner satisfaction due to the perceived relevance and adaptability of the experience (Wilson & Millar, 2021).

6.2. Support for Differentiated Learning and Inclusivity

AI-driven systems can tailor collaboration experiences to individual learner profiles, enabling differentiated support within team contexts. For instance, learners with low digital literacy or language proficiency may be matched with peers who have complementary skills, thereby facilitating scaffolded peer learning. Intelligent tutoring components can also provide content-level assistance without interrupting the team workflow. Inclusivity is further promoted by multimodal input support (e.g., voice, gesture, text), as well as by ensuring that learners from diverse backgrounds are not marginalized due to linguistic, cognitive, or behavioral differences. Group formation algorithms can include equity constraints to maintain demographic balance, while conversational agents can mitigate dominant discourse tendencies by regulating participation turns. These affordances position AI as a potential equalizer in otherwise inequitable collaborative dynamics (Hasanah et al., 2024).

6.3. Ethical Concerns

Despite its potential, AI deployment in collaborative learning raises significant ethical issues that require deliberate scrutiny and policy design.

6.3.1. Bias in AI-Driven Role Assignments

Algorithmic bias remains a critical concern in AI-based role distribution. If the training data reflect historical inequities, such as underrepresentation of minority learners in leadership roles, AI systems may perpetuate these biases. Additionally, overfitting on past behavioral patterns can lead to typecasting, where learners are consistently assigned the same roles, inhibiting skill development and reinforcing social hierarchies(Patel, 2024).

6.3.2. Privacy and Data Security in Team Interactions

AI-enhanced collaboration relies on continuous data collection, including communication logs, behavioral metrics, and sometimes affective signals. The granularity of this data raises questions about learner surveillance, consent, and data minimization. Without transparent governance frameworks, there is a risk of violating learner privacy and eroding trust in educational institutions. Moreover, breaches of team interaction data can expose sensitive discussions, academic disagreements, or psychological vulnerabilities to unauthorized actors (Zhan et al., 2024).

Table 5. Ethical Dilemmas in AI-Augmented Collaboration

Ethical Issue	Educational Impact	Mitigation Strategy
Bias in Role Assignment	Perpetuates inequity; restricts role diversity and leadership opportunities	Use fairness-aware algorithms; rotate roles periodically
Learner Profiling and Stereotyping	Reinforces past behavior; limits skill growth and learner autonomy	Include behavioral variability and growth metrics in models
Informed Consent and Data Transparency	Learners unaware of how data is used; erodes trust in the system	Provide clear data usage policies and opt-in mechanisms
Over-Surveillance of Group Interactions	Creates anxiety; suppresses natural learner interaction and expression	Limit data collection to essential metrics; anonymize logs
Inadequate Feedback Explainability	Reduces learner trust in AI recommendations and evaluations	Integrate XAI to justify feedback and decisions
Privacy Breach in Team Communication Logs	Exposes sensitive peer discussions and social dynamics to risks	Encrypt data and apply strict access control with audit trails

6.4. Pedagogical Implications

Beyond ethics, AI integration necessitates rethinking the instructor's role and the pedagogical architecture of collaboration.

6.4.1. AI as Co-Teacher vs. Support Tool

AI systems that autonomously mediate group interactions, assign roles, or resolve disputes challenge the conventional role of educators as facilitators and assessors. While some models envision AI as a co-teacher, such delegation risks undermining pedagogical authority and relational dynamics in learning. Clear boundaries must be established between instructor-led and AI-supported decisions to preserve educational accountability and learner trust (Malik & Shah, 2025).

6.4.2. Overdependence on Automation

A growing concern is that excessive reliance on AI tools may reduce learner initiative and critical thinking. When task coordination, resource curation, and feedback are entirely automated, learners may experience a loss of ownership and reduced metacognitive engagement. Pedagogically, this represents a shift from active knowledge construction to passive system navigation, which could hinder long-term skill development (Khlaif et al., 2025).

7. FUTURE DIRECTIONS AND RESEARCH OPPORTUNITIES

As AI continues to evolve, its role in shaping collaborative learning environments is poised for further expansion. The next decade will likely witness a transition from reactive, tool-based systems to deeply integrated, context-aware, and immersive AI ecosystems that co-evolve with learners and instructors. This section outlines five pivotal future directions, each representing a convergence of AI with novel technologies and learning theories. Together, these trajectories offer a roadmap for both academic inquiry and applied innovation in the domain of AI-supported virtual collaboration.

7.1. AI in Immersive Collaborative Environments

The integration of AI into immersive technologies such as Virtual Reality (VR) and Augmented Reality (AR) is redefining what collaborative learning can entail. In metaverse-based classrooms, learners interact through avatars in 3D environments that simulate real-world laboratories, design studios, or fieldwork settings. AI agents in these environments act as intelligent facilitators—guiding group tasks, modifying virtual spaces based on learner behavior, and dynamically adjusting difficulty levels to optimize group flow. Such AI-enhanced immersive collaboration enables embodied cognition, spatial awareness, and multisensory interaction, particularly valuable in engineering, medical, and architectural education (Sohail et al., 2023). Future research may focus on multi-agent coordination in 3D virtual spaces, as well as the ethical implications of long-term presence and data tracking in these environments (Zaidi & Faisal, 2018).

7.2. Neuroadaptive Collaboration Systems

The integration of neurotechnology and AI marks the emergence of neuroadaptive learning environments, where brain-computer interfaces (BCIs) inform real-time adaptations in group learning scenarios. Using sensors like EEG headsets, AI models can interpret effective and cognitive signals—such as attention, cognitive load, or frustration—and use this information to orchestrate team dynamics. For instance, if a learner in a group task shows signs of mental fatigue, the system could suggest a break or reassign tasks. Such capabilities offer a new paradigm in emotional regulation and distributed cognition. Research in this area must address signal reliability, personalization of thresholds, and ethical concerns surrounding brain data privacy (Abd-Alrazaq et al., 2023).

7.3. Cross-Cultural and Multilingual AI Facilitators

In globalized virtual classrooms, cultural and linguistic diversity presents both opportunities and barriers for collaboration. Future AI systems will incorporate cross-cultural communication models and multilingual NLP engines capable of translating not just words but intent, tone, and cultural nuance. For example, culturally adaptive chatbots may mediate group discussions using communication norms appropriate to each learner's background. This will improve equity in participation and reduce miscommunication in international teams. Key research challenges include sentiment modeling across languages, fairness in translation, and representation of non-Western communication patterns in AI training datasets(Faisal, 2024).

7.4. Blockchain for Team Contribution Tracking and Transparency

To enhance trust and transparency in collaborative evaluation, blockchain technology can be integrated with AI systems to maintain immutable records of learner contributions. Each interaction, whether a comment, submission, or peer review, can be timestamped and cryptographically secured on a distributed ledger. AI models can then analyze these records to compute fair contribution metrics, reduce plagiarism, and support transparent grading. This synergy enables decentralized learning analytics where students own and control their collaborative data. Research is needed to address interoperability with LMS, data scalability, and consensus protocols in educational contexts (Khlaif et al., 2025).

7.5. Hybrid AI–Human Facilitation Models

While AI continues to improve in decision-making and adaptability, the human element in education remains irreplaceable. Future systems will adopt hybrid facilitation models, where AI serves as a co-mediator alongside instructors. For example, AI may handle real-time data processing and feedback, while educators focus on emotional support and higher-order facilitation. This hybrid model supports augmentation over automation, ensuring that instructors remain in control of pedagogical direction. Research into trust calibration, delegation boundaries, and instructor-AI co-evolution will be critical in designing effective collaboration ecosystems(Ashraf et al., 2021; Sohail et al., 2023).

Table 6. Emerging Research Problems In AI-Powered Collaboration

Research Problem	Domain of Impact	Future Investigation Path
Emotion-aware AI in Group Dynamics	Affective computing, team cohesion, conflict resolution	Design of emotion recognition algorithms sensitive to collaboration context
Culturally Adaptive Communication Agents	Cross-cultural education, international virtual teams	Training NLP models on multicultural discourse datasets
Blockchain-Integrated Collaborative Analytics	Transparency, accountability, academic integrity	Developing smart contracts and privacy-preserving protocols for team logs
Neuroadaptive Feedback in Real-Time	Cognitive monitoring, personalized support	Integrating EEG/BCI data with adaptive learning systems
Multilingual Sentiment Modeling	Language equity, non-English collaborative environments	Building large-scale multilingual emotion datasets for education
Hybrid AI-Human Facilitation Protocols	Instructional design, teacher-AI interaction frameworks	Evaluating trust, control boundaries, and effectiveness of AI co-facilitators

8. CONCLUSION

AI has rapidly evolved from a supportive tool to a transformative force in enhancing collaboration and teamwork within VLEs. Through the integration of advanced computational models, ranging from NLP and RL to sentiment analysis and adaptive feedback, AI systems are now capable of personalizing interactions, facilitating group dynamics, and continuously optimizing the collaborative learning process. These intelligent systems do not merely automate tasks; they fundamentally reshape the way learners engage with one another by enabling real-time monitoring, equitable participation, and context-aware scaffolding. As this chapter has demonstrated, AI can act as a co-facilitator, capable of detecting affective states, redistributing cognitive load, and promoting reflective dialogue in a scalable, data-driven manner. However, as powerful as these systems are, the design and deployment of AI in collaborative education must remain resolutely human-centric. The goal is not to replace instructors or peer interactions, but to augment them in ways that are pedagogically meaningful and ethically sound. Human educators bring irreplaceable qualities to learning—empathy, intuition, cultural sensitivity, and moral judgment, that current AI systems are far from replicating. Thus, the design of AI-enabled collaboration tools must be rooted in principles of transparency, fairness, inclusivity, and learner agency. XAI, privacy-preserving computation, and equity-aware algorithms should be foundational to any system that influences educational experiences and outcomes.

For educators and curriculum designers, the implication is twofold. First, they must become active participants in the co-design of AI systems to ensure alignment with instructional goals and learner needs. Second, they must adopt an ecosystemic mindset, one that sees technology, pedagogy, and human relationships as interdependent. This means embedding AI not just as a backend service, but as a pedagogical partner whose capabilities and limitations are well understood and critically examined. Educators must also prepare learners to interact responsibly with AI systems by cultivating digital literacy, ethical awareness, and critical thinking. Moving forward, the call to action is clear: responsible innovation must be accompanied by rigorous empirical validation. The educational technology community must invest in longitudinal studies, randomized trials, and participatory design research to evaluate the long-term effects of AI-enhanced collaboration. Success must not be measured solely by efficiency or engagement metrics, but by deeper indicators of learning, such as metacognitive growth, social cohesion, and learner empowerment. Only through such a balanced approach can AI serve as a true catalyst for equitable, inclusive, and future-proof education.

REFERENCES

Abd-Alrazaq, A., AlSaad, R., Alhuwail, D., Ahmed, A., Healy, P. M., Latifi, S., Aziz, S., Damseh, R., Alrazak, S. A., & Sheikh, J. (2023). Large language models in medical education: Opportunities, challenges, and future directions. *JMIR Medical Education, 9*(1), e48291.

Ahmed, S. (2025). Integrating AI-Driven Automated Code Review in Agile Development: Benefits, Challenges, and Best Practices. *International Journal of Advanced Engineering Management Science, 11*(2), 593997.

Alrakhawi, H. A., Jamiat, N., & Abu-Naser, S. S. (2023). Intelligent tutoring systems in education: A systematic review of usage, tools, effects and evaluation. *Journal of Theoretical and Applied Information Technology, 101*(4), 1205–1226.

Ashraf, M. A., Yang, M., Zhang, Y., Denden, M., Tlili, A., Liu, J., Huang, R., & Burgos, D. (2021). A systematic review of systematic reviews on blended learning: Trends, gaps and future directions. *Psychology Research and Behavior Management*, •••, 1525–1541.

Bezzina, S., & Dingli, A. (2023). Rethinking gamification through artificial intelligence. *International Conference on Human-Computer Interaction*, 252–263.

Bhise, A., Munshi, A., Rodrigues, A., & Sawant, V. (2022). Overview of AI in education. In *Artificial Intelligence in Higher Education* (pp. 31–62). CRC Press.

Bradley, V. M. (2021). Learning Management System (LMS) use with online instruction. *International Journal of Technology in Education, 4*(1), 68–92.

Faisal, S. M. (2024). *Blockchain-Enabled Security Model for VANETs: A Novel Approach to Authentication and Position.*

Faisal, S. M., Gupta, B. K., & Zaidi, T. (2022). Detection and prevention of Sybil attack in VANET using modified ACO. *Proceedings of 4th International Conference on Cybernetics, Cognition and Machine Learning Applications, ICCCMLA 2022*, 78 – 84. DOI: 10.1109/ICCCMLA56841.2022.9989157

Faisal, S. M., Ishrat, M., & Khan, W. (2025). Digital twins in healthcare: Revolutionizing patient care and medical operations. In *Digital Twins for Smart Cities and Urban Planning*. From Virtual to Reality. DOI: 10.1201/9781003510338-4

Faisal, S. M., Jadhav, S. S., Ahlawat, A., Alam, M. S., Rama Krishna, B., Ranjan, R., & Bhoopathy, V. (2025). The Future of Wastewater Treatment Plant: Integrating HCNN-BiGRU-A Model for Superior Performance. *International Research Journal of Multidisciplinary Scope*, *6*(1), 151–161. DOI: 10.47857/irjms.2025.v06i01.02213

Faisal, S. M., & Zaidi, T. (2020). Timestamp Based Detection of Sybil Attack in VANET. *International Journal of Network Security*, *22*(3), 397–408.

Gan, A. W. J., Dang, Q., & Western, B. (n.d.). *AI-Mediated Group Ideation.*

Hasanah, R., Munawwaroh, I., Hasanah, M., & Mundiri, A. (2024). Fostering Inclusivity: Strategies for Supporting Students with Special Needs in Mainstream Classrooms. *FALASIFA: Jurnal Studi Keislaman*, *15*(1), 73–85.

Ishrat, M., Khan, W., & Faisal, S. M. (2025). AI and risk forecasting: Leveraging AI for environmental, social, and governance compliance. In *Artificial Intelligence for Financial Risk Management and Analysis*. DOI: 10.4018/979-8-3373-1200-2.ch015

Ishrat, M., Khan, W., Faisal, S. M., Al Farsi, M. M., & Farooqui, N. A. (2025). Digital twins future prospects in smart cities challenges of urban planning. In *Digital Twins for Smart Cities and Urban Planning*. From Virtual to Reality. DOI: 10.1201/9781003510338-3

Islam, M. H., & Ivy, J. S. (2022). Modeling the role of efficiency for the equitable and effective distribution of donated food. *OR-Spektrum*, *44*(2), 485–534.

Khlaif, Z. N., Hamamra, B., & Hussein, E. T. (2025). *AI Paradox in Higher Education: Understanding Over-Reliance*. Its Impact, and Sustainable Integration.

Malik, M. A., & Shah, R. (2025). *AI teachers (AI-based robots as*. Mueller, D., & Strohmeier, S. (2011). Design characteristics of virtual learning environments: State of research. *Computers & Education*, *57*(4), 2505–2516.

Nagel, L., Karras, O., Amiri, S. M., & Schneider, K. (2024). Turning asynchronicity into an opportunity: Asynchronous communication for shared understanding with vision videos. *Requirements Engineering*, *29*(1), 49–71.

Nami, F., Marandi, S. S., & Sotoudehnama, E. (2018). Interaction in a discussion list: An exploration of cognitive, social, and teaching presence in teachers' online collaborations. *ReCALL*, *30*(3), 375–398.

Ouyang, F., & Zhang, L. (2024). AI-driven learning analytics applications and tools in computer-supported collaborative learning: A systematic review. *Educational Research Review*, *44*, 100616.

Patel, K. (2024). Ethical reflections on data-centric AI: balancing benefits and risks. *Available at SSRN* 4993089.

Rahim, M. A. (2023). *Managing conflict in organizations*. Routledge.

Raihan, M. M. H., Subroto, S., Chowdhury, N., Koch, K., Ruttan, E., & Turin, T. C. (2024). *Dimensions and barriers for digital (in) equity and digital divide: A systematic integrative review*. Digital Transformation and Society.

Ryan, E., & Poole, C. (2019). Impact of virtual learning environment on students' satisfaction, engagement, recall, and retention. *Journal of Medical Imaging and Radiation Sciences*, *50*(3), 408–415.

Safkolam, R., Ahmad Zaky El Islami, R., & Sari, I. J. (2023). The Effects of Jigsaw Technique on Learning Achievement and Retention of Science Teacher Students. *Shanlax International Journal of Education*, *11*(2), 37–42.

Saqr, R. R., Al-Somali, S. A., & Sarhan, M. Y. (2024). Exploring the acceptance and user satisfaction of AI-driven e-learning platforms (Blackboard, Moodle, Edmodo, Coursera and edX): An integrated technology model. *Sustainability*, *16*(1), 204.

Shabani, K., Khatib, M., & Ebadi, S. (2010). Vygotsky's zone of proximal development: Instructional implications and teachers' professional development. *English Language Teaching*, *3*(4), 237–248.

Sheikh, H., Prins, C., & Schrijvers, E. (2023). Artificial intelligence: definition and background. In Mission, A. I. (Ed.), *The new system technology* (pp. 15–41). Springer.

Sohail, S. S., Farhat, F., Himeur, Y., Nadeem, M., Madsen, D. Ø., Singh, Y., Atalla, S., & Mansoor, W. (2023). Decoding ChatGPT: A taxonomy of existing research, current challenges, and possible future directions. *Journal of King Saud University. Computer and Information Sciences*, *35*(8), 101675.

Swart, K., Bond-Barnard, T., & Chugh, R. (2022). Challenges and critical success factors of digital communication, collaboration and knowledge sharing in project management virtual teams: A review. *International Journal of Information Systems and Project Management*, *10*(4), 84–103.

Varlamov, O. (2021). "Brains" for Robots: Application of the Mivar expert systems for implementation of autonomous intelligent robots. *Big Data Research*, *25*, 100241.

Wilson, K. E. S., & Millar, P. (2021). Intramural sport participation: An examination of participant benefits, service quality, program satisfaction, and student retention. *Recreational Sports Journal*, *45*(2), 149–160.

Zaidi, T., & Faisal, S. (2018). An overview: Various attacks in VANET. *2018 4th International Conference on Computing Communication and Automation (ICCCA)*, 1–6.

Zhan, C., Joksimović, S., Ladjal, D., Rakotoarivelo, T., Marshall, R., & Pardo, A. (2024). Preserving both privacy and utility in learning analytics. *IEEE Transactions on Learning Technologies*, *17*, 1615–1627.

Chapter 7
Levelling Up Learning: Gamification and LEGO-Based Strategies for Coaching and Peer Teaching in Higher Education in the Global South

Aradhana Ramnund-Mansingh
https://orcid.org/0000-0003-1995-6849
University of Free State, South Africa & MANCOSA, South Africa

Gareth Daniel Paul
https://orcid.org/0009-0001-5590-6841
MANCOSA, South Africa

ABSTRACT

Coaching and peer teaching are essential student skills that foster collaboration, leadership, and interpersonal communication while enhancing the quality and depth of individual learning and group dynamics. Despite their significance, innovative methods for cultivating these competencies remain underexplored in the Global South, particularly in resource-deficient educational contexts. This study examines gamification and concepts like LEGO Serious Play as engaging, flexible, and bespoke learning tools to foster coaching and peer teaching skills, emphasising their transformative impact on academic performance and personal growth. The research employs a secondary desktop study to analyse existing literature and case studies on experiential learning, gamified education, and hands-on approaches, such as LEGO-based learning. Data was collected using the PRISMA method and systematically appraised using the Critical Appraisal Skills Programme (CASP) framework to ensure methodological rigour and comprehensive evaluation. Findings are synthesised to identify effective strategies, enablers, and barriers to skill develop-

DOI: 10.4018/979-8-3373-9225-7.ch007

ment. Results show that gamification, achieved through rewards, leaderboards, and interactive challenges, enhances student motivation, engagement, and collaboration. Similarly, Lego provides a tactile and creative medium for simulating real-world problem-solving and teamwork, enabling students to practice coaching and peer teaching dynamically and experientially. Participants engaging in these methods reported increased confidence, critical thinking, and facilitation skills. However, challenges such as unequal access to resources and initial scepticism towards unconventional methods were observed. This study highlights the importance of incorporating gamified learning and LEGO-based activities into higher education curricula. Institutions can nurture a culture of shared learning and mutual growth by preparing students for academic and professional success. The findings contribute to the growing literature on peer learning, offering practical recommendations for scalable and context-sensitive interventions to effectively cultivate coaching and peer teaching skills in diverse educational environments.

INTRODUCTION

Higher education institutions globally are undergoing a paradigmatic shift from traditional, lecture-centric models towards more interactive, student-centred, and skills-based pedagogies. In this evolving educational landscape, coaching and peer teaching have emerged as transformative instructional strategies that not only enhance academic performance but also cultivate essential 21st-century skills such as collaboration, leadership, critical thinking, and emotional intelligence. These pedagogical approaches are particularly valuable in preparing students to navigate increasingly complex, interdependent, and technology-driven academic and professional environments (Aguilar-Ferrándiz et al., 2024).

This chapter examines the role of gamification and LEGO-based learning as innovative, low-cost, and high-impact methods for integrating coaching and peer teaching into higher education curricula, particularly in the Global South. These active learning strategies are grounded in contemporary learning theories, including Transformative Learning, Flow Theory, and Communities of Practice, to highlight their theoretical and empirical foundations. In doing so, the chapter seeks to demonstrate that gamified and tactile learning environments can foster inclusive, engaging, and reflective learning communities even in contexts challenged by infrastructural and pedagogical limitations.

The significance of this study lies in its focus on context-sensitive innovation, where strategies are tailored to local needs and constraints. The chapter offers practical, scalable, and culturally relevant pathways for educational transformation. While gamification and LEGO-based learning have gained momentum in Global North contexts, their potential in the Global South remains underexplored, particularly concerning peer teaching and coaching. The chapter, therefore, bridges this gap by offering evidence-based recommendations for educators, curriculum developers, and institutional leaders committed to enhancing student agency, engagement, and academic success through experiential learning. To guide this investigation, the chapter outlines a focused set of aims that shape its analytical approach and frame its contribution to both theory and practice.

The purpose of this chapter is to explore how innovative, low-cost pedagogical strategies, specifically gamification and LEGO-based learning, can be used to enhance coaching and peer teaching in higher education contexts within the Global South. By integrating theoretical insights with empirical evidence, the chapter provides a framework for designing experiential learning interventions that promote student engagement, collaboration, and critical reflection, even in resource-constrained environments.

The primary objectives of this study are:

1. To explore and evaluate the effectiveness of gamification and LEGO-based learning as innovative tools for fostering coaching and peer teaching skills in higher education in the Global South.
2. To analyse the challenges and barriers to implementing these methods in resource-constrained educational environments.
3. To propose practical, scalable recommendations for integrating gamified and LEGO-based activities into curricula to promote active learning and student collaboration.
4. To contribute to the body of knowledge on experiential and hands-on teaching strategies tailored to the unique needs of higher education institutions in the Global South.

BACKGROUND

Higher education in the Global South faces a distinctive constellation of challenges that impede the widespread adoption of innovative, student-centred pedagogies. These challenges include resource limitations, infrastructural deficits, rigid curricula, and a persistent emphasis on rote memorisation and didactic instruction (Shohel et al., 2022; Sareen & Mandal, 2024). Compounding these structural constraints are socio-cultural factors such as limited academic exposure to facilitation techniques, high student-to-faculty ratios, and a historical reliance on hierarchical classroom models that discourage collaborative learning and student agency.

However, these same environments also offer fertile ground for pedagogical innovation. Across countries such as India, South Africa, Nigeria, and Brazil, educators and institutions are beginning to experiment with contextually appropriate active learning strategies to overcome these barriers. Initiatives in South African universities have demonstrated that incorporating coaching circles into at-risk academic modules can significantly improve retention and student confidence (Nupen & Jagernath, 2024). In Nigeria, resistance to gamification in academic libraries has been directly linked to a lack of awareness, rather than cultural incompatibility, suggesting a latent openness to innovation once support systems are established (Adeyemi et al., 2021). Similarly, Ecuadorian classrooms have successfully introduced LEGO-based learning as a low-cost, engaging method to support students in under-resourced English language programs (Asanza et al., 2024).

Despite these isolated successes, a broader synthesis of how tools such as gamification and LEGO-based strategies can be systematically integrated into coaching and peer teaching frameworks remains underdeveloped in the literature. This gap is particularly concerning given the urgent need to develop pedagogies that are both scalable and inclusive, capable of reaching diverse learners across linguistic, cultural, and neurodiverse spectra, and resilient in the face of technological limitations.

This study responds to this need by evaluating the pedagogical affordances of gamification and LEGO-based learning within peer teaching and coaching contexts. It does so through a systematic review of global and regional literature, identifying best practices and barriers, and contextualising them within the unique structural and cultural conditions of the Global South. The goal is to provide an empirically grounded, theoretically robust, and practically actionable framework that educators can adapt to enhance learning outcomes, especially in resource-constrained and historically underserved academic environments.

THEORETICAL UNDERPINNING

This study is underpinned by a triadic theoretical foundation which includes Transformative Learning Theory, Flow Theory, and Communities of Practice. Together, these offer a multidimensional lens for designing and evaluating coaching and peer teaching interventions enhanced through gamification and LEGO-based learning. These frameworks were purposefully selected for their shared emphasis on learner agency, social interaction, and motivational engagement, which are essential attributes for pedagogical innovation in higher education contexts, within the Global South (Wenger-Trayner et al., 2023; Hamari & Koivisto, 2020; Taylor & Cranton, 2023).

Jack Mezirow's (2000) Transformative Learning Theory posits that adult learners experience deep learning when they critically reflect on their assumptions and reframe their perspectives. In the context of coaching and peer teaching, transformative learning is particularly evident when students engage in activities that challenge pre-existing beliefs about themselves as passive recipients of knowledge. Through LEGO-based modelling or peer-led coaching simulations, students are prompted to reconsider their learning roles and develop more autonomous and collaborative academic identities (Taylor & Cranton, 2023; Culpepper & Gauntlett, 2024). This theory aligns with gamified and tactile pedagogies in that both introduce what Mezirow (2000) refers to as "disorienting dilemmas", unexpected, reflective learning moments that prompt identity re-evaluation. Within institutions in the Global South, such moments can foster resilience, self-efficacy, and adaptive thinking, attributes essential for navigating unpredictable academic environments (Mavutha & Mansingh, 2024).

Flow Theory, developed by Csikszentmihalyi (1990), explains how learners become deeply immersed and intrinsically motivated when they engage in tasks that offer clear goals, real-time feedback, and an optimal balance between challenge and skill. Applied to educational contexts, gamification leverages flow dynamics to transform routine academic experiences into immersive, meaningful interactions (Hamari & Koivisto, 2020; Muñoz et al., 2023). When peer teaching activities are gamified through leaderboards, point systems, or competitive role-play, students experience heightened focus, reduced anxiety, and a sense of progress. This is particularly salient in Global South settings, where institutional constraints often reduce opportunities for interactive learning. Recent research by Duterte (2024) in the Philippines and Mbukanma et al. (2024) in South Africa has shown that even low-tech gamified interventions can significantly enhance student motivation and learning outcomes when aligned with local pedagogical needs. Flow Theory also supports the emotional and cognitive benefits of LEGO-based tasks. When learners engage in building metaphors or solving problems collaboratively using LEGO, they often enter a state of flow that amplifies concentration, creative risk-taking, and sustained participation (Lambert et al., 2023; Vardakosta et al., 2023).

Communities of Practice (CoP), conceptualised by Lave and Wenger (1991), offer a framework for understanding how knowledge is constructed through sustained social interaction within a shared domain. In the context of peer coaching and gamified group tasks, learners move from peripheral participation to central membership through iterative cycles of practice, reflection, and feedback. This communal approach to learning is particularly effective in low-resource higher education institutions, where formal mentorship may be limited (Wenger-Trayner et al., 2023; de Caux & Pretorius, 2024). Gamified and LEGO-based learning environments inherently support the development of CoPs by fostering recurring peer collaboration, accountability, and co-constructed meaning-making. In peer teaching scenarios, students act as facilitators, receiving and giving knowledge through structured dialogues, debriefs, and shared problem-solving (Hamilton-Hinch et al., 2023). The social architecture of these activities reinforces the value of mutual engagement and participatory learning, helping to build inclusive academic cultures. Emerging models such as Participatory Design Thinking (Simon, 2024) build on CoP principles to centre student voices in co-creating learning experiences, a particularly relevant innovation for Global South institutions striving for pedagogical equity.

These three theories form an interlocking theoretical scaffold that enables a comprehensive understanding of experiential, gamified, and peer-led learning strategies. Transformative Learning Theory explains how reflective practice catalyses personal and academic growth; Flow Theory illuminates how motivational engagement can be optimised through gamified design; and Communities of Practice frame the social dynamics that facilitate knowledge exchange and identity development among peers. This integrated framework supports the chapter's core argument that gamification and LEGO-based learning, when informed by coaching principles and grounded in these theoretical traditions, can offer scalable, inclusive, and contextually responsive pedagogical solutions for higher education in the Global South.

LITERATURE REVIEW

This section reviews existing scholarship, identifies current practice gaps, and highlights opportunities for innovation in fostering coaching and peer teaching skills. To ensure both contextual relevance and robustness, the study draws on global case studies from developed and developing regions. Research from higher-resource settings provides valuable benchmarks and transferable strategies that can inform practice, while also surfacing lessons adaptable to the structural, pedagogical, and socio-economic realities of the Global South. By engaging with these comparative perspectives, the study enhances its capacity to inform inclusive, scalable, and context-sensitive educational interventions. Recent large-scale reviews and meta-analyses further strengthen the empirical grounding for deploying peer coaching, peer teaching, and gamification in Global South universities. These quantitative syntheses not only demonstrate consistent positive effects but also highlight the importance of contextual factors such as infrastructure, cultural norms, and resource availability. As such, they justify a carefully phased, context-sensitive roll-out, beginning with low-tech or hybrid designs and monitoring effect sizes across cohorts and disciplines to account for cultural and institutional variation (Bengesai et al., 2023; Zhang & Maconochie, 2022).

Coaching and Peer Teaching in Higher Education

Coaching and peer teaching have been extensively studied as methods that foster active and flexible learning, leadership, and collaboration. Coaching involves guiding individuals to achieve personal and professional goals, emphasising self-awareness, critical thinking, and effective communication (Garvey et al., 2021). Aguilar-Ferrándiz et al. (2024) confirmed in their recent study of health science students in Spain that the practice of coaching reflected significant increases in cognitive empathy, emotional skills, understanding of patients' needs, stress management, communication, and connection-making with others. Furthermore, research conducted at a university in the United Kingdom (UK) confirmed that peer coaching enhanced students' confidence in managing their workloads and improved their academic performance (Andreanoff, 2016). According to Andreanoff (2016), retention rates improved due to coaching, with 20% of students who were not coached withdrawing from their studies, compared to 9.9% of students who were coached during the same period. Coaching was particularly effective for students with poor academic performance and for first-year students transitioning from high school to university (Andreanoff, 2016). The effectiveness of coaching for university students, however, depends on factors such as the timing of its conduct, avoiding exam and recess periods, and also the intensity that should be suited to the student's needs or level of development (Oreopoulos & Petronijevic, 2023).

Peer teaching, on the other hand, enables students to act as educators for their peers, reinforcing their understanding of the content while enhancing the quality of learning and collaborative problem-solving (Latifi et al., 2021). Böhm-Fischer and Luzi Beyer (2024) conducted a study in Germany, where a sample of 268 students in higher education found that peer teaching was highly effective in enhancing academic success, despite the students' demanding schedules, particularly in areas such as reducing procrastination towards their studies and improving students' assessment readiness. Another study in Oman (Shaikh, 2024), where students were studying English as a second language, also found peer-teaching to be a very valuable tool, with the majority agreeing that it enhanced their presentation and communication skills (85%), improved their understanding of the content that they taught their peers (95%), motivated them to write more on their chosen topic (75%). It also allowed them to utilise educational technology, such as PowerPoint presentations, videos, and Smartboards (85%) (Shaikh, 2024). Comparative research conducted in India found that the Global South faces significantly higher challenges in terms of these constraints relative to the Global North, and this has, consequently, resulted in the limited use of peer teaching, coaching, and blended learning in the former (Sareen & Mandal, 2024). Etomes and Nsem (2023) and Zickafoose et al. (2024) discuss that due to the uneven resource distribution in the Global South, 34.1% of educators stated that peer coaching is practised in their teaching, whereas, for public higher education institutions, a majority (65.9%) of educators indicated that peer coaching is a tool used in their teaching.

Recent quantitative syntheses confirm that peer-supported approaches deliver measurable academic gains in university settings, including Global South contexts. A higher-education meta-analysis of formal peer learning (PLTL, PASS/SI, PAL) reports weighted effects around $g \approx 0.40–0.42$ on course performance, with robustness across designs and disciplines (functional for positioning SI/peer coaching in at-risk modules) (Bengesai et al., 2023). In medical education, a meta-analysis of 13 RCTs (n=2,003) found that peer-assisted learning (PAL) improves exam performance in clinical knowledge/skills versus lecture-led instruction, and after sensitivity analysis, remains at least non-inferior to faculty-led teaching, underscoring PAL's viability where staff capacity is constrained (Zhang & Maconochie, 2022). Complementing this, an India-led systematic review and meta-analysis on near-peer tutoring concludes that learning outcomes (knowledge and skills) are comparable to expert teaching, with students reporting high comfort and engagement, relevant for resource-limited departments scaling support (Khapre et al., 2021). Cultural moderators also matter: meta-analytic evidence on Peer Instruction indicates larger gains in collectivist settings, which are helpful when interpreting results from Asia/ Latin America versus more individualist contexts.

Given the success of coaching and peer-teaching in higher education in other countries, these Supplemental Instruction (SI) tools can also be re-looked at and used in the South African higher education system to enhance retention rates, teaching and learning and promote equity, foster inclusivity and empower students both emotionally and mentally from all backgrounds by incorporating it's diverse languages as these tools are applied in collaborative learning and culturally responsive pedagogies. These tools can also be used at the beginning of each semester, allowing for different methods to be employed closer to assessments. They can be applied across students of varied academic strengths, especially when practised within at-risk modules, such as numeracy modules, to aid in understanding and, consequently, improve student pass rates (Nupen & Jagernath, 2024). Budget-effective yet adequate strategic planning and training, with workshops predominantly towards the second semester in preparation for the next year and continuous feedback during preparation and application, needs to be ensured to boost facilitators' or stakeholders' knowledge and expertise in the use of these SI tools, obtain their buy-in as a starting point and promote sustainability of such programmes.

Gamification in Education

Gamification, defined as the application of game design elements in non-game contexts, has emerged as a powerful tool to enhance student engagement and motivation (Krath et al., 2021). Research highlights the potential of gamification in higher education to transform passive learning environments into interactive and engaging experiences (Sharma et al., 2024; Slamet et al., 2024). James et al. (2024) found that gamified interventions significantly improved student engagement and learning outcomes in diverse educational contexts. The study by Adeyemi et al. (2021), conducted in Nigeria, aimed to introduce gamification in academic libraries and found a positive correlation between awareness and education regarding the application and perception of this tool. For academic librarians in Nigeria, a lack of awareness and education about gamification has led to predominantly negative perceptions of this tool, which in turn has influenced resistance to its application (Adeyemi et al., 2021). A significant geographical gap, particularly in Africa, was also identified in gamification research through a bibliometric analysis, with 83.33% of African countries having no research publications in this subject area (Guerrero-Alcedo et al., 2022). In contrast, however, an additional bibliometric analysis spanning 2013 – 2022 highlighted exponential growth in the use of gamification in higher education and research output in the Global North, particularly for leading countries in the field, Spain (78 publications), the United States (US) (29 publications), the UK (26 publications), Canada (21 publications) and Germany (17 publications) (Guerrero-Alcedo et al., 2022; Irwanto, 2023).

Large-scale syntheses similarly support gamification's learning impact, with regional nuances. A 2023 meta-analysis in BMC Medical Education (higher education) estimates a pooled Hedges' $g \approx 0.82$ for achievement; i.e., a sizeable improvement relative to traditional conditions (Li et al., 2024; Diaz & Estoque-Loñez, 2024). Zooming in regionally, a 2024 meta-analysis across Asian higher-education studies finds a substantial mean effect ($g \approx 1.30$) on academic performance, signalling strong potential where collaborative, competitive, and points/badges/leaderboards mechanics align with classroom norms. Broader SLRs also document consistent motivational gains and clarify design levers (e.g., task–mechanic alignment, feedback pacing), while noting mixed effects if designs are superficial or misaligned to outcomes, applicable caveats for staged adoption (Jaramillo-Mediavilla et al., 2024). From an equity lens, bibliometric mapping shows a documented publication gap in Africa (83% of countries without higher-ed gamification publications), which helps explain the scarcity of Nigeria-specific meta-analyses and underscores the value of pilot-plus-evaluation approaches when transferring designs (Guerrero-Alcedo et al., 2022).

Studies also indicate that gamification can be particularly impactful where traditional teaching methods fail to engage students (Shohel, 2022; Fransiska, 2024).

Mbukanma et al.'s (2024) study on gamification and student engagement was conducted in South African higher education institutions, which faced challenges, including technical barriers, concerns about game alignment and curricular objectives, and limited funding and student access to necessary tools. This study found that, when gamification was applied, student engagement was enhanced, as it tapped into students' intrinsic motivation, creating dynamic, immersive, and interactive learning experiences that captivated students' attention and fostered a sense of teamwork and healthy competition in their learning journey (Mbukanma et al., 2024). Duterte (2024) conducted a study in the Philippines that examined the effects of gamification on student engagement and motivation in higher education at three private universities. The results revealed that students faced challenges, including feeling overwhelmed by the competitive nature of gamification and technical difficulties due to resource constraints. However, student engagement and, subsequently, motivation increased significantly with continued practice and usage of gamification in their learning. This significant increase reflected a mean score increase from 3.2 to 4.1 in student motivation. The increase in engagement and motivation resulted in improved student test scores following the gamification intervention and learning (Duterte, 2024).

With the aforementioned, transitioning from traditional teaching methods to implementing game design elements is highly beneficial to students' learning journey and the consequent outcomes. Therefore, from a South African perspective, the initial potential of students' tendency to feel overwhelmed is high; hence, academics could consider low-tech gamification methods as a starting point, such as board games and offline activities (Moonsamy et al., 2022; Nwosu et al., 2023). This would ensure flexibility and inclusivity in their learning journey. In South African higher education, incorporating game design elements, such as badges, points, and leaderboards, would be particularly useful for theory-based modules, transforming traditional learning into more stimulating and interactive sessions (Hu & Razlog, 2023). More Edtech tools and innovations, such as the Ambani platform developed by a South African startup, could be incorporated into various areas of the syllabus and sectors in higher education to enhance the teaching of South Africa's indigenous languages (Manda, 2024). The Ambani platform offers augmented reality and gamified elements for teaching a range of languages, including those beyond the indigenous South African languages (Ambani Africa, 2024). Such innovations, which appeal to students and are implemented in higher education, can foster a more equitable, engaging, and effective learning environment for diverse students, supporting collaborative coaching and peer teaching. Similarly, at a limited-resource education institution in Ecuador, gamification was effectively incorporated by introducing simple games during lessons to create a stimulating, exciting, and collaborative learning environment for teaching English as a second language (Asanza et al., 2024). Implementing gamification enhanced student engagement, language acquisition, and collaborative learning by fostering subsequent student motivation.

LEGO-Based Learning

LEGO-based learning is an experiential teaching method that uses LEGO blocks as tools to facilitate problem-solving, teamwork, and creativity. This approach aligns with constructivist learning theories, which hold that learners build knowledge through hands-on experiences and collaboration (Piaget, 2005). Research by Culpepper and Gauntlett (2024) demonstrated the effectiveness of LEGO-based learning in fostering critical thinking and collaboration, particularly in group settings. A study based on five countries (Germany, South Korea, Australia, the UK and the United States of America) compared education institutions that did not use LEGO-based learning to those that did. In the former, this study reported that the lack of this interactive tool led to students becoming disengaged. This study also noted that the use of LEGO-based learning boosts students' grades (84%) and improves attendance rates and engagement (83%) (LEGO Education, 2024).

According to Mouratoglou (2018), research was conducted among undergraduate and postgraduate engineering and business students at universities in the UK and Greece, utilising LEGO-based learning for team building and entrepreneurship. This study also applied aspects of LEGO SERIOUS PLAY, which aims to stimulate creativity and imagination in work and entails a sequential process of steps when using the LEGO blocks, namely, challenge, build, share, and reflect (LEGO Education, 2024; Mouratoglou, 2018). The researcher encountered challenges related to the meticulous pre-planning required, time constraints, and the flexible nature of the LEGO blocks as an observer, particularly in how quickly the teams would modify their plans and ideas on the work-related 3D models (Mouratoglou, 2018). However, these were outweighed by the benefits of using LEGO and LEGO SERIOUS PLAY in higher education, as the researcher found that these tools created exposure for students to think outside the box, fostering creativity and agility, skills crucial in the job market (Mouratoglou, 2018).In higher education, LEGO-based methods have been successfully applied in engineering, business, and teacher training to develop communication and teamwork skills (Gordillo et al., 2024). Jiméneza et al.'s (2021) study in Colombia effectively utilised LEGO-based learning in higher education to develop industry skills in problem-solving, decision-making, and systematic thinking. This project was created by professors and is based on the usage of Lego Mindstorms by engineering students for gamification purposes. Students needed to use their Lego Mindstorms kit to build an aeroplane, and the success of this learning tool suggested that it was also a robust and reliable research approach (Jiménez et al., 2021).

The study (Lugaresi et al., 2020) conducted in Italy introduced LEGO-based learning at a Master's degree level to mechanical engineering students. This was offered as an additional course to enhance students' practical skills with a miniature production system made of LEGO MINDSTORMS (Lugaresi et al., 2020). LEGO MINDSTORMS are products developed by the LEGO Group, which include programmable miniature LEGO bricks equipped with sensors and electric motors, enabling the creation of interactive or automated systems (LEGO Education, 2024). According to Lugaresi et al. (2020), the LEGO-based learning course enhanced students' performance as they were tasked with introducing design modifications and developing technical solutions for their group-assigned production systems. This learning initiative successfully achieved its aim, enabling students to use peer teaching to enhance their teamwork skills and success by integrating different competencies and leveraging prior knowledge within their teams to solve problems during their learning experience. In addition, research indicates that the use of LEGO and LEGO SERIOUS PLAY in higher education serves as a bridge, connecting students within their respective teams through classroom activities in terms of ideas, creativity, concerns, reflection, and learning (Mouratoglou, 2018). An inviting and playful atmosphere is created with these tools, and they also encourage student engagement and the development of cultural cohesion among diverse participants with varied perspectives (Mouratoglou, 2018).

In the Global South, LEGO-based learning also presents an inclusive, cost-effective and versatile pedagogical approach to addressing the needs of neurodiverse students. Play-based learning in higher education appeals to a diverse student population and simplifies concepts for neurodiverse students. Similarly, this tactile tool can also support visually impaired students through its engaging use. It would be an effective tool to help foster coaching and peer teaching of neurodiverse students who already come into higher education institutions with a lack of motivation due to socially constructed norms (Mavutha & Mansingh, 2024). According to employers' perceptions in South Africa, university graduates lack crucial work-readiness skills; therefore, developmental interventions and tools that focus on this area in higher education are much needed (Nofemela & Winberg, 2020; Potgieter et al., 2023). LEGO-based learning has also proven effective in fostering creativity, critical thinking, and advanced thinking, as well as teamwork. Therefore, with the correct training for academics and adequate planning, graduates' work-readiness skills could be enhanced by coaching and peer teaching methodologies.

While the potential of LEGO-based learning and gamification is significant, specific recommendations in existing literature sometimes assume prior familiarity with advanced platforms such as LEGO Serious Play certification or sophisticated digital gamification tools (Kristiansen & Rasmussen, 2014). Such assumptions may limit applicability in Global South contexts, where many institutions face cost, training, and access barriers. To ensure broader relevance, this study emphasises a tiered model of interventions, beginning with low-tech, low-cost strategies (such as cards, bricks, or role-play) and gradually integrating more advanced tools where resources and expertise allow (Dichev & Dicheva, 2017; Oyelere et al., 2016). This approach avoids privileging well-resourced institutions and enhances the scalability and inclusivity of coaching and peer teaching interventions, aligning with UNESCO's (2021) call for equitable, context-sensitive education.

Digital Interventions and Graduate Employability

Recent research highlights the growing effectiveness of digital micro-credentials and mobile-first gamification in enhancing employability and learning engagement, even in low-resource contexts. For example, Gamage and Dehideniya (2025) present a critical narrative review showing how micro-credentials offer flexible, inclusive pathways for skill development and deepen institutional innovation. Complementing this, Kato et al. (2023) examine policy drivers behind the adoption of microcredentials for lifelong learning and employability, while Ahsan et al.'s (2023) systematic review outlines the opportunities and barriers to implementing microcredentials across diverse higher education systems. In parallel, gamification interventions tailored for low-bandwidth environments are gaining traction. Maryani et al. (2025) report that mobile-based gamified learning increases engagement and motivation, even where traditional infrastructure is limited. Additionally, Cheng et al. (2025) find that gamified reading interventions improve language performance and learner enjoyment in university settings. Together, these emerging studies strengthen the evidence base for designing accessible, scalable digital learning interventions—situating digital micro-credentials and mobile gamification as strategically viable tools for promoting employability and equitable learning in Global South contexts.

METHODOLOGY

This study employs a secondary desktop study to explore the effectiveness of gamification and LEGO-based learning in fostering coaching and peer teaching skills in higher education in the Global South. The methodology involves a systematic data collection process, critical appraisal, and synthesis of existing literature, reports, and case studies. The research is designed to ensure rigour, transparency, and relevance to the study's objectives. The study adopts a qualitative research design, using a narrative synthesis approach to evaluate and interpret findings from previous studies. This approach facilitates the integration of diverse data sources, including peer-reviewed articles, institutional reports, and case studies, to develop a comprehensive understanding of the potential and challenges of using gamification and LEGO-based methods in higher education. The Critical Appraisal Skills Programme (CASP) framework assesses the quality, reliability, and validity of the selected studies, ensuring a systematic and robust analysis.

Data was collected from academic databases, institutional repositories, and organisational reports to ensure a comprehensive review of relevant literature. The sources included academic databases such as PubMed, Scopus, ERIC, and Google Scholar, as well as grey literature from organisations such as UNESCO, the World Bank, and various educational NGOs. Institutional repositories were consulted, incorporating university research publications and case studies to provide insights into best practices and emerging trends. A systematic search strategy was employed, utilising targeted keywords to refine search results and ensure the inclusion of peer-reviewed studies and policy reports relevant to the study. To promote transparency and replicability, the study adopted a PRISMA-style reporting approach to document the screening and selection of sources. A flow diagram was developed to illustrate each stage of the review process, including identification, screening, eligibility, and inclusion. This ensures transparent reporting of how studies were selected, excluded, and retained, aligning with best practices in qualitative evidence synthesis (Page et al., 2021). Filters were applied to restrict results to peer-reviewed publications. Following this, duplicate records were removed, and a detailed screening process was conducted based on relevance to the research objectives. The PRISMA flow diagram (included in Figure 1) visually captures the total number of records retrieved, screened, excluded (with reasons), and included in the final review.

Figure 1. PRISMA Flow Diagram of Literature Screening and Inclusion

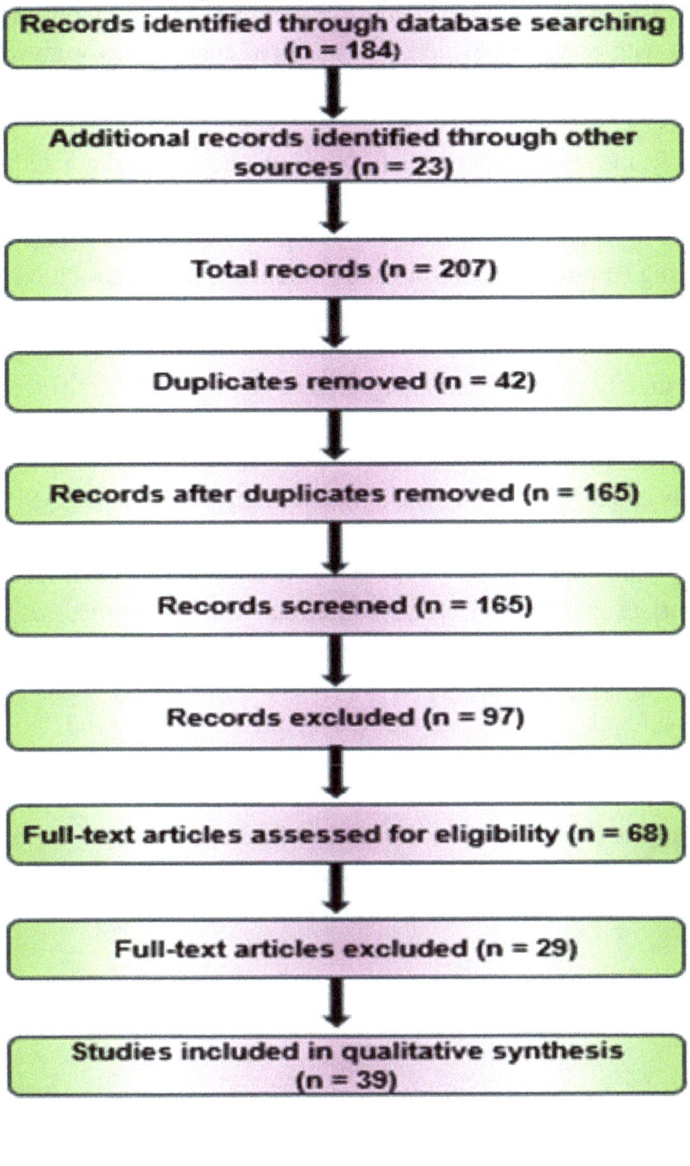

A set of inclusion and exclusion criteria was established to ensure the relevance, credibility, and applicability of the literature reviewed. These criteria guided the selection process, ensuring that only high-quality and contextually relevant studies were included in the analysis. The inclusion criteria focused on selecting studies directly aligned with the research objectives. Eligible sources included studies conducted in higher education settings within a global context, particularly those discussing gamification, LEGO-based learning, coaching, or peer teaching as innovative pedagogical approaches. Only peer-reviewed journal articles, institutional reports, and case studies were considered to maintain academic rigour and reliability. Publications with empirical evidence or practical applications were prioritised to ensure real-world relevance and potential for implementation in resource-constrained environments.

Conversely, the exclusion criteria filtered out studies that did not align with the research's scope. This included research focusing solely on primary or secondary education, as the study was limited to the higher education sector. Furthermore, articles lacking empirical data or methodological clarity were omitted to maintain the credibility and reliability of the study. Lastly, non-English publications were excluded due to resource limitations for translation, ensuring that all selected studies could be accurately analysed and interpreted. By applying these stringent selection criteria, the study ensures that its findings are contextually relevant, evidence-based, and practically applicable.

This study employs a systematic qualitative analysis using the CASP framework to evaluate the validity, relevance, and rigour of the selected literature. The CASP framework ensures that studies included in the review have clear research objectives, appropriate methodologies, and reliable data collection processes (Long et al., 2020). The selected literature was synthesised using thematic analysis, identifying key patterns, challenges, and best practices. Themes that emerged include enhanced engagement through gamification, the development of creative and critical thinking skills using LEGO blocks, increased confidence and communication skills, and the exploration of themes and patterns in student experiences (Table 1). This methodological approach ensures that the study's findings are based on high-quality, contextually relevant research, thereby contributing to a deeper understanding of pedagogical innovations in the Global South.

Table 1. Thematic Results Analysis

Theme	Refined Description	Frequency of Mentions	Key Supporting Literature
Enhanced Engagement through Gamification	Use of gamification (competitive quizzes, badges, point-based systems) improved motivation, sustained attention, and learner immersion across disciplines.	28	Csikszentmihalyi & Csikszentmihalyi (1990); Hamari et al. (2016); Bhatt & Chakrabarti (2022); Muñoz et al. (2023); Maryani et al. (2025)
Creative and Critical Thinking through LEGO-Based Learning	LEGO-based tasks fostered creativity, abstract reasoning, and supported problem-solving by enabling students to model and visualise complex concepts.	25	Tolba & Al-Osaimi (2023); Vardakosta et al. (2023); Simon (2024); Asanza et al. (2024)
Confidence and Communication Skills	Peer teaching and collaborative activities strengthened student confidence, enhanced articulation, and promoted clarity of thought through feedback loops.	22	Mezirow (2000); Taylor (2009); Wenger-Trayner et al. (2023); Guaman Quintanilla et al. (2022); Cheng (2025)
Cross-Cutting Patterns in Student Experience	Student feedback revealed recurring themes of inclusion, autonomy, enjoyment, and reflective learning, highlighting the holistic value of experiential pedagogy.	20	Lave & Wenger (1991); Sudirman et al. (2024); Gamage et al. (2025)

FINDINGS

The thematic analysis of selected studies revealed four interrelated areas of impact from gamification and LEGO-based strategies in higher education. These findings confirm their potential to foster engagement, creativity, confidence, and inclusion, but also highlight limitations that arise when such interventions are deployed in under-resourced Global South contexts. While learner experiences frequently reflected enhanced motivation and deeper critical engagement, the analysis also surfaces structural constraints such as overcrowded classrooms, uneven staff capacity, and digital divides. The themes below should be read not as universal successes but as contingent outcomes, dependent on careful alignment of interventions with context-specific challenges.

Enhanced Engagement through Gamification

One of the most prominent themes emerging from the analysis is the ability of gamification to enhance student engagement and motivation. Strategies such as competitive quizzes, digital badges, and point-based games consistently increased learner immersion, attention, and willingness to participate in class activities. These findings align with Csikszentmihalyi's (1990) concept of *flow*, where learners enter a state of heightened focus and intrinsic enjoyment when tasks are designed to balance challenge and skill. Empirical studies also support these outcomes, showing that gamified approaches sustain motivation and reinforce long-term learning behaviours (Hamari et al., 2016; Bhatt & Chakrabarti, 2022). More recently, Muñoz et al. (2023) demonstrated how gamification interventions improved academic persistence in blended learning environments, particularly among students who were previously disengaged.

Despite these gains, the implementation of gamification is not without limitations. A recurring challenge in the Global South is technological disparity: while advanced gamification platforms can integrate seamlessly in high-resource universities, many institutions in low-bandwidth contexts struggle with access to stable digital infrastructure. This creates a risk of reinforcing inequities, where only better-resourced students benefit from the full potential of gamified learning. Moreover, competitive elements, if poorly designed, can demotivate students who consistently underperform, thereby widening performance gaps rather than closing them. Faculty preparedness is another limiting factor; without adequate training, lecturers may reduce gamification to superficial "point-scoring exercises" rather than using it as a deep learning tool.

To overcome these challenges, several studies recommend context-sensitive adaptations. Low-tech gamification strategies, such as the use of flashcards, role-play, or analogue simulations, have proven effective alternatives in resource-constrained classrooms (Tolba & Al-Osaimi, 2023). These approaches preserve the motivational benefits of gamification without over-reliance on costly platforms or high-speed connectivity. Significantly, ensuring that gamification tasks incorporate collaboration, reflection, and critical thinking components can reduce the risk of shallow engagement. Taken together, these insights indicate that gamification has significant potential to transform learning cultures in higher education. However, its sustainability and inclusivity depend on careful contextualisation, ongoing lecturer development, and deliberate design choices that balance competition with collaboration.

Development of Creative and Critical Thinking through LEGO-Based Learning

Another significant finding relates to the role of LEGO-based learning in fostering creativity and critical thinking among students. The tactile and visual nature of LEGO blocks enables learners to externalise abstract ideas and conceptual frameworks, effectively "thinking with their hands" (Tolba & Al-Osaimi, 2023). This active construction process enhances students' ability to analyse, synthesise, and evaluate information which are core elements of higher-order thinking. Vardakosta et al. (2023) highlight that LEGO facilitates visualisation of complex concepts in fields such as engineering, business strategy, and healthcare training, while Simon (2024) demonstrates that structured LEGO Serious Play activities strengthen problem-solving and group-based reflection. These findings resonate with constructivist learning theories, which emphasise knowledge creation through doing and collaboration rather than passive reception.

The analysis also reveals that LEGO-based pedagogies are particularly effective in cultivating creative risk-taking. By encouraging students to test different configurations, fail safely, and rebuild models, the approach promotes resilience and adaptive thinking—competencies that are increasingly valued in the labour market (Asanza et al., 2024). Moreover, LEGO workshops foster inclusivity by appealing to diverse learning styles, accommodating students who may struggle with text-heavy or lecture-based content. This makes LEGO-based learning especially relevant in the Global South, where classrooms are often marked by high heterogeneity in language proficiency, prior knowledge, and socio-economic background.

Nevertheless, several challenges complicate the scalability of LEGO-based interventions. First, access to LEGO materials may be constrained in underfunded institutions, making the approach appear resource-intensive despite its relatively low-tech nature. Second, without adequate facilitator training, sessions can devolve into play without critical learning outcomes, reducing academic credibility. Finally, while LEGO Serious Play has gained popularity, its association with certification and commercial training packages risks limiting adoption in resource-constrained contexts. This creates an unintended barrier to inclusivity, privileging institutions with the means to invest in formalised programs.

To address these challenges, scholars advocate for locally adapted, low-cost alternatives such as using generic building blocks or recycled materials to replicate the tactile and visual affordances of LEGO (Vardakosta et al., 2023). Furthermore, embedding LEGO tasks within a structured reflective framework ensures that activities are not just playful but aligned to curricular objectives and assessment outcomes. When properly contextualised, LEGO-based learning holds strong potential to transform classrooms into dynamic, student-centred environments where creativity, collaboration, and critical inquiry flourish.

Increased Confidence and Communication Skills

A recurring theme across the reviewed literature is the enhancement of student confidence and communication skills through gamification and peer-led learning strategies. Collaborative tasks such as group challenges, peer feedback mechanisms, and reflective discussions provided safe spaces for students to articulate their ideas and refine their ability to communicate clearly (Mezirow, 2000; Taylor, 2009). These approaches align with transformative learning theory, which emphasises the role of dialogue and reflection in fostering personal growth and cognitive development. Wenger-Trayner et al. (2023) further demonstrate that participation in peer teaching communities of practice strengthens students' professional identity formation, equipping them with the communicative competencies necessary for the workplace.

The findings also suggest that confidence-building is not a passive by-product but a direct outcome of experiential interventions. For instance, gamified classroom activities that reward participation encourage previously hesitant students to engage actively, while structured peer coaching creates a supportive environment where students can test their knowledge without fear of failure. In this way, confidence and communication reinforce each other: as learners become more comfortable expressing themselves, they are more likely to engage in critical dialogue, which in turn improves clarity and persuasiveness in communication. Guaman Quintanilla et al. (2022) note that these competencies extend beyond academia, where effective communication is consistently ranked among the most sought-after employability skills by employers.

Despite these benefits, challenges persist in embedding communication-focused strategies systematically across curricula. Some students, particularly those from marginalised or linguistically diverse backgrounds, may initially perceive peer feedback as intimidating rather than supportive, especially in competitive classroom cultures. Additionally, time constraints within already dense curricula may limit opportunities for extended dialogue and reflective exercises, thereby reducing the transformative potential of peer coaching interventions. Another limitation arises when assessment practices remain overly summative, discouraging experimentation and open communication.

To overcome these barriers, researchers advocate for embedding communication skills development into formative assessment practices, ensuring that students view feedback as developmental rather than punitive. Facilitator scaffolding is also essential as educators need training to moderate discussions constructively and sensitively, creating environments where all students feel empowered to contribute.

When adequately resourced and systematically implemented, peer coaching and gamified dialogue activities hold significant potential to enhance both the academic and professional readiness of graduates in diverse higher education contexts.

Themes and Patterns in Student Experiences

Beyond the specific benefits of gamification, LEGO-based learning, and peer coaching, a set of cross-cutting themes emerged from student feedback and observational studies. These patterns, namely inclusion, enjoyment, reflection, and autonomy provide critical insights into how learners experience innovative pedagogies in practice. Students frequently described interventions as enjoyable and engaging, suggesting that fun and play are not peripheral but central to effective learning in higher education (Lave & Wenger, 1991). Enjoyment enhanced persistence and reduced learning fatigue, especially in disciplines traditionally characterised by rote memorisation or abstract theory (Sudirman et al., 2024).

A second recurring thread was inclusion, particularly in diverse classrooms where students reported feeling more connected and valued. Gamified and play-based methods allowed learners of varying academic strengths, learning styles, and cultural backgrounds to participate on more equal footing. This finding aligns with research on Universal Design for Learning (UDL), which advocates for multiple means of engagement and expression to accommodate diversity. In this sense, playful interventions functioned as levelling mechanisms, reducing barriers for neurodiverse or previously marginalised learners.

Reflection was another essential thread, with students identifying structured feedback and post-activity debriefs as opportunities to consolidate learning and link classroom exercises to real-world contexts. This reflective dimension is consistent with experiential learning cycles, where critical thinking emerges through iterative engagement with tasks and subsequent analysis. However, challenges persist: in some cases, students treated reflective exercises as perfunctory rather than transformative, underscoring the need for carefully scaffolded facilitation by educators.

Finally, autonomy featured prominently in student accounts, with learners valuing opportunities to take ownership of their learning. Whether through peer-led sessions, role-play, or self-directed gamified challenges, students highlighted the empowering effect of choosing how to engage with course material. Yet autonomy also carried risks: students who were weaker or less motivated sometimes disengaged when given too much freedom, suggesting that autonomy must be balanced with structured guidance.

These patterns highlight that the impact of gamification and LEGO-based interventions extends beyond discrete skills development. They foster a more holistic learning culture that values participation, inclusivity, and learner agency. However, their success depends on intentional design choices by educators, including how enjoyment is balanced with rigour, how reflection is scaffolded, and how autonomy is supported without leaving some students behind. These insights emphasise that educational innovation in the Global South must be both aspirational and pragmatic in pursuing inclusivity and creativity while remaining sensitive to contextual constraints.

Implications for Practice

The findings of this study demonstrate the considerable potential of innovative pedagogical strategies, notably gamification and LEGO-based tactile learning tools, in effectively developing coaching and peer teaching competencies within higher education contexts. These interactive methods facilitate deeper student engagement, promoting intrinsic motivation, critical thinking, and collaborative problem-solving skills vital for contemporary academic and professional success (Sharma et al., 2024; Krath et al., 2021).

To address challenges related to time management and curricular rigidity, institutions should proactively allocate dedicated time slots for gamified activities and tactile learning sessions within academic calendars, explicitly aligning these activities with learning outcomes and assessment frameworks (Hamilton-Hinch et al., 2023; Mbukanma et al., 2024). Furthermore, adopting flexible spatial settings and creating dedicated innovation or learning labs can significantly enhance student engagement and experiential learning outcomes, thereby challenging the rigidity of traditional classroom configurations and supporting dynamic, interactive experiences (Lee & Saw, 2021; Lambert et al., 2023). As higher education institutions increasingly recognise the critical importance of preparing students for collaborative, adaptive, and leadership-oriented roles, the scalable adoption of gamification and LEGO-based tactile learning approaches emerges as a robust and practically viable strategy. Through intentional curriculum redesign, structured academic training, and strategic resource investment, institutions can leverage these methodologies to foster essential student competencies and ensure sustainable, inclusive, and meaningful educational transformations aligned with contemporary and future workforce demands (UNESCO, 2019; Saro et al., 2024).

Design Thinking: Methodological Integration of Theory and Practice

Design thinking serves as a robust methodological framework for translating contemporary educational theories into practical, learner-centred pedagogical strategies, particularly gamification and LEGO-based learning. It offers an iterative, structured process that operationalises inclusive and motivational principles into tangible educational interventions. Its prototyping and iterative testing phases parallel the cyclical reflection central to Transformative Learning Theory, allowing students to critically engage with new perspectives and reframe their identities through experiential, peer-led activities (Mezirow, 2000; Taylor, 2009). Flow Theory underpins the design of engaging and optimally challenging learning experiences that sustain intrinsic motivation and concentration, particularly through game-based mechanics and tactile, immersive tasks (Csikszentmihalyi & Csikszentmihalyi, 1990; Hamari et al., 2016). Simultaneously, Communities of Practice are cultivated throughout the design process as students collaborate, share knowledge, and co-construct meaning in authentic, socially grounded learning environments (Lave & Wenger, 1991; Wenger-Trayner et al., 2023). In this way, design thinking serves as a methodological bridge that not only integrates theory and practice but also promotes agency, inclusivity, and innovation, particularly within the Global South.

According to Guaman-Quintanilla et al. (2022), when design thinking was applied in higher education in Ecuador as a course that required completion to analyse and solve real-life problems, enhancing student problem-solving skills and creativity, both hypotheses of the study were accepted, reflecting the improved student problem-solving skills and creativity. Similarly, a quantitative study conducted at a University in Switzerland involving 342 students demonstrated that integrating design thinking into higher education curricula significantly develops critical socio-emotional and cognitive competencies that are increasingly demanded in contemporary workplaces (Saro et al., 2024). Students who participated in experimentation, problem reframing, and a learning-oriented mindset as part of design thinking at university subsequently displayed enhanced resilience, collaborative effectiveness, and adaptability (Saro et al., 2024).

The strategies outlined in this research relate directly to design thinking. This research commenced by identifying resource constraints and the limitations of traditional teaching and pedagogical tools prevalent in higher education in the Global South, addressing the "define the problem" phase. The research further extended to empathising and understanding, adopting a human-centred approach that focuses explicitly on diverse learner needs and acknowledges cultural resistance to non-traditional educational methods within the Global South. According to Simon (2024), this approach in Kenya was described as Participatory Design Thinking (PDT), primarily due to its inclusivity, deeper engagement, and innovative solution generation beyond traditional design thinking. PDT places students directly and continuously at the heart of the design process (e.g., peer teaching or analysis of LEGO MINDSTORM models), fostering empathy, amplifying student voices and experiences, and generating deeper student understanding and ownership of solutions compared to passive, recipient-based models (Simon, 2024).

Gamification and LEGO-based learning correspond closely to the solution ideation and prototyping phases in the design thinking process. These pedagogical practices encourage students to explore multiple solutions, reflect collectively, and engage experientially and tangibly with concepts. Strategies such as LEGO-based learning particularly align with design thinking, allowing learners to externalise thoughts through physical prototyping as they build or analyse models, critically assess abstract concepts, and collaborate meaningfully to solve problems (Tolba & Al-Osaimi, 2023; Vardakosta et al., 2023). Applying tactile approaches in the Global South's higher education settings, where written and verbal articulation may be limited due to language barriers, limited access to technology, and inadequate training, enhances accessibility, inclusion, and learner engagement (Asanza et al., 2024). Gamification as a learning tool explicitly links to design thinking by facilitating real-time iteration through feedback loops, rewards, and role-play scenarios, encouraging low-risk experimentation and continuous improvement (Bhatt & Chakrabarti, 2022; Muñoz et al., 2023; Patrício et al., 2020).

Reflective aspects of learning, such as coaching sessions and peer feedback, align with the fourth phase of design thinking: iterative reflection for solution development. This phase involves a cyclical process of testing, reflection, and refinement of solutions (Guaman-Quintanilla et al., 2022). A study at a university in Indonesia found that iterative thinking ensured structured and guided opportunities for students to reflect critically on their learning journey, enhancing or correcting strategies through self-analysis, peer analysis, and constructive collaboration (Sudirman et al., 2024). The tools and strategies in this study explicitly incorporate iterative reflection, closely aligning with the reflective phase of design thinking. Lastly, the learning tools and concepts in this study align with the final design thinking phase—testing solutions. Here, prototypes are evaluated, and real-user feedback refines solutions (Guaman-Quintanilla et al., 2022). PDT's clear emphasis on stakeholder feedback shifts theoretical assessments toward practical, user-focused evaluations that integrate marginalised communities, thus ensuring relevance, ethical grounding, social acceptance, and sustainability in the Global South.

Future Direction for Quality, Open and Flexible Learning in the Global South

This research and its suggestions align directly with the changing future of education in the Global South, where systemic challenges constrain quality learning. Large class sizes limit lecturers' ability to provide personalised feedback, making structured peer teaching and coaching critical for cultivating a culture of shared learning, ownership, and responsibility (Hlatshwayo et al., 2023). Resource constraints often prevent institutions from investing in costly digital infrastructure; low-tech, affordable tools such as LEGO-based activities, role-play, and card games offer a viable pathway to active learning in these contexts. Similarly, reliance on lecture-driven pedagogy contributes to student disengagement, whereas gamified simulations and peer-led workshops foster collaboration, critical thinking, and inclusivity. Collectively, these interventions transform classrooms into safe, engaging spaces for mentorship, reflection, and creativity, aligning with UNESCO's recommendations for equitable and quality education (Awan et al., 2023).

The abovementioned learning tools also facilitate learning outside of the classroom environment to cater for asynchronous learning, given the nature of students in the Global South who have challenges with connectivity and a lack of technology to join classes live, are employed due to commitments and overwhelming expenses but are studying (Hlatshwayo et al., 2023; Walton, 2023). Students can, therefore, engage with bespoke learning tools, such as peer coaching, peer teaching, LEGO-based learning, and gamification, and the feedback mechanisms will assist in providing constructive corrections or suggestive improvements, ensuring flexibility in learning and inclusivity under tight resource constraints. The future trajectory of higher education in the Global South, characterised by growing enrolment demands, limited resources, and increasing calls for inclusive, flexible, and quality learning, necessitates pedagogical innovation and adaptive frameworks. As identified, traditional teaching methods alone cannot adequately address these systemic educational constraints, nor can they sufficiently engage and prepare students for the multifaceted demands of contemporary professional environments. The insights from this study underscore that innovative educational practices, specifically gamification, LEGO-based learning, peer teaching, and coaching, are not merely supplemental but essential components of future-focused education strategies.

Institutions must, therefore, move decisively from theoretical discussions and exploratory phases towards systematic integration and institutionalisation of these evidence-supported practices. To realise the transformative potential highlighted in the previous section, there must be deliberate, structured interventions aligned with clearly defined goals and supported by robust governance frameworks. This requires practical measures, targeted resources, and sustained capacity-building initiatives that support educators, engage students effectively, and ensure scalability and sustainability. In bridging the identified future directions with the realities of current institutional challenges, this study presents actionable implications and recommendations. The recommendations that follow are strategically aligned with practical implementation frameworks, grounded in the empirical evidence and theoretical foundations explored earlier. These recommendations address critical leverage points, including policy reform, curriculum integration, academic training, technological enhancement, community engagement, and evaluative processes, necessary for fostering scalable, inclusive, and impactful peer teaching and coaching ecosystems.

By adopting and operationalising these evidence-informed recommendations, higher education institutions in the Global South can create dynamic, inclusive, and learner-centred environments that not only respond proactively to current educational challenges but also anticipate future demands, preparing students comprehensively for academic, personal, and professional success. These implications highlight the necessity for higher education institutions to embed innovative, learner-centred strategies within both curriculum design and institutional structures. To translate these insights into sustainable transformation, practical recommendations are required. The following section outlines specific strategies for implementation, grounded in the empirical findings and theoretical frameworks of this study.

RECOMMENDATIONS

Building on the implications outlined above, it is evident that innovative pedagogies such as gamification, LEGO-based learning, and structured peer teaching cannot remain peripheral enhancements within higher education. Instead, they must be strategically embedded into institutional frameworks to overcome persistent barriers such as curricular rigidity, resource constraints, and limited faculty preparedness. The following recommendations are designed to translate these implications into actionable strategies. Each recommendation directly addresses an identified challenge while advancing the broader goal of fostering inclusive, engaging, and employability-focused learning environments in the Global South.

Systematically Embed Gamification to Address Engagement Gaps

As highlighted in the implications for practice, gamification enhances motivation but risks being treated as a one-off add-on rather than a core learning tool. To overcome this, higher education institutions should systematically embed gamification into curricula. Scenario-based simulations, competitive challenges, and point-based leaderboards should be linked directly to learning outcomes and assessment frameworks (Krath et al., 2021; Sharma et al., 2024). In low-bandwidth settings, scalable tools such as Kahoot or Quizizz can be used, while physical role-plays and card-based activities provide inclusive, low-tech alternatives (Hamari et al., 2016). This ensures sustained engagement across diverse learning environments.

Employ LEGO-Based Learning to Mitigate Barriers to Creativity and Abstraction

The implications section noted that traditional classroom structures limit opportunities for tactile, collaborative learning. To counter this, institutions should formalise LEGO-based learning as a structured pedagogical strategy in courses that demand abstract reasoning, creativity, and problem-solving. LEGO Serious Play, when paired with reflective debriefs, enables students to externalise and visualise complex ideas, fostering both individual creativity and group collaboration (Vardakosta et al., 2023; Culpepper & Gauntlett, 2024). Tailored toolkits and staff training can help contextualise activities for discipline-specific learning outcomes while addressing cultural resistance to non-traditional methods.

Develop Targeted Faculty Training to Overcome Pedagogical Inertia

The findings underscored that innovative pedagogies often fail due to a lack of lecturer confidence and institutional buy-in. Institutions should therefore invest in structured professional development programmes focused on experiential facilitation, gamified instructional design, and inclusive coaching principles (Hamilton-Hinch et al., 2023). Embedding digital micro-credentials in gamification and tactile learning skills can incentivise adoption, ensure coherence across departments, and provide formal recognition of pedagogical innovation (Topping, 2005).

Allocate Dedicated Time, Flexible Spaces, and Resources to Address Structural Constraints

Curricular rigidity and resource limitations emerged as recurring barriers in the implications. To overcome these, institutions must explicitly allocate time, flexible space, and budget for gamified and tactile learning activities. Timetabling should include extended coaching and gamified sessions, while learning labs and collaborative classroom layouts should support experimentation (Muñoz et al., 2023). Even in resource-constrained contexts, pilot programmes can model cost-effective pathways for scaling, ensuring sustainability.

Institutionalise Reflection and Peer Feedback to Enhance Coaching Mindsets

The implications highlighted the need to deepen student agency through reflective practice. Institutions should therefore embed structured reflection and peer feedback as core elements of pedagogy. Models such as Gibbs' Reflective Cycle or Brookfield's Critical Incident Questionnaire can scaffold student reflection (Mezirow, 2000; Taylor, 2009). Peer evaluations and coaching debriefs create accountability and mutual learning, while lecturer facilitation ensures reflection is meaningful rather than superficial.

Forge Industry and Community Partnerships to Ensure Real-World Relevance

Employability emerged as a critical driver in the implications section. To align pedagogy with labour market demands, higher education institutions should establish partnerships with industry, alumni, and community stakeholders. Reciprocal mentorship, internship opportunities, and service-learning projects can situate coaching and facilitation skills in authentic contexts (Tibingana-Ahimbisibwe et al., 2022). These partnerships also ensure that curricula adapt to evolving workforce needs.

Implement Participatory Monitoring and Evaluation to Strengthen Accountability

Finally, the implications stressed the importance of sustainability and inclusivity. Institutions should adopt participatory evaluation frameworks to assess the long-term effectiveness of gamification and LEGO-based learning (Guaman Quintanilla et al., 2022; Sudirman et al., 2024). Key metrics should track student engagement, confidence, employability, and inclusivity, with disaggregated data to capture impacts on underrepresented or neurodiverse learners. Involving students, faculty, and external stakeholders in evaluation fosters responsiveness and continuous improvement.

Table 2. Intervention and Practicalisation Plan: Fostering Coaching and Peer Teaching Skills

Key Area	Strategic Action	Stakeholders	Timeframe	Expected Outcomes
Policy and Governance	Advocate inclusion of coaching and peer teaching in institutional policies aligned with experiential learning and SDGs (Goal 4: Quality Education).	Higher Education Regulatory Bodies, University Leadership, UNESCO	24 months	Institutional buy-in, policy alignment
Curriculum Integration	Embed gamification and LEGO-based activities into accredited modules or electives, aligning clearly with course objectives.	Academic Deans, Curriculum Committees, Accreditation Agencies	12-18 months	Structured experiential curricula, improved skill relevance
Academic Development	Conduct regular training on facilitation techniques, gamified learning methods, and LEGO Serious Play frameworks.	Academic Development Units, Academic Staff	3-6 months (pilot), then annually	Enhanced academic competence, reduced resistance
Technology and Infrastructure	Provide accessible, low-tech and digital platforms for implementing gamification and peer learning, ensuring inclusivity.	IT Departments, Technology Partners	18 months	Greater student participation, equitable learning opportunities
Industry and Community Partnerships	Establish mentorship schemes, internships, and community engagement projects that are explicitly linked to coaching initiatives.	Local Businesses, NGOs, Alumni Networks	12-24 months	Strengthened industry connections, enhanced employability
Monitoring and Evaluation	Implement participatory evaluation methods, reflective assessments, and longitudinal research studies.	Researchers, Quality Assurance Teams, Assessment Bodies	Ongoing, Review Annually	Data-informed continuous improvement, enhanced sustainability
Scalability and Sustainability	Develop scalable pilot models, share open-access materials, implement Train-the-Trainer initiatives.	University Exco, Alumni Community, Academics	18-36 months	Long-term program viability, reduced external dependency

The following example programs and activities illustrate how higher education institutions can operationalise gamification, LEGO-based learning, and peer coaching strategies in practice. These initiatives are designed with scalability, inclusivity, and employability outcomes in mind, particularly for the Global South, where resource constraints demand flexible and context-sensitive approaches.

Table 3. Example Programs and Activities

Program/Activity	Description & Implementation Steps	Challenges	Solutions	Expected Outcomes
Peer Coaching Circles	Establish senior-to-junior mentoring groups (4–6 students). Regular meetings structured around goal setting, problem-solving, and reflective practices using gamified scenarios.	Low student participation and inconsistent meeting attendance.	Use digital scheduling tools, incentivise with recognition/badges, and allocate staff mentors to monitor engagement.	Improved academic outcomes, enhanced leadership, stronger peer networks.
Industry Mentorship Integration	Pair industry experts with student peer-teachers. Integrate LEGO-based simulations reflecting authentic workplace challenges.	Securing consistent industry participation and alignment with academic timetables.	Leverage alumni networks and CSR programmes; align mentorship projects with industry-specific needs.	Practical industry skills, enhanced employability, career insights.
Digital Knowledge Sharing Platforms	Create low-cost online platforms (Moodle, Google Classroom) for virtual peer teaching, gamified feedback, and resource sharing.	Digital divide (low connectivity, limited devices) hinders inclusivity.	Develop offline/low-bandwidth features; provide downloadable resources; allow blended (online + offline) access.	Greater accessibility, increased student engagement, self-directed learning.
Annual Peer Teaching Conference	Organise student-led events showcasing case studies, research, and gamified/LEGO-based teaching methodologies. Offer academic credits or awards.	High resource demands (logistics, funding, time).	Begin with department-level pilot events; secure sponsorship from industry and professional bodies.	Recognition of peer teaching excellence, motivation, innovation sharing.
Cross-Disciplinary Collaborative Projects	Form interdisciplinary teams to engage in coaching and peer teaching tasks using LEGO and gamification.	Institutional silos discourage collaboration across faculties.	Establish cross-faculty committees; introduce shared credits or assessment for joint projects.	Interdisciplinary collaboration, enhanced problem-solving skills
Gamified Peer Teaching Challenges	Run competitive scenarios (leaderboards, badges, points, Kahoot/Quizizz quizzes) integrated into curricula.	Risk of overemphasis on competition creating stress or exclusion	Design challenges with both collaborative and competitive elements; integrate reflective debriefs.	Higher motivation, dynamic and inclusive learning environment.

Practicalisation Notes for Higher Education Institutions

Employability Alignment: Design programs explicitly linked to industry-relevant competencies. Use coaching scenarios, gamified role-plays, and LEGO-based simulations that mirror workplace challenges.

Interdisciplinary Integration: Encourage collaboration across departments by embedding joint projects into curricula. Shared credits or assessment weightings can reduce siloed approaches and incentivise cross-disciplinary engagement.

Incentives for Participation: Recognise student and staff contributions formally. Credits, badges, or micro-credentials tied to innovative pedagogy signal institutional commitment and motivate sustained involvement.

Scalable Rollout: Pilot interventions in select courses or faculties. Use data-driven evaluation to refine approaches before expanding institution-wide, ensuring cost-effectiveness and adaptability.

Inclusive Access: Address resource and connectivity gaps by designing low-tech, blended alternatives alongside digital tools. This ensures equity across diverse student populations in the Global South.

CONCLUSION

This study has highlighted the transformative potential of gamification, LEGO-based learning, coaching, and peer teaching in addressing persistent challenges within higher education in the Global South. These approaches not only enhance student engagement and creativity but also develop critical employability skills such as problem-solving, leadership, and adaptability. Importantly, the evidence demonstrates that low-cost, scalable, and inclusive interventions can serve as practical alternatives to technology-heavy solutions, which remain inaccessible in many resource-constrained contexts.

At the same time, the findings underline that meaningful integration requires overcoming structural barriers. Institutional inertia, rigid curricula, and limited training opportunities for academics often impede innovation. Without deliberate alignment of these pedagogies to curricula, recognition systems, and resource allocation, such interventions risk remaining fragmented or unsustainable. The practical roadmap outlined in this study focused on employability alignment, interdisciplinary integration, incentivisation, scalable rollouts, and inclusive access—offers a realistic framework for institutions to bridge these gaps.

For the Global South, the stakes are particularly high. Expanding student enrolments, increasing demands for work-ready graduates, and ongoing equity concerns necessitate bold pedagogical redesign. By embedding gamified and tactile strategies into mainstream curricula and creating supportive ecosystems for peer-led learning, institutions can shift from theoretical aspiration to measurable impact. The challenge lies not in proving their effectiveness—evidence from this study and related literature is clear—but in institutionalising these practices through policy reform, professional development, and participatory evaluation.

Ultimately, the future of higher education in the Global South depends on moving beyond traditional didactic methods toward dynamic, inclusive, and employability-focused models. Gamification, LEGO-based learning, and structured peer teaching are not peripheral innovations; they are essential strategies for preparing students to thrive in complex and uncertain professional environments. If implemented with foresight and commitment, these interventions can play a pivotal role in reshaping higher education into a more equitable, relevant, and resilient system.

LIMITATIONS AND FUTURE RESEARCH

While this study offers important insights into the value of gamification, LEGO-based learning, and peer teaching in higher education, several limitations must be acknowledged. First, the review relied primarily on secondary sources, meaning that findings are shaped by the availability and quality of existing literature rather than direct empirical data. Although efforts were made to ensure rigour through systematic screening and thematic analysis, the absence of primary, longitudinal evidence limits the ability to capture the sustained impact of these interventions over time.

Second, while the study highlights low-cost, scalable strategies suitable for Global South contexts, implementation challenges such as institutional resistance, uneven digital access, and limited staff training remain underexplored. These contextual nuances suggest that success may vary significantly across institutions, depending on governance structures, policy alignment, and resource availability.

Future research should therefore prioritise longitudinal and mixed-methods studies that track the long-term effectiveness of gamification and LEGO-based strategies on student employability, resilience, and career trajectories. Comparative research across Global South regions could further illuminate how cultural, institutional, and resource-specific factors shape implementation. Additionally, studies that examine digital micro-credentials, mobile-first gamification, and the integration of these pedagogies in hybrid or low-bandwidth learning environments will provide much-needed insights for scalability and inclusivity. Finally, participatory research involving students and academics as co-designers of interventions can enhance contextual fit and sustainability, ensuring these innovations are not only theoretically sound but also practically embedded within higher education systems.

REFERENCES

Adeyemi, I. O., Esan, A. O., & Aleem, A. (2021). Application of gamification to library services: Awareness, perception, and readiness of academic librarians in Nigeria. *The Electronic Library*, *39*(5), 767–781. Retrieved March 31, 2025, from. DOI: 10.1108/EL-05-2021-0096

Aguilar-Ferrándiz, M. E., Toledano-Moreno, S., Casas-Barragán, A., Albornoz-Cabello, M., Tapia-Haro, R., & Correa-Rodríguez, M. (2024). Implementation of a coaching training for enhancing empathy and emotional intelligence skills in health science students: A prospective study. *BMC Medical Education*, *24*(76), 2–9. Retrieved April 01, 2025, from. DOI: 10.1186/s12909-024-05076-z

Ahsan, K., Akbar, S., Kam, B., & Abdulrahman, M. D. A. (2023). Implementation of micro-credentials in higher education: A systematic literature review. *Education and Information Technologies*, *28*(10), 13505–13540. DOI: 10.1007/s10639-023-11739-z

Ambani Africa. (2024). AMBANI. [Accessed 12 May, 2025] https://www.ambaniafrica.com/copy-of-about

Andreanoff, J. (2016). The Impact of Peer Coaching on the Academic Performance of Undergraduate Students: A Mixed Methods Study. *Journal of Learning Development in Higher Education Special Edition*, *1-5*(2). Advance online publication. Retrieved April 23, 2025, from. DOI: 10.47408/jldhe.v0i0.358

Asanza, T. E. P., Asanza, M. V. P., Martínez, M. A. M., & García, F. A. R. (2024). Gamification as a Didactic Motivator in Low-Resource Public English as a Foreign Language (EFL) Classrooms in Ecuador. *Ciencia Latina Education*, *8*(2), 5393–5399. Retrieved May 05, 2025, from. DOI: 10.37811/cl_rcm.v8i2.10951

Awan, S., Anthony, N., & Shahbaz, K. (2023). Inclusive and Equitable Quality Education: The Context of Constitution of Pakistan and International Commitments. *Voyage Journal of Educational Studies (VJES) 3*(1), 88-89. [Accessed 23 April, 2025] https://vjes.voyageams.com/index.php/vjes/article/download/28/26

Bengesai, A. V., Amusa, L. B., & Dhunpath, R. (2023). A meta-analysis on the effect of formal peer learning approaches on course performance in higher education. *Cogent Education*, *10*(1), 2203990. DOI: 10.1080/2331186X.2023.2203990

Bhatt, N., & Chakrabarti, A. (2022). Gamification of design thinking: A way to enhance effectiveness of learning. *Artificial Intelligence for Engineering Design, Analysis and Manufacturing*, *36*(29). Advance online publication. Retrieved April 07, 2025, from. DOI: 10.1017/S0890060422000154

Böhm-Fischer, A., & Beyer, L. (2024). Blended Learning, Flipped Classroom, and Peer Teaching as a Combination to Meet the Increasing Diversity in Higher Education. *International Journal of Information and Education Technology (IJIET), 14*(2), 310–314. Retrieved April 01, 2025, from. DOI: 10.18178/ijiet.2024.14.2.2053

Cheng, J., Lu, C., & Xiao, Q. (2025). Effects of gamification on EFL learning: A quasi-experimental study of reading proficiency and language enjoyment among Chinese undergraduates. *Frontiers in Psychology, 16*, 1448916.

Csikszentmihalyi, M., & Csikzentmihaly, M. (1990). *Flow: The psychology of optimal experience* (Vol. 1990). Harper & Row.

Culpepper, M. K., & Gauntlett, D. (2024). The construction of everyday creative identity. *Journal of Creativity, 34*(2), 100085. Retrieved January 05, 2025, from. DOI: 10.1016/j.yjoc.2024.100085

de Caux, B. C., & Pretorius, L. (2024). Learning together through collaborative writing: The power of peer feedback and discussion in doctoral writing groups. *Studies in Educational Evaluation, 83*, 101379. DOI: 10.1016/j.stueduc.2024.101379

Diaz, A. F., & Estoque-Loñez, H. (2024). A Meta-Analysis on the Effectiveness of Gamification on Student Learning Achievement. *International Journal of Education in Mathematics. Science and Technology, 12*(5), 1236–1253.

Dichev, C., & Dicheva, D. (2017). Gamifying education: what is known, what is believed and what remains uncertain: a critical review. *International Journal of Educational Technology in Higher Education, 14*(9). Advance online publication. DOI: 10.1186/s41239-017-0042-5

Duterte, J. P. (2024). The Impact of Educational Gamification on Student Learning Outcomes. [IJRISS]. *International Journal of Research and Innovation in Social Science, 8*(10), 481–482. Retrieved May 12, 2025, from. DOI: 10.47772/IJRISS.2024.8100040

Etomes, E. S., & Nsem, M. C. (2023). Strategies for Improving Teachers' Professional Development in Higher Education Institutions in the Southwest Region of Cameroon. *Cultivating International Connections Through Education, 49*(2), 6–10. Retrieved April 03, 2025, from. DOI: 10.4148/0146-9282.2366

Fransiska, F. W. (2024). Game On! Teaching English with Fun and Creativity: Gamification Implementation in Remote Rural Areas (Sukaraja Village, South Lampung). *Jurnal Pengabdian Masyarakat, 1*(1), 40–46. Retrieved February 21, 2025, from. DOI: 10.62207/vwastn89

Gamage, K. A., & Dehideniya, S. C. (2025). Unlocking Career Potential: How Micro-Credentials Are Revolutionising Higher Education and Lifelong Learning. *Education Sciences*, *15*(5), 525.

Garvey, R., Garvey, B., & Stokes, P. (2021). *Coaching and mentoring: Theory and practice* (4th ed.). Sage.

Gordillo, A., López-Fernández, D., & Mayor, J. (2024). Examining and Comparing the Effectiveness of Virtual Reality Serious Games and LEGO Serious Play for Learning Scrum. *Applied Sciences (Basel, Switzerland)*, *14*(2), 830. Retrieved February 21, 2025, from. DOI: 10.3390/app14020830

Guerrero-Alcedo, J. M., Espina-Romero, L. C., & Nava-Chirinos, A. A. (2022). Gamification in the University Context: Bibliometric Review in Scopus (2012-2022). *International Journal of Learning. Teaching and Educational Research*, *21*(5), 311–134. Retrieved May 01, 2025, from. DOI: 10.26803/ijlter.21.5.16

Hamari, J., Shernoff, D. J., Rowe, E., Coller, B., Asbell-Clarke, J., & Edwards, T. (2016). Challenging games help students learn: An empirical study on engagement, flow and immersion in game-based learning. *Computers in Human Behavior*, *54*, 170–179. DOI: 10.1016/j.chb.2015.07.045

Hamilton-Hinch, B. A., Stilwell, C., Manuel, C., Hutchinson, S., Woodford, K. & Ellis, A. (2023). Peer Assisted Learning: What Can Students Teach Us and Each Other?. *SCHOLE: A Journal of Leisure Studies and Recreation Education, 38*(3), 161-174. [Accessed 07 March, 2025] https://doi.org/DOI: 10.1080/1937156X.2021.1969527

Hlatshwayo, M. N., Zondi, T., & Mokoena, T. (2023). It gives me anxiety! Black Academics' experiences of teaching large classes during the Covid-19 pandemic in a South African university. *Perspectives in Education*, *41*(2). Advance online publication. Retrieved April 23, 2025, from. DOI: 10.38140/pie.v41i2.6837

Hu, Z., & Razlog, R. (2023). The use of game-based learning to enhance student engagement in the acupuncture programme: South African students' opinions. *Journal for the Education of Gifted Young Scientists*, *11*(2), 137–152. Retrieved April 10, 2025, from. DOI: 10.17478/jegys.1277401

Irwanto, I., Wahyudiati, D., Saputro, A. D., & Laksana, S. D. (2023). Research Trends and Applications of Gamification in Higher Education: A Bibliometric Analysis Spanning 2013–2022. *International Journal of Emerging Technologies in Learning*, *18*(5), 3–7. Retrieved May 01, 2025, from. DOI: 10.3991/ijet.v18i05.37021

James, W., Oates, G., & Schonfeldt, N. (2024). Improving retention while enhancing student engagement and learning outcomes using gamified mobile technology. *Accounting Education*, •••, 1–21. Retrieved March 12, 2025, from. DOI: 10.1080/09639284.2024.2326009

Jaramillo-Mediavilla, L., Basantes-Andrade, A., Cabezas-González, M., & Casillas-Martín, S. (2024). Impact of gamification on motivation and academic performance: A systematic review. *Education Sciences*, *14*(6), 639.

Jiméneza, I. A. C., Gonzálezb, J. P. C., & Ruiz, C. E. C. (2021). Developing Systemic Thinking through Gamification with Invention System Kits: Case of an Aircraft Assembly Line. *Academia y Virtualidad*, *14*(1), 27–30. Retrieved May 03, 2025, from. DOI: 10.18359/ravi.4888

Kato, S., Gyorfi, R., & Weko, T. (2023). Micro-credentials for lifelong learning and employability: Uses and possibilities. OECD. https://www.oecd.org/content/dam/oecd/en/publications/reports/2023/03/micro-credentials-for-lifelong-learning-and-employability_13dd81a9/9c4b7b68-en.pdf

Khapre, M., Deol, R., Sharma, A., Badyal, D., & Badyal, D. K. (2021). Near-peer tutor: A solution for quality medical education in faculty constraint setting. *Cureus*, *13*(7). Advance online publication. DOI: 10.7759/cureus.16416

Krath, J., Schürmann, L., & Von Korflesch, H. F. (2021). Revealing the theoretical basis of gamification: A systematic review and analysis of theory in research on gamification, serious games and game-based learning. *Computers in Human Behavior*, *125*, 106963. Retrieved March 22, 2025, from. DOI: 10.1016/j.chb.2021.106963

Kristiansen, P., & Rasmussen, R. (2014). *Building a better business using the Lego serious play method*. John Wiley & Sons.

Lambert, N. J., Xiaoting, L., & Akinyo, O. (2023). Knowing Me, Knowing You: Self-Reflection and Understanding Diversity for Effective Teamwork—A LEGO® Building Activity. *Management Teaching Review*, *10*(1), 24–26. Retrieved April 16, 2025, from. DOI: 10.1177/23792981231119058

Latifi, S., Noroozi, O., & Talaee, E. (2021). Peer feedback or peer feedforward? Enhancing students' argumentative peer learning processes and outcomes. *British Journal of Educational Technology*, *52*(2), 768–784. Retrieved March 22, 2025, from. DOI: 10.1111/bjet.13054

Lave, J., & Wenger, E. (1991). *Situated learning: Legitimate peripheral participation*. Cambridge University Press.

Lee, S. W. H., & Saw, P. S. (2021). The Use of Building Blocks to Teach Communication and Social Skills to First-year Pharmacy Students. *American Journal of Pharmaceutical Education*, *85*(8), 5–7. Retrieved April 20, 2025, from. DOI: 10.5688/ajpe8464

LEGO Education. (2024). MINDSTORMS. [Accessed 31 March, 2025] https://www.prnewswire.com/news-releases/lego-education-report-examines-the-state-of-classroom-engagement-302237279.html

Li, L., Hew, K. F., & Du, J. (2024). Gamification enhances student intrinsic motivation, perceptions of autonomy and relatedness, but minimal impact on competency: A meta-analysis and systematic review. *Educational Technology Research and Development*, *72*(2), 765–796. DOI: 10.1007/s11423-023-10337-7

Long, H. A., French, D. P., & Brooks, J. M. (2020). Optimising the value of the critical appraisal skills programme (CASP) tool for quality appraisal in qualitative evidence synthesis. *Research Methods in Medicine & Health Sciences*, *1*(1), 31–42. Retrieved March 31, 2025, from. DOI: 10.1177/2632084320947559

Lugaresi, G., Frigerio, N., & Matta, A. (2020). A New Learning Factory Experience Exploiting LEGO For Teaching Manufacturing Systems Integration. *Procedia Manufacturing*, *45*, 271–276. Retrieved May 02, 2025, from. DOI: 10.1016/j.promfg.2020.04.106

Manda, S. (2024). Ambani takes African languages digital. [Accessed 12 May, 2025] https://www.vukuzenzele.gov.za/ambani-takes-african-languages-digital

Maryani, I., Suyatno, S., Arfiani, I., Nizaar, M., Astuti, I. A. D., & Sulisworo, D. (2025). Gamified Mobile-Based Learning Approach: Efforts to Improve Students' Engagement and Learning Quality in Remote Schools in Indonesia. *Educational Process: International Journal*, *15*, e2025179. DOI: 10.22521/edupij.2025.15.179

Mavutha, W., & Mansingh, A. R. (2024). Online Education Adaptability for South African Learners with Dyscalculia and Dyslexia using Digital Learning Methods. *Chinese Sociological Review*, *19*(1), 51–80.

Mbukanma, I., Manganyi, M., & Vellem, B. & Neliswa Gqoli. (2024). Unlocking Potential: The Transformative Role of Gaming in Rural Higher Learning Institutions of South Africa - A Systematic Exploration. *Research in Social Sciences and Technology*, *9*(3), 141–143. Retrieved May 01, 2025, from. DOI: 10.46303/ressat.2024.52

Mezirow, J. (2000). *Learning as Transformation: Critical Perspectives on a Theory in Progress. The Jossey-Bass Higher and Adult Education Series*. Jossey-Bass Publishers, 350 Sansome Way, San Francisco, CA 94104.

Moonsamy, M., Nkomo, S., & Matli, W. (2022). New Education Technologies in Higher Education: E-Leadership Perspectives on South African Student Learning During and Post-Covid Reality. *International Conference on Multidisciplinary Research 2022*(20), 241-249. [Accessed 07 May, 2025] https://doi.org/DOI: 10.26803/MyRes.2022.20

Mouratoglou, N. (2018). LEGO®, Learning, And Facilitation: A Reflective Approach. *International Journal of Management and Applied Research, 5*(4). Advance online publication. Retrieved April 07, 2025, from. DOI: 10.18646/2056.54.18-021

Muñoz, C. B., Nanclares, N. H., Zamorano, L. R. M., & Sánchez, J. A. L. (2023). *Gamification and Design Thinking in Higher Education Case Studies for Instructional Innovation in the Economics Classroom* (1st ed.). Routledge Taylor Francis Group.

Nofemela, F. R., & Winberg, C. (2020). The relevance of Kaizen-based work-readiness training for South African University of Technology students. *The Journal for Transdisciplinary Research in Southern Africa, 16*(1), 1–2. Retrieved April 23, 2025, from. DOI: 10.4102/td.v16i1.729

Nupen, D. M., & Jagernath, J. (2024). Digital Integration Insights: Exploring Highlights and Challenges of Numeracy Lecturers in Higher Education. *International Conference on Education Research 1(*1):254-262. [Accessed 23 April, 2025] https://doi.org/DOI: 10.34190/icer.1.1.2834

Nwosu, L. I., Berengb, M. C., Segotsoa, T., & Blessing, E. N. (2023). Fourth Industrial Revolution Tools to Enhance the Growth and Development of Teaching and Learning in Higher Education Institutions: A Systematic Literature Review in South Africa. *Research in Social Sciences and Technology, 8*(1), 57–59. Retrieved May 02, 2025, from. DOI: 10.46303/ressat.2023.4

Oreopoulos, P., & Petronijevic, U. (2023). The Promises and Pitfalls of Using (Mostly) Low-Touch Coaching Interventions to Improve College Student Outcomes. *Economic Journal (London), 133*(656), 7–15. Retrieved April 24, 2025, from. DOI: 10.1093/ej/uead064

Oyelere, S. S., Suhonen, J., & Sutinen, E. (2016). M-learning: A new paradigm of learning ICT in Nigeria. *International Journal of Interactive Mobile Technologies, 10*(1). Advance online publication. DOI: 10.3991/ijim.v10i1.4872

Page, M. J., McKenzie, J. E., Bossuyt, P. M., Boutron, I., Hoffmann, T. C., Mulrow, C. D., Shamseer, L., Tetzlaff, J. M., Akl, E. A., Brennan, S. E., & Chou, R. (2021). The PRISMA 2020 statement: An updated guideline for reporting systematic reviews. *British Medical Journal, 372*. Advance online publication. DOI: 10.1136/bmj.n71

Piaget, J. (2005). *The Psychology of Intelligence*. Routledge.

Potgieter, I., Coetzee, M., & Ferreira, N. (2023). University students' digital world of work readiness in relation to their employability competency. *Journal of Learning Development in Higher Education, 27*. Advance online publication. Retrieved April 07, 2025, from. DOI: 10.47408/jldhe.vi27.922

Sareen, S., & Mandal, S. (2024). Challenges of blended learning in higher education across global north-south: A systematic and integrative literature review. *Social Sciences & Humanities Open*, *10*, 1–10. Retrieved March 31, 2025, from. DOI: 10.1016/j.ssaho.2024.101011

Saro, N., Muhiddin, N. I., Anwar, N. S. S., Karim, N. A., & Hisham, N. A. B. (2024). Analysis of Correlation Factors on The Effectiveness of Design Thinking Mindset Reflection. [IJRISS]. *International Journal of Research and Innovation in Social Science*, *8*(3). Advance online publication. Retrieved April 23, 2025, from. DOI: 10.47772/IJRISS.2024.803421S

Shaikh, S. (2024). Peer Teaching for Peer Learning and Sharing: A study on students' attitudes towards implementing peer teaching and learning in the ESL classroom at the University of Technology and Applied Sciences. *International Journal of English Language Teaching*, *15*(5), 9–10. Retrieved April 05, 2025, from. DOI: 10.37745/ijelt.13/vol12n5117

Sharma, W., Lim, W. M., Kumar, S., Verma, A., & Kumra, R. (2024). Game on! A state-of-the-art overview of doing business with gamification. *Technological Forecasting and Social Change*, *198*, 122988. Retrieved May 06, 2025, from. DOI: 10.1016/j.techfore.2023.122988

Shohel, M. M. C., Ashrafuzzaman, M., Azim, F., Naomee, I., Rahman, M. S., & Siddik, M. A. B. (2022). *Blended learning space for primary and secondary education: Challenges and opportunities in resource-constrained contexts. Designing effective distance and blended learning environments in K-12*. IGI Global Scientific Publishing., DOI: 10.4018/978-1-7998-6829-3.ch012

Simon, N. O. (2024). Participatory Design Thinking: A User-Centered Approach to Computer Science Innovation. *European Journal of Information Technologies and Computer Science*, *4*(3). Advance online publication. Retrieved May 10, 2025, from. DOI: 10.24018/compute.2024.4.3.125

Slamet, T., Brush, T., & Kwon, K. (2024). The Effects of Competition in Gamified Online Discussions on Learners' Behavioural and Cognitive Engagement. *Technology. Knowledge and Learning*, *30*, 1–27. Retrieved May 06, 2025, from. DOI: 10.1007/s10758-024-09740-7

Sudirman, A., Gemilang, A. V., Kristanto, T. M. A., Robiasih, H., Hikmah, I., Nugroho, A. D., Karjono, J. C. S., Lestari, T., Widyarini, T. L., & Prastanti, A. D. (2024). Reinforcing Reflective Practice through Reflective Writing in Higher Education: A Systematic Review. *International Journal of Learning. Teaching and Educational Research, 23*(5). Advance online publication. Retrieved April 07, 2025, from. DOI: 10.26803/ijlter.23.5.24

Taylor, E. W. (2009). Fostering transformative learning. In Mezirow, J., & Taylor, E. W. (Eds.), *Transformative learning in practice: Insights from community, workplace, and higher education* (pp. 3–17). Jossey-Bass.

Tibingana-Ahimbisibwe, B., Willis, S., Catherall, S., Butler, F., & Harrison, R. (2022). A systematic review of peer-assisted learning in fully online higher education distance learning programmes. *Open Learning, 37*(3), 251–272. DOI: 10.1080/02680513.2020.1758651

Tolba, E. G. A., & Al-Osaimi, A. M. (2023). The effectiveness of using the model-based thinking strategy in developing first-grade high school students' physical concepts and inquiry thinking skills. *Eurasia Journal of Mathematics, Science and Technology Education, 19*(4), 8–10. Retrieved May 10, 2025, from. DOI: 10.29333/ejmste/13111

Topping, K. J. (2005). Trends in peer learning. *Educational Psychology, 25*(6), 631–645. DOI: 10.1080/01443410500345172

UNESCO. (2019). *Global education monitoring report: Migration, displacement, and education – Building bridges, not walls.* UNESCO. https://www.unesco.org/gem-report/en/migration

UNESCO. (2021). *Reimagining our futures together: A new social contract for education.* UNESCO Publishing. International Commission on the Futures of Education. https://doi.org/ https://unesdoc.unesco.org/ark:/48223/pf0000379707.locale =enDOI: 10.54675/ASRB4722

Vardakosta, E., Priniotakis, G., Papoutsidakis, M., Sigala, M., Tsikritsis, A., & Nikolopoulos, D. (2023). Design Thinking as a Co-Creation Methodology in Higher Education. A Perspective on the Development of Teamwork and Skill Cultivation. *European Journal of Educational Research, 12*(2), 1030–1031. Retrieved April 23, 2025, from. DOI: 10.12973/eu-jer.12.2.1029

Walton, E. (2023). Why inclusive education falters: A Bernsteinian analysis. *International Journal of Inclusive Education, 29*(4). Advance online publication. Retrieved April 23, 2025, from. DOI: 10.1080/13603116.2023.2241045

Wenger-Trayner, E., Wenger-Trayner, B., Reid, P., & Bruderlein, C. (2023). *Communities of practice within and across organisations: a guidebook.* Social Learning Lab. https://www.wenger-trayner.com/wp-content/uploads/2024/03/24-02-21-CoP-guidebook-second-edition-final-2.pdf

Zhang, Y., & Maconochie, M. (2022). A meta-analysis of peer-assisted learning on examination performance in clinical knowledge and skills education. *BMC Medical Education*, *22*(1), 147. DOI: 10.1186/s12909-022-03183-3

Zickafoose, A., Ilesanmi, O., Diaz-Manrique, M., Adeyemi, A. E., Walumbe, B., Strong, R., Wingenbach, G., Rodriguez, M. T., & Dooley, K. (2024). Barriers and Challenges Affecting Quality Education (Sustainable Development Goal #4) in Sub-Saharan Africa by 2030. *Sustainability*, *16*(2657), 5–17. Retrieved April 11, 2025, from. DOI: 10.3390/su16072657

KEY TERMS AND DEFINITIONS

Coaching (in Higher Education Context): Educational strategy that enables students to guide their peers or mentees toward achieving academic and personal goals by fostering self-awareness, promoting problem-solving, and facilitating effective communication (Garvey et al., 2021).

Communities of Practice: Theory that focuses on students' collaboration, sharing of knowledge and the co-construction of meaning in authentic, socially grounded learning environments (Lave & Wenger, 1991; Wenger-Trayner et al., 2023).

Design Thinking: Design thinking serves as a robust methodological framework for translating contemporary educational theories into practical, learner-centred pedagogical strategies. It comprises five stages (Empathise, Define, Ideate, Prototype and Test) and offers an iterative, structured process that operationalises inclusive and motivational principles into tangible educational interventions (Guaman-Quintanilla et al., 2022).

Flow Theory: Theory that underpins the design of engaging and optimally challenging learning experiences that sustain intrinsic motivation and concentration, particularly through game-based mechanics and tactile, immersive tasks (Csikszentmihalyi & Csikszentmihalyi, 1990; Hamari et al., 2016).

Gamification: The application of game design elements in non-game contexts has emerged as a powerful tool to enhance student engagement and motivation (Krath et al., 2021).

LEGO® SERIOUS PLAY®: Learning methodology tool that aims to stimulate creativity and imagination in work and entails a sequential process of steps when using the LEGO blocks, namely, challenge, build, share, and reflect (LEGO Education, 2024; Mouratoglou, 2018).

LEGO-Based Learning: An experiential teaching method that uses LEGO blocks as tools to facilitate problem-solving, teamwork, and creativity. This approach aligns with constructivist learning theories, which hold that learners build knowledge through hands-on experiences and collaboration (Piaget, 2005).

Low-Tech Gamification: Gamification tools that are simpler, more accessible and cost-effective, such as board games and offline activities (Moonsamy et al., 2022; Nwosu et al., 2023).

Participatory Design Thinking (PDT): A learning tool that involves advanced Design Thinking, due to its inclusivity, deeper engagement, and innovative solution generation beyond traditional design thinking (Simon, 2024).

Peer Teaching: Educational strategy that enables students to assume the role of educators, thereby encouraging their knowledge while enriching the learning experiences of their peers (Aguilar-Ferrándiz et al., 2024).

Supplemental Instruction (SI) tools: Tools such as coaching and peer-teaching are used in support of the primary teaching and learning pedagogy to enhance learning, promote equity, foster inclusivity, and empower students (Nupen & Jagernath, 2024).

Tactile Learning: A physical or hands-on approach to education whereby students engage with concepts and materials through movement and touch to enhance their understanding and learning (Topping, 2005).

Transformative Learning Theory: Theory that provides a critical framework for understanding how coaching and peer teaching foster personal growth and cognitive development in students (Mezirow's, 2000).

Chapter 8
Perceptions of ChatGPT-Assisted Writing in the Stages of the Writing Process: An Exploratory Study

Jessica Ruiz Quiñonero
https://orcid.org/0009-0007-6108-8025
University of Murcia, Spain

Aitor Garcés-Manzanera
https://orcid.org/0000-0002-1789-9046
University of Murcia, Spain

ABSTRACT

Artificial intelligence chatbots have recently drawn considerable attention for their potential to revolutionise education systems in myriad ways. Notwithstanding the growing interest in examining the use of chatbots in Foreign Language Teaching (FLT), research on Chatbot-Assisted Writing remains scarce. This study explores how 16 first-year upper secondary students from a Spanish high school interact with ChatGPT while writing an argumentative essay. Specifically, it gathers perceptions about the impact of this tool on the main stages of the Writing Process, namely Planning, Translating, and Reviewing. For this purpose, data on students' interactions with the tool, written essays, and responses to two different questionnaires were collected. Findings revealed that students predominantly used the chatbot

DOI: 10.4018/979-8-3373-9225-7.ch008

for Planning, particularly when they lacked ideas or arguments. Consequently, their overall perceptions after completing the Chatbot-Assisted Writing Task were remarkably positive, suggesting that learners value their use in education and FLT.

INTRODUCTION

Recent advances in artificial intelligence have opened new avenues in education, particularly in supporting writing skills among language learners. ChatGPT, a conversational tool developed by OpenAI, has attracted significant attention for its ability to offer immediate feedback and guidance (Lo, 2023; Murphy et al., 2023). Through vocabulary suggestions, illustrative examples, and alternative perspectives, ChatGPT has the potential to enrich language instruction and promote more effective learning strategies (Huang & Li, 2023). In foreign language teaching, its capacity for real-time interaction enables learners to practice all four language skills—reading, writing, speaking, and listening—beyond the confines of the traditional classroom (Yan, 2023).

Despite the growing interest in chatbot-assisted learning, research has yet to fully explore the specific contributions of ChatGPT across the different stages of the writing process. While prior studies have generally examined the role of AI in educational contexts (Javier & Moorhouse, 2023; Montenegro-Rueda et al., 2023), the distinct functions of ChatGPT during planning, composing, and reviewing have not been sufficiently addressed. This gap is notable given the importance of each stage in developing coherent and well-structured written texts, as described in classical writing models (Hayes & Flower, 1980).

In this study, we investigate students' perceptions of ChatGPT as they engage with the three phases of the writing process: planning, composing, and reviewing. Our research seeks to clarify how the tool supports idea generation, facilitates language formulation, and aids in the refinement of text. By examining the experiences of language learners, the study aims to contribute to a more detailed understanding of how AI tools can be integrated into foreign language writing instruction to improve both process and product.

The findings of this research are expected to inform pedagogical practices and provide a framework for effectively incorporating ChatGPT into language classrooms. In what follows, we outline the background and rationale for the study, positioning our approach within the broader context of AI-supported education.

ARTIFICIAL INTELLIGENCE AND ITS IMPACT ON EDUCATION

Artificial intelligence (AI) is reshaping education by modifying traditional teaching methods and learning experiences. AI-driven technologies, particularly chatbots like ChatGPT, enhance student engagement and personalize instruction (Adiguzel et al., 2023). These systems analyze large datasets, tailor content to individual needs, and provide instant feedback, making learning more accessible and efficient. ChatGPT, one of the most advanced AI-powered conversational tools, offers real-time support to help students understand complex concepts, generate ideas, and refine their work (Rathod, 2023).

While AI streamlines certain tasks, it does not replace teachers. Educators remain central to learning due to their role in fostering critical thinking, creativity, and interpersonal engagement (García-Peñalvo, 2023). AI often handles routine tasks, such as grading or providing basic feedback, allowing teachers to focus on mentoring and higher-order instruction (Zayoud et al., 2023).

Despite its benefits, integrating AI into education presents challenges. Concerns about data privacy, ethics, and misinformation require careful oversight (Bit et al., 2024). Initially, some schools banned ChatGPT over fears of cheating and unreliable information. However, institutions and policymakers are shifting from outright bans to establishing ethical guidelines, recognizing AI's potential when used appropriately (Patel et al., 2023; UNESCO, 2023). Some schools have reversed initial restrictions, integrating AI with proper oversight. As AI evolves, students must develop skills to critically evaluate AI-generated content and use these tools responsibly (Karan & Bakina, 2024).

AI can complement rather than replace traditional teaching by supporting personalized instruction while preserving the human aspects of education, such as reasoning and meaningful interaction. A balanced approach—using AI's strengths while addressing risks through digital literacy and clear policies—guarantees responsible integration (Banks, 2023).

THE VALUE OF CHATGPT IN L2 LEARNING

Among AI applications in education, ChatGPT's role in foreign language teaching (FLT) stands out. As a conversational agent capable of generating fluent text, it provides rich linguistic input and interactive practice, which can improve learner engagement and motivation (Huang et al., 2022; Irzawati et al., 2024). ChatGPT offers extensive examples and resources on demand, including lists of expressions, model texts across genres, grammar explanations, and vocabulary suggestions—materials that may not always be available from human instructors (Huang et al., 2022).

In FLT, ChatGPT can support all four core language skills: listening (through AI-generated audio or dialogues), reading (via level-appropriate texts), speaking (through interactive prompts and role-plays; e.g., Stampfl et al., 2024), and writing (by assisting with composition and revision; Zhang et al., 2023). Writing has drawn particular attention in recent research, giving rise to the concept of *chatbot-assisted writing*, which refers to the use of AI chatbots at different stages of the writing process.

Studies highlight ChatGPT's role as a collaborative writing assistant that provides targeted feedback, suggests improvements, and enhances text quality (Teng, 2024). It can identify complex grammatical and syntactical errors, propose structural adjustments, and improve coherence. These functions are especially valuable in EFL contexts, where students often struggle with self-expression and accuracy. By handling repetitive tasks such as grammar checks and rephrasing, ChatGPT allows learners to focus on more complex aspects of writing (Teng, 2024). This support can improve time management and productivity.

Beyond assisting students, ChatGPT can complement teacher feedback in L2 writing instruction. Research suggests that AI-generated feedback covers content, organization, and language use in greater volume than a single instructor can provide (Guo et al., 2022). For example, Guo et al. (2022) found that ChatGPT helped students develop argumentative writing by prompting elaboration and structuring their essays, effectively acting as a supplementary tutor. Additionally, it can generate personalized recommendations and practice exercises (Zadorozhnyy & Lai, 2024), reinforcing its instructional value.

An important secondary effect of using ChatGPT in language learning is the development of AI literacy. Engaging with AI encourages students to evaluate the reliability of information, refine their prompts, and use AI-generated suggestions appropriately—skills that are increasingly relevant in education (Teng, 2024; Kang & Yi, 2023). For instance, ChatGPT can function as a reformulation tool, similar to dedicated rewriting applications like Wordtune, providing alternative phrasings to help students overcome writer's block or refine their work (Zhao et al., 2024). Other documented benefits include improved clarity and cohesion. Many EFL learners use AI tools for editing, and ChatGPT's ability to produce texts in different genres and adjust output complexity makes it a versatile aid (Allen & Mizumoto, 2024). It can also assist beyond the classroom, generating practice questions and model answers for standardized tests (TOEFL, IELTS) or simulating job interview Q&A for speaking practice.

Despite these advantages, gaps remain in understanding ChatGPT's impact across specific stages of the writing process—*planning, translating, and reviewing* (Hayes & Flower, 1980). Most research has focused on its overall influence on writing quality and student motivation (Raheem et al., 2023; Yildiz, 2023), with generally positive findings. However, less is known about how these benefits vary across writing stages. Do students rely on ChatGPT more for brainstorming, drafting, or revision? This study aims to address that gap by analyzing how ChatGPT supports each phase of writing. A clearer understanding of these patterns will help educators integrate AI tools more effectively into FLT curricula to enhance writing development at every stage.

THE CONCEPT OF CHATBOT-ASSISTED WRITING

Chatbot-Assisted Writing refers to writing tasks in which students use AI chatbot tools, such as ChatGPT, for support, feedback, or content generation. Chatbots simulate human-like interactions, providing learners with immediate access to language resources. For instance, ChatGPT can evaluate grammar, suggest ideas, and assist with revisions at any time, bypassing the constraints of teacher availability. Prior research highlights its effectiveness in facilitating timely revisions and iterative writing practice (Zou & Huang, 2023). Athanassopoulos et al. (2023) demonstrated this in a multi-stage writing task where students drafted an email, received corrective feedback on grammar and vocabulary, and then submitted a revised version. The process mirrored a draft-reflect-revise cycle, similar to traditional tutoring.

Well-structured chatbot-assisted tasks also enable learners to negotiate meaning with AI, treating the chatbot as an interactive partner. For example, students might ask ChatGPT to generate arguments for and against a topic and then evaluate these points in discussion—deepening their understanding of content (Songsiengchai, 2023). Barrot (2023) found that ChatGPT can address a wide range of writing constructs, including pragmatics, coherence, cohesion, and style. It can remind students of essay format conventions, suggest more cohesive transitions, or adjust wording for tone. However, Barrot cautions that ChatGPT's usefulness depends on the quality of student prompts; vague or overly broad queries often lead to irrelevant or incoherent responses. This underscores the importance of *prompt literacy*—the ability to craft precise queries to elicit useful AI-generated responses (Kang & Yi, 2023). Recent research emphasizes that teaching students how to write effective prompts significantly improves AI-assisted learning outcomes (Kim et al., 2023).

Working with chatbots can also increase students' awareness of their own linguistic gaps. ChatGPT's immediate feedback allows learners to compare their initial output with more target-like phrasing. For instance, if a grammatically correct sentence sounds awkward, ChatGPT might propose a more natural alternative, prompting students to reflect on why the change improves fluency. These interactions, particularly when recorded as transcripts, offer insights into the writing process (Guo et al., 2022). Teachers can analyze AI-student dialogues to identify areas where students struggle—such as vocabulary choice or argument clarity—and provide targeted instruction. Moreover, the low-stakes nature of chatbot interaction can boost confidence. Hsu et al. (2021) found that chatbots create a risk-free environment where students experiment with language more freely, knowing they can receive immediate, non-judgmental feedback. This increased confidence can lead to greater willingness to revise and refine their writing.

Recent studies have begun quantifying these benefits. Research indicates improvements in essay organization, vocabulary richness, and grammatical accuracy when students use AI during writing (Rahim et al., 2023; Zhang et al., 2023). Baskara and Mukarto (2023) found that ChatGPT-generated outlines and idea prompts help students write more fluently and produce more coherent essays. However, students may still struggle with abstract or complex concepts that AI has difficulty simplifying. Additionally, chatbot-assisted writing has been linked to increased motivation and reduced anxiety (Silitonga, 2023), with many students reporting greater confidence when revising their work (Yildiz, 2023).

Despite these advantages, researchers caution against over-reliance on AI. Bin Hady et al. (2023) highlighted ChatGPT's potential for interactive writing tasks, such as debates and dialogues, where it can assume various personas. However, Hong (2023) warned that without structured guidance, students might rely too heavily on AI-generated content, bypassing critical thinking. ChatGPT can assist with academic writing tasks such as literature reviews and citation formatting (Almusharraf, 2023), but its output requires human evaluation to ensure accuracy. Instructors should teach students to verify AI-generated suggestions rather than accepting them uncritically.

To address these concerns, some scholars propose integrating AI within a structured pedagogical framework. Yang and Li (2024) advocate for clear task objectives that define AI's role within writing instruction. They also suggest incorporating multimodal AI support (e.g., combining text-based chatbots with visual or auditory elements) to enrich writing activities. Additionally, researchers stress the need for explicit training in AI tool use. Kang and Yi (2023) and Kim et al. (2023) recommend practical guides on prompt writing, demonstrating how specifying genre, expected length, or key vocabulary improves AI-generated responses. Fagbohun et al. (2024) have developed instructional materials to help students refine their chatbot interactions. Meanwhile, Kohnke et al. (2023) found that while ChatGPT adapts its output to different proficiency levels, its explanations can be repetitive or lack depth, reinforcing the need for human oversight.

The research suggests that ChatGPT can enhance L2 writing when integrated thoughtfully. AI excels in speed, accessibility, and volume of feedback, while human instructors provide judgment, personalization, and contextual guidance. Used effectively, ChatGPT can support formative assessment by identifying errors and weaknesses in student writing (Kostka & Toncelli, 2023; Steiss et al., 2024). For instance, Pfau et al. (2023) demonstrated that ChatGPT can be fine-tuned to detect linguistic patterns and flag grammatical errors, though human verification remains necessary to ensure accuracy.

Chatbot-assisted writing presents significant potential for language learning, offering structured support at various stages of the writing process—from idea generation to revision. However, maximizing its benefits requires students to engage critically with AI rather than passively relying on its output. The present study builds on this foundation by investigating how students perceive and use ChatGPT across different writing stages, examining whether these theoretical benefits translate into practice.

LINKING THE COGNITIVE WRITING PROCESS WITH CHATGPT-ASSISTED WRITING

Writing is widely recognized as one of the most complex language skills, requiring writers to coordinate multiple cognitive processes during composition (Gautam, 2011). Classical cognitive models of writing provide a structured framework for understanding these processes. In particular, Hayes and Flower's (1980) model conceptualizes writing as a hierarchical yet recursive activity involving three interacting components: *the task environment, the writer's long-term memory, and the writing process itself.* Within the writing process component, the model delineates three primary phases – *Planning*, *Translating*, and *Reviewing* – each with distinct cognitive activities (Flower & Hayes, 1980). *Planning* involves generating ideas, organizing them, and setting goals for the text. *Translating* refers to the act of converting ideas into written language (drafting sentences and paragraphs). *Reviewing* entails evaluating and revising the text to improve it, which can include editing for grammar, refining word choice, and reorganizing content for clarity. Crucially, Hayes and Flower noted that these phases are not strictly linear; writers often loop back – for example, while reviewing one might realize a need to plan more or rephrase (translating again). This model was chosen as a foundation for the present research because its clear segmentation of writing activities allows us to examine how ChatGPT's functionalities map onto each phase. If we structure our investigation around these defined stages, we can directly focus on our core question: *How does ChatGPT support (or fail to support) the writer during Planning, Translating, and Reviewing?*

Building on the Hayes and Flower model, Berninger and Swanson's (1994) modified model of writing introduces additional granularity by distinguishing three levels of processing within each phase: the *word*, *sentence*, and *discourse* levels. This added detail is particularly relevant for analyzing how ChatGPT might help with different linguistic units. For instance, at the *word level* (micro-level), ChatGPT can serve as a dictionary or thesaurus, suggesting synonyms or clarifying meanings – thus aiding vocabulary development. At the *sentence level*, ChatGPT might help with syntax and grammar; for example, a student can ask if a sentence is well-formed or how to combine two simple sentences into a more complex one. At the *discourse level* (macro-level), the AI can assist with organizing paragraphs, creating outlines, or ensuring coherence across an entire essay. By considering these levels, our study can more precisely identify what kind of help ChatGPT provides: Is it mostly word-level (e.g., giving synonyms), sentence-level (fixing grammar), or discourse-level (suggesting the next paragraph's content)? Such specificity is essential to fully understand ChatGPT's role in L2 writing and directly informs our research questions, which probe not only the overall impact of ChatGPT but its phase-specific contributions in Planning, Translating, and Reviewing.

Applying these cognitive writing models to *ChatGPT-assisted writing* reveals distinct roles for the tool at each stage of the process. During the *Planning* phase, ChatGPT can function as a brainstorming partner. For example, a student uncertain how to start an essay can prompt ChatGPT with the essay topic to generate ideas or an outline. This can help overcome writer's block by quickly providing content to work with. The AI might list pros and cons for an argumentative essay, offer examples or anecdotes relevant to the topic, or suggest a possible thesis statement. All these uses are in line with Planning activities: idea generation, organization, and goal setting. In the *Translating* (or drafting) phase, ChatGPT's support shifts to language formulation. Here, students might use it to get help with vocabulary (asking for a more precise word or a translation of a term), to check sentence structure, or even to generate a sample sentence as a model. For instance, if a learner has an idea but isn't sure how to express it in English, they could ask ChatGPT, "How can I say that my friend's suggestion is helpful in a formal way?" ChatGPT's suggestions can then guide the student in composing their own sentence, thereby aiding the *translating of ideas into text*. Finally, in the *Reviewing* phase, ChatGPT can assist with editing and revising. Students might paste a draft (or part of it) into the chat and ask for feedback: "Can you check this paragraph for mistakes or clarity?" ChatGPT can then point out grammatical errors, suggest rephrasing for clarity, or highlight sentences that seem out of place. It might also help with higher-order concerns like coherence ("Does the argument flow well?") or style ("Make the tone more academic"). In sum, ChatGPT has the potential to provide tailored assistance at each key stage of writing: generating and organizing content (Planning), converting ideas to well-formed text (Translating), and refining the draft (Reviewing).

It is important to emphasize, however, that ChatGPT should be viewed as a *complementary tool* rather than a replacement for the writer's own cognitive efforts. While it can increase efficiency by handling specific sub-tasks (e.g., quickly supplying synonyms or catching typos), it does not eliminate the need for the writer's critical thinking, creativity, and decision-making. Effective writing still requires the student to decide which ideas to use, how to structure their argument, and which of the AI's suggestions to accept or ignore. In fact, one could argue that using ChatGPT effectively *increases* the demand on a student's metacognitive skills: the student must evaluate the AI's output, integrate it with their own intent, and perhaps even reconcile differing options (their original phrasing vs. ChatGPT's suggestion). Thus, rather than doing the work for the student, a well-integrated ChatGPT acts like a cognitive assistant or a sounding board, supporting learners as they develop their own writing abilities. This perspective adheres to the notion of *scaffolding* in educational theory, where a tool or tutor provides temporary support to extend the learner's current skills, with the goal of eventually fading that support as the learner becomes more proficient.

Integrating the above models with our study's aims, we see a clear justification for examining ChatGPT's influence on L2 writing at multiple levels and stages. The research questions driving this study focus on whether ChatGPT's support is most pronounced during the early stages of writing (especially for idea generation in Planning and word choice in Translating) and where it might be underutilized or less effective (possibly in the Reviewing stage for deep revision). This focus is particularly relevant given the increasing presence of AI tools in language learning (Yan, 2023; Ghafar, 2023) and the need to assess both their benefits and limitations in practice (Guo et al., 2022; Zou & Huang, 2023). Notably, very recent empirical work has started to adopt similar frameworks. For example, one *2024 study* categorized students' ChatGPT queries according to the cognitive writing stages and found that queries often clustered around *Planning* and *Translating*, with far fewer purely for Reviewing. This kind of evidence supports our approach to structure observations by writing phase. In that study, students who primarily used ChatGPT for brainstorming (Planning) tended to take more ownership of writing the content themselves, whereas those who leaned on ChatGPT for everything (even drafting full sentences or paragraphs) felt a lower sense of ownership over their work. Such findings underline why it's crucial to guide students in *how* to use ChatGPT – ideally as a helper for generating and refining ideas, not as an auto-pilot for entire essays.

Our theoretical framework connects a well-established cognitive model of writing with the capabilities of a modern AI tool, offering a foundation for predicting and interpreting how ChatGPT might influence each stage of the writing process. It also helps define stage-specific research questions. For example, both theory and emerging research suggest that ChatGPT's effects will be most pronounced in the Planning stage, where generating ideas and overcoming blank-page anxiety are common challenges AI can address. In contrast, its influence is likely to be minimal in the Reviewing stage unless students receive explicit instruction on how to use it for careful revision. The following sections will examine these questions empirically, analyzing students' perceptions and uses of ChatGPT at each stage and assessing whether these correspond to the theoretical possibilities and concerns outlined earlier.

METHODOLOGY

Research Questions

This study examines how ChatGPT supports the three phases of the writing process—Planning, Translating, and Reviewing (Hayes & Flower, 1980)—and explores students' perceptions of its usefulness in foreign language education. Specifically, the study will determine which phase is most supported by ChatGPT, what functions the tool serves in each phase, and how students use the information it provides. In addition, it will assess whether students' overall views of ChatGPT's utility change after they complete a Chatbot-Assisted Writing Task.

Hence, the main research questions of this study are as follows:

RQ1 How do students perceive their utilisation of ChatGPT throughout the stages of Planning, Translating, and Reviewing in their Writing Cognitive Process?

RQ2 To what extent did the general perception of ChatGPT's utility change among students after using it for a Chatbot-Assisted Writing Task?

Research Design

Given the innovative and under-researched nature of this study, which explores research questions that have not been examined in depth, an exploratory research design was adopted in accordance with the principles outlined by Stebbins (2001). This investigation specifically follows a classroom-based laboratory study approach (DeKeyser & Prieto-Botana, 2019), conducted within a natural educational setting to capture ChatGPT's impact on students' writing in an authentic manner. Although the study took place in a regular classroom rather than a conventional laboratory, all participants consented to spending two hours in a dedicated session for the experimental treatment. This single-cycle data collection allowed for the immediate administration of retrospective questionnaires, enabling participants to provide fresh reflections on the writing task. Furthermore, the study draws on Guo et al.'s (2024) research on Chatbot-Assisted Argumentative Writing, replicating and extending their methodological approach.

To ensure a comprehensive analysis, a mixed-methods approach was employed (Creswell, 2014), integrating both quantitative and qualitative data to examine ChatGPT-assisted writing. While the primary data were qualitative, pre- and post-tests using Likert-scale responses were converted into numerical codes for statistical analysis. This strategy conforms to the principles of mixed-methods research (Creswell, 2014; Teddlie & Tashakkori, 2009), allowing for a more complete examination of the research problem (Greene et al., 1989). Integrating both data types allows the study to address RQ1 and RQ2 directly, providing a detailed account of students' interactions with ChatGPT and how their perceptions of its usefulness develop over time. To strengthen the validity and reliability of the findings, data triangulation was applied through an analysis of students' written outputs and records of their interactions with ChatGPT during the writing tasks.

Participants and Context

This study involved an intact sample of sixteen students in the first year of Upper Secondary Education at a public high school in Spain. Participants were between sixteen and eighteen years old, with 94% of them aged sixteen. Additionally, 75% identified as female. All were native Spanish speakers and received four hours of English as a Foreign Language (EFL) instruction per week.

According to their English instructor, although the prescribed textbook was *Great Thinkers B2 Student's Book (Gateway)*, the class's average proficiency level corresponded to B1 on the Common European Framework of Reference for Languages (CEFR). In terms of L2 writing instruction, students practiced writing for at least one hour per week as part of their regular coursework. Their prior experience with AI tools was minimal, limited to basic interactions with chatbots in non-academic contexts.

The study was conducted in a regular EFL classroom, following a "classroom-based laboratory" approach. Students used their own mobile devices to access ChatGPT, with internet access provided through the school's Wi-Fi. No restrictions were placed on how they could interact with the chatbot beyond the parameters of the study task. This setup ensured that students engaged with ChatGPT in an authentic learning environment, reflecting the conditions under which they might realistically integrate AI assistance into their writing processes.

Ethical considerations were carefully addressed. Written consent was obtained from participants' legal guardians, authorizing their involvement in the study. Students were explicitly informed that their participation was *voluntary* and that their *grades or academic standing would not be affected* by their responses or performance in the study.

To address potential privacy concerns related to AI tools, strict *data protection measures* were in place. No *personal data* were input into ChatGPT beyond the essay content so that student identities remained anonymous. Additionally, all interactions with ChatGPT were conducted in a controlled environment, and the platform was used in a manner that complied with *data security standards*. Collected data, including questionnaire responses and ChatGPT interaction logs, were *kept confidential* and used solely for research purposes.

Instruments and Procedures

Writing Task

The participants completed an argumentative writing task with the assistance of a chatbot, as illustrated in Figure 1. The task required them to write a "for and against" essay on the topic of animal testing. Students were explicitly instructed to use ChatGPT during the Planning, Translating, and Reviewing stages, which represent the cognitive phases of writing analyzed in this study. They were allotted fifty minutes to compose a 150-word essay on paper while interacting with ChatGPT on their mobile devices.

The writing task was specifically designed for the purposes of this investigation. Argumentative writing is the most commonly examined genre in previous studies on chatbot-assisted writing (e.g., Guo et al., 2024; Su et al., 2023). The term "Chatbot-Assisted Writing Task" will be used throughout this study to refer to this specific essay-writing activity, in which students engaged with ChatGPT at different stages of the writing process. Finally, the students' compositions were collected to cross-check their alignment with questionnaire responses and recorded interactions with ChatGPT.

Figure 1. ChatGPT-Assisted Writing Task

Writing task

Write a for and against essay on animal testing of approximately 100-150 words. You can use ChatGPT in order to ask for help during the planning, composing or revising stage of your writing process.

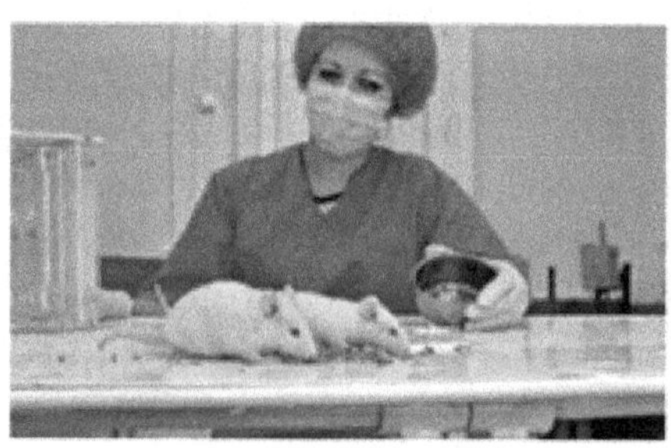

ChatGPT

Students were permitted to use the free version of ChatGPT-3.5 on their mobile devices. All interactions were systematically recorded for subsequent analysis, allowing ChatGPT to serve as a key tool for data validation and triangulation, consistent with its use in prior experimental studies (e.g., Yan, 2023).

Although participants indicated familiarity with ChatGPT and required minimal guidance, an initial prompt was provided to standardize interactions. All students began with the same prompt: *"Today you are my English teacher. Help me with my for-and-against essay on animal testing."* This approach ensured a common starting point while allowing flexibility in how they engaged with the tool. The prompt was designed to enhance ChatGPT's response quality, as suggested in prior research (Fagbohun et al., 2024).

Once introduced to the tool, students interacted with ChatGPT autonomously, moving through different stages of the writing process at their own pace. During the planning stage, they used ChatGPT to generate vocabulary lists and develop arguments for and against the topic. In the translation phase, they relied on ChatGPT to suggest synonyms, refine sentence structures, and provide transition words. In the reviewing phase, ChatGPT assisted in proofreading, identifying spelling errors, and offering grammatical corrections. The study did not impose a fixed sequence or time allocation for each stage, allowing students to navigate the process fluidly.

While students were expected to engage with ChatGPT throughout the writing process, the extent of their reliance on the tool varied. Their interactions were recorded and submitted via email at the end of the session, facilitating a comprehensive record of how they integrated ChatGPT into their writing.

Questionnaires

Given the exploratory nature of this study, no standardized questionnaires fully aligned with its objectives. Therefore, *ad hoc instruments* were developed, drawing on *Tick et al. (2023)* for inspiration (see Appendix), to capture both general perceptions and task-specific experiences.

Pre-Test and Post-Test Questionnaires

This instrument assessed students' general use of and perceptions regarding ChatGPT in educational settings and foreign language teaching (FLT). It comprised eight items: two introductory yes/no questions regarding prior familiarity with ChatGPT, followed by six Likert-scale items (rated 1–5, where 1 = not at all and 5 = a lot). These items evaluated:

- ChatGPT's ease of use (Q1)
- Its perceived utility in educational settings (Q2)
- Its effectiveness for learning English (Q3)
- Students' interest in integrating ChatGPT into English lessons (Q4)
- Its potential support for their English classes (Q5)
- Its ability to improve their writing skills (Q6)

Pre-test responses provided baseline insights into students' initial knowledge and impressions, while post-test responses revealed changes following the *Chatbot-Assisted Writing Task.* The *internal consistency* of these questionnaires was assessed using McDonald's omega, yielding $\omega = .84$ (95% CI [.72, .96]) for the Pre-test and $\omega = .86$ (95% CI [.76, .96]) for the Post-test, which indicates good reliability.

Immediate Retrospective Questionnaire

This *19-item* questionnaire, administered immediately after the writing task, was structured into sections corresponding to each phase of the writing process: *Initial, Planning, Translating, Reviewing, and Final.*

- **Likert-scale items** (e.g., Q1, Q2, Q7, Q12, Q17): These measured students' perceptions of ChatGPT's usefulness, as well as the time spent using the tool overall and within each phase.
- **Multiple-response items** (e.g., Q3, Q8, Q13): These allowed students to indicate the various functions for which they used ChatGPT—such as searching for vocabulary lists, translating terms, generating arguments, receiving grammar suggestions, organizing ideas, modeling texts, or setting objectives. Students also identified the most useful function in each phase (e.g., Q5, Q10, Q15) and reported whether they incorporated ChatGPT responses verbatim or modified them (e.g., Q4, Q9, Q14).
- **Level-specific items** (e.g., Q6, Q11, Q16): These required students to specify whether ChatGPT was used at the **word, sentence, or discourse level** during each phase.
- **Final items** (Q18 and Q19): These asked students to indicate the phase in which ChatGPT was most helpful and to report any errors observed during their interactions.

See Appendix (Tables 3 and 4) for a detailed overview of the Pre-/Post-Test and Immediate Retrospective Questionnaire items, respectively.

Data Collection

The study employed a single-session data collection approach, lasting approximately 90 minutes (see Table 1). Participants completed all study components in sequence: the pre-test questionnaire, the Chatbot-Assisted Writing Task, the Immediate Retrospective Questionnaire (IRQ), and the post-test questionnaire. Due to time constraints and limited access to digital devices, both the questionnaires and the writing task were administered on paper, while participants submitted their ChatGPT interaction records via email.

Although the Chatbot-Assisted Writing Task was conducted in English (L2), the questionnaires were distributed in Spanish (L1) to ensure accurate comprehension and enhance ecological validity. Providing the questionnaires in the participants' first language minimized potential misunderstandings that could have influenced their responses.

Table 1. Data Collection Protocols and Specifications

Order of distribution	Time allotted	Format
1. Pre-test	10 minutes	Paper
2. Chatbot-Assisted Writing Task	50 minutes	Paper (Writing Task) & Mail (ChatGPT Interaction)
3. IRQ	20 minutes	Paper
4. Post-test	10 minutes	Paper

Data Analysis

To address *RQ1 ("How do students perceive their utilization of ChatGPT throughout the stages of Planning, Translating, and Reviewing in their Writing Cognitive Process?")*, data from the Immediate Retrospective Questionnaire were analyzed using Microsoft Excel. Given that the questionnaire contained both single-answer and multiple-answer items, not all responses could be converted into standard numerical measures (e.g., mean, standard deviation). Consequently, responses were manually coded as counts and percentages, and results were visualized through charts. Frequencies for multiple-response items were calculated to capture the range of ways in which students engaged with ChatGPT at each stage. To further verify these findings, we triangulated them with an analysis of students' written tasks and logs of their interactions with ChatGPT.

To examine differences in ChatGPT utilization at different linguistic levels (*word, sentence, and discourse*) across the three writing phases, a Friedman test was conducted. Given that normality tests indicated a non-normal distribution, a non-parametric approach was required. Additionally, the small sample size (n=16) and the ordinal nature of Likert-scale data further supported the decision to use rank-based tests over parametric alternatives. Post hoc pairwise comparisons were carried out using Conover's test, with Kendall's W (*Field, 2018*) reported as an effect size for the Friedman test and rank-biserial correlation (rrb) (*Tomczak & Tomczak, 2014*) used for post hoc comparisons.

To address *RQ2 ("To what extent did the general perception of ChatGPT's utility change among students after using it for a Chatbot-Assisted Writing Task?")*, data from the Pre- and Post-test questionnaires were analyzed using both Microsoft Excel and JASP 0.18.3.0. Likert-scale responses were converted into numerical codes, and descriptive statistics—including median, mean, standard deviation, minimum, and maximum—were computed. The Wilcoxon Signed Rank Test was employed to compare Pre- and Post-test responses, as it is appropriate for non-normally distributed and ordinal data, particularly with small sample sizes (*n=16*).

To assess the practical significance of any observed differences, Cohen's d was calculated following the benchmarks established by Plonsky & Oswald (2014) for effect size interpretation in applied linguistics research. While Wilcoxon tests do not inherently provide standardized effect sizes, reporting Hedges' g offers a clearer indication of the magnitude of change beyond statistical significance.

For a more precise interpretation of p-values, the Vovk-Sellke Maximum p-ratio (VS-MPR) was included. The VS-MPR provides a measure of the maximum possible odds in favor of the alternative hypothesis over the null hypothesis, allowing for a more transparent evaluation of marginal p-values (*Leppink, 2019*). This is particularly relevant in educational research, where traditional p-value thresholds may not fully reflect the strength of the evidence. Incorporating VS-MPR allows the study to facilitate a more informed assessment of the results, avoiding binary interpretations of significance.

RESULTS AND DISCUSSION

RQ1 explored how students engage with ChatGPT during different writing stages—Planning, Translating, and Reviewing. As shown in Figure 2, the majority of students used ChatGPT most frequently in the Planning phase, with 44.83% of its use dedicated to generating arguments and 31.03% to building vocabulary lists. These findings suggest that learners perceive ChatGPT as a valuable tool for brainstorming and expanding their lexical resources, which resonates with prior research on AI-supported early-stage writing (Huang & Li, 2023; Montenegro-Rueda et al., 2023).

Figure 2. Heatmap of the Uses of ChatGPT as per the Writing Process (Planning, Translation and Revision)

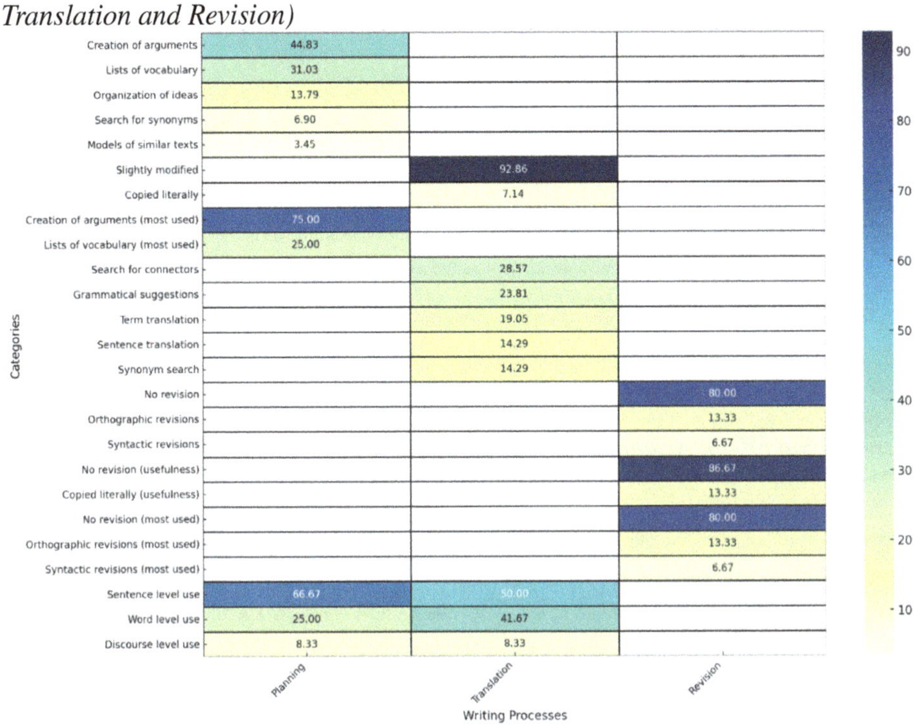

As an illustration, Figures 3 and 4 capture two students' interactions with ChatGPT during the Planning stage. S4 requested a vocabulary list ("give me a vocabulary list") and received not only a set of items but also advice on integrating them into the essay—for instance, "Vital Research: emphasize the importance of certain experiments for scientific advancements." Subsequently, S4 incorporated these suggestions into the final text by writing, "Firstly, animal testing has several arguments in favor. First of all, scientific advancements because animal testing is crucial for scientific progress which leads to breakthroughs in medicine and technology," thus demonstrating how ChatGPT's output can be adapted without copying verbatim.

In contrast, S2 sought both for and against arguments ("can you give me some for and against arguments?"). Among ChatGPT's suggestions was "Limited translatability. Findings from animal studies may not always translate to humans due to species differences in biology, metabolism, and genetics." The student then wrote, "However, the results are not always reliable as we have biological differences between species," reflecting the process of rephrasing and selectively incorporating ChatGPT's input.

Figure 3. Example of a Vocabulary List (Interaction between ChatGPT and S4)

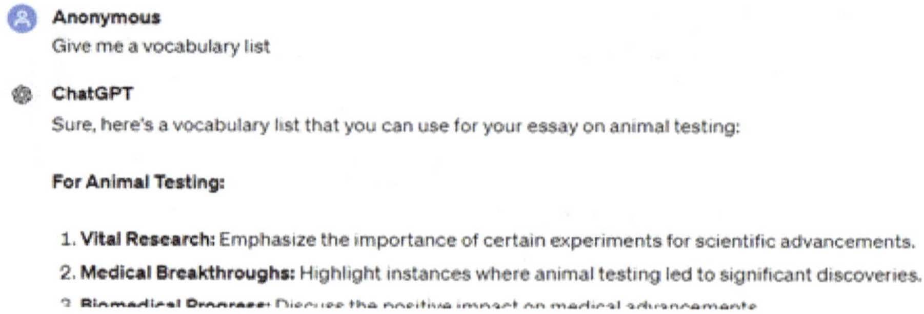

Anonymous
Give me a vocabulary list

ChatGPT
Sure, here's a vocabulary list that you can use for your essay on animal testing:

For Animal Testing:

1. **Vital Research:** Emphasize the importance of certain experiments for scientific advancements.
2. **Medical Breakthroughs:** Highlight instances where animal testing led to significant discoveries.
3. **Biomedical Progress:** Discuss the positive impact on medical advancements

Figure 4. Example of Arguments Against (Interaction between ChatGPT and S2)

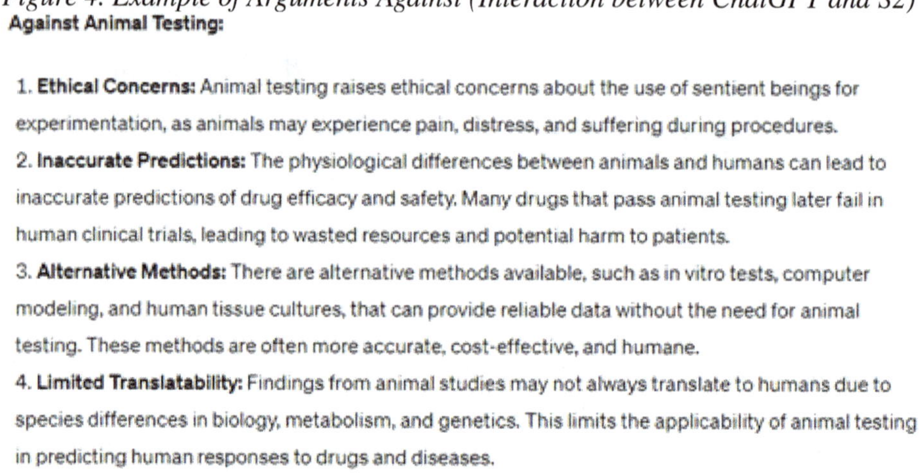

Against Animal Testing:

1. **Ethical Concerns:** Animal testing raises ethical concerns about the use of sentient beings for experimentation, as animals may experience pain, distress, and suffering during procedures.
2. **Inaccurate Predictions:** The physiological differences between animals and humans can lead to inaccurate predictions of drug efficacy and safety. Many drugs that pass animal testing later fail in human clinical trials, leading to wasted resources and potential harm to patients.
3. **Alternative Methods:** There are alternative methods available, such as in vitro tests, computer modeling, and human tissue cultures, that can provide reliable data without the need for animal testing. These methods are often more accurate, cost-effective, and humane.
4. **Limited Translatability:** Findings from animal studies may not always translate to humans due to species differences in biology, metabolism, and genetics. This limits the applicability of animal testing in predicting human responses to drugs and diseases.

During the Translating stage, students shifted their focus to refining their drafts, with 28.57% of users employing ChatGPT to search for connectors and 23.81% using it for grammatical corrections. This reliance on ChatGPT for sentence-level adjustments and clarity is consistent with the observations of Zhang et al. (2023) and Hong (2023), who noted that AI tools often address learners' immediate needs for grammatical accuracy and cohesive text.

Figures 5 and 6 illustrate this phase. S15 requested a list of linkers ("give me a list of linkers") and received 20 items, subsequently integrating "for example" and "likewise" into the final text. The same student also asked ChatGPT to translate the term "likewise" into Spanish, then added, "Likewise, animal feel a lot of pain (…)." Although the student's sentence remains grammatically imperfect, ChatGPT's role in providing connectors and translation options appears to facilitate more cohesive writing.

Figure 5. Example of a List of Linkers (Interaction between ChatGPT and S15)

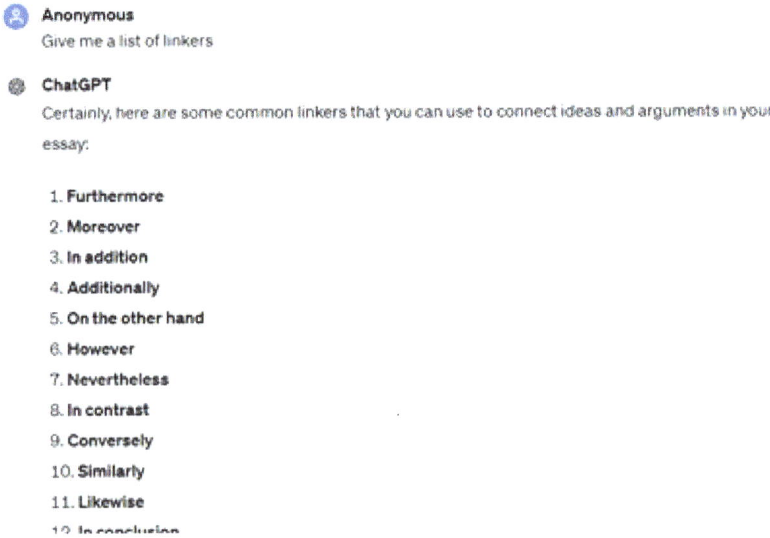

Figure 6. Example of the Translation of a Term (Interaction between ChatGPT and S15)

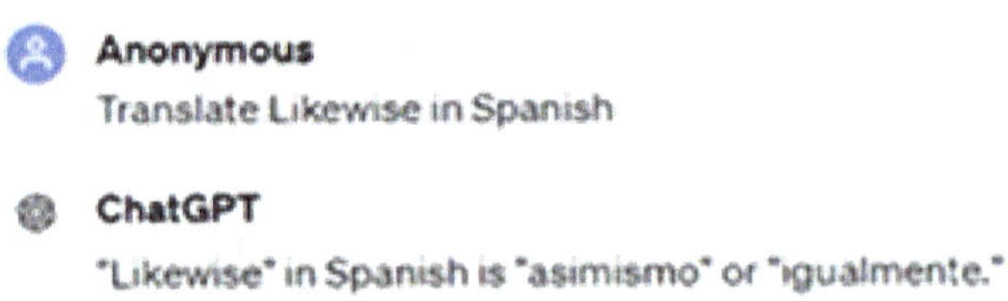

However, the Reviewing phase showed the lowest engagement, with 80% of participants reporting no use of ChatGPT for revision. This underutilization suggests a gap in students' awareness of ChatGPT's capabilities for metalinguistic reflection and deeper cognitive tasks. Guo et al. (2022) and Fitria (2023) observed a similar pattern, indicating that while learners readily use AI for idea generation and sentence construction, they may be hesitant to rely on it for complex aspects such as coherence, style, or overall organization. This hesitancy could stem from a preference for traditional revision methods, skepticism regarding AI's reliability, or insufficient training on how to employ ChatGPT effectively for higher-order writing tasks. Our findings suggest a need to reframe students' perceptions of ChatGPT from not just a brainstorming buddy, but also a revision aide. Future writing classes could incorporate mini-lessons on how to prompt ChatGPT for editing suggestions (e.g., asking it to critique a paragraph's clarity or correctness) to normalize using AI in the revision stage.

Figure 7 exemplifies a rare instance in which S2 asked ChatGPT if a particular sentence was grammatically correct. After receiving confirmation, the student incorporated the sentence—"However, the results are not always reliable as we have biological differences between species"—into the essay. Beyond this isolated example, students appeared to rely on conventional self-editing strategies or peer/teacher feedback, indicating that ChatGPT's potential for revision may be underused.

Figure 7. Example of Grammatical Revision (Interaction between ChatGPT and S2)

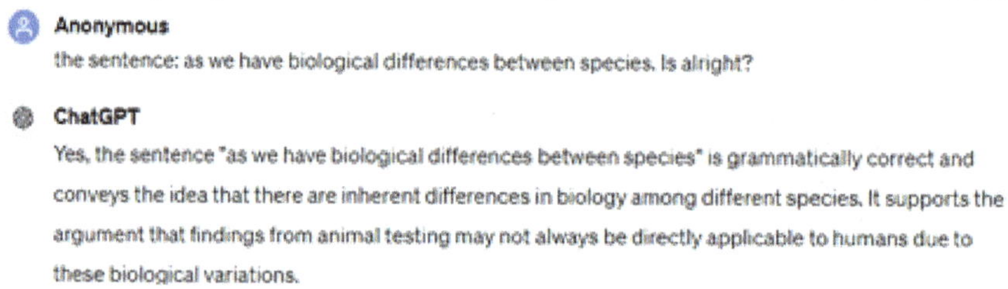

A Friedman test was conducted to assess whether ChatGPT usage differed significantly across the three writing stages. The results revealed a statistically significant difference, $\chi^2(2) = 22.842$, $p < .001$, with a large effect size (Kendall's $W = 0.714$). Post hoc comparisons using Conover's test indicated that usage during Reviewing was significantly lower than in both Planning ($p < .001$, rrb = 1.000) and Translating ($p < .001$, rrb = 1.000), with large effect sizes for both comparisons. However, no significant difference emerged between Planning and Translating ($p = .138$, rrb = –0.500).

In light of the Cognitive Writing Process model (Hayes & Flower, 1980; Berninger & Swanson, 1994), these findings highlight ChatGPT's effectiveness in reducing cognitive load during Planning and Translating, particularly in idea organization and sentence-level refinement. By contrast, its minimal use in Reviewing points to a need for instructional strategies that encourage students to explore ChatGPT's potential for more advanced revision. Explicit training on how to employ AI tools for coherence, style, and metalinguistic analysis may help learners fully capitalize on ChatGPT's capabilities, thereby supporting a more comprehensive integration of AI across the entire writing process.

RQ2 examined how students' perceptions of ChatGPT's usefulness evolved after completing the Chatbot-Assisted Writing Task. As presented in Table 2, no significant change was observed in students' views regarding ChatGPT's ease of use (Q1), with consistently high mean scores from the pre-test (M = 4.37, SD = 0.61) to the post-test (M = 4.43, SD = 0.62). This consistency suggests that participants already considered the tool user-friendly, likely due to their prior experience with AI-driven platforms (Montenegro-Rueda et al., 2023).

Table 2. Pre- and Post-Test Descriptive Statistics and Statistical Analysis for Students' Perceptions of ChatGPT

Variable	Pre	Post	Statistic	z	p	VS-MPR	Hedges' g
	M (SD)	*M (SD)*					
Q1	4.37 (0.61)	4.43 (0.62)	2.000	–0.535	0.773	1.000	0.09
Q2	3.81 (0.65)	4.62 (0.50)	0.000	–2.934	0.002	28.721	1.39
Q3	3.50 (0.73)	4.31 (0.60)	0.000	–2.934	0.002	28.721	1.21
Q4	3.75 (0.77)	4.43 (0.62)	4.000	–2.395	0.015	5.952	0.97
Q5	3.75 (0.68)	4.43 (0.62)	0.000	–2.934	0.001	49.501	1.04
Q6	3.68 (0.60)	4.37 (0.50)	0.000	–2.803	0.003	22.750	1.24

In contrast, perceptions of ChatGPT's educational value (Q2) increased significantly, rising from M = 3.81 (SD = 0.65) to M = 4.62 (SD = 0.50). This shift indicates that direct engagement with the chatbot during the writing task strengthened students' recognition of its role in learning (Huang & Li, 2023). A similar trend emerged for its perceived usefulness in learning English (Q3), which increased from M = 3.50 (SD = 0.73) to M = 4.31 (SD = 0.60). These findings are consistent with previous studies (Fitria, 2023; Yan, 2023), which highlight ChatGPT's effectiveness in providing immediate feedback, suggesting vocabulary, and improving sentence structure. Exposure to ChatGPT across different stages of the writing process may have helped students develop a clearer understanding of how AI can support language learning, which could explain the shift in attitudes toward the tool.

Students also expressed a stronger preference for integrating ChatGPT into their English lessons (Q4), with mean scores increasing from M = 3.75 (SD = 0.77) to M = 4.43 (SD = 0.62). This result is consistent with studies showing that AI-based tools can reduce language anxiety and increase motivation (Rawas, 2023; Zhang et al., 2023). The ability to generate ideas, refine text, and receive real-time feedback appears to have reinforced students' perception of ChatGPT's benefits in classroom settings, further encouraging its adoption.

Notable improvements were also observed in perceptions related to writing skills (Q5) and ChatGPT's overall contribution to the writing process (Q6). These results suggest that students recognize ChatGPT's effectiveness in addressing common writing difficulties, such as idea generation, vocabulary selection, and basic error correction (Zou & Huang, 2023). Specifically, mean scores for writing skills (Q5) increased from M = 3.75 (SD = 0.68) to M = 4.43 (SD = 0.62), while scores for overall impact on writing (Q6) rose from M = 3.68 (SD = 0.60) to M = 4.37 (SD = 0.50). These improvements support the cognitive writing models proposed by Hayes and Flower (1980) and Berninger and Swanson (1994), which emphasize the importance of external support during Planning, Translating, and Reviewing. Engaging with AI-generated feedback at each stage may have reinforced students' understanding of writing as a recursive process, leading to a stronger appreciation of ChatGPT's role in writing development.

None of the participants in our study reported feeling that ChatGPT 'wrote the essay for them' – an important distinction, as other research has warned that over-reliance on AI can diminish students' sense of authorship (see Weber et al., 2024). Our approach of having students generate content with ChatGPT in a controlled manner (and on a topic that required their own arguments) might have helped maintain a feeling of ownership. Future studies should continue to monitor this aspect, allowing for the role of AI as a support rather than a substitute for student-generated writing

Taken together, these results address RQ2 by demonstrating that although students initially found ChatGPT easy to use, the Chatbot-Assisted Writing Task significantly increased their awareness of its educational value, its role in English learning, and its contribution to writing development. This outcome is consistent with the Technology Acceptance Model (Davis, 1989), which suggests that direct engagement with AI tools enhances perceptions of their usefulness and encourages wider adoption in language education.

CONCLUSION

This study examined how students interacted with ChatGPT across the distinct phases of the Writing Process—Planning, Translating, and Reviewing—and how their perceptions of its utility evolved after completing a Chatbot-Assisted Writing Task. The findings indicate that ChatGPT was used primarily during the Planning and Translating phases. Specifically, 44.83% of students relied on the tool for generating arguments, while 31.03% used it for building vocabulary during Planning. ChatGPT also played a notable role in refining language at the Translating stage. These results are consistent with classical Cognitive Writing Process models (Hayes & Flower, 1980; Berninger & Swanson, 1994), which propose that external tools can reduce cognitive load at the early stages of writing by supporting idea generation and sentence construction.

In contrast, the Reviewing phase was significantly underutilized, with 80% of students reporting no engagement with ChatGPT for revision. This gap underscores a potential instructional challenge, as it suggests that learners may lack awareness or confidence in using AI for higher-order revision tasks such as metalinguistic reflection, coherence enhancement, and style adjustments. These findings reinforce concerns raised in prior research (Guo et al., 2022; Fitria, 2023) regarding the inconsistent use of AI tools for complex writing tasks. Addressing this gap requires explicit training on how to integrate ChatGPT effectively across all writing stages, making sure that learners benefit from AI not only in content development but also in text refinement and revision.

Furthermore, an analysis of Pre- and Post-test data (RQ2) reveals that students' perceptions of ChatGPT's ease of use remained consistently high, while their views on its educational value, effectiveness for learning English, and role in improving writing skills showed significant improvement after completing the writing task. These shifts suggest that direct engagement with AI tools enhances learners' awareness of their benefits, making them more willing to incorporate ChatGPT into their language learning practices. This result is consistent with previous studies highlighting the role of AI in enriching learning experiences (Montenegro-Rueda et al., 2023; Huang & Li, 2023).

The theoretical implications of these findings contribute to a broader understanding of AI's role in cognitive writing processes within L2 contexts. While ChatGPT demonstrates clear benefits for idea generation and linguistic refinement, its limited application in the Reviewing phase raises critical questions about how AI can be better utilized for advanced cognitive tasks in writing. Future research should investigate structured AI-assisted revision techniques that help learners engage more deeply with discourse-level writing improvements.

From a practical standpoint, these results emphasize the need for structured opportunities that guide students in using AI tools at every stage of writing. Educators should provide direct instruction on how to use ChatGPT for revision and metalinguistic analysis, helping students develop the ability to critically evaluate AI-generated content and improve their writing on their own.

Despite these promising results, this study is subject to several limitations. The small sample size and focus on a single writing task restrict the generalizability of findings. Additionally, the short-term nature of the intervention does not fully capture the long-term impact of AI integration on L2 writing development. Future research should address these limitations by conducting longitudinal studies and comparing different AI tools and instructional methods to determine the most effective approaches for enhancing L2 writing proficiency.

In conclusion, as AI technology develops, teaching strategies must adapt to incorporate it meaningfully into language education. This study provides initial evidence that secondary school EFL students benefit most from using ChatGPT during the planning stage of writing and that even a brief, structured introduction to AI can lead to a more positive perception of its role in learning.

This is one of the first studies conducted in Spain examining how secondary students engage with AI in writing tasks, addressing a gap in the literature, where most research has focused on university-level learners or different educational contexts. Expanding the scope to younger students offers a broader perspective on AI's role in language learning. A structured approach to AI integration allows educators to help students develop the skills needed to use AI tools effectively, promoting that technology enhances rather than displaces the cognitive processes fundamental to L2 writing.

Author Contributions

The work was a collaborative effort with equal contributions from both authors across all roles, including conceptualization, methodology, formal analysis, original draft preparation, and review and editing.

Conflict of Interest

The authors have no conflicts of interest to declare.

ACKNOWLEDGEMENTS

This study was done under the auspices of one competitive program of research: I+D+i Grants PID2022-137544NB-I00, funded by the Spanish National Research Agency and the Ministry of Science, Innovation and Universities.

REFERENCES

Adiguzel, T., Kaya, M. H., & Cansu, F. K. (2023). Revolutionizing education with AI: Exploring the transformative potential of ChatGPT. *Contemporary Educational Technology*. Advance online publication. DOI: 10.30935/cedtech/13152

Allen, T. J., & Mizumoto, A. (2024). ChatGPT over my friends: Japanese English-as-a-foreign-language learners' preferences for editing and proofreading strategies. *RELC Journal*. Advance online publication. DOI: 10.1177/00336882241262533

Almusharraf, I. (2023). Analyzing the role of ChatGPT as a writing assistant at higher education level: A systematic review of the literature. *Contemporary Educational Technology*, *15*(4), ep464. DOI: 10.30935/cedtech/13265

Athanassopoulos, S., Manoli, P., Gouvi, M., Lavidas, K., & Komis, V. (2023). The use of ChatGPT as a learning tool to improve foreign language writing in a multilingual and multicultural classroom. *Advances in Mobile Learning Educational Research*, *3*(2), 818–824. DOI: 10.25082/AMLER.2023.02.009

Barrot, J. S. (2023). Using ChatGPT for second language writing: Pitfalls and potentials. *Assessing Writing*, *57*, 100745. DOI: 10.1016/j.asw.2023.100745

Baskara, R., & Mukarto, M. (2023). Exploring the implications of ChatGPT for language learning in higher education. *Indonesian Journal of English Language Teaching and Applied Linguistics*, *7*(2), 343–358. DOI: 10.21093/ijeltal.v7i2.1387

Berninger, V., & Swanson, H. (1994). Modifying Hayes and Flower's model of skilled writing to explain beginning and developing writing. In Butterfield, E. C. (Ed.), *Children's writing: toward a process of development of skilled writing* (Vol. 2, pp. 57–81). JAI Press.

Bin Hady, W. R. A., Al-Kadi, A., & Alzubi, M. (2023). Exploring the dimensions of ChatGPT in English language learning: A global perspective. *Library Hi Tech*. Advance online publication. DOI: 10.1108/LHT-05-2023-0200

Bit, D., Biswas, S., & Nag, M. (2024). The impact of artificial intelligence in the educational system. *International Journal of Scientific Research in Science and Technology*. Advance online publication. DOI: 10.32628/ijsrst2411424

Creswell, J. W. (2014). *Research design: Qualitative, quantitative, and mixed methods approaches* (4th ed.). SAGE Publications.

Davis, F. (1989). Perceived Usefulness, Perceived Ease of Use, and User Acceptance of Information Technology. *Management Information Systems Quarterly*, *13*, 319–340. DOI: 10.2307/249008

DeKeyser, R. M., & Prieto Botana, G. (Eds.). (2019). *Doing SLA research with implications for the classroom: Reconciling methodological demands and pedagogical applicability*. John Benjamins Publishing Company., DOI: 10.1075/lllt.52

Fagbohun, O., Harrison, R. M., & Dereventsov, A. (2024). An empirical categorization of prompting techniques for large language models: A practitioner's guide. *Journal of Artificial Intelligence. Machine Learning and Data Science*, *1*(4), 1–11. DOI: 10.51219/JAIMLD/Oluwole-Fagbohun/15

Field, A. P. (2018). *Discovering Statistics Using IBM SPSS Statistics* (5th ed.). Sage.

Fitria, T. N. (2023). Artificial intelligence (AI) technology in OpenAI ChatGPT application: A review of ChatGPT in writing English essay. *ELT Forum: Journal of English Language Teaching, 12*(1), 44-58. https://doi.org/DOI: 10.15294/elt.v12i1.64069

Flower, L., & Hayes, J. R. (1980). A cognitive process theory of writing. *College Composition and Communication*, *32*(4), 365–387. DOI: 10.2307/356600

García-Peñalvo, F. J. (2023). La percepción de la inteligencia artificial en contextos educativos tras el lanzamiento de ChatGPT: Disrupción o pánico. *Education in the Knowledge Society*, *24*, 1–9. DOI: 10.14201/eks.31279

Gautam, P. (2011). Writing skill: An instructional overview. *Journal of NELTA Gandaki*, *2*, 74–90. DOI: 10.3126/jong.v2i0.26605

Ghafar, Z. N. (2023). ChatGPT: a new tool to improve teaching and evaluation of second and foreign languages. A review of ChatGPT: the future of education. *International Journal of Applied Research and Sustainable Sciences*, *1*(2), 73–86. DOI: 10.59890/ijarss.v1i2.392

Greene, J. C., Caracelli, V. J., & Graham, W. F. (1989). Toward a conceptual framework for mixed – method evaluation designs. *Educational Evaluation and Policy Analysis*, *11*(3), 255–274. DOI: 10.3102/01623737011003255

Guo, K., Li, Y., Li, Y., & Chu, S. K. W. (2024). Understanding EFL students' chatbot-assisted argumentative writing: An activity theory perspective. *Education and Information Technologies*, *29*, 1–20. DOI: 10.1007/s10639-023-12230-5

Guo, K., Wang, J., & Chu, S. K. W. (2022). Using chatbots to scaffold EFL students' argumentative writing. *Assessing Writing*, *54*, 100666. DOI: 10.1016/j.asw.2022.100666

Hayes, J. R., & Flower, L. S. (1980). Identifying the organisation of writing processes. In Gregg, L., & Steinberg, E. R. (Eds.), *Cognitive processes in writing* (1st ed., pp. 3–30). Routledge., DOI: 10.4324/9781315630274

Hong, W. C. H. (2023). The impact of ChatGPT on foreign language teaching and learning: Opportunities in education and research. *Journal of Educational Technology and Innovation*, *5*(1), 37–45.

Hsu, M.-H., Chen, P.-S., & Yu, C.-S. (2021). Proposing a task-oriented chatbot system for EFL learners speaking practice. *Interactive Learning Environments*, *31*(7), 4297–4308. DOI: 10.1080/10494820.2021.1960864

Huang, J., & Li, S. (2023). Opportunities and challenges in the application of ChatGPT in foreign language teaching. *International Journal of Education and Social Science Research*, *6*(4), 75–89. DOI: 10.37500/IJESSR.2023.6406

Huang, W., Hew, K. F., & Fryer, L. K. (2022). Chatbots for language learning—Are they really useful? A systematic review of chatbot-supported language learning. *Journal of Computer Assisted Learning*, *38*(1), 237–257. DOI: 10.1111/jcal.12610

Irzawati, I., Unamo, A. F., Agnes, A., & Angelika, V. (2024). The use of Chat GPT in ELT. *International Journal of Education, Language, Literature, Arts, Culture, and Social Humanities*, *2*(1), 32–44. DOI: 10.59024/ijellacush.v2i1.674

Javier, D. R. C., & Moorhouse, B. L. (2023). Developing secondary school English language learners' productive and critical use of ChatGPT. *TESOL Journal*, *755*, 1–9. DOI: 10.1002/tesj.755

Kang, S., & Yi, Y. (2023). Beyond ChatGPT: Multimodal generative AI for L2 writers. *Journal of Second Language Writing*, *62*, 101071. DOI: 10.1016/j.jslw.2023.101071

Karan, K., & Bakina, W. (2024). *Generative artificial intelligence (AI) in education: A cross-national survey on university teachers' perceptions on the use of ChatGPT*. Education and New Developments 2024 – Volume 1. https://doi.org/ DOI: 10.36315/2024v1end035

Kim, S., Park, E., & Lee, J. (2023). A study on the utilization of OpenAI ChatGPT as a second language learning tool. *Journal of Multimedia Information System, 10*(1), 79–86. DOI: 10.33851/JMIS.2023.10.1.79

Kohnke, L., Moorhouse, B. L., & Zou, D. (2023). ChatGPT for language teaching and learning. *RELC Journal.* Advance online publication. DOI: 10.1177/00336882231162868

Kostka, I., & Toncelli, L. (2023). Integrating AI tools into instructed second language acquisition. In Marsden, M., & Mason, S. E. (Eds.), *AI in Language Learning and Teaching* (pp. 45–67). Iowa State Digital Press., DOI: 10.31274/isudp.154

Leppink, J. (2019). *Statistical methods for experimental research in education and psychology*. Springer.

Lo, C. K. (2023). What is the impact of ChatGPT on education? A rapid review of the literature. *Education Sciences, 13*(4), 1–15. DOI: 10.3390/educsci13040410

Montenegro-Rueda, M., Fernández-Cerero, J., Fernández-Batanero, J. M., & López-Meneses, E. (2023). Impact of the implementation of ChatGPT in education: A systematic review. *Computers, 12*(8), 1–13. DOI: 10.3390/computers12080153

Murphy, R. S., Wotley, D., & Minn, D. (2023). Integrating ChatGPT into the EFL classroom: Benefits and challenges. *Center for Fundamental Education, 40*, 97–166.

Patel, R., Bajaj, P., Kumar, A., Kumari, A., Rai, V., & Kumar, S. (2023). *ChatGPT in the classroom: A comprehensive review of the impact of ChatGPT on modern education*. 2023 11th International Conference on Intelligent Systems and Embedded Design (ISED), 1–6. https://doi.org/DOI: 10.1109/ISED59382.2023.10444568

Pfau, A., Polio, C., & Xu, Y. (2023). Exploring the potential of ChatGPT in assessing L2 writing accuracy for research purposes. *Research Methods in Applied Linguistics, 2*(3), 100083. DOI: 10.1016/j.rmal.2023.100083

Plonsky, L., & Oswald, F. L. (2014). How big is "big"? Interpreting effect sizes in L2 research. In *Language learning,* (Vol. 64, pp. 878-912). https://www.doi.org/10.1111/lang.12079

Raheem, B. R., Anjum, F., & Ghafar, Z. N. (2023). Exploring the profound impact of artificial intelligence applications (Quillbot, Grammarly and ChatGPT) on English academic writing: A Systematic Review. [IJIR]. *International Journal of Integrative Research, 1*(10), 599–622. DOI: 10.59890/ijir.v1i10.366

Rathod, K. (2023). *A review of ChatGPT in promoting teaching and learning*. International Journal of Scientific Research in Engineering and Management., DOI: 10.55041/ijsrem24976

Rawas, S. (2023). ChatGPT: Empowering lifelong learning in the digital age of higher education. *Education and Information Technologies*, *29*, 6895–6908. DOI: 10.1007/s10639-023-12114-8

Silitonga, L. M., Hawanti, S., Aziez, F., Furqon, M., Zain, D. S. M., Anjarani, S., & Wu, T. T. (2023, August). The impact of AI chatbot-based learning on students' motivation in English writing classroom. *International Conference on Innovative Technologies and Learning* (pp. 542-549). Cham: Springer Nature Switzerland.

Songsiengchai, S., Sereerat, B. O., & Watananimitgul, W. (2023). Leveraging artificial intelligence (AI): ChatGPT for effective English language learning among Thai students. *English Language Teaching*, *16*(11), 1–68. DOI: 10.5539/elt.v16n11p68

Stampfl, R., Ivkić, I., & Geyer, B. (2024). Role-playing simulation games using ChatGPT. *ERCIM News*, *136*, 14–15. DOI: 10.48550/arXiv.2402.09161

Stebbins, R. A. (2001). *Exploratory research in the social sciences: What is exploration? 48, 1-14.* Sage Publications., DOI: 10.4135/9781412984249

Steiss, J., Tate, T., Graham, S., Cruz, J., Hebert, M., Wang, J., Moon, Y., Tseng, W., Warschauer, M., & Olson, C. B. (2024). Comparing the quality of human and ChatGPT feedback of students' writing. *Learning and Instruction*, *91*, 101894. Advance online publication. DOI: 10.1016/j.learninstruc.2024.101894

Su, Y., Lin, Y., & Lai, C. (2023). Collaborating with ChatGPT in argumentative writing classrooms. *Assessing Writing*, *57*, 1–11. DOI: 10.1016/j.asw.2023.100752

Teddlie, C., & Tashakkori, A. (2009). *Foundations of mixed methods research: Integrating quantitative and qualitative approaches in the social and behavioral sciences*. Sage Publications.

Teng, M. F. (2024). A Systematic Review of ChatGPT for English as a Foreign Language Writing: Opportunities, Challenges, and Recommendations. *International Journal of TESOL Studies*, *6*(3), 36–57. DOI: 10.58304/ijts.20240304

Tick, A., Toktosunova, A., Fallah, H., Toutouchi, Z., & Tadzhibaeva, Z. (2023). The Impact of ChatGPT on Learning in Higher Education–Results of a Pilot Study. *Practice and Theory in Systems of Education*, *18*(1), 31–50.

Tomczak, M., & Tomczak, E. (2014). The need to report effect size estimates revisited. An overview of some recommended measures of effect size. *Trends in Sport Sciences*, *1*, 19–25.

UNESCO (2023). *ChatGPT and artificial intelligence in higher education: Quick start guide*, 1-14.

Weber, A., Meyer, B., & Schmidt, R. (2024). Enhancing legal writing skills: The impact of formative feedback in a hybrid intelligence learning environment. *British Journal of Educational Technology*, *55*(2), 215–233. DOI: 10.1111/bjet.13560

Yan, D. (2023). Impact of ChatGPT on learners in a L2 writing practicum: An exploratory investigation. *Education and Information Technologies*, *28*(11), 13943–13967. DOI: 10.1007/s10639-023-11742-4

Yang, , LLi, , R. (2024). ChatGPT for L2 learning: Current status and implications. *System, 124*, 103351. https://doi.org/10.1016/j.system.2024.103351

Yildiz, T. A. (2023). The impact of ChatGPT on language learners' motivation. *Journal of Teacher Education and Lifelong Learning*, *5*(2), 582–597. DOI: 10.51535/tell.1314355

Zadorozhnyy, A., & Lai, W. Y. (2024). ChatGPT and L2 written communication: A game-changer or just another tool? *Languages (Basel, Switzerland)*, *9*(1), 5. DOI: 10.3390/languages9010005

Zayoud, M., Oueida, S., Awad, P., & Ionescu, S. (2023). *Impact of ChatGPT on education: Challenges and opportunities.* Towards Increased Business Resilience: Facing Digital Opportunities and Challenges. https://doi.org/DOI: 10.56177/11icmie2023.18

Zhang, Z., Gao, J., Dhaliwal, R. S., & Li, T. J.-J. (2023). VISAR: A human-AI argumentative writing assistant with visual programming and rapid draft prototyping. *In Proceedings of the 36th Annual ACM Symposium on User Interface Software and Technology* (Article No. 5, pp. 1–30). Association for Computing Machinery. https://doi.org/DOI: 10.1145/3586183.3606800

Zhao, Y., Chen, Q., Zhou, X., & Cheng, G. (2024). Integrating AI Tools into Instructed Second Language Acquisition. *Exploring Artificial Intelligence in Applied Linguistics*, 9-235.

Zou, M., & Huang, L. (2023). The impact of ChatGPT on L2 writing and expected responses: Voice from doctoral students. *Education and Information Technologies*, *29*, 13201 – 13219. DOI: 10.1007/s10639-023-12397-x

APPENDIX

Questionnaires Created Ad Hoc for the Specific Purposes of the Present Research

The questionnaires below were previously mentioned, explained, and discussed throughout this paper. Nevertheless, we would like to present the specific questions answered by our students to facilitate a clearer understanding for future research.

On one level, Table 3 presents the questions used in this study's Pre-test and Post-test. Notably, the Pre-test includes two additional introductory questions regarding ChatGPT's prior use.

Table 3. Pre- and Post-test on ChatGPT General Use

Number	*Question*
ChatGPT Prior Use – Introductory Questions (Pre-test)	
I-Q1	Are you familiar with the tool ChatGPT?
I-Q2	Have you ever used the tool ChatGPT?
ChatGPT General Use – Pre- and Post-test Questions	
Q1	Do you think it is easy to use?
Q2	Do you think it could be useful in educational contexts?
Q3	Do you think it could be useful to learn English?
Q4	Would you like to use it in your own English lessons?
Q5	Do you think it could help improve your writing skills?
Q6	Do you think it could impact your writing process?

On another level, Table 4 displays the questions from the Immediate Retrospective Questionnaire on the Chatbot-Assisted Writing Task. This questionnaire was administered only once, immediately after the completion of the task. It is subdivided into various categories: Initial, Planning, Translating, Reviewing, and Final Sections.

Table 4. Immediate Retrospective Questionnaire on the Chatbot-Assisted Writing Task

Number	*Question*
Initial Section	
Q1	Has ChatGPT been helpful during the writing process?
Q2	Has using ChatGPT taken a long time during the writing process?

continued on following page

Table 4. Continued

Number	*Question*
Planning Section	
Q3	Have you employed ChatGPT to plan your writing? (Please tick the options you have used)
Q4	Have these options been useful to plan your writing?
Q5	What has been the option you have used the most when planning?
Q6	At which level have you used ChatGPT the most when planning the text?
Q7	Has using ChatGPT taken a long time while planning the text?
Translating Section	
Q8	Have you employed ChatGPT to compose your writing? (Please tick the options you have used)
Q9	Have these options been useful to compose your writing?
Q10	What has been the option you have used the most when translating?
Q11	At which level have you used ChatGPT the most when translating the text?
Q12	Has using ChatGPT taken a long time while composing the text?
Reviewing Section	
Q13	Have you employed ChatGPT to review your writing? (Please tick the options you have used)
Q14	Have these options been useful to review your writing?
Q15	What has been the option you have used the most when reviewing?
Q16	At which level have you used ChatGPT the most when reviewing the text?
Q17	Has using ChatGPT taken a long time while reviewing the text?
Final Section	
Q18	For which stage of the writing process has ChatGPT been the most useful?
Q19	Have you noticed any instances where ChatGPT failed during the process?

Chapter 9 Perceived Usability, Usefulness, and Satisfaction of Educational Virtual Assistant Chatbots: Teachers' and Students' Perception Study

Anil Kumar Nayak
https://orcid.org/0000-0002-8907-5732
Christ University, India

Ayushi Zina
https://orcid.org/0000-0001-8959-2310
Christ University, India

Nilesh Kumar
Amity University, Ranchi, India

ABSTRACT

Artificial Intelligence (AI) is changing education with tools like chatbots and virtual assistants. These tools provide personalized support and make academic tasks easier. This study examines how teachers and students view chatbot usability, usefulness, and satisfaction in different educational settings. The researcher used a quantitative survey design and collected data from 238 participants across various institutions and fields. The results are promising. About 59.2% of participants found chatbots

DOI: 10.4018/979-8-3373-9225-7.ch009

easy to use. Additionally, 78.2% said these tools helped them work more efficiently, and 79% reported having positive experiences. ChatGPT and Grammarly were the most commonly used platforms. While the overall opinions were positive, the study highlights the need for organized integration, ethical guidelines, and training to improve engagement and learning results. These findings indicate that educational chatbots are not just trends; they are becoming vital parts of modern teaching, suggesting ways to create more inclusive and adaptable learning environments.

1. INTRODUCTION

In recent years, the rapid development of artificial intelligence has begun to transform not only the process of teaching and learning but also the very essence of being pedagogical or a learner. AI applications contribute largely to building flexible environments that are sensitive to the particularities of each student by considering their needs, styles, and degrees of attention. Students benefit from AI-powered chatbots in three significant areas: homework and study assistance, personalised learning experiences, and skill development. At a macro level, such systems will be able to dynamically respond to student learning by providing immediate feedback and adjustments to content when appropriate, based on individual paths discovered for all learners (Li & Wong, 2023). AI developers have actively taken the lead in changing the education landscape by continuously assessing how effective, usable, and satisfying these tools are to people who depend on them (Almufarreh, 2024). This results in more responsive digital learning environments, whereby automatic grading systems can now provide instant feedback to the student. In the process of evolution, intelligent tutors and generative and language-based AI create flexibility and dynamism in learning to suit the uniqueness of individual learners' needs (Das et al., 2024). This renaissance was reflected bibliometrically by a surge of scholarly publishing that started building momentum in 2020 and peaked three years later in 2023—a shift reflected in research involving students, machine learning, and higher education (Kavitha & Joshith, 2024).

It saves time for teachers and helps improve pedagogy. The greater the role AI plays in classrooms, the more likely it is to become a true educational shift (Zawacki-Richter et al., 2019). AI innovations such as intelligent tutoring systems and adaptive learning platforms have transformed instructional methods by automating significant administrative tasks. This global research momentum comes from traditional powerhouses China and the US and newer players like Saudi Arabia, India, and Malaysia. There has been a discernible pivot since 2022 to longitudinal studies tracing AI's evolution and its impacts, especially concerning intelligent tutoring systems, ChatGPT, and machine learning. As a result, significant efforts and resources have gone into developing the right kinds of algorithms to bring AI into classrooms and support teaching and learning in meaningful ways" (Cope et al., 2020).

Educators increasingly view AI chatbots as a promising solution to many pressing challenges in education. More and more schools use these tools to improve learning and change how help is given (Labadze, Grigolia, & Machaidze, 2023, p. 56). The growing presence of AI in education is evident from its integration into daily teaching routines and a surge in research highlighting its impact. Tools like chatbots and virtual helpers have taken the lead in online learning setups, offering fresh ways to involve students and aid their learning paths.

1.1 Rationale

The fast infusion of AI into pedagogies and andragogies causes major restructuring of drives toward teaching and learning. The introduction of tailored AI tools, such as chatbots and virtual assistants, changes the way and transforms education by delivering instant feedback and creating a more adaptive and engaging learning environment. The advancement profoundly affects education, making a difference in teaching and learning. More particularly, artificial intelligence holds out the promise of revolutionising classrooms through individualised learning opportunities it can provide, along with automation of mundane tasks and timely feedback to students (Moreno-Guerrero et al., 2020). All these enhance the burden of routine tasks from teachers so that they may very well concentrate on building strong ties with the students and instructing in a customised manner for each. When AI becomes an integral part of education, not just the method but the entire experience regarding learning and teaching will change for all the stakeholders involved. Teachers, in particular, have a critical role in this transformation. Their voice is vital. Understanding how they feel about the use of AI, what excites them, and what scares them will provide a better way to know how these tools become part and parcel of their everyday lives as teachers. As AI continues to play an increasing role in education, we must listen to teachers and students to design AI to support teachers, enhance student learning, and create a more thoughtful and inclusive educational system (Alwaqdani, 2025). A persuasive case exists for creating appropriate methodologies to evaluate primary users' perceptions and experiences interacting with AI-driven educational tools.

1.2 Research Gap

AI technology is changing how we live, work, and learn, making its mark in various fields like marketing, content creation, legal work, and more (Zhang & Aslan,

2021). In education, its impact is particularly significant, transforming how classrooms operate, the roles of professionals, and students' overall learning experiences.

Even though AI tools are widely adopted, much of the research has concentrated on their technical capabilities, leaving a gap in understanding how users, especially students and teachers, interact with these technologies. This study aims to bridge that gap by looking into personal factors such as age, prior knowledge, and learning styles influencing how people engage with educational chatbots.

By considering the viewpoints of both students and teachers, the study reveals significant differences in what each group values. Students appreciate quicker feedback and tailored support while teachers navigate new roles and responsibilities. Together, these findings provide a more comprehensive understanding of how AI is reshaping education and how it can be improved to better meet the needs of those who depend on it (Alwaqdani, 2025).

This study aims to assess the overall user experience of educational chatbots for both students and teachers, focusing on usability, perceived usefulness, and satisfaction. It investigates how individual factors, like user background, learning styles, and previous experiences, affect interactions with chatbots and how these tools support teaching and learning. By comparing the perspectives of students and teachers, the study highlights differing priorities: students often prioritise ease of use and quick feedback, while teachers focus on the potential for personalised learning support. Additionally, the research points out current limitations, especially regarding the chatbots' ability to engage in more profound and complex educational discussions.

The following research questions were sought to be answered:

- How do students and teachers perceive chatbot usability, usefulness, and satisfaction?
- What role do age, prior knowledge, and learning styles play in shaping chatbot interaction experiences, and how can these factors be leveraged to enhance user experience?
- What improvements can be made to chatbot design for better user engagement and deeper learning interactions?

2. LITERATURE REVIEW

2.1 AI in Education

The idea of Artificial Intelligence (AI) has been around since the 1950s, ignited by Alan Turing's iconic question: "Can machines think?" (Gonçalves, 2023). The journey of AI in education kicked off decades ago, with early innovations like Intelligent Tutoring Systems and Computer-Assisted Instruction emerging in the 1960s and 70s (Perrotta & Selwyn, 2020). By the 1980s, AI had started to gain formal recognition in academia, highlighted by significant milestones such as the launch of the International Journal of Artificial Intelligence in Education in 1989 and the founding of the International AI in Education Society (IAIED) in 1993 (Aldeman et al., 2021). These developments marked a collective effort to investigate how intelligent technologies could revolutionise learning.

This exploration laid the groundwork for years of research into what intelligent machines can do. AI is no longer just a concept from the future; it is actively changing how we live, work, and learn. Education, in particular, has experienced incredible transformations as AI shapes classrooms, teaching methods, and student support systems.

Since then, AI has transitioned from labs to everyday classrooms, especially in general and higher education (Edtech, 2020). It changes how students interact with content and how teachers craft their lessons. However, while these advancements bring exciting possibilities, they also pose significant challenges, especially regarding equity, accessibility, and the role of traditional teaching methods (Hennekeuser et al., 2024).

Today, AI makes its presence felt in classrooms in two main ways. First, it acts as a hands-on learning tool, encouraging students to experiment with algorithms, explore concepts in creative ways, and deepen their understanding through interactive experiences. Second, it enhances personalised learning by tailoring lessons to meet each student's goals, learning style, and pace (Chounta et al., 2022). Platforms like Canvas are stepping up by incorporating chatbots that provide real-time help and create a more natural way for students to engage with their learning environment. These AI systems monitor student engagement and performance, allowing learners to gain insights into their study habits and make necessary improvements.

Teachers are also receiving valuable support from AIED tools. By visualising student data, educators can track progress, pinpoint areas that need attention, and make timely, informed decisions. These technologies empower teachers to manage their classrooms more effectively and deliver meaningful, responsive instruction, turning AI into a helpful ally rather than a replacement (Chounta et al., 2022; Alwaqdani, 2025).

Overall, the emergence of AI in education is not just a tech trend; it is a move towards more responsive, inclusive, and personalised learning experiences that support both students and the educators guiding them.

Now, let us dive into educational chatbots and virtual assistants—tools designed to mimic human conversation and provide on-demand support in learning settings. These advanced software agents (bots) use text or voice interaction to create an intuitive, user-friendly experience, responding to student inquiries with personalised, context-sensitive explanations and recommending resources tailored to each learner's skill level (Adamopoulou & Moussiades, 2020; Labadze, Grigolia, & Machaidze, 2023). These conversational bots represent a significant leap in education, offering instant feedback, scalable guidance, and continuous availability to enhance teaching and learning processes.

From the early days of rule-based systems to the advanced large language models, chatbots have come a long way regarding their capabilities and how we use them. A significant turning point occurred with the launch of ChatGPT in November 2022, which is based on OpenAI's GPT-3.5 and GPT-4 architectures and trained on a massive array of books, academic papers, and code. This latest generation of AI chatbots can produce coherent and contextually relevant text for various tasks. In classrooms, students turn to ChatGPT for instant tutoring, creating personalised study guides, and engaging in Socratic-style discussions. Meanwhile, teachers use it for lesson planning, designing assessments, and simplifying everyday tasks. Its fluency, flexibility, and extensive knowledge have made personalised support more accessible and have enriched the teaching and learning experience (Rahman et al., 2025; Rudolph et al., 2023; Labadze, Grigolia, & Machaidze, 2023).

On a broader scale, chatbots—called Conversational User Interfaces (CUIs)—are software applications enabling real-time interactions with users through text or voice, frequently acting as virtual assistants (Luo, Tong, Fang, & Qu, 2019). These systems, from rule-based logic to sophisticated machine learning and NLP techniques, are built on diverse technological foundations that enable adaptive and intelligent behaviour. A key player in modern Generative AI, Generative Pre-trained Transformers (GPTs) equip CUIs with the ability to provide context-aware, dynamic responses, making them powerful tools in both educational and commercial settings (Rahman, Ismail, Hossain, & Hossen, 2025).

Generative AI-powered chatbots are making their way into various fields, with education an up-and-coming area. Even though these technologies are becoming more common, research on them is still in its infancy. There is a significant lack of 'empirical literature examining teacher educators' attitudes towards and use of instructional and web-based technologies within the country's teacher preparation programs' (Ibrahim & Shiring, 2022, p. 535). Only a handful of studies have examined how these chatbots fit into teacher education programs. Students and teachers are crucial players in this scenario—they are not just the ones who will use these technologies in the future. However, they can also be champions for meaningful changes in education. Their ability to apply new skills and digital know-how in the classroom makes their involvement with generative AI all the more critical. However, there is still a gap in research regarding how these AI chatbots can effectively assist students and teachers in their academic and professional journeys. This study aims to evaluate usability and gather insights from student teachers about how they view the scholarly uses of educational chatbots and virtual assistants (Nikou, Guliya, Van Verma, & Chang, 2024, p. 45). With a solid understanding of how chatbots operate and their roles for students and teachers, we will explore broader attitudes toward AI as an educational partner.

2.2 AI as a Teacher's Aid

Teachers acted as cautious gatekeepers in the early stages of educational technology adoption. By the late 2000s, many educators approached AI with skepticism, perceiving it as a potential threat to their professional authority and classroom expertise (Prensky, 2008). This hesitance usually came from a fear of the unknown, a lack of confidence in navigating unfamiliar systems, and worries about losing control over their established teaching methods (Zimmerman, 2006). Naturally, teachers leaned towards familiar materials and strategies, which inadvertently slowed the adoption and scaling of innovative AI applications in schools (Tallvid, 2016; Hébert et al., 2021).

However, over the last decade, things have changed as research has begun to showcase AI's ability to enhance teaching rather than detract from it. Educators now say that their openness to AI tools depends on several factors: their teaching philosophies, years of experience in the classroom, previous exposure to educational technologies, and their assessments of an application's relevance and effectiveness (Gilakjani et al., 2013; Ryu & Han, 2018; Panigrahi, 2020; Roll & Wylie, 2016). As teachers get hands-on experience with adaptive platforms and intelligent tutoring systems, many realise these innovations can relieve them from mundane tasks, allowing for more meaningful student engagement.

Indeed, when we integrate AI thoughtfully, it transforms from just a teaching aid into a true partner in the educational journey. Today's adaptive learning platforms are impressive; they assess how students are doing in real time and tailor lessons to fit each individual's pace, preferences, and areas where they might need extra help. On top of that, intelligent tutoring systems provide immediate, focused feedback, allowing students to practice until they grasp the concepts. Plus, AI analytics can spot early signs of academic struggles, allowing teachers to step in before minor issues turn into major obstacles (Blanuša, Maričić, & Ćurić, 2024; Holmes et al., 2019; Qin et al., 2020; Heffernan & Heffernan, 2014). However, these exciting advancements come with their own set of challenges. Not everyone has equal access to the necessary hardware, software, and fast internet, which could widen the educational gap and leave disadvantaged students even further behind. Teachers also have a tough road ahead as they adapt to new roles as knowledge providers and guides in AI-enhanced learning experiences. Finding the right balance between automation and genuine human connection is crucial; without the warmth, empathy, and mentorship that make teaching effective, AI risks turning education into a series of cold transactions.

In the end, the real success of AI in education hinges less on how advanced the technology is and more on the values that shape its use. When we prioritise equity, transparency, and empathy in our decision-making, AI can enhance what educators do best, empower students to take charge of their learning, and enrich classroom interactions without taking away the personal touch essential for meaningful educational change.

2.3 Theoretical Framework

2.3.1 Technology Acceptance Model (TAM)

The Technology Acceptance Model (TAM) is a widely accepted theoretical framework that explains how users accept and use technology. It outlines the relationships between external variables, user beliefs, attitudinal constructs, and usage behaviour (Hubona & Kennick, 1996). TAM has been applied in various contexts, including education, to understand stakeholders' responses to new technological products and services (Musa et al., 2024). This study adapts the Technology Acceptance Model (TAM) to explore how teachers and students engage with educational technologies, focusing on their perceptions of usability, usefulness, and satisfaction with current tools.

Fundamentally, it is reasonable to assume that a technology must be easy to use before users are willing to adopt it. Users' perceptions of usability, usefulness, and satisfaction are central to the successful integration and diffusion of technology in education. Prensky (2006) emphasises that the information age has reshaped how educators teach children growing up in the digital era. Understanding the interaction between humans and machines becomes essential, as this interaction shapes the acceptance of and resistance to technology. These dynamics, in turn, influence the development of subsequent stages in the design and implementation process.

Davis et al. (1989) developed the Technology Acceptance Model (TAM) based on Fishbein and Ajzen's Theory of Reasoned Action (TRA). TAM has since gained widespread recognition for illustrating how different components interact in forming attitudes and adopting technology. These components include external variables, perceived usefulness (PU), perceived ease of use (PEU), attitude toward the technology (A), behavioural intention to use (BI), and actual system use. In this study, external variables refer to the different technology tools that educators can use. The variable "A" stands for a specific technology used for a particular purpose in the classroom. The Technology Acceptance Model (TAM) gives special importance to

PEU and PU, as both play a key role in shaping a person's attitude towards accepting or rejecting a technology (Ibrahim & Shiring, 2022, p. 537).

Therefore, this study explores how teachers and students perceive chatbots and virtual assistants through usability testing and evaluation. The primary objective is to assess whether users find these technologies efficient, effective, and satisfactory. Sevilla et al. (2006) clarify that.

'When we speak of a positive or negative attitude toward an object, we refer to its evaluative component. Such evaluations shape the cognitive, affective, and behavioural intentions related to the object. Often, these evaluations are stored in memory independently of the original cognitions and emotions that led to their formation' (p. 358).

Additionally, the study aims to investigate users' psychological attitudes and reactions, highlighting their mental orientation towards adopting such tools (Holden & Rada, 2011, p. 343).

3. METHODOLOGY

Teachers' and students' opinions on educational chatbots and virtual assistants in terms of their usability, utility, and general satisfaction were investigated in this study using a quantitative survey design. Participants' experiences in diverse educational settings were captured and comprehended with a descriptive approach. The methodology's components were the research design, population and sample, instruments, data collection strategy, and data analysis techniques. Teachers and students with prior experience using AI-powered educational tools from schools, colleges, universities, and other academic institutions made up the study's population. The researchers employed convenience and voluntary participation methods to recruit 238 respondents. Among the participants, 128 were teachers (53.8%) and 110 were students (46.2%), providing a well-rounded view from both teaching and learning perspectives. This dual perspective is vital for understanding how AI-based tools are accepted. Teachers mainly focus on teaching methods, while students look at the tools from a user experience and learning improvement angle.

Data gathering used a structured questionnaire to measure three main aspects: perceived usability, perceived usefulness, and satisfaction with educational chatbots and virtual assistants. The questionnaire had two sections. The first section collected demographic information such as the participant's role (teacher or student), type of institution (school, college, university, or other), academic discipline, and the specific chatbot or virtual assistant they used the most (for example, ChatGPT, Grammarly, Microsoft Copilot, QuillBot, Socratic, or others). The second section featured eight items rated on a five-point Likert scale, from Strongly Disagree (1) to Strongly Agree (5). These items examined participants' views on ease of use, clarity of instructions, navigational simplicity, efficiency in academic tasks, meaningful learning or teaching support, relevance and informativeness of responses, overall satisfaction, and willingness to use such tools in education. Three academic experts validated the instrument's content to ensure it was clear and relevant to the research goals.

Data collection occurred online, using Google Forms to connect with respondents from various institutions and fields. The study uses survey links shared through institutional networks, academic mailing lists, and social media groups to reach as many participants as possible. The researchers informed participants about the study's purpose, assured them that their responses would remain confidential, and clarified that participation was voluntary. The researchers spent over three weeks collecting participant responses. After thoroughly inspecting the dataset for completeness, they selected 238 valid responses for analysis.

4. DATA ANALYSIS

Data analysis involved descriptive statistical methods to summarise and interpret the results. Moreover, the researchers calculated frequencies and percentages for each item to analyse response patterns, which revealed insights into participants' perceptions of usability, usefulness, and satisfaction. Furthermore, the researchers studied demographic data to create a profile of respondents and identify trends in chatbot usage across various roles, disciplines, and types of institutions. The results were presented in tables and narrative interpretations, followed by a discussion that connected the findings to the research goals.

The methodology selected fits the research purpose because it enables the systematic collection of measurable data. This approach ensured that the perceptions of a diverse group of respondents were thoroughly compiled, analysed, and interpreted clearly. Combining a structured survey with descriptive statistical analysis provided concrete evidence of how teachers and students interact with educational chatbots and highlighted areas of high satisfaction and potential challenges for future use.

Table 1. Respondents Details

Role	No. of Respondents	Total
Teacher	128	
Student	110	238

The study included 238 respondents, comprising 128 teachers (53.8%) and 110 students (46.2%). This distribution ensures that the views collected represent both educators' teaching perspective and learners' experiences. Therefore, assessing the usability, usefulness, and satisfaction with educational chatbots and virtual assistants is important. Teachers share insights on integrating these tools into their teaching methods, while students discuss their daily interactions and the effectiveness of AI-assisted learning. This dual representation strengthens the study's conclusions by highlighting both sides of the teaching and learning process.

Table 2. Institutional Representation

Your Educational Institution/Organisation	No. of Respondents
University	93
College	76
School	53
Institution	16

4.1 Institutional Representation

Respondents came from various educational institutions. This diversity helps make the findings more relevant. Universities made up the largest group at 39.1%, followed by colleges at 31.9%, schools at 22.3%, and other institutions at 6.7%. These findings suggest that people in higher education are more engaged with AI-based educational tools than those in primary and secondary schools. The strong participation from universities and colleges reflects more exposure to new technologies in higher education, where digital skills and resources are better. In contrast, fewer school responses indicate that the use of chatbots in primary and secondary education is still developing, possibly due to infrastructure or policy challenges.

Table 3. Academic Discipline Distribution

Subject/Discipline	No. of Respondents	Total
Arts	32	238
Science	25	
Engineering	48	
Humanities	17	
Management	58	
Law	27	
Journalism	18	
Social Science	13	

4.2 Academic Discipline Distribution

Participants came from a wide range of academic fields, which adds depth to the study. Management (24.4%) and Engineering (20.2%) were the most represented disciplines, followed by Arts (13.4%), Law (11.3%), Science (10.5%), Journalism (7.6%), Humanities (7.1%), and Social Sciences (5.5%). This variety is important because views on chatbot usefulness and satisfaction may differ across fields. For instance, Management and Engineering often involve problem-solving, report generation, and data analysis, where AI tools can significantly help. In contrast, Humanities and Social Sciences may focus more on critical thinking and interpretive responses, which could affect how respondents view chatbot accuracy and relevance (Luo, H., Luo, H., Li, Z., Li, Z., Liang, J., Li, G., & Yan, Y., 2024). Law and journalism enrich the sample, as these fields demand high factual accuracy and ethical considerations in assessing AI-driven assistance.

Table 4. Chatbot and Virtual Assistant Usage

Educational chatbot/virtual assistant	No. of respondents	Total
ChatGPT	87	238
Microsoft Copilot	41	
Socratic by Google	17	
Grammarly	58	
Quilbot	25	
Deepseek	7	
Other	3	

4.3 Chatbot and Virtual Assistant Usage

The study also examined which educational chatbots and virtual assistants participants used most often. ChatGPT (36.6%) was the most popular platform, reflecting its global reach and ability to support various academic tasks like content generation, problem-solving, and language help. Grammarly (24.4%) came in second, mainly used for writing support, proofreading, and improving language, which shows that participants often rely on AI tools to enhance communication and academic writing. Microsoft Copilot (17.2%) was another important tool, showing the increased use of AI in productivity software and professional settings. Smaller percentages of respondents reported using QuillBot (10.5%), Socratic by Google (7.1%), and DeepSeek (2.9%), while 1.3% used other tools. This distribution prefers multifunctional and well-known tools that meet teaching and learning needs.

4.4 Interpretation and Implications

This diverse demographic profile lays a strong foundation for the study's analysis. Including teachers and students from various institutions and fields ensures that the perceptions gathered are broad and well-rounded. The higher number of university and college participants suggests that AI adoption is more widespread in higher education, likely due to greater technological readiness and access to digital resources. Also, the wide range of disciplines suggests the study can shed light on how different academic areas interact with AI tools, spanning from quantitative problem-solving in STEM fields to critical and interpretive work in the humanities.

The chatbot usage data shows that participants already use AI-driven tools, with ChatGPT being the key platform. The development indicates that students and teachers are increasingly open to using AI in learning and that these tools are transitioning from novelty items to functional parts of education. The varying levels of familiarity with different platforms may also affect views on usability and satisfaction. The upcoming analysis sections examine this in greater detail.

In summary, the demographic profile reflects a diverse, digitally aware, and multidisciplinary group of participants, providing a solid basis for interpreting usability, usefulness, and satisfaction levels regarding educational chatbots and virtual assistants. This diversity enhances the reliability of the findings and offers valuable insights into the changing role of AI in education across various contexts.

Table 5. Chatbots' Ease of Use

The chatbot/assistant was easy to use.	No. of respondents
Strongly Disagree	6
Disagree	24
Neutral	67
Agree	76
Strongly Agree	65

The findings show that 59.2% of respondents (Agree + Strongly Agree) viewed the chatbot/virtual assistant as easy to use, indicating high usability and minimal technical barriers. Only 12.6% reported difficulties, suggesting that usability issues are generally minor. The 28.2% neutral responses may come from participants who are new to the technology or have used it only a little, resulting in no strong opinion. Ease of use is vital for technology acceptance in education, as users are more likely to engage with tools that require little effort or technical assistance. These results suggest that the chatbots are intuitive and accessible, supporting positive user adoption trends.

Table 6. Navigate Chatbot Interface with Ease

I could navigate the chatbot interface without much help	No. of respondents
Strongly Disagree	9
Disagree	17
Neutral	48
Agree	79
Strongly Agree	85

The results show that 68.9% of respondents (Agree + Strongly Agree) could navigate the chatbot interface independently, highlighting the tool's intuitive design and user-friendly nature. Only 10.9% reported difficulties, which may indicate limited prior exposure to AI tools or issues accessing specific features. The 20.2% neutral responses suggest that some users may need help or more time to become familiar with the interface. Effective navigation is crucial for perceived usability, and these findings reinforce that most users can operate educational chatbots with minimal guidance, enabling smooth integration in academic settings.

Table 7. Effective Clarity in Chatbot Interaction

Instructions and outputs from the chatbot were clear and understandable.	No. of respondents
Strongly Disagree	3
Disagree	23
Neutral	49
Agree	85
Strongly Agree	78

The findings reveal that 68.5% of respondents (Agree + Strongly Agree) found the instructions and outputs from the chatbots to be clear and understandable, showcasing the effectiveness of the tools' communication and language processing. A small percentage, 11% of respondents, had difficulty interpreting the outputs, which might be due to technical jargon, ambiguous replies, or limited familiarity with AI interactions. Around 20.6% responded neutrally, suggesting mixed clarity depending on the task. Clarity in instructions is essential for task efficiency and learning support, and the high agreement suggests that the chatbots effectively deliver understandable and helpful responses, promoting a positive user experience.

Table 8. Improved Efficiency with Chatbot Help

The chatbot helped me complete academic tasks more efficiently.	No. of respondents
Strongly Disagree	3
Disagree	18
Neutral	31
Agree	79
Strongly Agree	107

The data shows that 78.2% of respondents (Agree + Strongly Agree) believed the chatbot improved their efficiency in completing academic tasks. Therefore, it highlights its value as a time-saving tool. Only 8.9% disagreed, which shows minimal dissatisfaction with task support. A small 13% stayed neutral, possibly including users who did not use the chatbot for task-related questions or did not explore its full features. These findings suggest that chatbots can help simplify routine academic tasks like drafting responses, generating explanations, or clarifying concepts. Hence, it contributes to effective teaching and learning. High perceived efficiency is important for the continued use of AI tools in education.

Table 9. Improved Effectiveness in Teaching/Learning Activities

It supported my learning/teaching process in a meaningful way.	No. of respondents
Strongly Disagree	3
Disagree	8
Neutral	19
Agree	97
Strongly Agree	111

An overwhelming 87.4% of respondents (Agree + Strongly Agree) stated that the chatbot helped their learning or teaching meaningfully. Therefore, it indicates a high relevance and impact in educational settings. Only 4.7% disagreed, suggesting negative perceptions are minimal. A small fraction (8% neutral) may reflect participants who used the tool for limited purposes or who have not fully integrated it into their academic activities. This positive feedback highlights that educational chatbots can enhance knowledge acquisition, provide timely academic help, and support teaching efforts. Such meaningful assistance emphasises their potential as a practical edtech resource that can enhance teaching strategies and student engagement.

Table 10. Informative and Relevant Chatbot Responses

I found the responses generated to be relevant and informative.	No. of respondents
Strongly Disagree	1
Disagree	11
Neutral	17
Agree	92
Strongly Agree	117

The responses indicate that 87.9% of participants (Agree + Strongly Agree) viewed the chatbot outputs as relevant and informative, confirming the quality and accuracy of its responses. Only 5% expressed dissatisfaction, showing minimal concerns about irrelevant or misleading outputs. A small 7.1% were neutral, including participants who used the chatbot for exploratory or non-critical tasks. High relevance and informativeness are essential for building user trust and supporting effective decision-making in academic work. These findings underscore that educational chatbots can provide helpful content, reinforcing their value as reliable academic helpers in learning and teaching situations.

Table 11. Positive Experience Using the Chatbot

I am satisfied with my experience of using the chatbot/assistant.	No. of respondents
Strongly Disagree	12
Disagree	15
Neutral	23
Agree	84
Strongly Agree	104

The data reveals that 79% of respondents (Agree + Strongly Agree) expressed overall satisfaction with their chatbot experience, indicating a positive acceptance of these tools in education. Only 11.3% reported dissatisfaction, which may stem from occasional inaccuracies or unmet expectations. A moderate 9.7% were neutral, likely representing users who engaged little with the chatbot or had mixed experiences. High satisfaction levels are crucial for technology adoption, suggesting that the chatbots effectively met the academic support needs of teachers and students. These results show that positive user experiences can encourage ongoing use and wider integration of AI tools in educational practices.

Table 12. Optimistic about Integrating Digital Learning Tools

Overall, I feel positive about integrating such tools in education.	No. of respondents
Strongly Disagree	6
Disagree	11
Neutral	21
Agree	87
Strongly Agree	113

The results demonstrate a strong positive attitude toward integrating chatbots and virtual assistants in educational contexts, with 84.1% of respondents (Agree + Strongly Agree) feeling optimistic. Therefore, it shows broad acceptance and readiness for AI-driven tools in teaching and learning settings. Only 7.1% expressed concerns about accuracy, potential over-reliance, or institutional readiness. A small 8.8% were neutral, indicating some participants are cautiously attentive to long-term effects. The overwhelmingly positive sentiment emphasises that AI tools are seen as complementary rather than disruptive, and with the proper support, when thoughtfully implemented, educational technologies enrich instructional practices and foster more profound learning experiences to enhance educational practices.

4.5 Results and Analysis

The study included 238 respondents, consisting of 128 teachers (53.8%) and 110 students (46.2%). This mix allowed for a deeper look into chatbots' role in education. Teachers shared their ideas on integrating these tools into teaching, while students discussed their learning experiences and the practical value of these tools in their schoolwork. Having both groups represented made the findings more reliable, as it included viewpoints from both sides of the teaching-learning relationship.

Respondents came from various educational institutions. The highest share came from universities (39.1%), followed by colleges (31.9%), schools (22.3%), and other institutions (6.7%). Moreover, the analysis shows that AI-driven educational tools are more common in higher education than in schools. The larger presence of university and college respondents may be due to better access to technology, greater exposure to new tools, and more infrastructure that supports AI in academics. In contrast, the smaller number of school respondents indicates that chatbot use in early education is still developing, possibly because of infrastructure issues or a cautious approach at the pre-university level.

The respondents represented various academic disciplines, adding variety to the study. Management and Engineering participants comprised the largest groups, accounting for 24.4% and 20.2% of the total sample. These fields often relate to problem-solving, analytical tasks, and professional writing, where AI tools can offer immediate benefits. Arts (13.4%) and Law (11.3%) had significant representation as well, while Science (10.5%), Journalism (7.6%), Humanities (7.1%), and Social Science (5.5%) brought in perspectives from areas that value critical thinking, creativity, and interpretation. The diverse academic backgrounds of respondents ensured that perceptions captured in the study were not limited to one area but reflected various expectations and uses of chatbots across STEM, management, and humanities.

Researchers recorded participants' responses regarding their use of chatbots and virtual assistants. ChatGPT was the most widely used tool at 36.6%, showcasing its versatility and accessibility. Its functions in generating content, problem-solving, and clarifying concepts make it a logical choice for teaching and learning tasks. Grammarly was the second most popular platform at 24.4%, showing that users often depend on AI tools for language improvement and proofreading to meet academic writing standards. Microsoft Copilot made up 17.2% of usage, showing the increasing role of AI in popular productivity tools for creating documents, analysing data, and making presentations. Other tools like QuillBot (10.5%), Socratic by Google (7.1%), and DeepSeek (2.9%) attracted fewer users, with just 1.3% of respondents mentioning other platforms. This trend indicates a preference for multifunctional, reliable, and user-friendly tools. It suggests that users prefer platforms with good reputations offering practical educational uses. The demographic profile provides a solid and diverse foundation for examining users' opinions on usability, usefulness, and satisfaction with educational chatbots.

The usability analysis showed that most respondents found the chatbots easy to use. A majority, 59.2%, agreed that the chatbot was simple, while only 12.6% reported difficulties. About 28.2% of participants remained neutral, meaning some may not have interacted with the tools enough or needed more experience to form a clear opinion. Ease of use is crucial for technology adoption. Users tend to favour straightforward tools that do not require extensive technical skills. Similarly, 68.9% of respondents stated they could navigate the chatbot interface independently, suggesting that the design promotes self-use. The low percentage of users who struggled with navigation, just 10.9%, might indicate either first-time use or unfamiliarity with certain advanced features. Finally, 68.5% of participants found the chatbot's instructions and results transparent and understandable. Only 11% noted some ambiguity, which could come from technical terms or unclear questions. Overall, the usability findings suggest that most users can operate chatbots effectively. The combination of user-friendly interfaces and clear outputs leads to positive user experiences.

Participants rated the usefulness of chatbots highly, highlighting a significant strength of these tools. 78.2% agreed that chatbots helped them complete academic tasks more quickly, showcasing AI's time-saving and productivity-boosting roles in education. Only 8.9% disagreed, indicating that most people saw real benefits in completing their work. Furthermore, 87.4% of participants felt that the chatbots greatly supported their learning or teaching processes. This finding underscores the educational value of these tools. They enhance traditional teaching by providing on-demand explanations, academic guidance, and learning help. Another important factor for usefulness is the quality of the outputs. In this study, 87.9% rated the chatbot responses as relevant and informative. The small number of dissatisfied users (5%) suggests that most participants trust the content provided, which is key for adequate academic support. These findings show that educational chatbots can significantly improve academic efficiency, boost engagement, and deliver reliable, appropriate responses.

User satisfaction and acceptance of chatbot use in education were largely positive. 79% of respondents felt satisfied with their overall experience, with 43.7% strongly agreeing. Only 11.3% expressed dissatisfaction, likely due to occasional errors or unmet expectations. Satisfaction is a key factor in ongoing usage, and the high approval rates seen in this study suggest that these tools have met the expectations of teachers and students. Acceptance of integration into education was even higher, with 84.1% of respondents expressing a positive view on using AI tools in classrooms and academic tasks. The small minority with reservations (7.1%) may have concerns about reliance, reliability, or ethical issues surrounding AI in education. Still, the overwhelming positivity shows that educators and learners see chatbots as helpful rather than disruptive, and their inclusion in academic settings seems feasible and welcome.

The analysis views educational chatbots as highly usable, valuable, and well-accepted tools. Respondents consistently stated that these platforms improved efficiency, provided meaningful learning and teaching support, and delivered relevant, clear outputs. The study points to a trend where AI tools are moving from being a novelty to a necessity in education. The strong connection between usability, usefulness, and satisfaction indicates that chatbots could become partners in teaching and learning, enhancing human effort rather than replacing it. With proper backing from institutions, training for teachers and students, and attention to ethical guidelines, these tools can boost productivity, engagement, and access to academic resources in various educational environments.

5. CONCLUSION AND RECOMMENDATIONS

The current study explored teachers' and students' views on the usability, usefulness, and satisfaction of educational chatbots and virtual assistants. Based on responses from 238 participants, including 128 teachers and 110 students, the research provided valuable insights into how these tools are viewed in education today and their potential for future use. The study clarifies the role of chatbots in modern learning environments by examining demographic distribution, usage patterns, and survey feedback about usability, usefulness, and satisfaction.

The findings showed a consistently positive response to educational chatbots and virtual assistants. The participant pool included various roles, institutions, and subjects. The balance between teachers and students ensured the analysis captured both the instructional perspective of those designing learning experiences and the firsthand experience of users interacting with AI tools. Representation from universities, colleges, and schools indicated that higher education is leading the way in chatbot adoption, likely due to better infrastructure, support for technological exploration, and a willingness from both faculty and students to engage with new tools. In contrast, schools are at the early stages of adoption, suggesting a need for more investment in resources and awareness at the foundational education level.

Diversity in academic disciplines enriched the analysis, showing that chatbot usage spans STEM and non-STEM fields. Participants from Management and Engineering exhibited particularly high engagement with these tools, likely due to their analytical and productivity-focused work. Educators and learners from Arts, Law, Humanities, Journalism, and Social Sciences also provided important insights, demonstrating that even fields centred on critical thinking and creativity find value in chatbots as supportive tools. This wide range of representation indicates that educational chatbots can be helpful across various learning experiences, not confined to specific subjects.

Regarding usability, the results were mostly positive. Most participants found the chatbots easy to use and navigate, providing clear and understandable outputs. These findings are significant since usability is crucial for adopting new technologies. Complicated or confusing tools that take too long to learn are less likely to see consistent use, especially in educational settings where teachers juggle multiple responsibilities, and students may avoid tools that add to their workload. The significant number of users who navigated the chatbots with little difficulty indicates that these tools have reached a user-friendly design level that promotes broad access. However, the small percentage of users facing challenges highlights the need for onboarding resources, tutorials, and ongoing training to improve ease of use and lower barriers for first-time users.

Perceived usefulness emerged as the strongest aspect of the study, showing that participants view chatbots as not just new tools but valuable aids in their academic work. Most agreed that these tools help them work more efficiently, provide meaningful support for learning and teaching, and generate relevant, informative responses. This combination of efficiency, pedagogical support, and informational value shows that chatbots are starting to fulfil the long-anticipated role of AI in education: boosting productivity, supporting instructional delivery, and enhancing the student learning experience. The observed efficiency gains are noteworthy since they suggest that chatbots can streamline repetitive tasks. Thus, teachers can focus on more complex educational activities while enabling students to dedicate more time to understanding concepts rather than searching for information. The high ratings of response relevance and informativeness further indicate that chatbots can deliver content that meets user expectations, which is essential for building trust and encouraging continued use.

Satisfaction and acceptance levels were also high, indicating that users benefit from chatbots in practical ways while forming a positive overall impression of the tools. The strong satisfaction ratings suggest that the experiences of teachers and students mostly met or exceeded their expectations, which is critical for any technology seeking lasting use in education. The positive sentiment toward integration shows that both groups are eager to incorporate chatbots more fully into academic processes. This finding is vital because even the best technological tools will not work effectively if end users hesitate to adopt them. The high satisfaction and openness to future integration make it clear that educational institutions are well-positioned to explore official adoption strategies for AI tools in teaching and learning.

The implications of these findings extend to various aspects of educational practice and policy. For teachers, positive experiences with chatbots highlight opportunities to integrate these tools into lesson planning, assessment preparation, and student support. For students, reliable and informative chatbots enhance independent learning, encourage exploration, and provide immediate help that supports traditional classroom teaching. For institutions, the widespread acceptance and satisfaction revealed by the study suggest that investing in AI-driven educational technologies could lead to tangible benefits, such as increased productivity, more personalised learning experiences, and greater engagement with digital learning environments.

However, the findings also emphasise the need for careful and structured integration. While most participants reported positive experiences, the small number reporting difficulties indicates that some challenges remain. These include concerns about response accuracy, ethical implications like over-reliance or plagiarism, and proper guidance to ensure students and teachers use chatbots effectively rather than using them instead of critical thinking. Institutions must consider these issues when developing policies and frameworks for AI adoption.

From these insights, several key recommendations for future practice arise. First, educational institutions should focus on structured integration strategies beyond casual or individual use. Resulting in embedding chatbot use in specific academic tasks, such as research guidance, formative assessment, or writing support, to ensure the tools align with learning goals. Second, training and awareness programs for both teachers and students are crucial. While most users reported ease of use, structured guidance can build confidence, tackle ethical issues, and enhance tool interactions. Training sessions could also teach strategies for verifying chatbot outputs, helping to foster critical digital literacy skills.

Third, institutions should create clear ethical guidelines and policies for using AI in education. These guidelines should address issues such as academic integrity, data privacy, responsible usage, and the importance of using chatbots as supplements rather than replacements for human effort. Such frameworks will help mitigate risks from over-reliance and ensure that AI integration aligns with education's broader mission to develop independent, critical thinkers. Fourth, it is essential to continuously evaluate and refine chatbot and virtual assistant selection based on user feedback and technological progress. Popular platforms like ChatGPT, Grammarly, and Microsoft Copilot dominate usage due to their versatility and accessibility, but new tools with improved features or specific capabilities may emerge and deserve consideration.

Future research could include long-term studies to see how views on usability, usefulness, and satisfaction shift over time as users gain experience and as AI technologies evolve. Comparative studies across different educational levels and subjects would provide deeper insights into the contexts where chatbots are most effective. Additionally, examining learning outcomes and performance metrics alongside user perceptions would offer more substantial evidence for the educational impact of these tools.

In conclusion, the study indicates that educational chatbots and virtual assistants are quickly becoming recognised as valuable tools in the teaching and learning environment. They offer high usability, provide meaningful academic support, and create positive user experiences for teachers and students. The overwhelmingly positive views on efficiency, relevance, and satisfaction suggest that these tools are well-positioned to become essential parts of educational practice. Institutions must implement structured integration strategies to fully leverage this potential, provide thorough training, and establish ethical guidelines promoting responsible use. By doing so, educational stakeholders can harness the power of AI-driven chatbots to enhance engagement, productivity, and learning outcomes while upholding the principles of academic integrity and critical thinking at the core of education.

REFERENCES

Adamopoulou, E., & Moussiades, L. (2020). Chatbots: History, technology, and applications. *Machine Learning with Applications*, *2*, 100006. DOI: 10.1016/j.mlwa.2020.100006

Aldeman, N. L. S., Urtiga, D. S., Aita, K. M., Machado, V. P., Mata, D., Sousa, L. C. D., & Coelho, A. G.B., Da, Silva, A. S., Silva, D., Mendes, A. P., Neres, F. J. D. O., & Monte, S. J. H. D. (2021). Smartpathk: A platform for teaching glomerulopathies using machine learning. *BMC Medical Education*, *21*, 248–248.

Almufarreh, A. (2024). Determinants of Students' Satisfaction with AI Tools in Education: A PLS-SEM-ANN Approach. *Sustainability*, *16*(13), 5354. DOI: 10.3390/su16135354

Alwaqdani, M. (2025). Investigating teachers' perceptions of artificial intelligence tools in education: Potential and difficulties. *Education and Information Technologies*, *30*, 2737–2755. DOI: 10.1007/s10639-024-12903-9

Blanuša Trošelj, D., Maričić, S., & Ćurić, A. (2024). *Growing interest in AI in education: Systematic literature review*. In Shelley, M., & Ozturk, O. T. (Eds.), *Proceedings of ICRES 2024 – International Conference on Research in Education and Science* (pp. 56–73). International Society for Technology, Education, and Science.

Chounta, I. A., Bardone, E., Raudsep, A., & Pedaste, M. (2022). Exploring teachers' perceptions of artificial intelligence as a tool to support their practice in Estonian K-12 education. *International Journal of Artificial Intelligence in Education*, *32*, 725–755.

Cope, B., Kalantzis, M., & Searsmith, D. (2020). Artificial intelligence for education: Knowledge and its assessment in AI-enabled learning ecologies. *Educational Philosophy and Theory*, *52*(8), 786–800. DOI: 10.1080/00131857.2020.1728732

Das, S., Anowar, S., & Ghosh, B. (2024). The Rise of Artificial Intelligence in Education: Current Trends and Future Prospects (pp. 57–67). https://doi.org/DOI: 10.52756/lbsopf.2024.e01.006

Davis, F. D., Bagozzi, R. P., & Warshaw, P. R. (1989). User acceptance of computer technology: A comparison of two theoretical models. *Management Science*, *35*(8), 982–1003. DOI: 10.1287/mnsc.35.8.982

EdTech Magazine. (2020). *Successful AI examples in higher education that can inspire our future*. EdTech Magazine. Retrieved from https://edtechmagazine.com/higher-ed/article/2020/07/successful-ai-examples-higher-education-can-inspire-our-future

Gilakjani, A. P., Leong, L. M., & Ismail, H. N. (2013). Teachers'. *Use of Technology And Constructivism. Int. J. Mod. Educ. Comput. Sci.*, *5*, 49–63. DOI: 10.5815/ijmecs.2013.04.07

Gonçalves, B. (2023). Can machines think? The controversy that led to the Turing test. *AI & Society*, *38*(6), 2499–2509. DOI: 10.1007/s00146-021-01318-6

Hébert, C., Jenson, J., & Terzopoulos, T. (2021). "Access to technology is the major challenge": Teacher perspectives on barriers to DGBL in K-12 classrooms. *E-Learning and Digital Media*, *18*, 307–324. DOI: 10.1177/2042753021995315

Heffernan, N. T., & Heffernan, C. L. (2014). The ASSISTments ecosystem: Building a platform that brings scientists and teachers together for minimally invasive research on human learning and teaching. *International Journal of Artificial Intelligence in Education*, *24*, 470–497. DOI: 10.1007/s40593-014-0024-x

Hennekeuser, D., Vaziri, D. D., Golchinfar, D., Schreiber, D., & Stevens, G. (2024). Enlarged education – Exploring the use of generative AI to support lecturing in higher education. *International Journal of Artificial Intelligence in Education*. Advance online publication. DOI: 10.1007/s40593-024-00424-y

Holden, H., & Rada, R. (2011). Understanding the influence of perceived usability and technology self-efficacy on teachers' technology acceptance. *Journal of Research on Technology in Education*, *43*(4), 343–367. DOI: 10.1080/15391523.2011.10782576

Holmes, W., Bialik, M., & Fadel, C. (2019). *Artificial intelligence in education*. Centre for Curriculum Redesign., DOI: 10.1007/978-3-319-60013-0_107-1

Hubona, G., & Kennick, E. (1996). The impact of external variables on information technology usage behaviour. In Sprague, R. (Ed.), *Proceedings of the 29th Annual Hawai'i International Conference on System Sciences* (Vol. 4, pp. 166–176). Washington, DC: IEEE Computing Society Press.

Ibrahim, A., & Shiring, E. (2022). The relationship between educators' attitudes, perceived usefulness, and perceived ease of use of instructional and web-based technologies: Implications from Technology Acceptance Model (TAM). *International Journal of Technology in Education*, *5*(4), 535–551. DOI: 10.46328/ijte.285

Kavitha, K., & Joshith, V. P. (2024). The Transformative Trajectory of Artificial Intelligence in Education: The Two Decades of Bibliometric Retrospect. *Journal of Educational Technology Systems*. Advance online publication. DOI: 10.1177/00472395241231815

Labadze, L., Grigolia, M., & Machaidze, L. (2023). Role of AI chatbots in education: Systematic literature review. *International Journal of Educational Technology in Higher Education, 20*(1), 56.

Li, K. C., & Wong, B. T. M. (2023). Artificial intelligence in personalised learning: A bibliometric analysis. *Interactive Technology and Smart Education, 20*(3), 422–445. DOI: 10.1108/ITSE-01-2023-000

Luo, H., Luo, H., Li, Z., Li, Z., Liang, J., Li, G., & Yan, Y. (2024). Creating an immersive virtual reality game space for multiuser, synchronous co-located collaboration: Design considerations and influencing factors. *Applied Sciences (Basel, Switzerland), 14*(5), 2167. DOI: 10.3390/app14052167

Luo, X., Tong, S., Fang, Z., & Qu, Z. (2019). Machines vs. humans: The impact of artificial intelligence chatbot disclosure on customer purchases. *Marketing Science, 38*(6), 937–947. DOI: 10.1287/mksc.2019.1192

Moreno-Guerrero, A. J., López-Belmonte, J., Marín-Marín, J. A., & Soler-Costa, R. (2020). Scientific development of educational artificial intelligence in Web of Science. *Future Internet, 12*, 124–124.

Musa, H. G., Fatmawati, I., Nuryakin, N., & Suyanto, M. (2024). *Marketing research trends using technology acceptance model (TAM): a comprehensive review of research (2002–2022)*. https://doi.org/DOI: 10.1080/23311975.2024.2329375

Nikou, S. A., Guliya, A., Van Verma, S., & Chang, M. (2024). A generative artificial intelligence empowered chatbot: System usability and student teachers' experience. In Intelligent Tutoring Systems: 20th International Conference, ITS 2024, Thessaloniki, Greece, June 10–13, 2024, Proceedings (pp. 330–340). Springer. https://doi.org/DOI: 10.1007/978-3-031-63028-6_27

Panigrahi, C. M. A. (2020). Use of artificial intelligence in education. *Management Accounting (London), 55*, 64–67. DOI: 10.1371/journal.pone.0229596

Perrotta, C., & Selwyn, N. (2020). Deep learning goes to school: Toward a relational understanding of AI in education. *Learning, Media and Technology, 45*, 251–269.

Prensky, M. (2006). Listen to the natives. *Educational Leadership, 63*(4), 8–13. https://eric.ed.gov/?id=EJ745468

Prensky, M. (2008). Backup Education? Too many teachers see education as preparing kids for the past, not the future. *Educational Technology, 48*, 1–3.

Qin, F., Li, K., & Yan, J. (2020). Understanding user trust in artificial intelligence-based educational systems: Evidence from China. *British Journal of Educational Technology*, *51*, 1693–1710. DOI: 10.1111/bjet.12994

Rahman, M. K., Ismail, N. A., Hossain, M., & Hossen, M. M. (2025). Students' mindset to adopt AI chatbots for the effectiveness of online learning in higher education. *Future Business Journal*, *11*(1), 30. DOI: 10.1186/s43093-025-00459-0

Roll, I., & Wylie, R. (2016). Evolution and revolution in artificial intelligence in education. *International Journal of Artificial Intelligence in Education*, *26*, 582–599. DOI: 10.1007/s40593-016- 0110-3

Rudolph, J., Tan, S., & Tan, S. (2023). ChatGPT: Bullshit spewer or the end of traditional assessments in higher education? *Journal of Applied Learning and Teaching*, *6*(1), 9. Advance online publication. DOI: 10.37074/jalt.2023.6.1.9

Ryu, M., & Han, S. (2018). The educational perception of artificial intelligence by elementary school teachers. *J. Korean Assoc. Inform. Educ.*, *22*, 317–324. DOI: 10.1016/j.ridd.2019.01.002

Sevilla, C. G., Punsalan, T. G., Rovira, L. G., & Vendivel, F. G. (2006). *General psychology with values development lesson*. Rex Book Store, Inc.

Tallvid, M. (2016). Understanding teachers' reluctance to the pedagogical use of ICT in the 11th grade classroom. *Education and Information Technologies*, *21*, 503–519. DOI: 10.1007/s10639-014-9335-7

Zawacki-Richter, O., Marín, V. I., Bond, M., & Gouverneur, F. (2019). Systematic review of research on artificial intelligence applications in higher education—Where are the educators? *International Journal of Educational Technology in Higher Education*, *16*(1), 39. Advance online publication. DOI: 10.1186/s41239-019-0171-0

Zhang, K., & Aslan, A. B. (2021). AI technologies for education: Recent research & future directions. *Computers and Education: Artificial Intelligence*, *2*, 100025–100025.

Zimmerman, J. (2006). Why some teachers resist change and what principals can do about it. *NASSP Bulletin*, *90*, 238–249. DOI: 10.1177/0192636506291521

Chapter 10
The Rise of the Digital Tutor:
AI Chatbots and Virtual Assistants in Education

Goh Ying Yingsoon
https://orcid.org/0000-0002-6654-2887
Universiti Teknologi MARA, Malaysia

Liu Wenpang
https://orcid.org/0009-0009-1542-4870
Teesside University, UK

Zhang Suyan
https://orcid.org/0009-0003-4518-1650
Shandong Jianzhu University, China

Nurul Ain Chua Binti Abdullah
https://orcid.org/0000-0003-2915-1577
University Terengganu Malaysia, Malaysia

Nurul Ajleaa Abdul Rahman
Universiti Teknologi MARA, Malaysia

ABSTRACT

This chapter delves into the burgeoning role of AI chatbots and virtual assistants within the educational landscape. As artificial intelligence continues to advance, these tools are increasingly being integrated into classrooms and online learning environments, promising to revolutionize how students learn and educators teach. This chapter will explore the various applications of AI chatbots and virtual as-

DOI: 10.4018/979-8-3373-9225-7.ch010

sistants in education, including personalized learning, automated feedback, 24/7 student support, and the creation of immersive learning experiences. It will discuss the benefits and challenges associated with their implementation, such as improved student engagement, accessibility, and efficiency, while also addressing concerns regarding data privacy, algorithmic bias, and the potential impact on human interaction. Finally, it will explore the future trajectory of AI in education, considering the ethical and pedagogical implications of these technologies and their potential to reshape the future of learning.

1) INTRODUCTION

The landscape of education is undergoing a profound transformation, driven by the rapid advancement of artificial intelligence (AI). From early computer-aided instruction to the sophisticated algorithms of today, AI's role has evolved from a supplementary tool to a potentially transformative force. This evolution is particularly evident in the emergence of AI chatbots and virtual assistants, which are designed to interact with students in a personalized and adaptive manner. These technologies represent a significant leap forward, offering the potential to address some of the most persistent challenges in education, such as individualized learning, accessibility, and scalability (Noonia et al., 2024).

In the context of education, AI chatbots and virtual assistants are software applications that utilize natural language processing (NLP) and machine learning (ML) to simulate human-like conversations. They can provide students with instant answers to questions, offer personalized feedback, guide them through learning materials, and even facilitate collaborative learning experiences (Darwish, 2024). These tools can be integrated into various educational platforms, including learning management systems (LMS), mobile apps, and online learning environments. By automating routine tasks and providing on-demand support, AI chatbots and virtual assistants can free up educators' time, allowing them to focus on more complex and creative aspects of teaching.

This chapter aims to explore the multifaceted role of AI chatbots and virtual assistants in education. It will delve into their capabilities, benefits, and limitations, examining how they are being implemented in various educational settings. Furthermore, it will discuss the ethical considerations and potential challenges associated with their widespread adoption, including issues related to data privacy, equity, and the evolving role of human educators. By providing a comprehensive overview of this rapidly developing field, this chapter seeks to offer insights into the future of AI-powered education and its potential to reshape the learning experience.

2) APPLICATIONS OF AI CHATBOTS AND VIRTUAL ASSISTANTS IN EDUCATION

In the realm of personalized tutoring, AI chatbots are emerging as powerful tools capable of providing tailored educational support (Sajja et al., 2024). These intelligent systems can engage students in one-on-one interactions, adapting their teaching methods to suit individual learning styles and paces. By breaking down complex concepts, answering student queries in real-time, and generating bespoke examples, AI tutors can address specific learning gaps and foster deeper understanding. The advantages of this approach are manifold, including heightened student engagement, customized learning experiences that cater to unique needs, and the invaluable benefit of 24/7 availability, ensuring students can access assistance whenever they require it.

The application of AI In automated feedback and grading is revolutionizing the assessment process in education (Atherton et al., 2024). AI-powered systems can meticulously analyze student assignments, offering immediate feedback on aspects like grammar, style, and content, thereby accelerating the learning cycle. Furthermore, these technologies automate the grading of objective assessments, such as quizzes and multiple-choice tests, significantly reducing the workload for educators. This automation not only saves valuable time but also ensures that students receive faster feedback, enabling them to promptly address their areas of improvement. Additionally, AI-driven assessments provide consistent and objective evaluations, minimizing human bias and promoting fairness in the grading process.

In the domain of language learning, AI chatbots offer a dynamic and interactive approach to mastering new languages (Öncü, S. E., & Süral, 2024). These chatbots can engage students in simulated conversations, providing opportunities for practical application of language skills. They also serve as valuable resources for vocabulary acquisition, offering definitions, synonyms, and contextual usage. Moreover, AI's ability to provide real-time feedback on pronunciation allows learners to refine their spoken language skills effectively. This interactive and personalized practice leads to increased student engagement, tailored learning experiences, and ultimately, greater fluency in the target language.

Virtual assistants are proving to be invaluable tools in educational administration, effectively handling routine tasks that often consume significant time (Al-Jaf et al., 2024). These AI-driven assistants can efficiently address student inquiries, provide accurate information about schedules and deadlines, and streamline the course registration process. By automating these tasks, virtual assistants significantly free up time for educators and administrative staff, allowing them to focus on more strategic and complex responsibilities. This shift not only improves overall efficiency within educational institutions but also enhances communication between students, faculty, and administration, leading to a more organized and productive learning environment.

AI tools are significantly enhancing accessibility and inclusion in education by providing personalized support for students with disabilities (Chandramma et al., 2025). Technologies like text-to-speech and speech-to-text enable students with visual or auditory impairments to engage more effectively with learning materials. Furthermore, AI facilitates personalized learning adaptations, tailoring educational content and delivery to meet the unique needs of each student. This application of AI leads to increased accessibility for diverse learners, ensuring that all students can access and benefit from educational opportunities. By providing individualized support, AI fosters a more inclusive learning environment, promoting equity and empowering students to reach their full potential.

AI chatbots are playing a crucial role in bolstering student support and guidance within educational institutions (Martinez-Requejo et al., 2024). These chatbots act as readily available resources, providing students with answers to frequently asked questions, delivering valuable study tips, and offering emotional support when needed. By providing this consistent support, educational institutions can enhance student well-being and increase student retention rates. Moreover, chatbots can facilitate a smoother transition and acclimation process for new students, offering information and guidance that helps them navigate the academic and social aspects of their educational journey. This readily accessible support system ensures that students feel supported and connected, fostering a more positive and productive learning environment.

In the realm of course content delivery, AI chatbots are proving to be effective tools for enhancing student access and engagement (Abdallah et al., 2024). These chatbots can provide students with on-demand access to course materials, summaries, and relevant information, ensuring that learning resources are readily available whenever needed. Additionally, they can facilitate the distribution of quizzes and practice questions, reinforcing learning and promoting active recall. This greater availability of materials increases the chances of student content retention, as information is accessible at their fingertips. Furthermore, chatbots facilitate student-guided studies by allowing students to review and practice material at their own pace and convenience. This approach promotes independent learning and empowers students to take ownership of their educational journey.

AI chatbots and virtual assistants are being implemented across various educational domains, offering personalized tutoring, automated feedback, and administrative support. These applications aim to enhance student engagement, improve accessibility, and free up educators' time, ultimately leading to more efficient and effective learning experiences. (see Table 1).

Table 1. Various applications of AI chatbots and virtual assistants in education

Application area	Description	Benefits
Personalized tutoring	AI chatbots can provide one-on-one tutoring, adapting to individual student learning styles and paces. They can explain complex concepts, answer questions, and provide tailored examples.	Increased student engagement, personalized learning experiences, ability to address individual learning gaps, 24/7 availability.
Automated feedback and grading	AI can analyze student assignments and provide instant feedback on grammar, style, and content. They can also automate the grading of quizzes and multiple-choice tests.	Reduced teacher workload, faster feedback for students, consistent and objective assessment.
Language learning	Chatbots can engage students in conversational practice, provide vocabulary assistance, and offer real-time feedback on pronunciation.	Interactive and engaging language learning, personalized practice opportunities, increased fluency.
Administrative support	Virtual assistants can handle routine administrative tasks, such as answering student inquiries, providing information about schedules and deadlines, and assisting with course registration.	Freed up time for educators and administrative staff, improved efficiency, streamlined communication.
Accessibility and inclusion	AI tools can provide support for students with disabilities, such as text-to-speech, speech-to-text, and personalized learning adaptations.	Increased accessibility for diverse learners, personalized support to meet individual needs, greater inclusion.
Student support and guidance	Chatbots can provide students with resources, answer frequently asked questions, offer study tips, and offer emotional support.	Enhanced student support, increased student retention, readily available information, easier transition and acclimation to schools.
Course content delivery	Chatbots can give students access to course materials, summaries, and information when needed. They can also aid in the distrubution of quizes and practice questions.	Greater availability of materials, increased chances of student content retention, and allows for student guided studies.

3) PERSONALIZED LEARNING

Adaptive learning platforms and human-driven individualized instruction both strive to personalize education, but they differ significantly in their approaches (Chiriboga et al., 2025; Yekollu et al., 2024). Adaptive platforms leverage algorithmic analysis to collect and utilize granular student data, enabling real-time adjustments to content, pacing, and feedback, and facilitating scalability through automation. In contrast, human-driven instruction relies on teacher observation and manual adaptation, allowing for nuanced, contextual understanding but demanding substantial teacher time and resources. While adaptive platforms excel in data-driven efficiency and scalability, human instruction offers unparalleled flexibility and emotional intelligence, highlighting a potential synergy between technology and human expertise for optimal individualized learning. (see Table 2).

Table 2. The intersection of adaptive learning platforms and individualized instruction

Feature	Adaptive learning platforms	Individualized instruction (human-driven)
Data collection & analysis	Collect granular data on student performance, learning patterns, and knowledge gaps through algorithmic analysis.	Relies on teacher observation, assessments, and feedback to understand individual student needs. Requires intensive teacher effort.
Personalized content delivery	Adjusts content difficulty, pacing, and modality (text, video, interactive exercises) in real-time based on student progress.	Teachers create custom learning plans, use differentiated materials, and provide one-on-one support tailored to each student.
Feedback mechanism	Provides instant, automated feedback on student performance, highlighting areas for improvement and offering targeted remediation.	Teachers deliver personalized feedback during instruction, in written form, or through meetings, requiring considerable teacher time.
Pacing	Enables students to progress at their own pace, adjusting the learning path as needed.	Accommodates varied pacing through flexible assignment deadlines or differentiated instruction, but heavily dependent on instructor awareness and planning.
Flexibility and scalability	Can be deployed at scale to reach a large number of students, offering consistent and personalized learning experiences.	Demands significant instructor time and resources, making it challenging to scale effectively for larger classrooms or diverse populations.
Automation	Automates administrative tasks, such as generating reports and tracking student progress.	Requires educators to manually handle most administrative tasks, which may diminish instructional focus.
Student agency	Allows students increased control over their learning path with some degree of self directed learning.	Empowers student's through the incorporation of choices relating to the learning process; allowing students to control various parts of their learning.
Data utilization	Aggregates and analyzes student data to improve curriculum design and predict potential student challenges, allowing educators to address issues proactively.	Relies heavily on individual teacher interpretation and application of student data, which may lead to inconsistencies in implementation and support across students.
Technology integration	Highly integrated with digital tools and resources to deliver dynamic and interactive learning experiences.	Can incorporate technology but may rely more on traditional teaching methods and resources.

4) AUTOMATED FEEDBACK AND ASSESSMENT

Grading essays and providing instant feedback

Automated feedback and assessment tools, powered by AI, offer a range of functionalities from analyzing grammar and style to detecting plagiarism and providing instant scoring. While these tools provide significant benefits, such as instant feedback, reduced teacher workload, and consistent grading, they also present challenges. AI algorithms may struggle with nuanced language, creative writing, and complex arguments, and there's a risk of over-reliance on automated feedback, potentially hindering the development of critical thinking skills. Moreover, the accuracy of content analysis depends heavily on database completeness, and ethical considerations surrounding data use and potential false positives in plagiarism detection must be carefully addressed. (see Table 3).

Automated feedback and assessment tools, powered by AI, offer a range of functionalities from analyzing grammar and style to detecting plagiarism and providing instant scoring (Fidan & Gencel, 2022; Ifelebuegu, 2023). While these tools provide significant benefits, such as instant feedback, reduced teacher workload, and consistent grading, they also present challenges. AI algorithms may struggle with nuanced language, creative writing, and complex arguments, and there's a risk of over-reliance on automated feedback, potentially hindering the development of critical thinking skills. Moreover, the accuracy of content analysis depends heavily on database completeness, and ethical considerations surrounding data use and potential false positives in plagiarism detection must be carefully addressed.

Table 3. Automated feedback and assessment, specifically focusing on grading essays and providing instant feedback

Feature	Description	Benefits	Challenges
Grammar & mechanics analysis	AI algorithms analyze essays for grammatical errors, punctuation mistakes, and sentence structure issues.	Instant identification and correction of basic errors, improved writing clarity, helps students understand structural rules.	Potential for misinterpretation of stylistic choices, may not capture subtle nuances in language, focus mainly on surface-level errors.
Style & cohesion analysis	AI analyzes writing style, flow, and coherence, providing feedback on sentence variety, transitions, and overall organization.	Enhances writing organization and style, provides insights into improving essay structure, develops better writing techniques.	Subjectivity in style analysis, struggle with creative or non-standard writing, less effective with complex or abstract ideas.
Content relevance & accuracy	AI can check if content is relevant to the prompt and if facts are accurate, using databases and semantic analysis.	Provides quick feedback on adherence to prompt requirements and factual accuracy, aids in research and content development.	Difficulty in judging nuanced arguments and complex analyses, accuracy dependent on database completeness, may overlook logical fallacies outside factual errors.
Instant scoring/ grading	Automates grading based on predefined rubrics, analyzing specific features of the essay.	Saves teachers time, ensures consistent and objective grading, provides quick feedback for students.	Difficulty in capturing the complexity of written expression, potential to undervalue creativity and originality, rubric creation complexity
Personalized feedback reports	Generates detailed reports highlighting strengths and weaknesses, offers suggestions for improvement, and provides targeted resources.	Facilitates individualized learning, aids in targeted revision, provides a comprehensive overview of writing skills.	Requires sophisticated AI to provide meaningful and accurate suggestions, possibility of students becoming reliant on AI feedback rather than critical thought.
Plagiarism detection	Scans submitted work for similarity to existing text using large databases.	Helps ensure academic integrity, deters plagiarism, can aid in teaching proper citation practices.	Possibility of false positives, inability to detect all forms of paraphrasing, ethical consideration in data use.

Formative assessment and progress tracking

AI-driven formative assessment and progress tracking offer significant advantages through real-time data collection, instant feedback, and personalized reporting (Tao, 2025; Rizvi, 2024; Martínez-Requejo & Ruiz-Lazaro, 2024; Rym, 2024). These tools provide valuable insights into student comprehension, facilitate immediate intervention, and enable customized learning paths, ultimately enhancing the learning experience. However, challenges such as data overload, the need for accurate algorithms, and potential biases in predictive analytics must be carefully addressed. Over-reliance on automated tools, ethical concerns regarding data privacy, and the complexity of data interpretation also pose significant considerations. Ensuring effective integration of AI into pedagogical practices and maintaining a balance between technology and human interaction are crucial for maximizing the benefits of these tools while mitigating potential drawbacks. (see Table 4).

Table 4. Formative assessment and progress tracking through AI

Feature	Description	Benefits	Challenges
Real-time Data Collection	AI-driven platforms gather data during the learning process through quizzes, interactive exercises, and responses to questions.	Provides immediate insights into student comprehension, enabling timely adjustments to instruction.	Potential for data overload, difficulty in interpreting complex interaction data, relying solely on surface data instead of deeper understanding.
Instant Feedback & Adjustments	AI analyzes student responses and provides instant feedback, identifying areas of misunderstanding. It also adjusts the subsequent material based on real time data.	Facilitates immediate intervention, promotes active learning, personalized pace adjustment.	Dependence on accurate algorithms, possible distraction through over-stimulation with instant feedback, needs strong pedagogical design to function effectively.
Personalized Progress Reports	AI creates detailed reports outlining individual student progress, including strengths and weaknesses.	Enables teachers to monitor individual development over time, facilitates targeted support, keeps students informed and motivated.	Potential for over-reliance on reports to guide teaching (rather than direct interaction), raises questions concerning data privacy, data visualization complexity for some educators and students.
Learning Path Adaptation	AI modifies the learning path based on ongoing performance, recommending specific resources or adjusting the difficulty level of tasks.	Provides individualized learning experiences, caters to diverse learning speeds, supports mastery learning.	Requires sophisticated algorithms to ensure appropriate modifications, may lead to fragmentation if not integrated into a structured curriculum.
Predictive Analytics	AI uses historical data to predict student performance and identify at-risk students.	Enables early intervention to prevent learning difficulties, helps in planning personalized interventions, proactively addresses concerns.	Potential for bias in historical data, ethical concerns surrounding algorithmic prediction, risk of labeling students early based on predictive algorithms.
Automated Question Generation	AI can create practice questions and formative assessments based on learning materials and past performance data.	Provides varied and customized practice, helps students in spaced repetition, simplifies teacher workload by automating simple tasks.	Can over generate questions, requiring quality control, risk of overly repetitive question types, may not be able to produce nuanced and creative prompts.

5) 24/7 STUDENT SUPPORT

24/7 student support, powered by AI chatbots and virtual assistants, offers numerous benefits, including instant access to information, flexible tutoring outside traditional hours, and technical troubleshooting (Roca et al., 2024 ; Razak et al., 2024 ; Gayathri et al., 2024). While this enhances student convenience and reduces administrative burdens, it also presents challenges. AI systems require accurate and comprehensive knowledge bases, and they may struggle with nuanced questions or complex problems. There's also the risk of student over-dependence, the limitations of AI in providing emotional support, and the need for careful resource curation to prevent information overload. Ultimately, the successful implementation of 24/7 support requires a balance between leveraging AI's capabilities and acknowledging its limitations, ensuring that human intervention remains a critical component of student assistance. (see Table 5).

Table 5. 24/7 student support

Feature	Description	Benefits	Challenges
Answering faqs and providing technical assistance	AI chatbots provide instant answers to frequently asked questions related to course logistics, deadlines, technical issues, and university policies.	Instant access to information, reduced waiting times, decreased administrative burden on staff, helps ensure students find easy answers.	Requires accurate and comprehensive knowledge bases, potential for misinterpreting nuanced questions, limited ability to handle complex or unique problems.
Tutoring and academic support (outside hours)	AI tutors offer assistance with coursework, study materials, and concept clarification beyond traditional classroom hours, providing individualized support.	Flexible learning schedule, caters to diverse student needs, helps students reinforce learning at their own pace, consistent support whenever needed.	Potential for student dependence, difficulty in addressing complex or subjective questions, possible lack of emotional and social cues.
Technical troubleshooting	AI assistants guide students through common technical problems related to learning platforms, software, and hardware.	Reduces downtime during learning, facilitates independent problem-solving, improves student digital literacy.	Needs up-to-date and accurate problem-solving databases, possible frustration for students when addressing novel tech issues, assumes consistent hardware between users.

continued on following page

Table 5. Continued

Feature	Description	Benefits	Challenges
Resource and information provision	AI can provide links, documents, and helpful guides to students when needed 24/7.	Increases the accessibility of materials, students can easily gain deeper understanding in a topic at any time.	Students could feel overwhelmed by a large amount of undifferentiated information, there is a requirement of careful curation.
Emotional and wellbeing support (basic)	Chatbots can provide resources and refer students to proper help centers relating to students' personal wellbeing 24/7.	Students feel supported and have access to resources at any point, potentially reduces students feelings of isolation.	There are limitations on the depth of emotional intelligence of chat bots, cannot replace proper mental health professionals, need to have ethical safeguards.

6) IMMERSIVE LEARNING EXPERIENCES

Immersive learning experiences powered by AI offer significant benefits, including enhanced experiential learning through virtual simulations, accelerated language acquisition via cultural exchange, and increased accessibility to scientific explorations and historical Recreations (Knihová, 2024 ; Garg et al., 2024 ; Chheang et al., 2024). However, these experiences also present challenges. High development costs, the need for sophisticated algorithms, and potential technical glitches can hinder widespread adoption. Additionally, ensuring authentic cultural representations and avoiding algorithmic bias in language learning, as well as maintaining historical accuracy and avoiding distraction in gamified learning, require careful consideration. Striking a balance between the immersive potential of AI and the essential human elements of education is critical to maximize the benefits while mitigating the risks. (see Table 6).

Table 6. Immersive learning experiences powered by AI

Feature	Description	Benefits	Challenges
Virtual Simulations and Interactive Learning Environments	AI drives realistic virtual simulations, allowing students to interact with complex scenarios, conduct experiments, and experience practical applications of knowledge in a safe and engaging virtual setting.	Enhanced experiential learning, deeper understanding through hands-on interaction, safe exploration of potentially dangerous or expensive scenarios, increased student engagement and motivation.	High development costs, requires sophisticated AI algorithms and robust infrastructure, potential for technical glitches, possibility of virtual experiences overshadowing real-world applications.
Language Learning and Cultural Exchange	AI-powered virtual environments facilitate language immersion and cultural exchange by simulating real-world interactions, including conversations, cultural scenarios, and cross-cultural collaborations.	Accelerated language acquisition, deeper understanding of cultural nuances, increased intercultural competence, accessible international collaboration opportunities.	Ensuring authentic cultural representations, navigating cultural sensitivities, limitations in capturing non-verbal cues and social dynamics, potential for algorithmic bias in representing diverse cultures.
Virtual Labs and Scientific Explorations	AI generates customized virtual labs and scientific explorations, allowing students to conduct experiments they may otherwise not be able to.	Makes learning more accessible, customizable labs, and makes complicated scientific processes easier to interact with.	Can have large memory and computing power requirements, could take long periods of time to design complex virtual worlds, and may miss the human element of science.
Historical Recreations and Explorations	Allows students to experience and explore history in an immersive, interactive experience.	Learning comes alive, increases understanding and content retention, and enhances student enjoyment of learning.	Accuracy relating to historical points must be monitored closely, may have issues representing all historical groups, could distract student from core learning objective.
Gamified Learning Experiences	Adds game like elements to a learning experience to make it more engaging. Students can control in world avatars, participate in team activities, and earn points or rewards relating to progress.	Encourages active learning, can greatly increase students' enjoyment, promotes in class competition.	Need to create strong learning frameworks around game elements, the gaming elements of some programs may distract students, requires planning to avoid "learning through play" being the only method of learning.

7) BENEFITS AND CHALLENGES

Benefits

AI chatbots and virtual assistants offer a multitude of benefits to the educational landscape (Naik et al., 2024 ; Gökçearslan et al., 2024 ; Dastani & Mohseni, 2024). They significantly increase student engagement and motivation through personalized, interactive learning experiences, fostering a deeper connection with the material. Furthermore, these technologies enhance accessibility and equity by providing tailored support to diverse learners, removing barriers related to disabilities, language, and location. Educators benefit from reduced workloads as AI automates administrative tasks and assessment, allowing them to focus on personalized instruction and creative teaching. Additionally, AI-driven personalized and adaptive learning caters to individual student needs, improving content mastery and motivation. Finally, data-driven insights from AI analytics enable educators and administrators to make informed decisions, leading to more effective curriculum design and intervention strategies, ultimately improving educational outcomes for all students. (see Table 7).

Table 7. The benefits of AI chatbots and virtual assistants in education

Benefit	Description	Specific examples	Impact
Increased student engagement and motivation	AI-driven interactive tools and personalized learning experiences make learning more enjoyable and relevant.	Virtual simulations and gamified learning platforms that capture student interest; chatbots that provide immediate feedback and encouragement; personalized learning paths that cater to individual interests and learning styles.	Higher participation rates, improved focus and retention of knowledge, increased intrinsic motivation to learn, students feel more connected to the material.
Improved accessibility and equity in education	AI tools provide personalized support for students with diverse needs, breaking down barriers to learning.	Text-to-speech and speech-to-text tools for students with disabilities; language translation tools for multilingual learners; 24/7 access to resources for students with demanding schedules or remote locations; personalized learning for student needing individualized instruction.	Equitable access to quality education for all learners, regardless of physical or learning differences, geographical location, or socioeconomic background; reduces gaps in educational outcomes.
Enhanced efficiency and reduced workload for educators	AI automates administrative tasks and provides assistance with assessment, allowing educators to focus on more complex and creative aspects of teaching.	Chatbots that handle routine inquiries and provide administrative support; automated grading tools that provide instant feedback; AI-driven learning analytics that track student progress and identify areas for intervention.	More time for educators to engage in personalized instruction, develop innovative lesson plans, and provide meaningful feedback; reduced administrative burden and burnout; teachers are enabled to concentrate on student-educator interactions.
Personalized and adaptive learning	AI adapts the pace and content of the lesson for each student.	Algorithmic learning that increases in difficulty based upon successful performance.	Increased content mastery, increased ease for struggling students, and allows advanced students to maintain motivation.
Data-driven insights	AI tools analyze learning data to provide actionable insights for educators and administrators.	Learning analytics platforms that visualize student progress, identify learning patterns, and predict potential challenges.	Data-informed decision-making for curriculum design, intervention strategies, and resource allocation; improved understanding of student needs and learning effectiveness.

Challenges

The integration of AI chatbots and virtual assistants in education presents several significant challenges (Storey & Wagner, 2024 ; Casheekar et al., 2024). Data privacy and security concerns arise from the storage and potential misuse of sensitive student data, leading to decreased trust and legal ramifications. Algorithmic bias can perpetuate systemic inequities, unfairly impacting student assessment and learning experiences. Over-reliance on AI may also diminish human interaction, hindering the development of crucial social-emotional skills. Implementation costs and the digital divide further exacerbate inequalities, limiting access to these technologies for underserved communities. Lastly, the ease of access to digital answers can lead to a decline in students' critical thinking abilities, as they may prioritize quick solutions over deep learning and problem-solving. Addressing these challenges requires careful consideration of ethical implications, equitable access, and the preservation of essential human elements in education. (see Table 8).

Table 8. The challenges associated with AI chatbots and virtual assistants in education

Challenge	Description	Specific examples	Impact
Data privacy and security concerns	The collection and storage of sensitive student data, including learning patterns and personal information, raise concerns about unauthorized access and misuse.	Storage of student assessment data, learning progress, and personal details on cloud servers; the use of student data for targeted advertising or other purposes outside of educational improvement.	Potential for identity theft, privacy breaches, and misuse of student information; decreased trust in educational institutions and technology providers; legal and ethical ramifications.
Algorithmic bias and ethical considerations	AI algorithms may perpetuate or amplify existing biases in data, leading to unfair or discriminatory outcomes.	AI-driven assessment tools that score students unfairly based on race or socioeconomic status; AI tutoring systems that reinforce stereotypes or provide culturally insensitive content.	Systemic inequities in education, unfair assessment of students, erosion of trust in AI-powered tools, ethical dilemmas related to fairness and accountability.
The potential impact on human interaction and social-emotional learning	Over-reliance on AI can reduce human interaction, potentially hindering the development of crucial social and emotional skills.	Chatbots that replace face-to-face interactions between students and teachers; virtual learning environments that isolate learners from social interactions.	Diminished social skills, reduced empathy and emotional intelligence, difficulty in building relationships; decreased opportunities for collaboration and teamwork; decline in crucial hands on experiences.

continued on following page

Table 8. Continued

Challenge	Description	Specific examples	Impact
Implementation costs and the digital divide	The cost of developing, implementing, and maintaining AI-powered educational tools can create barriers to access, especially for schools with limited resources.	High upfront costs for advanced AI software and hardware; limited access to reliable internet and digital devices in underserved communities.	Exacerbated inequalities in education, unequal access to AI-driven learning tools, widening the gap between well-resourced and under-resourced schools.
Over-reliance and decreased critical thinking	When students can always find a digital answer, there is a risk of them stopping developing deep thinking skills.	Students relying on chat bot help instead of seeking answers within a text or through creative problem solving.	Diminishing in class critical thinking abilities, decreased ability to self-evaluate without a given rubric.

8) CASE STUDIES AND REAL-WORLD EXAMPLES

The University of Southern California, collaborating with Georgia Tech, implemented "Jill Watson," an AI chatbot, into an online graduate-level AI course to provide 24/7 support to students in the course forum (Design & Intelligence Laboratory (DILab), n.d.; Goel & Joyner, 2024). This initiative significantly reduced the instructor's workload while offering students instant assistance, leading to increased engagement. The project highlighted critical lessons: the necessity of thorough chatbot training and clear communication about its role to manage student expectations, and the understanding that while efficient, AI should complement, not replace, human interaction. The technology leveraged IBM Watson and custom LMS chatbot integrations to facilitate this seamless support system.

Duolingo's innovative approach to language learning leverages AI to create a highly personalized and interactive experience (Handini et al., 2022). By integrating AI-powered chatbot interactions, the platform provides students with contextual feedback on their language use and simulates real-world conversational scenarios. This application of AI has demonstrably increased student engagement and time spent learning, highlighting the effectiveness of personalized and adaptive learning pathways. Duolingo's success underscores the importance of continuous data analysis and iterative improvement in refining AI models, while also revealing a strong demand for more interactive and engaging language learning tools, all facilitated by their proprietary AI language model.

University successfully implemented a chatbot to streamline admissions and student support services, providing instant answers to frequently asked questions regarding admissions, financial aid, and academic advising (Ardimento & Scalera,

2024). This initiative resulted in a significant reduction in administrative inquiries, freeing up staff time and improving student satisfaction by delivering consistent and immediate information. The project demonstrated the potential of chatbots to enhance accessibility to essential student services, while also emphasizing the critical importance of creating a user-friendly interface and establishing clear escalation paths for complex student inquiries. This university utilized platforms such as AdmitHub and Oracle chatbot platforms to achieve these positive outcomes.

These case studies illustrate the successful integration of AI chatbots and virtual assistants in diverse educational settings, demonstrating their ability to enhance student support and streamline administrative tasks. The examples highlight key lessons in AI implementation, including the importance of personalized learning, effective communication, and the need for a balanced approach that combines AI efficiency with human interaction. (see Table 9).

Table 9. Three case studies showcasing real-world implementations of AI chatbots and virtual assistants in educational settings, alongside lessons learned and software examples

Case study	Implementation	Results and lessons learned	Software examples
University of southern california (usc) - jill watson (georgia tech course implementation)	AI chatbot integrated into an online graduate-level AI course. "Jill Watson" provided 24/7 answers to student questions in the course forum.	- Significantly reduced instructor workload. - Provided students with instant support, increasing engagement. - Highlighted the importance of careful training and clear communication about the chatbot's role to manage expectations. - Showed that while efficient, a chatbot shouldn't replace all Human interaction.	- IBM Watson - Custom LMS chatbot integrations
Duolingo's ai-powered language learning	Integration of AI to personalize language learning experience. Chatbot interactions provide contextual feedback on language use and provide real world conversational opportunities.	- Dramatically increased student engagement and time spent learning. - Demonstrated the effectiveness of using AI for personalized and adaptive learning pathways. - Emphasized the value of iterative improvement and continuous data analysis to refine the AI model's performance. - Shows the demand for a more interactive language learning experience.	- Duolingo's proprietary AI language model.
University - admissions and student support chatbot	Implemented a chatbot to provide instant answers to frequently asked questions from prospective and current students relating to admissions, financial aid, and academic advising.	- Reduced administrative inquiries, freeing up staff time. - Provided consistent and immediate information, improving student satisfaction. - Proved that chatbots can enhance accessibility to essential student services. - Showed the importance of creating a user-friendly interface and providing clear escalation paths for complex inquiries.	- AdmitHub - Oracle chatbot platforms

9) THE FUTURE OF AI IN EDUCATION

The future of AI in education is being shaped by several emerging trends and technologies (Alam & Hasan, 2024; Graefen & Fazal, 2024). Enhanced Natural Language Processing (NLP) is paving the way for more sophisticated and personalized AI tutors, while deep learning facilitates the creation of highly adaptable educational content. The increasing development of AI-driven Virtual Reality (VR) and Augmented Reality (AR) learning environments promises to deliver immersive and engaging educational experiences. Furthermore, the integration of AI-powered learning analytics, coupled with the expansion of 5G connectivity, enables real-time data-driven decisions for curriculum development and the deployment of AI learning on localized networks through edge computing. These advancements collectively point towards a future where education is more personalized, interactive, and efficient.

AI is poised to fundamentally reshape the future of learning by driving personalized and adaptive educational experiences at scale (Kayyali, 2024; Baker et al., 2023). This transformation will make learning more engaging and efficient, tailoring educational content and delivery to individual student needs. Moreover, AI has the potential to create lifelong learning ecosystems, providing continuous educational support throughout a person's life. This shift will lead to classrooms becoming dynamic hubs of personalized learning, where students are empowered with data-driven tools to take control of their educational journeys. Additionally, AI-enabled career guidance will emerge, offering students tailored pathways to professional development, ensuring they are equipped with the skills and knowledge needed for future success.

The integration of AI into education necessitates careful consideration of ethical and pedagogical factors (Pappagallo, 2024; Kooli, 2023). Key among these are safeguarding student data privacy, mitigating algorithmic biases, and ensuring the continued presence of the human element in learning. Effective AI implementation also requires designing systems that support diverse learning styles and promoting transparent AI decision-making. To address these concerns, the development of robust ethical guidelines and regulations is crucial. Incorporating diverse datasets during AI development can help mitigate bias, while curriculum design should prioritize fostering human interaction alongside AI assistance. Furthermore, educators and AI developers require comprehensive training in responsible AI design to ensure that these technologies are used ethically and effectively in educational settings.

The future of AI in education hinges on the crucial concept of human-AI collaboration, emphasizing that AI should augment, rather than replace, human educators (Hutson & Plate, 2023; Fui-Hoon Nah et al., 2023; Sowa et al., 2021). This collaborative model envisions teachers evolving into facilitators, leveraging AI to deliver personalized and adaptive learning experiences. Such a partnership fosters a synergistic learning environment, seamlessly blending the unique strengths of human creativity and empathy with AI's efficiency and data-processing capabilities. This approach not only optimizes learning outcomes but also creates a renewed focus on nurturing students' creative potential, ensuring that technology enhances, rather than diminishes, the essential human aspects of education.

The future of AI in education highlights emerging technologies that promise personalized learning and data-driven insights, while also emphasizing the crucial need for ethical guidelines and human-AI collaboration. As AI transforms educational landscapes, it's vital to balance technological advancements with human-centric pedagogy, ensuring equitable access and responsible implementation. (see Table 10).

Table 10. The future of AI in education, focusing on emerging trends, its role in shaping learning, ethical considerations, and human-AI collaboration

Topic	Description	Implications and considerations
Emerging trends and technologies	Includes advances like enhanced Natural Language Processing (NLP), deep learning for personalized content creation, increased development of AI-driven VR/AR learning, and the integration of AI-powered learning analytics with the growth of 5g connectivity.	Personalized AI tutors become more prevalent, AI-driven content is more adaptable, immersive learning increases, data-driven decisions relating to curriculum occur in real time, edge computing allows AI learning on localized networks.
The role of ai in shaping the future of learning	AI will drive personalized, adaptive learning at scale, transforming the learning experience to be more engaging and efficient. AI can help create lifelong learning ecosystems, providing continuous educational support.	Classrooms become hubs of personalized learning facilitated by AI, students empowered with data driven tools for their own learning, AI enabled career guidance develops.
Ethical and pedagogical considerations	Focuses on safeguarding student data privacy, mitigating algorithmic biases, maintaining human element in learning, designing AI that supports diverse learning styles, and ensures transparent AI decision-making.	Development of ethical guidelines and regulations around AI in education, incorporation of diverse data sets to avoid bias, curriculum designed to foster human interaction along with AI assistance, training in responsible AI design needed.
The importance of human-ai collaboration	Stresses the necessity of AI augmenting, not replacing, human educators. Teachers will become facilitators, using AI to provide personalized student learning experiences.	Fosters a synergistic learning environment that blends the best of human creativity and empathy with AI's efficiency and data-processing capabilities. Creates a focus on creativity.

10) CONCLUSION

The exploration of AI chatbots and virtual assistants in education reveals a landscape brimming with potential and complexity. Key findings underscore their capacity to personalize learning, automate tasks, and enhance accessibility. From providing 24/7 student support to creating immersive learning experiences, these technologies are transforming traditional educational paradigms. However, the journey is not without its challenges. Ethical considerations, data privacy, and the preservation of human interaction remain paramount. Ultimately, the successful integration of AI hinges on a balanced approach that leverages its efficiency while safeguarding the essential human elements of teaching and learning. (Chen et al., 2023).

Reflecting on the potential impact, it is clear that AI chatbots and virtual assistants can significantly democratize education, offering tailored support to diverse learners and freeing educators to focus on higher-level pedagogical activities (Kuzmanov, 2024 ; Luckyardi et al., 2024). The ability to provide instant feedback, adapt learning paths, and offer personalized tutoring can dramatically improve student outcomes and engagement. However, the risk of over-reliance and the potential for exacerbating existing inequalities must be addressed through careful planning and implementation. The future of education is not about replacing human educators but about empowering them with AI tools that augment their capabilities and enhance the learning experience.

Instructional design plays a pivotal role in the successful integration of AI chatbots and virtual assistants within educational settings (Chang et al, 2023; Chen et al., 2023). It ensures that these technologies are not merely adopted as novel tools, but are strategically implemented to enhance learning outcomes. Effective instructional design frameworks guide the creation of AI-driven learning experiences that are pedagogically sound, engaging, and aligned with educational objectives. This involves carefully considering how AI can personalize learning, provide meaningful feedback, and facilitate interactive experiences while also addressing ethical considerations such as data privacy and algorithmic bias. By designing learning experiences that prioritize human-AI collaboration, instructional designers help create environments where AI augments, rather than replaces, the essential role of human educators, ultimately fostering a more effective and equitable learning ecosystem.

In conclusion, AI chatbots and virtual assistants represent a powerful force in the evolution of education. As these technologies continue to advance, it is imperative that we prioritize ethical development, equitable access, and human-centered design. By fostering collaboration between educators, technologists, and policymakers, we can harness the transformative potential of AI to create a more inclusive, effective, and engaging learning environment for all. The goal is to create a future where AI serves as a catalyst for human potential, enriching the educational experience and preparing students for the challenges and opportunities of the 21st century.

REFERENCES

Abdallah, A. K., Alkaabi, A. M., Mehiar, D. A. F., & Aradat, Z. A. J. (2024). Chatbots in Classrooms: Tailoring Education and Boosting Engagement. In *Cutting-Edge Innovations in Teaching, Leadership, Technology, and Assessment* (pp. 166-181). IGI Global. Can be accessed at https://library.oapen.org/bitstream/handle/20.500.12657/88268/9798369308813.pdf?sequence=3#page=187

Al-Jaf, K., Öz, C., Mahmud, H., & Rashid, T. A. (2024). *Leveraging Chatbots for Effective Educational Administration: A Systematic Review*. Can be accessed at https://www.preprints.org/frontend/manuscript/89d7afca4e6f6e3b8ac319f446f7030c/download_pub

Alam, M., & Hasan, M. (2024). Applications and future prospects of artificial intelligence in education. *International Journal of Humanities & Social Science Studies*, pp. 209-218. DOI: DOI: 10.29032/ijhsss.v10.i1.2024.209-218

Ardimento, P., & Scalera, M. (2024). Enhancing Higher Education with AI: Balancing Personalized Learning and Ethical Responsibility. In *Book of Abstracts* (p. 164). Can be accessed at https://air.unimi.it/bitstream/2434/1121742/3/BOA_HELMETO2024.pdf#page=180

Atherton, P., Topham, L., & Khan, W. (2024). AI and student feedback. *EDULEARN24 Proceedings*. Can be accessed at https://researchonline.ljmu.ac.uk/id/eprint/23757/1/AI%20AND%20STUDENT%20FEEDBACK.pdf

Baker, B., Mills, K. A., McDonald, P., & Wang, L. (2023). AI, concepts of intelligence, and chatbots: The "Figure of Man," the rise of emotion, and future visions of education. *Teachers College Record*, *125*(6), 60–84. DOI: 10.1177/01614681231191291

Casheekar, A., Lahiri, A., Rath, K., Prabhakar, K. S., & Srinivasan, K. (2024). A contemporary review on chatbots, AI-powered virtual conversational agents, ChatGPT: Applications, open challenges and future research directions. *Computer Science Review*, *52*, 100632. DOI: 10.1016/j.cosrev.2024.100632

Chandramma, R., Babu, K. S., Ranjith, K. S., Sinha, A. K., Neerugatti, V., & Reddy, D. S. (2025, January). Enhancing E-learning Accessibility through AI (Artificial Intelligence) and Inclusive Design. In *2025 6th International Conference on Mobile Computing and Sustainable Informatics (ICMCSI)* (pp. 1466-1471). IEEE. Doi: DOI: 10.1109/ICMCSI64620.2025.10883148

Chang, D. H., Lin, M. P. C., Hajian, S., & Wang, Q. Q. (2023). Educational design principles of using AI chatbot that supports self-regulated learning in education: Goal setting, feedback, and personalization. *Sustainability, 15*(17), 12921. Can be accessed at https://www.mdpi.com/2071-1050/15/17/12921

Chen, Y., Jensen, S., Albert, L. J., Gupta, S., & Lee, T. (2023). Artificial intelligence (AI) student assistants in the classroom: Designing chatbots to support student success. *Information Systems Frontiers, 25*(1), 161–182. DOI: 10.1007/s10796-022-10291-4

Chheang, V., Sharmin, S., Márquez-Hernández, R., Patel, M., Rajasekaran, D., Caulfield, G., . . . Barmaki, R. L. (2024, January). Towards anatomy education with generative AI-based virtual assistants in immersive virtual reality environments. In *2024 IEEE international conference on artificial intelligence and eXtended and virtual reality (AIxVR)* (pp. 21-30). IEEE. Can be accessed at https://arxiv.org/pdf/2306.17278

Chiriboga, S. P. J., Burgos, A. L. T., Avila, M. M. R., Chida, J. L. C., Macias, K. J. A., Morante, Y. E. C., & Párraga, A. P. B. (2025). Artificial Intelligence and Personalized Learning in Foreign Languages: An Analysis of Chatbots and Virtual Assistants in Education. *Revista Científica de Salud y Desarrollo Humano, 6*(1), 882-905. Can be accessed at http://revistavitalia.org/index.php/vitalia/article/download/515/1062

Darwish, D. (2024). Chatbots vs. AI Chatbots vs. Virtual Assistants. In *Design and Development of Emerging Chatbot Technology* (pp. 26–50). IGI Global., DOI: 10.4018/979-8-3693-1830-0.ch002

Dastani, M., & Mohseni, M. (2024). Artificial intelligence chatbots in medical education: a literature review of potential benefits and challenges. *International Journal of Medical Reviews, 11*(2), 710-715. Can be accessed at https://www.ijmedrev.com/article_201393_9d2970d16312f91f0fe2c44b87ef5562.pdf

Design & Intelligence Laboratory (DILab). (n.d.). *Jill Watson.* Georgia Tech. Retrieved from https://dilab.gatech.edu/jill-watson/

Fidan, M., & Gencel, N. (2022). Supporting the instructional videos with chatbot and peer feedback mechanisms in online learning: The effects on learning performance and intrinsic motivation. *Journal of Educational Computing Research, 60*(7), 1716–1741. DOI: 10.1177/07356331221077901

Fui-Hoon Nah, F., Zheng, R., Cai, J., Siau, K., & Chen, L. (2023). Generative AI and ChatGPT: Applications, challenges, and AI-human collaboration. *Journal of information technology case and application research, 25*(3), 277-304. Can be accessed at https://www.tandfonline.com/doi/pdf/10.1080/15228053.2023.2233814

Garg, N., Kaur, A., & Dutta, R. (2024, November). Immersive Learning: Evaluating the Effectiveness of AI Chatbots and AR in Education. In *2024 3rd Edition of IEEE Delhi Section Flagship Conference (DELCON)* (pp. 1-7). IEEE. DOI: DOI: 10.1109/DELCON64804.2024.10866724

Gayathri, B., Kumar, G. S., Prashanth, T., & Kumar, B. M. (2024, May). Vardhagenie: Advancing student support through ai. In *2024 International Conference on Smart Systems for applications in Electrical Sciences (ICSSES)* (pp. 1-6). IEEE. DOI: DOI: 10.1109/ICSSES62373.2024.10561262

Goel, A. K., & Joyner, D. A. (2024). *Jill Watson: A Virtual Teaching Assistant powered by ChatGPT*. arXiv preprint arXiv:2405.11070. Retrieved from https://arxiv.org/pdf/2405.11070?

Gökçearslan, S., Tosun, C., & Erdemir, Z. G. (2024). Benefits, challenges, and methods of artificial intelligence (AI) chatbots in education: A systematic literature review. *International Journal of Technology in Education, 7*(1), 19-39. Can be accessed at https://files.eric.ed.gov/fulltext/EJ1415037.pdf

Graefen, B., & Fazal, N. (2024). From Chat bots to Virtual Tutors: An Overview of Chat GPT's Role in the Future of Education. *Archives of pharmacy practice, 15*(2-2024), 43-52. Can be accessed at https://archivepp.com/storage/files/article/70559ce0-c956-43a3-a971-1a56e7eff80f-2by3H9rq0zQArGpf/FmZ0HtMuPZUFl4k.pdf

Handini. B.S., Nurhasanah, & Panly. F.I., (2022). The Effect of Artificial Intelligent Technology Used (Duolingo Application) to Enhance English Learning. ELLITE. *Journal of English Language, Literature, and Teaching,1* 7(2), 86-94. Doi:.DOI: 10.32528/ellite.v7i2.8354

Hutson, J., & Plate, D. (2023). *Human-AI collaboration for smart education: Reframing applied learning to support metacognition*. IntechOpen. Can be accessed at https://digitalcommons.lindenwood.edu/cgi/viewcontent.cgi?article=1481&context=faculty-research-papers

Ifelebuegu, A. (2023). Rethinking online assessment strategies: Authenticity versus AI chatbot intervention. *Journal of Applied Learning and Teaching, 6*(2), 385-392. Can be accessed at https://jalt.journals.publicknowledgeproject.org/index.php/jalt/article/download/875/601

Kayyali, M. (2024). Future possibilities and challenges of AI in education. In *Transforming education with generative AI: Prompt engineering and synthetic content creation* (pp. 118-137). IGI Global Scientific Publishing. Can be accessed at https://www.researchgate.net/profile/Mustafa-Kayyali/publication/378032423_Future_Possibilities_and_Challenges_of_AI_in_Education/links/65c397c71bed776ae337490f/Future-Possibilities-and-Challenges-of-AI-in-Education.pdf

Knihová, L. (2024). *AI-Powered Immersive Learning: Transforming Tertiary Education*. Can be accessed at https://dspace.zcu.cz/bitstreams/35815e42-c43b-4315-ad30-46d238e2cdae/download

Kooli, C. (2023). Chatbots in education and research: A critical examination of ethical implications and solutions. *Sustainability*, *15*(7), 5614.

Kuzmanov, I. (2024). *Reform The Ivory Tower: AI And The Democratization Of Higher Education*. Can be accessed at https://www.researchgate.net/profile/Iliyan-Kuzmanov/publication/388156030_Reform_The_Ivory_Tower_AI_And_The_Democratization_Of_Higher_Education/links/678c181195e02f182e9cb6d9/Reform-The-Ivory-Tower-AI-And-The-Democratization-Of-Higher-Education.pdf

Luckyardi, S., Karin, J., Rosmaladewi, R., Hufad, A., & Haristiani, N. (2024). Chatbots as Digital Language Tutors: Revolutionizing Education Through AI. *Indonesian Journal of Science and Technology, 9*(3), 885-908. Can be accessed at https://ejournal.upi.edu/index.php/ijost/article/download/79514/30035

Martinez-Requejo, S., García, E. J., Duarte, S. R., Lázaro, J. R., Sanz, E. P., & Vivas, G. M. (2024). AI-driven student assistance: chatbots redefining university support. In *INTED2024 Proceedings* (pp. 617-625). IATED. Can be accessed at https://www.researchgate.net/profile/Sara-Redondo-Duarte/publication/378902826_AI-DRIVEN_STUDENT_ASSISTANCE_CHATBOTS_REDEFINING_UNIVERSITY_SUPPORT/links/65f0d4cb32321b2cff69e669/AI-DRIVEN-STUDENT-ASSISTANCE-CHATBOTS-REDEFINING-UNIVERSITY-SUPPORT.pdf?utm_source=chatgpt.com

Martínez-Requejo, S. R. D. S., & Ruiz-Lazaro, E. J. G. J. (2024). *The potential of educational chatbots for the support and formative assessment of students*. Can be accessed at https://www.researchgate.net/profile/Sara-Redondo-Duarte/publication/377299168_THE_POTENTIAL_OF_EDUCATIONAL_CHATBOTS_FOR_THE_SUPPORT_AND_FORMATIVE_ASSESSMENT_OF_STUDENTS/links/670cf1541a0a901a3e71629f/THE-POTENTIAL-OF-EDUCATIONAL-CHATBOTS-FOR-THE-SUPPORT-AND-FORMATIVE-ASSESSMENT-OF-STUDENTS.pdf

Naik, I., Naik, D., & Naik, N. (2024, July). Investigating the benefits and barriers of using AI chatbots in education. In *The International Conference on Computing, Communication, Cybersecurity & AI* (pp. 510-524). Cham: Springer Nature Switzerland. Can be accessed at https://www.techrxiv.org/doi/pdf/10.36227/techrxiv.173121417.72328214

Noonia, A., Beg, R., Patidar, A., Bawaskar, B., Sharma, S., & Rawat, H. (2024). Chatbot vs Intelligent Virtual Assistance (IVA). *Conversational Artificial Intelligence*, 655-673. DOI: DOI: 10.1002/9781394200801.ch36

Öncü, S. E., & Süral, İ. (2024). Leveraging AI for Enhanced Support: Satisfaction Levels of Users Utilizing Virtual Assistant in Open Education. *Asian Journal of Distance Education, 19*(1). Can be accessed at https://www.asianjde.com/ojs/index.php/AsianJDE/article/download/778/428

Pappagallo, S. (2024). Chatbots in education: A dual perspective on innovation and ethics. *Journal of Digital Pedagogy, 3*(1), 3-10. Can be accessed at https://www.researchgate.net/profile/Sergio-Pappagallo/publication/379984812_Chatbots_in_Education_A_Dual_Perspective_on_Innovation_and_Ethics/links/66cdeb9764f7bf7b1944c83e/Chatbots-in-Education-A-Dual-Perspective-on-Innovation-and-Ethics.pdf

Razak, M. A., Kumar, M. M., Nirmala, C. R., Naseer, R., Prashanth, B. S., & Sneha, H. R. (2024, August). Enhancing Student Support with AI: A College Assistance Chatbot Using NLP and ANN. In *2024 Second International Conference on Networks, Multimedia and Information Technology (NMITCON)* (pp. 1-8). IEEE. Can be accessed at https://www.scribd.com/document/771718552/2024206868

Rizvi, N. (2024). *From Chalkboards to Chatbots: The Role of Generative AI in Education*. Can be accessed at https://www.researchgate.net/profile/Nusrat-Rizvi-2/publication/382143399_From_Chalkboards_to_Chatbots_The_Role_of_Generative_AI_in_Education/links/668f1675b15ba559074f6bd0/From-Chalkboards-to-Chatbots-The-Role-of-Generative-AI-in-Education.pdf

Roca, M. D. L., Chan, M. M., Garcia-Cabot, A., Garcia-Lopez, E., & Amado-Salvatierra, H. (2024). The impact of a chatbot working as an assistant in a course for supporting student learning and engagement. *Computer Applications in Engineering Education, 32*(5), e22750. Can be accessed at https://onlinelibrary.wiley.com/doi/pdf/10.1002/cae.22750

Rym, L. (2024). *Exploring the Student s Perception on Use of Artificial Intelligence Writing Programs in Writing Essay: The Case of Third Year English foreign language students at Biskra University*. Can be accessed at http://archives.univ-biskra.dz/bitstream/123456789/29066/1/Laouni_Rym.pdf

Sajja, R., Sermet, Y., Cikmaz, M., Cwiertny, D., & Demir, I. (2024). Artificial intelligence-enabled intelligent assistant for personalized and adaptive learning in higher education. *Information, 15*(10), 596. Can be accessed at https://www.mdpi.com/2078-2489/15/10/596

Sowa, K., Przegalinska, A., & Ciechanowski, L. (2021). Cobots in knowledge work: Human–AI collaboration in managerial professions. *Journal of Business Research, 125*, 135–142. DOI: 10.1016/j.jbusres.2020.11.038

Storey, V. A., & Wagner, A. (2024). Integrating artificial intelligence (ai) into adult education: opportunities, challenges, and future directions. *International Journal of Adult Education and Technology (IJAET), 15*(1), 1-15. Can be accessed at https://www.igi-global.com/viewtitle.aspx?titleid=345921

Tao, W. (2025). Fostering Inspirational Learning Through AI-Enhanced Formative Assessment: Strategies and Challenges in Higher Education. *Educational Assessments in the Age of Generative AI*, 207-250. Can be accessed at https://www.researchgate.net/profile/Tao-Wu-119/publication/387721559_Fostering_Inspirational_Learning_Through_AI-Enhanced_Formative_Assessment/links/67cbadeecc055043ce6f3f1f/Fostering-Inspirational-Learning-Through-AI-Enhanced-Formative-Assessment.pdf

Yekollu, R. K., Bhimraj Ghuge, T., Sunil Biradar, S., Haldikar, S. V., & Farook Mohideen Abdul Kader, O. (2024, February). AI-driven personalized learning paths: Enhancing education through adaptive systems. In *International Conference on Smart data intelligence* (pp. 507-517). Singapore: Springer Nature Singapore. https://doi.org/DOI: 10.1007/978-981-97-3191-6_38

ADDITIONAL READING

Davar, N. F., Dewan, M. A. A., & Zhang, X. (2025). AI chatbots in education: challenges and opportunities. Information, 16(3), 235. Can be accessed at https://www.mdpi.com/2078-2489/16/3/235

Gill, S. S., Xu, M., Patros, P., Wu, H., Kaur, R., Kaur, K., . . . Buyya, R. (2024). Transformative effects of ChatGPT on modern education: Emerging Era of AI Chatbots. *Internet of Things and Cyber-Physical Systems, 4*, 19-23. Can be accessed at https://www.sciencedirect.com/science/article/pii/S2667345223000354

Graefen, B., & Fazal, N. (2024). From Chat bots to Virtual Tutors: An Overview of Chat GPT's Role in the Future of Education. *Archives of pharmacy practice, 15*(2-2024), 43-52. Can be accessed at https://archivepp.com/storage/files/article/70559ce0-c956-43a3-a971-1a56e7eff80f-2by3H9rq0zQArGpf/FmZ0HtMuPZUFl4k.pdf

Korda, D. R., Dapaah, E. O., & Akolgo, E. A. (2024). The Role of AI Chatbots in Education: A Review. *Academy Journal of Science and Engineering, 18*(1), 79-87. Can be accessed at https://www.ajol.info/index.php/ajse/article/view/291461/274383

KEY TERMS AND DEFINITIONS

Adaptive Learning: An educational method that uses technology to adjust learning experiences based on a student's performance. AI algorithms analyze student data to provide tailored instruction and feedback, ensuring optimal learning outcomes.

AI Chatbots: Software programs powered by artificial intelligence, particularly natural language processing (NLP), designed to simulate human conversation. In education, they can answer student questions, provide learning support, and offer interactive learning experiences.

Automated Feedback: The use of AI and software to provide students with evaluations and guidance on their work without direct human intervention. This can include grading assignments, providing suggestions for improvement, and highlighting areas of strength or weakness.

Education: The process of receiving or giving systematic instruction, especially at a school or university. In the context of AI, it refers to the application of technology to enhance teaching and learning.

Personalized Learning: An educational approach that aims to customize learning for each student's strengths, needs, skills, and interests. AI contributes to personalized learning by adapting content and pace to individual student progress.

Virtual Assistants: AI-powered software applications that can perform tasks or provide services based on user commands or questions. In educational settings, they can manage schedules, deliver information, and assist with administrative tasks, as well as interact with students to deliver learning support.

Chapter 11
The Role of Artificial Intelligence in Bridging the Gap Between Academia and Labor Markets

Dania Mohammad Waleed Sagheer
https://orcid.org/0009-0003-6189-8598
Al-Shahbaa Private University, Syria

ABSTRACT

This chapter investigates the persistent gap between academic education and labor market demands, using theoretical frameworks and empirical studies to analyze its underlying causes. A conceptual model defines the scope of the mismatch, highlighting structural barriers such as outdated curricula and limited industry engagement. The chapter introduces artificial intelligence (AI) and data science as potential tools to bridge this gap, showcasing applications like predictive analytics and intelligent recommendation systems. International and regional case studies demonstrate how AI technologies can help align educational outcomes with job requirements. A localized example from Syria illustrates a hypothetical data-driven approach to enhance graduate employability. The chapter concludes by outlining implementation challenges and offering policy recommendations. Overall, it advocates for strategic collaboration between academia and industry to develop AI-supported, skill-based learning environments responsive to evolving workforce needs.

DOI: 10.4018/979-8-3373-9225-7.ch011

INTRODUCTION

We are living in a new era—one that is markedly different from the past. This era brings with it entirely new types of jobs, emerging opportunities, and unique challenges. With the rise of digital transformation, traditional tools and methods have become obsolete, and new skills are now essential to thrive in the evolving workforce. Despite this dramatic shift, many educational institutions—particularly universities and schools—continue to operate under outdated curricula that no longer align with the demands of the modern labor market. This disconnect is not entirely new, yet it remains unresolved: the persistent misalignment between academic programs and real-world labor requirements continues to hinder graduates' readiness for employment.

University graduates often encounter a critical challenge: a significant misalignment between the academic education they receive and the practical skills demanded by the labor market. This disconnect not only contributes to increased levels of frustration and psychological distress among graduates—sometimes leading to depression—but also results in students losing confidence in the relevance and value of university-provided knowledge. Consequently, many students find themselves caught between two conflicting paths: striving to meet academic requirements to obtain their degrees, while simultaneously struggling to develop the competencies necessary for professional success.

In light of the ongoing digital transformation and the emergence of the AI era, it becomes essential to explore how artificial intelligence can serve as a bridge to close the gap between academic education and labor market demands. AI technologies offer powerful capabilities in identifying, classifying, and analyzing skill sets—ranging from technical and professional skills to soft skills. Through advanced data analytics, AI can predict future labor market needs by modeling emerging skill trends across industries. Moreover, AI-powered systems can guide students in choosing academic or career pathways by analyzing individual student data such as performance, interests, and behavioral patterns. This enables more personalized and data-informed decisions that align with both student potential and market expectations. In addition to educational applications, AI tools are increasingly used to analyze employee feedback, salary trends, and workplace satisfaction data. When applied to labor studies in specific regions or industries, AI can identify challenges and propose targeted solutions, offering valuable recommendations to policymakers, educators, and employers alike.

Curriculum designers are therefore urged to take AI-generated insights and recommendations into serious consideration. These recommendations are grounded in the analysis of labor market data and student data, aiming to uncover meaningful relationships that can inform more relevant and responsive educational strategies.

The growing use of AI in education and labor market forecasting raises ethical and regulatory issues, such as data privacy and algorithmic fairness. This chapter addresses these challenges by examining foundational concepts, applications, and critical reflections

This chapter provides a comprehensive exploration of the gap between academic education and labor market needs. In Section Two, we present a contextual overview of this long-standing challenge. Section Three offers a theoretical foundation of artificial intelligence and its core technologies. Section Four discusses the role and value of data analysis in understanding skill demands. Section Five delves into how AI tools can support decision-making and generate actionable recommendations based on data-driven insights. Section Six highlights real-world applications, and Section Seven addresses the limitations and ongoing challenges of applying AI in educational contexts. Finally, Section Eight concludes the chapter with reflections and future directions.

FOUNDATIONS

Theoretical Framework

Bridging Education and Labor Market Needs The relationship between academic education and the labor market can be understood through several foundational theories.

To better understand the persistent gap between academic education and labor market demands, it is essential to examine several foundational theories that explain how education shapes workforce readiness and economic outcomes.

Human Capital Theory

Human Capital Theory offers a foundational framework for analyzing the relationship between education and labor market outcomes. According to Becker (1993), education is viewed as an investment in human capital that enhances individual productivity, improves employability, and contributes to economic growth. However, this investment is only effective when the skills and competencies developed through academic programs align with the evolving demands of the labor market. A mismatch between educational outputs and labor market requirements leads to a decline in the return on educational investment, resulting in the underutilization of human resources. In such cases, graduates may lack the practical skills necessary for employment, limiting both their career prospects and the broader economic benefits of education. Addressing this misalignment is essential to maximizing the efficiency of human capital development and narrowing the gap between academic institutions and the world of work.

Supply and Demand Theory

The Supply and Demand Theory provides a foundational economic framework for analyzing labor market dynamics. According to Borjas (2016), the labor market operates through the interaction between the supply of workers—typically represented by graduates—and the demand for labor—represented by available job opportunities. A skills mismatch arises when the competencies provided by the education system do not align with the practical requirements of employers. In such cases, an oversupply of graduates in fields with limited market demand can coexist with labor shortages in more technical or vocational sectors.

This misalignment not only leads to underemployment and increased competition among job seekers but also results in inefficiencies in workforce utilization and lost economic potential. Furthermore, employers may resort to using educational attainment as a proxy for skills, despite its limited predictive power in assessing actual job readiness. Thus, the persistence of a gap between academic qualifications and market expectations exacerbates labor market imbalances and highlights the need for adaptive education policies that are informed by real-time labor market trends.

Vocational Learning Theory

Vocational Learning Theory emphasizes the importance of acquiring skills through hands-on experience and engagement with real-world work environments, rather than relying solely on abstract theoretical knowledge. According to Kolb (1984), effective learning is based on a cycle involving concrete experience, reflective observation, active experimentation, and the application of knowledge in practical contexts. Through this approach, learners gain a deeper understanding of required competencies by solving problems, engaging in project-based learning, and participating in field activities.

This theory supports the integration of vocational training within academic curricula, thereby preparing graduates for the evolving demands of the labor market. It enhances employability by developing practical skills such as communication, teamwork, and critical thinking. In the context of a rapidly changing global economy, this approach is essential for building a workforce that is both adaptable and innovative. Researchers emphasize the importance of partnerships between universities and industry sectors to design training programs aligned with actual labor market needs, thereby contributing to the reduction of the gap between academic education and employment requirements. These theories stress aligning academic programs with market needs, highlighting workforce development's economic and practical aspects. They provide the basis for exploring how AI can help bridge the education-employment gap, as discussed next.

Retrieval Review

Causes of the Gap Between Academic Education and Labor Market Needs

A growing body of literature has identified multiple root causes behind the persistent gap between higher education outcomes and labor market expectations. (Pervez et al., 2024) highlight that university curricula in many contexts remain misaligned with evolving job market demands, often due to outdated content and insufficient emphasis on hands-on skills. Similarly, Jaiswal, Kuzminykh, and Modgil (2024) focus on the artificial intelligence sector in the UK, revealing a significant mismatch between graduates' competencies and the dynamic requirements of the tech industry. Dobslaw et al. (2023) further support this view by examining the software industry, where technological advancements outpace curriculum updates, leading to graduates being underprepared for real-world tasks. Collectively, these studies emphasize the need for continuous curriculum reform and closer collaboration between academic institutions and industry stakeholders.

Strategies to Bridge the Gap Between Academic Education and Labor Market Needs

Multiple strategies have been proposed to bridge the persistent gap between higher education outcomes and labor market expectations. One major approach involves enhancing vocational education and training (VET), which has been shown to significantly support youth employability, especially in contexts of high unemployment and skill shortages (Zylfijaj & Shaqiri, 2024). Another effective measure is the implementation of cooperative (co-op) education programs. According to Wyonch (2020), such programs substantially improve graduates' employability, particularly when aligned with their fields of study.

In addition, embedding soft skills into academic curricula is crucial. (Namjildorj, 2025) argue that communication, teamwork, and problem-solving skills must be integrated into higher education to meet industry demands. Public-private partnerships (PPPs) also play a vital role in strengthening the educational infrastructure and fostering more market-relevant training, as illustrated by (Arellano et al., 2008). Finally, providing tailored career services, such as individualized counseling, labor market information, and skill development workshops, can help guide students toward viable career paths (Khurumova & Pinto, 2024).

The Role of Technology and Artificial Intelligence in Bridging the Skills Gap

Technology, and particularly Artificial Intelligence (AI), has emerged as a transformative force in aligning academic education with the evolving demands of the labor market. AI-driven personalized learning platforms allow for adaptive content delivery, catering to individual student needs and enhancing the relevance and efficiency of skill acquisition (Zawacki-Richter et al., 2019). In the context of vocational education, AI applications have revolutionized competency-based assessments and curriculum development, enabling more targeted and data-informed learning pathways (Yan et al., 2025). Recent studies also highlight the potential of generative AI in instructional system design—such as automated content creation, adaptive feedback, and efficient curriculum planning—which may support scalable and individualized learning solutions (Chai et al., 2025).

Moreover, national AI strategies play a critical role in ensuring long-term workforce readiness. (Shi, 2025) analyzed AI policies across 50 countries and highlighted a significant gap in comprehensive strategies that integrate AI competence development in both education and employment sectors. In organizational settings, AI has catalyzed the need for continuous upskilling and reskilling, pushing institutions to revise training models and invest in human-AI collaboration (Morandini et al., 2023).

Furthermore, AI-powered educational tools, such as intelligent tutoring systems and automated assessment technologies, contribute to closing learning gaps by offering real-time feedback and individualized support (Eling et al., 2025). These innovations collectively underline the potential of AI not only to modernize education but also to serve as a critical bridge to industry-aligned competencies

Challenges and Gaps in the Literature

Despite the growing body of research addressing the gap between academic education and labor market demands, several challenges and gaps persist:

Limited Scalability of Initiatives: Many successful models—such as dual vocational systems or AI-driven learning platforms—have shown promise in specific regions but face difficulties when adapted to different socio-economic contexts (OECD, 2021).

Weak Integration of Soft Skills: While technical skill development has advanced, several studies highlight that essential soft skills like communication, adaptability, and critical thinking are often underemphasized in both traditional and technology-driven education programs (World Economic Forum, 2023).

Insufficient Public-Private Collaboration in Developing Countries: Although partnerships are key to aligning education with market needs, many developing nations lack strong frameworks for cooperation between academic institutions and industries (UNESCO, 2022).

Digital Divide and Technological Infrastructure: The lack of robust infrastructure in low-income regions hampers the equitable adoption of advanced educational technologies, further widening the global skills gap (World Bank, 2020).

AI Readiness and Ethical Concerns: The integration of AI in education raises concerns related to data privacy, bias in algorithms, and the preparedness of educators to use such tools effectively. For instance, educators often lack proper training to leverage AI-driven analytics responsibly, which may affect pedagogical outcomes (Holmes et al., 2019).

Recent literature highlights the critical importance of ethical frameworks in deploying AI technologies within education and employment sectors. Concerns around data privacy, algorithmic bias, and transparency are prominent (Zawacki-Richter et al., 2019; UNESCO, 2023). Regulations such as the General Data Protection Regulation (GDPR)—a European law that protects individuals' personal data and grants strict rights regarding its use—and the Family Educational Rights and Privacy Act (FERPA)—a U.S. law that safeguards the privacy of student educational records—underscore the necessity for protecting individuals' data rights in educational contexts. Moreover, ethical considerations extend to ensuring fairness and accountability in AI-driven decision-making systems.

In addition to ethical issues, social frameworks are essential for understanding the broader impact of AI on educational equity. The digital divide, which reflects disparities in access to technology and internet connectivity, disproportionately affects marginalized communities, limiting their ability to benefit from AI-powered learning tools (Davidoff, 2024). Addressing these socio-economic inequalities is crucial for the inclusive and effective integration of AI in education and labor market alignment.

Conclusion

The reviewed literature suggests that bridging the gap between academic education and the labor market requires a multifaceted approach that includes curriculum reform, strategic partnerships, and the integration of advanced technologies. However, the effectiveness of these strategies depends largely on local economic, cultural, and policy conditions. This highlights the need for context-specific solutions, continuous evaluation, and inclusive policies that consider both technological and human factors.

Building on this foundation, this chapter aims to contribute to closing the gap by employing a data-driven approach, analyzing student data alongside labor market trends and job vacancy announcements. This approach seeks to propose precise, evidence-based interventions that better align higher education outcomes with real employment needs.

Conceptual Framework

This conceptual framework explores the interconnections between academic education, labor market requirements, and the skills gap—three key concepts that are central to understanding the misalignment between education systems and employment outcomes. It further introduces artificial intelligence (AI) and data analytics as mediating tools that can support the alignment of educational outputs with real-time labor market needs. The framework is visually represented in Figure 1, which highlights the centrality of AI in integrating educational objectives with market needs and skill development.

Figure 1. Conceptual Venn diagram illustrating the interplay between academic education, labor market demands, and skill development, with artificial intelligence as the central enabling factor.

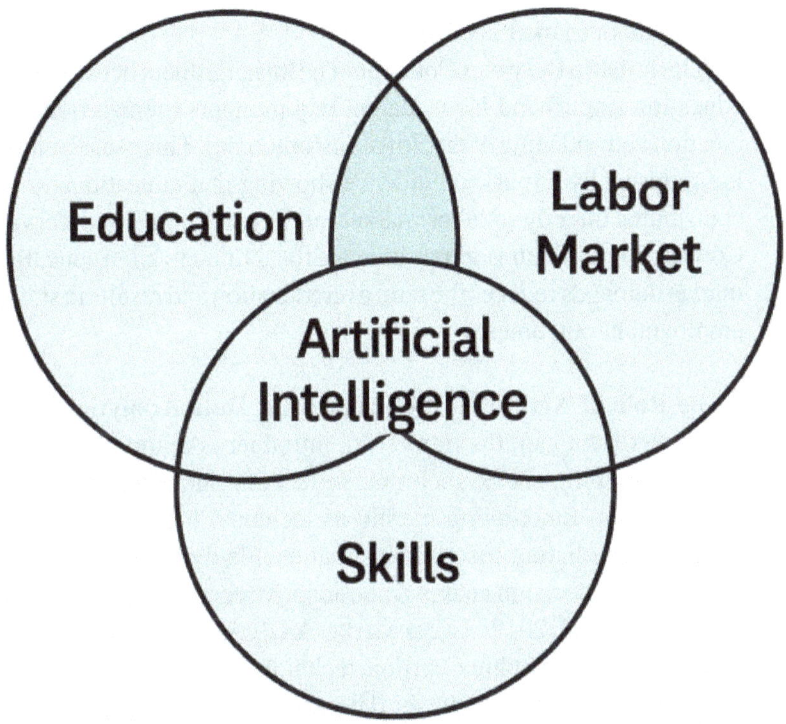

1. **Academic Education** Academic education refers to the formal training and instruction provided by schools, colleges, and universities. While these institutions equip students with theoretical knowledge and general competencies, they often lack sufficient integration of practical, job-relevant skills (UNESCO, 2023). This limited orientation toward applied skills can hinder students' ability to transition effectively into the workforce.
2. **Labor Market Requirements** Labor market requirements denote the set of skills, behaviors, and technical competencies demanded by employers. These requirements are dynamic, shaped by technological advancements, globalization, and changing business models (OECD, 2021). When academic curricula fail to respond to such shifts, a mismatch between graduate qualifications and job expectations emerges.

3. **The Skills Gap** The skills gap arises when educational systems do not provide students with the competencies required in the labor market. This leads to high rates of graduate underemployment, skill shortages in key sectors, and a general inefficiency in workforce deployment (UNESCO, 2023). The skills gap is thus the direct outcome of a disconnect between the first two concepts—academic education and labor market needs.

4.Relationship Between Concepts The misalignment between academic education (input) and labor market requirements (demand) leads to the creation and widening of the skills gap (outcome). This causal relationship is supported by empirical evidence showing that educational mismatch contributes directly to labor market inefficiencies (Varona Cervantes & Cooper, 2022). Their findings indicate that failure to align education with market demands reduces the return on education and results in suboptimal employment outcomes.

5. **The Role of Artificial Intelligence and Data Analytics** To address this persistent gap, the framework introduces AI and data analytics as key enablers that help synchronize education and employment systems. Rather than functioning merely as technical tools, AI and analytics serve as mediating mechanisms that enable dynamic feedback loops, data-driven decision-making, and adaptive curriculum design (Holmes, Bialik, & Fadel, 2019). Labor Market Analytics employ natural language processing and machine learning techniques to extract insights from job advertisements and employer data, thereby identifying emerging skill trends across sectors (Zhang, M, 2024). Educational Data Mining helps evaluate student performance, detect learning gaps, and support curricular adjustments aligned with labor market needs (Baker & Inventado, 2024). AI-Powered Career guidance offers personalized recommendations for learning pathways based on predicted employment patterns and individual student profiles (Senger et al., 2024). University–Industry Collaboration, underpinned by real-time data, enables co-development of training modules, certifications, and internship programs tailored to evolving labor demands. Collectively, these technologies support curriculum innovation, promote lifelong learning, and enhance the responsiveness of educational systems to labor market dynamics. This results in a more adaptive and responsive education-to-employment pipeline, capable of evolving with labor market dynamics.

6 . Ethical and Regulatory Considerations Importantly, the integration of AI into education and workforce development also introduces significant ethical and regulatory challenges that must be proactively addressed. Concerns such as data privacy, algorithmic bias, lack of transparency, and automated decision-making can compromise equity and trust if left unchecked (UNESCO, 2021). Compliance with global data protection frameworks—such as the General Data Protection Regulation (GDPR) in Europe (European Commission, 2018) and the Family Educational Rights and Privacy Act (FERPA) in the United States (U.S. Department of Education, 2020)—is essential to safeguard student information and maintain institutional accountability. Moreover, ethical guidelines issued by international organizations like UNESCO emphasize the importance of fairness, inclusivity, and human oversight in the deployment of AI systems in education. Without these ethical safeguards, the same technologies designed to close educational and labor gaps could unintentionally reinforce existing inequalities or exclude marginalized populations (UNESCO, 2021).

In conclusion, the successful application of AI and data analytics depends not only on technical efficacy but also on a robust ethical and regulatory foundation. These technologies must be implemented responsibly to ensure that they advance social justice, equity, and long-term alignment between education and employment.

THE GAP BETWEEN ACADEMIC EDUCATION AND THE LABOR MARKET

The university graduate represents the human capital essential to industry and market development. The value of this capital varies depending on the skills acquired by the degree holder. While the market economy is driven by supply and demand, many graduates entering the job market offer only academic qualifications without possessing the practical skills required by employers. Often, their knowledge remains theoretical.

When there is a high number of applicants for a particular job, employers may differentiate candidates based on academic degrees or the number of years spent in education. Unfortunately, these criteria do not necessarily reflect the candidate's competence or ability to meet the actual needs of the market.

Therefore, providing education and training to graduates becomes a crucial investment in developing human capital. Several training strategies can be employed, including brainstorming, critical thinking, and problem-based learning. Field visits and practical training can also serve as effective methods for vocational development.

In professional training, experiential learning plays a vital role. Since the labor market is constantly evolving and the needs of industries and consumers are continually shifting, trainees must adapt to changing market conditions. This necessitates adopting a lifelong learning strategy—where individuals remain continuously engaged in learning, stay updated on developments, and are able to propose innovative solutions in response to emerging challenges.

To deepen the understanding of AI's role within this framework, the following sections present foundational insights into AI technologies and their applications in decision-making and data analysis.

ARTIFICIAL INTELLIGENCE: A FOUNDATIONAL OVERVIEW

Artificial Intelligence (AI) is a branch of computer science concerned with developing systems that can emulate human cognitive functions such as reasoning, learning, decision-making, and problem-solving. At its core, AI seeks to create intelligent agents—software or hardware systems that can perceive their environment, analyze information, and take goal-directed actions.

Early AI efforts focused on expert systems and rule-based reasoning, relying on human experts to codify domain-specific knowledge into structured rules (Russell & Norvig, 2020). These systems, however, lacked adaptability and learning capabilities. The emergence of machine learning marked a significant paradigm shift, enabling systems to learn patterns and behaviors from data without being explicitly programmed. Inspired by the human brain, artificial neural networks were introduced as mathematical models simulating the behavior of biological neurons. As data complexity increased, deep learning—a subfield of machine learning—rose to prominence. Deep learning utilizes multilayered neural networks to perform complex tasks such as image recognition, natural language processing (NLP), and predictive analytics (Goodfellow, Bengio, & Courville, 2016). AI encompasses several major subfields, each focusing on different aspects of intelligence and data processing. Natural Language Processing (NLP) enables machines to understand, interpret, and generate human language, essential for applications like chatbots and language translation. Computer Vision deals with the automatic extraction, analysis, and understanding of information from images and videos, supporting technologies like facial recognition and autonomous vehicles. Machine Learning, as mentioned earlier, allows systems to learn from data and improve over time without explicit programming. Together, these subfields expand AI's capabilities and practical applications across diverse domains.

Today, AI plays a critical role in applications that demand automation, real-time decision-making, and personalized experiences. Its integration into fields like education and workforce development provides transformative opportunities for aligning academic training with dynamic labor market needs.

DATA SCIENCE

Data science is a multidisciplinary field that leverages methods from statistics, computer science, and information theory to extract actionable insights from data. Data can be structured (e.g., numerical databases, spreadsheets) or unstructured (e.g., text, images, video), and the ability to process and interpret such data has become vital across domains.

At its core, data science encompasses data collection, cleaning, analysis, visualization, and interpretation. It integrates advanced techniques such as machine learning and deep learning to build predictive models and automate decision-making processes. According to Provost & Fawcett (2013), data science plays a key role in transforming raw data into strategic knowledge, especially in sectors where complexity and volume of information are rapidly increasing.

As education systems and labor markets become more data-driven, data science serves as a fundamental enabler for aligning academic programs with real-time market trends, enhancing both curriculum design and workforce planning.

ARTIFICIAL INTELLIGENCE APPROACHES IN DECISION SUPPORT

With the rapid advancement of artificial intelligence, various analytical approaches have become essential in supporting decision-making processes across individual, organizational, and societal levels. The strength of AI lies in its ability to process large-scale data, identify patterns, and generate evidence-based recommendations or predictions—shifting decisions from intuition-based to insight-driven (Russell & Norvig, 2020; Shalev-Shwartz & Ben-David, 2014).

Among the most prominent approaches contributing to this capability are Machine Learning, Data Mining, and Predictive Analytics. These approaches have been widely adopted across multiple domains, including education, workforce development, and institutional planning, where data-informed decisions are increasingly vital (Han, Pei, & Kamber, 2011; Kelleher, Mac Carthy, & Korvir, 2015; Provost & Fawcett, 2013).

The following sections will provide a brief overview of each approach, highlighting their core mechanisms and practical applications in decision support.

Machine Learning

Machine learning (ML) is a core approach within artificial intelligence that focuses on the development of algorithms capable of learning patterns from data and making decisions or predictions without being explicitly programmed for each task. Unlike traditional rule-based systems, ML models improve their performance as they are exposed to more data over time (Shalev-Shwartz & Ben-David, 2014).

In the context of decision support, ML enables systems to analyze complex datasets, detect trends, and offer real-time recommendations. For example, classification algorithms can be used to predict student success or identify at-risk learners, while regression models may forecast enrollment trends or labor market demands. Additionally, unsupervised learning techniques, such as clustering, can help reveal hidden groupings in educational or workforce data, aiding in targeted policy design (Kelleher, Mac Carthy, & Korvir, 2015).

The adaptability and scalability of ML make it especially valuable in dynamic environments where decision-makers need to respond to constantly evolving data.

Data Mining and Information Retrieval

Data mining and information retrieval are complementary techniques widely used in educational and labor market data analysis. Data mining refers to the process of discovering meaningful patterns, correlations, and structures within large datasets through a combination of statistical, machine learning, and database techniques (Han, Pei, & Kamber, 2011; Tan, Steinbach, & Kumar, 2019). It focuses on exploratory analysis to uncover previously unknown insights, such as identifying factors influencing student success or shifts in labor market skill demands.

Information retrieval, on the other hand, involves searching within large datasets or document collections to find and extract relevant information based on specific queries (Manning, Raghavan, & Schütze, 2008; Baeza-Yates & Ribeiro-Neto, 2011). For example, educational institutions may use information retrieval systems to locate specific research articles or student records, while labor market analysts can retrieve job descriptions matching particular skills.

By integrating both approaches, decision-makers can benefit from a comprehensive understanding of data: data mining reveals hidden trends and predictive factors, whereas information retrieval allows quick access to precise information needed for timely decisions. Together, these techniques significantly enhance evidence-based decision-making in education and workforce planning.

Predictive Analytics

Predictive analytics is a data-driven approach that leverages historical data, statistical algorithms, and machine learning techniques to forecast future outcomes or behaviors (Kelleher, Mac Carthy, & Korvir, 2015; Provost & Fawcett, 2013). Unlike descriptive analytics, which focuses on understanding past events, predictive analytics aims to anticipate what is likely to happen, thereby enabling proactive decision-making.

In educational and workforce planning contexts, predictive analytics can be used to estimate student enrollment trends, forecast graduation rates, or predict workforce demand in specific industries. These forecasts can support strategic decisions such as curriculum development, resource allocation, and policy formulation.

By quantifying uncertainty and highlighting probable future scenarios, predictive analytics empowers decision-makers to take action before issues arise, increasing both efficiency and responsiveness.

In summary, this framework underscores the complex link between education and labor market needs. By incorporating AI and data science, it supports building a more adaptive and aligned education-to-employment pathway.

The Role of Artificial Intelligence in Bridging the Gap Between Academia and Labor Markets

After reviewing the concept of the gap between education and the labor market in the conceptual framework, we now turn to examine the effective role that artificial intelligence can play in narrowing this gap. AI technologies provide innovative tools and strategies that contribute to aligning educational curricula with the evolving demands of the labor market, thereby enhancing employment opportunities and fostering the development of future competencies.

The Role of Artificial Intelligence in Analysis and Prediction

Artificial intelligence plays a crucial role in analyzing vast amounts of educational and labor market data to uncover patterns, trends, and emerging skill requirements. Through techniques such as machine learning and predictive analytics, AI systems can forecast future workforce demands and student performance outcomes, enabling educational institutions and policymakers to make data-driven decisions. These predictive insights help in proactively adjusting curricula, designing targeted training programs, and allocating resources more effectively to meet evolving labor market needs (Baker & Inventado, 2014; Chen, Chiang, & Storey, 2012).

Moreover, recent research underscores the predictive power of AI in forecasting emerging labor market needs. OECD (2024) reports that while specialized AI roles remain niche, AI exposure is reshaping demand even in non-technical occupations—boosting demand for managerial, cognitive, and digital skills (Green, 2024). In addition, a pan-OECD study (Borgonovi et al., 2023) documents that across 14 countries, machine learning remains the most in-demand AI skill, but employers increasingly demand complementary soft skills such as leadership and problem-solving (Borgonovi et al., 2023).

However, the effectiveness of such predictive systems depends on ensuring digital equity—so that students from marginalized or low-resource backgrounds are not systematically underrepresented in training data or underserved by algorithmic decisions (UNESCO, 2023).

Consequently, AI-driven analysis supports a dynamic and responsive education system aligned with economic and technological developments.

AI-Powered Recommendation Systems and Personalized Learning

Artificial intelligence enables personalized learning experiences through recommendation systems that tailor educational content and career guidance to individual learner profiles. By analyzing students' strengths, weaknesses, and preferences alongside labor market trends, these systems suggest optimal learning pathways and skill development opportunities (Drachsler, Verbert, & Santos, 2015; Romero & Ventura, 2020). This personalization enhances student engagement and effectiveness, while ensuring that learners acquire competencies aligned with current and future workforce demands. Consequently, AI-driven recommendation systems contribute significantly to bridging the education-to-employment gap.

These systems support personalized and responsive education, yet their effectiveness depends not only on technical performance but also on adherence to ethical standards related to data privacy and algorithmic transparency, as discussed in recent educational policy frameworks (UNESCO, 2023; European Commission. (2020)

Continuous Interaction Between Educational Institutions and the Labor Market Through AI

Artificial intelligence facilitates ongoing communication and collaboration between educational institutions and labor market stakeholders via digital platforms and data-sharing tools. AI-powered systems enable real-time feedback loops where employers can communicate evolving skill requirements directly to educators, who in turn can adapt curricula accordingly (Luckin et al., 2016; Popenici & Kerr, 2017). Virtual meetings, online collaboration environments, and intelligent dashboards help maintain this dynamic relationship, ensuring education remains relevant and responsive to economic changes.

Moreover, ensuring that this AI-mediated communication includes voices from marginalized communities and low-resource institutions is vital to promoting equity. True responsiveness requires not just efficient data exchange, but also inclusive participation that helps prevent the reinforcement of existing inequalities.

Such continuous interaction strengthens workforce readiness and supports lifelong learning aligned with market needs.

CASE STUDIES: PRACTICAL APPLICATIONS OF AI IN BRIDGING THE EDUCATION-EMPLOYMENT GAP

To complement the theoretical and strategic perspectives discussed in the previous sections, this part presents selected case studies that highlight how artificial intelligence has been effectively applied to reduce the gap between education and labor market demands. These real-world examples demonstrate the practical use of AI techniques such as machine learning, data mining, and predictive analytics in improving educational decision-making, personalizing learning experiences, and fostering continuous interaction with employers.

Importantly, the case studies also serve to illustrate key components of the conceptual framework—particularly the role of AI as an intermediary mechanism enabling dynamic feedback loops, data-informed interventions, and adaptive curriculum design. They offer empirical support for the framework's premise that ethically grounded, data-driven AI applications can enhance system responsiveness and promote equitable alignment between academic training and labor market realities

By examining these cases, we gain deeper insights into the transformative potential of AI in aligning curricula, skills development, and career pathways with evolving workforce needs.

CASE STUDIES

1. Institutional Interventions

Case Study 1: Enhancing Student Success Through Predictive Analytics – Georgia State University's AI-Powered Intervention

Context

In August 2012, Georgia State University (GSU) launched a pioneering initiative to address high dropout rates and achievement gaps among its diverse student population. With over 52,000 students—many from historically underrepresented or low-income backgrounds—GSU faced systemic challenges in student retention and timely graduation. To combat these issues, the university implemented an AI-driven predictive analytics system designed to proactively identify at-risk students and provide timely, targeted support.

AI Techniques Used

GSU's system, known as the Graduation and Progression Success (GPS) advising system, relied on predictive analytics powered by machine learning algorithms. These algorithms processed over 800 academic and behavioral variables per student daily, including GPA trends, course performance, class attendance, registration patterns, and financial aid status. The system continuously scanned for signs of academic risk and generated alerts when a student deviated from successful patterns. University staff then intervened with personalized guidance, academic planning, and resource recommendations.

Data Handling and Analysis

The GPS system aggregated vast amounts of student data from institutional systems and learning platforms, ensuring compliance with data privacy standards. Data was cleaned, structured, and updated daily to maintain real-time accuracy. Statistical models were trained on historical student success patterns to identify correlations between specific behaviors and academic outcomes. This enabled GSU to predict potential obstacles before they became critical issues, allowing staff to prioritize interventions based on risk severity.

Decision-Making Process

When the system detected an academic or administrative anomaly—such as a student enrolling in a course outside their degree path or failing a prerequisite—an alert was sent to academic advisors. These advisors used a dashboard interface to review each case and respond with tailored support. The decision-making process blended automated risk detection with human judgment, ensuring that interventions were contextually appropriate and student-centered.

Results and Impact

By 2019, GSU reported significant outcomes from the implementation of the GPS system (Association of Governing Boards of Universities and Colleges, 2019):

The university conferred 67% more undergraduate degrees than it did six years prior.

Achievement gaps between high-risk student populations and the total student body were eliminated, with African-American, Hispanic, and low-income students graduating at the same rates as their white and middle- to upper-income peers.

Over 200,000 advisor interventions were prompted by the GPS system.

These results underscore the effectiveness of GSU's data-informed approach to student success, demonstrating how AI can drive equitable outcomes in higher education.

However, the initiative also highlighted the importance of maintaining transparency in data practices and ensuring ongoing advisor training to avoid over-reliance on algorithmic alerts. While GSU benefited from strong infrastructure and institutional support, replicating this model in low-resource settings may require scaled-down, open-source alternatives and tailored capacity-building measures.

Case Study 2: Developing an Intelligent Recruitment Model Using AI for the Saudi Labor Market

Context

As part of Saudi Arabia's Vision 2030, the kingdom aims to reduce unemployment by improving recruitment mechanisms and guiding graduates toward suitable job opportunities. This requires bridging the gap between job seekers' skills and labor market demands efficiently.

AI Model Description

The Intelligent Recruitment Model (AIRM) utilizes artificial intelligence techniques such as machine learning and natural language processing to analyze and match job seekers with vacancies. The model is designed to understand complex patterns in both candidate profiles and job requirements, enabling more accurate and personalized job recommendations

Data Handling and Analysis

Data was collected from various sources, including resumes submitted by job seekers and detailed job descriptions from employers. The data underwent preprocessing steps such as cleaning, normalization, and feature extraction. Advanced algorithms analyzed skill sets, experience levels, and preferences to create detailed candidate profiles. Similarly, job descriptions were parsed to extract required skills and qualifications. Matching algorithms then compared these profiles with job requirements using similarity metrics and pattern recognition to identify optimal.

Decision-Making Process

Based on the analysis, the system generates recommendations for both job seekers and employers. Job seekers receive tailored suggestions for job opportunities that best fit their skills and preferences, while employers receive ranked lists of potential candidates matching their criteria. This decision support system streamlines the recruitment process, reduces time-to-hire, and enhances the quality of employment matches.

Results and Impact

Initial trials demonstrated an 84% accuracy rate in matching candidates to suitable jobs, significantly reducing recruitment time compared to traditional methods. The model contributes to improving the efficiency of the Saudi labor market and better aligns graduate skills with available opportunities, supporting national employment goals (Aleisa et al., 2023).

Critical Reflection, Ethics, and Future Directions

While the model shows promise, it may inherit biases from training data, potentially disadvantaging some candidates. Transparency in AI decision-making is essential to foster trust. Ethical concerns—particularly regarding data privacy and fairness—must be carefully addressed.

Future efforts should emphasize bias monitoring, human oversight, and adaptability across job sectors. Collaboration among policymakers, technologists, and labor stakeholders is key to ensuring the model supports equitable employment in line with Vision 2030.

Case Study 3: EduBridge Platform in India – Bridging Academia and Industry through Digital Collaboration

Context

EduBridge is an Indian platform designed to bridge the gap between academic institutions and the labor market by facilitating digital collaboration between universities and companies. It aims to provide practical, industry-oriented training and employment opportunities to students, aligning educational outcomes with real-world job demands.

AI Techniques Used

EduBridge leverages data analytics and AI-driven recommendation systems to analyze student profiles, skills, and labor market trends. The platform uses machine learning algorithms to personalize training pathways and job placements for each learner.

Data Handling and Analysis

The platform collects data from multiple sources, including student academic records, skill assessments, and employer requirements. This data is processed and analyzed to identify skill gaps and match students to tailored training modules and job opportunities. Continuous feedback from employers and learners helps refine the recommendations and training content.

Decision-Making Process

Based on the analyzed data, EduBridge generates personalized learning and career recommendations for students. The system also informs companies about suitable candidates whose skills align with their current vacancies. This data-driven matching accelerates recruitment and improves employment outcomes.

Results and Impact

EduBridge has successfully enhanced employability for thousands of students by providing customized training and facilitating direct connections with employers. The platform's AI-powered insights ensure that curricula remain relevant to evolving industry needs, reducing the education-to-employment gap significantly (EduBridge, 2022).

Critical Reflection, Ethical Considerations, and Future Recommendations

Despite EduBridge's positive impact on employability, concerns persist around data privacy and ethical use of personal information. Transparent data practices and strong security measures are vital.

AI-driven recommendations may also risk reinforcing bias if based on skewed data, making human oversight and algorithm audits essential.

Future directions should ensure inclusive access, adaptive training content, and stronger collaboration among academia, industry, and government to enhance EduBridge's role in narrowing the education-employment gap.

Case Study 4: The ODIN Platform in Denmark – Enhancing University-Industry Collaboration through Open Innovation

Context

Launched in 2020, the Open Discovery Innovation Network (ODIN) is an initiative led by Aarhus University in Denmark (Novo Nordisk Foundation, 2024). It aims to foster collaboration between universities and companies in the fields of drug discovery and diagnostics. The platform promotes an "open innovation" approach, where research projects are conducted without intellectual property restrictions, enabling seamless knowledge sharing among participants.

AI and Digital Technologies Used

ODIN utilizes digital platforms to facilitate communication and collaboration between academic researchers and industry professionals. Data analytics and AI technologies support matchmaking processes between industrial needs and academic expertise, increasing the efficiency of joint research efforts.

Data Handling and Analysis

Data from various collaborative research projects is collected and analyzed using advanced analytical methods to identify trends and innovation opportunities. The open-access model allows data and results to be shared freely, enabling broader use and further development by other researchers and companies.

Decision-Making Process

Project funding decisions are made through a rigorous scientific evaluation conducted by an independent panel. Researchers are encouraged to submit proposals targeting specific industrial challenges, and projects demonstrating high potential for innovation and impact are selected for support.

Results and Impact

Since its inception, ODIN has funded 11 collaborative research projects, leading to over 40 scientific publications and the creation of a new startup. The platform has significantly strengthened ties between academia and industry, and accelerated advancements in drug discovery and diagnostics. In 2024, ODIN received an additional DKK 180 million in funding from the Novo Nordisk Foundation to extend its operations until 2029.

Critical Analysis, Ethical Considerations, and Future Recommendations

ODIN has enhanced university-industry collaboration and drug discovery innovation. However, its open model raises data privacy and intellectual property concerns, requiring clear ethical and legal protections.

Reliance on private funding risks research independence, stressing the need for diversified support.

Future efforts should expand ODIN to new fields, improve AI alignment with industry needs, and foster international partnerships and community engagement for greater impact.

2. National and Regional Initiatives

Case Study 1: Using Artificial Intelligence to Identify and Support At-Risk Students of Dropout in Morocco

Context:

The Moroccan Ministry of National Education launched an innovative initiative utilizing artificial intelligence techniques to analyze student data and identify those at risk of dropping out. This initiative aims to improve educational outcomes and ensure students' continuity in their academic paths.

AI Techniques Used:

Advanced machine learning models were applied, including algorithms such as Naïve Bayes, Random Forest, and J48. The SMOTE technique was used to balance the dataset, enhancing the models' accuracy in predicting dropout cases.

Data Handling and Analysis:

Comprehensive data were collected, covering academic performance, attendance, socio-economic background, and participation in school activities. Data cleaning and preprocessing ensured data quality, after which the models identified patterns and key factors influencing dropout risk.

Decision-Making Process:

Based on predictions, alerts were sent to teachers and administrators to provide appropriate support to at-risk students, such as academic counseling, psychological support, or career guidance. These cases were monitored regularly to ensure effective intervention.

Results and Impact:

The initiative showed a significant improvement in student retention rates and a reduction in dropout rates, reflecting the effectiveness of using AI to enhance educational quality and ensure students remain on their academic trajectories.

Critical Analysis, Ethical Considerations, and Future Recommendations

While AI offers promise, challenges persist—such as biased data reflecting social inequalities and overdependence on automation without human oversight.

Ethical use requires transparency, privacy protection, and equitable access, particularly for marginalized groups, aligned with UNESCO and local data regulations.

Future priorities include ongoing AI monitoring to mitigate bias and strengthening educator training to interpret insights and guide interventions. These steps support sustainable, scalable AI use in low-resource educational settings.

This case study is based on the research conducted by Elbouknify et al. (2025), which utilized real data provided by the Moroccan Ministry of National Education.

Case Study 2: Mapping the AI Skills Gap – A Collaboration Between Frontier Economics and Glass.AI

Context

In 2020, Frontier Economics and Glass.AI launched a collaborative study in the United Kingdom to explore how artificial intelligence can be used to analyze labor market trends and identify skill gaps in the AI sector. The goal was to provide insights into how job market demand for AI-related skills is evolving and how this demand compares with available training and educational offerings.

AI Techniques Used

The study employed advanced artificial intelligence tools to scan and interpret thousands of online job postings in real time. Glass.AI's proprietary technology used natural language processing (NLP) and machine learning to extract relevant skill requirements from job advertisements. This helped in mapping the skills most frequently mentioned by employers across various industries.

Data Handling and Analysis

The system parsed job descriptions to identify high-frequency AI-related terms, including “machine learning,” “data science,” “Python,” and “AI ethics.” These were then analyzed using statistical models to detect trends and emerging demand. The study emphasized the increasing requirement for hybrid skill sets combining technical abilities with domain-specific knowledge. While the study didn’t directly compare these findings to specific academic curricula, it provided a clear picture of the rapidly changing demand landscape for AI talent.

Decision-Making Process

The findings were communicated through an accessible and interactive report aimed at decision-makers in education, government, and business. The insights encouraged stakeholders to rethink workforce planning strategies and align training programs with the dynamic needs of the digital economy. The study also highlighted the importance of using AI as a tool not only for analysis but for informing policy and curriculum development.

Recommendations and Conclusions

The report recommended that training providers and educational institutions incorporate AI skills into their programs, with a particular focus on real-world applications and interdisciplinary competencies. It stressed the need for more agile and responsive curriculum development and advocated for continuous monitoring of labor market trends using AI-based tools. These approaches were proposed as vital to ensuring that the future workforce remains competitive and well-equipped for an AI-driven economy (Frontier Economics & Glass.AI, 2020).

Critical Reflection and Future Directions

Although the study offers valuable data-driven insights, critical reflection highlights limitations such as potential bias in job postings data that may miss emerging or non-traditional AI roles. Ethical concerns around data privacy and algorithmic transparency require stronger emphasis to build stakeholder trust and ensure fairness.

Promoting inclusivity and preventing the widening of inequalities should be central to workforce planning. Future efforts must embed ethical frameworks and maintain human oversight alongside AI tools to guarantee equitable access to AI education and employment opportunities.

Ongoing collaboration among academia, industry, and policymakers is vital to develop flexible curricula and responsive policies that meet evolving skill demands, supporting both economic growth and social equity.

Local Perspective: The Need for Collaboration Between Universities and the Business Sector in Syria

After reviewing a range of case studies illustrating how artificial intelligence can help bridge the gap between education and the labor market, it is essential to consider the local context in Syria to better understand the existing challenges and potential opportunities. The UNICEF (2024) report highlights that Syrian youth lack practical and vocational skills upon graduation, creating a gap between academic education and labor market demands, which hinders their effective entry into employment. The report recommends strengthening training programs and aligning curricula with life and job skills.

This pattern is also evident through social media posts and field observations drawn from my direct communication with students and graduates in my academic role and my involvement in supervising training and capacity-building programs at the Syrian Computer Society. Many graduates struggle to find practical training opportunities post-graduation, due to the heavy theoretical focus of university curricula contrasted with employers' demands for prior practical experience, thereby creating a barrier to entry for fresh graduates.

Consequently, numerous graduates resort to enrolling in private institutes or training centers to acquire the required skills, which incurs additional time and financial costs without guaranteeing actual employment. These efforts remain largely individual initiatives in the absence of a coordinated framework between higher education institutions and the labor market sectors.

This gap underscores the urgent need for strategic partnerships between universities and the private sector, where practical training and real-world projects are integrated into academic programs. Such collaboration enables companies to identify talented and highly skilled individuals early, while universities can better prepare graduates who are ready to meet labor market demands.

Furthermore, companies can contribute to graduation projects by providing professional supervision and real industry challenges, thus enhancing the practical learning environment.

Initiatives of this nature contribute to producing graduates capable of meeting evolving market demands, including digital skills, teamwork, and problem-solving abilities, while providing companies with a competitive advantage through early access to qualified and well-trained talent. Although this proposal does not represent a direct application of artificial intelligence, it constitutes a fundamental prerequisite for the successful future deployment of AI technologies. Providing a genuine training environment and effective interaction between students and the labor market generates the essential data and insights that AI systems can analyze to guide training and improve employment decisions.

Hypothetical Case Study 3: A Syrian Model for Bridging the Gap Between Education and the Labor Market Using Artificial Intelligence

Context

Syria faces an urgent need to modernize higher education outcomes and align them with labor market requirements, especially in the post-crisis phase characterized by limited job opportunities and a rapidly evolving digital economy. The lack of organized coordination between academic institutions and the private sector has exacerbated the skills gap among graduates. Building on current national initiatives and the growing interest in AI-based solutions, this study proposes a pilot project that utilizes artificial intelligence to deliver personalized training recommendations and connect students with practical training opportunities. The initiative would be implemented in collaboration with selected Syrian universities and private companies, aiming to establish a scalable, data-driven model that helps bridge the education-to-employment gap in the country.

Proposed AI Techniques

Although this initiative has not yet been implemented, it presents a practical vision for how AI can help address the education-employment mismatch by analyzing data generated through real-world training and interaction between students and the labor market. The proposed model offers fertile ground for applying various AI techniques in the future, including:

Smart recommendation systems to guide students toward the most relevant skills and academic courses aligned with their career paths.

Predictive models based on machine learning to analyze the local labor market and forecast future skill demands.

Intelligent matching tools that link students with internships and graduation projects tailored to their abilities and interests.

Data Handling and Analysis

To activate these systems, data will be collected from various sources, including academic records, skill assessments, company requirements, and graduate feedback on training and employment. This data will be analyzed using AI algorithms to customize training plans and align academic curricula with labor market needs.

Decision-Making Process

The proposed systems will analyze student profiles and market needs to generate personalized recommendations that enhance students' employability. Companies can also benefit from this data to identify suitable candidates for internships and job placements, fostering better integration between academic and professional sectors.

Results and Expected Impact

This foundational model aims to produce graduates better equipped to meet labor market demands, reduce the time gap between graduation and employment, and provide universities with real-time data to update their curricula. While this initiative has not yet been implemented, it lays the groundwork for the effective use of AI in the future to bridge the gap between education and employment in Syria.

Critical Reflection and Future Directions

The proposed AI-based education-to-employment model in Syria holds great promise but depends on key structural and ethical factors such as data availability, infrastructure readiness, and stakeholder engagement. Transparency in algorithms and ethical guidelines are vital to build trust. Next steps should include piloting the model, evaluating results, and adapting AI tools to local needs.

Ethical and Regulatory Considerations for AI Implementation

A focused ethical analysis is crucial to address issues like data privacy, algorithmic bias, and fairness in AI applications for education and labor markets. Frameworks such as GDPR, FERPA, and UNESCO's AI ethics recommendations provide essential guidance on consent, transparency, non-discrimination, and human oversight.

In low-resource settings like Syria, where regulations may be weak, clear guidelines on data handling—especially for vulnerable groups—are urgently needed. Collaboration between educational institutions and private sectors should extend beyond technology to include ethical protocols such as:

- Ethical impact assessments before deployment
- Transparency in AI recommendations and data sources
- Appeal processes for affected users
- Regular bias audits

In conclusion, ethical governance is fundamental, not optional, especially given AI's impact on individuals' educational and employment opportunities.

Challenges

Despite the promising potential of artificial intelligence in bridging the gap between education and the labor market, several challenges hinder its full implementation and effectiveness. First, the quality and availability of relevant data remain a major obstacle; incomplete, outdated, or biased data can reduce the accuracy of AI models (Khosravi et al., 2023). Second, there is often a lack of integration between educational institutions and labor market platforms, limiting real-time data exchange and collaboration (Luckin et al., 2016). Third, ethical and privacy concerns related to handling sensitive student and employment data require strict regulations and transparency (Khalil et al., 2025). Furthermore, the digital divide and unequal access to advanced technologies pose risks of exacerbating educational inequalities (Selwyn, 2019). Finally, resistance to change within institutions and insufficient training for educators and administrators may delay AI adoption and reduce its impact (Holmes et al., 2019).

CONCLUSION AND RECOMMENDATIONS

Artificial intelligence offers powerful capabilities to analyze, predict, and personalize educational and labor market dynamics, thus playing a pivotal role in aligning academic curricula with workforce needs. The case studies presented illustrate diverse applications of AI that have demonstrated improvements in student success, employment matching, and continuous interaction between education and industry. However, realizing the full potential of AI requires addressing challenges related to data quality, ethical considerations including privacy, transparency, and institutional readiness.

To maximize AI's impact, policymakers and educators should focus on:

Enhancing data infrastructure and promoting open data sharing between education and labor sectors.

Implementing clear ethical guidelines and privacy protections in AI applications.

Developing and enforcing clear ethical guidelines and privacy protections to safeguard student and worker data, ensuring transparency and fairness in AI applications.

Investing in capacity building for educators and administrators to effectively use AI tools.

Encouraging collaboration between academia, industry, and government to ensure AI solutions meet real market needs.

Addressing the digital divide by investing in infrastructure and affordable access to AI technologies, especially in underserved and resource-limited communities.

Designing scalable and adaptable AI solutions tailored to low-resource environments, providing practical training and support to educators and administrators.

Prioritizing equitable access to technology to avoid deepening existing inequalities.

By embracing these recommendations, AI can be a transformative force in closing the education-to-employment gap and preparing learners for the future workforce, especially as labor markets increasingly demand up-to-date digital skills and adaptable competencies. Continuous curriculum updates and skill mapping are essential to ensure graduates remain relevant in a rapidly evolving digital economy.

By integrating ethical frameworks, bridging the digital divide, and tailoring AI solutions to diverse educational contexts, AI can truly become a transformative force in closing the education-to-employment gap and preparing learners for the demands of the future workforce.

REFERENCES

Aleisa, M. A., Beloff, N., & White, M. (2023). Implementing AIRM: A new AI recruiting model for the Saudi Arabia labour market. *Journal of Innovation and Entrepreneurship, 12*(1), 59. DOI: 10.1186/s13731-023-00324-w

Arellano, F. A., Felgueroso, F., Vázquez, P., & González, E. (2008). Public-private partnerships in labour markets (IESE Business School Working Paper No. D/744). IESE Business School. https://www.iese.edu/media/research/pdfs/DI-0744-E.pdf

Association of Governing Boards of Universities and Colleges. (2019). Case study: Georgia State University. https://agb.org/wp-content/uploads/2019/01/case_study_innovation_georgia.pdf

Baker, R. S., & Inventado, P. S. (2014). Educational data mining and learning analytics. In *Learning Analytics* (pp. 61–75). Springer., DOI: 10.1007/978-1-4614-3305-7_4

Becker, G. S. (1993). *Human capital: A theoretical and empirical analysis, with special reference to education* (3rd ed.). University of Chicago Press.

Borgonovi, F., Calvino, F., Criscuolo, C., Samek, L., Seitz, H., Nania, J., Nitschke, J., & O'Kane, L. (2023). *Emerging trends in AI skill demand across fourteen OECD countries. OECD Artificial Intelligence Papers, No. 2*. OECD Publishing., DOI: 10.1787/7c691b9a-

Borjas, G. J. (2016). *Labor economics* (7th ed.). McGraw-Hill Education.

Chai, D. S., Kim, H.-S., Kim, K.-N., Ha, Y., Shin, S. S., & Yoon, S. W. (2025). Generative artificial intelligence in instructional system design. *Human Resource Development Review*. Advance online publication. DOI: 10.1177/15344843251320256

Chen, H., Chiang, R. H. L., & Storey, V. C. (2012). Business intelligence and analytics: From big data to big impact. *Management Information Systems Quarterly, 36*(4), 1165–1188. DOI: 10.2307/41703503

Davidoff, M. (2024). How broadening AI access can help bridge the digital divide. EDUCAUSE Review. https://er.educause.edu/articles/2024/11/how-broadening-ai-access-can-help-bridge-the-digital-divide

Dobslaw, F., Angelin, K., Öberg, L.-M., & Ahmad, A. (2023). The gap between higher education and the software industry: A case study on technology differences. arXiv preprint. https://arxiv.org/abs/2303.15597

Drachsler, H., Verbert, K., & Santos, O. C. (2015). Panorama of recommender systems to support learning. In *Recommender Systems Handbook* (pp. 421–451). Springer., DOI: 10.1007/978-1-4899-7637-6_14

EduBridge. (2022). Empowering students through AI-driven skill development and employment. EduBridge Official Website. https://www.edubridgeindia.com

Elbouknify, I., Berrada, I., Mekouar, L., Iraqi, Y., Bergou, E. H., Belhabib, H., Nail, Y., & Wardi, S. (2025). AI-based identification and support of at-risk students: A case study of the Moroccan education system. arXiv.

Eling, F., & Ogwal, A. (2025). Bridging learning gaps: The role of AI-powered technologies in enhancing quality education. *International Journal of Research and Innovation in Social Science*, *9*(3), 45–52. DOI: 10.47772/IJRISS.2025.903SEDU0155

European Commission. (2020). White paper on artificial intelligence: A European approach to excellence and trust. Publications Office of the European Union. https://ec.europa.eu/info/sites/default/files/commission-white-paper-artificial-intelligence-feb2020_en.pdf

Frontier Economics & Glass. AI. (2020). A new way to read the jobs market: Using AI to map the AI skills gap. Frontier Economics. https://www.frontier-economics.com/uk/en/news-and-insights/articles/article-i21335-a-new-way-to-read-the-jobs-market-using-ai-to-map-the-ai-skills-gap/

Goodfellow, I., Bengio, Y., & Courville, A. (2016). *Deep learning*. MIT Press.

Green, A. (2024). *Artificial intelligence and the changing demand for skills in the labour market. OECD Artificial Intelligence Papers, No. 14*. OECD Publishing., DOI: 10.1787/88684e36-

Han, J., Pei, J., & Kamber, M. (2011). *Data mining: Concepts and techniques* (3rd ed.). Morgan Kaufmann.

Holmes, W., Bialik, M., & Fadel, C. (2019). *Artificial intelligence in education: Promises and implications for teaching and learning*. Center for Curriculum Redesign.

Jaiswal, K., Kuzminykh, I., & Modgil, S. (2024). Understanding the skills gap between higher education and industry in the UK in the artificial intelligence sector. arXiv preprint. https://arxiv.org/abs/2408.10788

Kelleher, J. D., Mac Carthy, M., & Korvir, R. (2015). *Fundamentals of machine learning for predictive data analytics: Algorithms, worked examples, and case studies*. MIT Press.

Khalil, M., Shakya, R., & Liu, Q. (2025). Towards Privacy-Preserving Data-Driven Education: The Potential of Federated Learning. arXiv preprint arXiv:2503.13550. https://arxiv.org/abs/2503.13550

Khosravi, H., Sadiq, S., & Amer-Yahia, S. (2023). Data management of AI-powered education technologies: Challenges and opportunities. *Learning Letters*, *1*(2). Advance online publication. DOI: 10.59453/XLUD7002

Khurumova, V., & Pinto, J. C. (2024). Career services at HEI's: What are they offering? *Frontiers in Education*, *9*, 1410628. Advance online publication. DOI: 10.3389/feduc.2024.1410628

Kolb, D. A. (1984). *Experiential learning: Experience as the source of learning and development*. Prentice Hall.

Luckin, R., Holmes, W., Griffiths, M., & Forcier, L. B. (2016). *Intelligence Unleashed: An Argument for AI in Education*. Pearson Education.

Morandini, S., Fraboni, F., De Angelis, M., Puzzo, G., Giusino, D., & Pietrantoni, L. (2023). The impact of artificial intelligence on workers' skills: Upskilling and reskilling in organisations. Informing Science. *The International Journal of an Emerging Transdiscipline*, *26*, 39–68. https://www.informingscience.org/Publications/5078

Namjildorj, O. (2025). The requirements of integrating soft skills into higher education curricula within the context of transformative education. International Journal of Learning. *Teaching and Educational Research*, *24*(3), 725–739. DOI: 10.26803/ijlter.24.3.34

Novo Nordisk Foundation. (2024). Open Discovery Innovation Network (ODIN). Retrieved from https://novonordiskfonden.dk/en/projects/open-discovery-innovation-network-odin/

OECD. (2021). The future of education and skills 2030: OECD learning compass 2030. https://www.oecd.org/education/2030-project/

Pervez, N., Mahmood, W., Akram, M., & Waqas, M. (2024). Analyzing the alignment between university curriculum and job market requirements in Pakistan: Challenges and opportunities. *Indus Journal of Social Sciences*, *2*(2), 397–410. DOI: 10.59075/ijss.v2i2.269

Popenici, S. A. D., & Kerr, S. (2017). Exploring the impact of artificial intelligence on teaching and learning in higher education. *Research and Practice in Technology Enhanced Learning*, *12*(1), 22. DOI: 10.1186/s41039-017-0062-8 PMID: 30595727

Provost, F., & Fawcett, T. (2013). *Data science for business: What you need to know about data mining and data-analytic thinking*. O'Reilly Media.

Romero, C., & Ventura, S. (2020). Educational data mining and learning analytics: An updated survey. *Wiley Interdisciplinary Reviews. Data Mining and Knowledge Discovery*, *10*(3), e1355. DOI: 10.1002/widm.1355

Russell, S., & Norvig, P. (2020). *Artificial intelligence: A modern approach* (4th ed.). Pearson.

Selwyn, N. (2019). *Should robots replace teachers? AI and the future of education*. Polity Press.

Senger, E., Zhang, M., van der Goot, R., & Plank, B. (2024, March). Deep learning-based computational job market analysis: A survey on skill extraction and classification from job postings. In Proceedings of the First Workshop on Natural Language Processing for Human Resources (NLP4HR 2024) (pp. 1–15). Association for Computational Linguistics.

Shalev-Shwartz, S., & Ben-David, S. (2014). *Understanding machine learning: From theory to algorithms*. Cambridge University Press.

Shi, L. (2025). Global perspectives on AI competence development: Analyzing national AI strategies in education and workforce policies. *Human Resource Development Review*, *24*(1), 123–145. DOI: 10.1177/15344843251332360

UNESCO. (2022). Reimagining our futures together: A new social contract for education. https://unesdoc.unesco.org/ark:/48223/pf0000379707

UNESCO. (2023). Global education monitoring report 2023: Technology in education. https://unesdoc.unesco.org/ark:/48223/pf0000385723

UNESCO. (2023). Guidance for generative AI in education and research. United Nations Educational, Scientific and Cultural Organization. https://unesdoc.unesco.org/ark:/48223/pf0000386693

UNESCO. (2023). Digital learning holds great promise to transform education, but its benefits are not evenly distributed. https://www.unesco.org/en/articles/unesco-spotlights-how-digital-learning-can-promote-equity-low-resource-contexts

UNESCO. (2023). Ethics of Artificial Intelligence in Education. UNESCO. https://unesdoc.unesco.org/ark:/48223/pf0000380455

UNICEF. (2024). Adolescent development and participation in the Syrian Arab Republic. Retrieved from https://www.unicef.org/syria/adolescent-development-and-participation

U.S. Department of Education. (2025). Protecting Student Privacy: FERPA. Retrieved July 2025.

Varona Cervantes, C., & Cooper, R. (2022). Labor Market Implications of Education Mismatch. *European Economic Review*, *148*, 104179. DOI: 10.1016/j.euroecorev.2022.104179

World Bank. (2020). The COVID-19 pandemic: Shocks to education and policy responses. https://www.worldbank.org/en/topic/education/publication/the-covid19-pandemic-shocks-to-education-and-policy-responses

World Economic Forum. (2023). The future of jobs report 2023. https://www.weforum.org/reports/the-future-of-jobs-report-2023

Wyonch, R. (2020). Work-ready graduates: The role of co-op programs in labour market success. C.D. Howe Institute. https://cdhowe.org/publication/work-ready-graduates-role-co-op-programs-labour-market-success

Yan, J., Tian, H., Sun, X., & Song, L. (2025). Role of artificial intelligence in enhancing competency assessment and transforming curriculum in higher vocational education. *Frontiers in Education*, *10*, 1551596. DOI: 10.3389/feduc.2025.1551596

Zawacki-Richter, O., Marín, V. I., Bond, M., & Gouverneur, F. (2019). Systematic review of research on artificial intelligence applications in higher education: Where are the educators? *International Journal of Educational Technology in Higher Education*, *16*(1), 39. DOI: 10.1186/s41239-019-0171-0

Zhang, M. (2024). Computational Job Market Analysis: with Natural Language Processing.

Zylfijaj, K., & Shaqiri, M. (2024). The Role of Vocational Education and Training in Bridging the Skills Gap in the Labor Market. Paper presented at the UBT International Conference on Management, Business and Economy. Retrieved from https://www.researchgate.net/publication/382250381_The_Role_of_Vocational_Education_and_Training_in_Bridging_the_Skills_Gap_in_the_Labor_Market

Compilation of References

Abdallah, A. K., Alkaabi, A. M., Mehiar, D. A. F., & Aradat, Z. A. J. (2024). Chatbots in Classrooms: Tailoring Education and Boosting Engagement. In *Cutting-Edge Innovations in Teaching, Leadership, Technology, and Assessment* (pp. 166-181). IGI Global. Can be accessed at https://library.oapen.org/bitstream/handle/20.500.12657/88268/9798369308813.pdf?sequence=3#page=187

Abd-Alrazaq, A., AlSaad, R., Alhuwail, D., Ahmed, A., Healy, P. M., Latifi, S., Aziz, S., Damseh, R., Alrazak, S. A., & Sheikh, J. (2023). Large language models in medical education: Opportunities, challenges, and future directions. *JMIR Medical Education*, *9*(1), e48291.

Abubakari, M. S., Shafik, W., & Hidayatullah, A. F. (2024b). Evaluating the Potential of Artificial Intelligence in Islamic Religious Education: A SWOT Analysis Overview. In *AI-Enhanced Teaching Methods* (pp. 216–239). IGI Global.

Abubakari, M. S., Shafik, W., & Hidayatullah, A. F. (2024a). Evaluating the Potential of Artificial Intelligence in Islamic Religious Education. In *AI-Enhanced Teaching Methods* (pp. 216–239). IGI Global., DOI: 10.4018/979-8-3693-2728-9.ch010

Adamopoulou, E., & Moussiades, L. (2020). Chatbots: History, technology, and applications. *Machine Learning with Applications*, *2*, 100006. DOI: 10.1016/j.mlwa.2020.100006

Adeniyi, F. B., & Akinsuroju, O. E. (2024). Harnessing artificial intelligence (AI) for strategic human resource planning, educational commercialization, and navigating marketization dynamics. FUOYE Journal of Educational Management, 1(2).

Adeyemi, I. O., Esan, A. O., & Aleem, A. (2021). Application of gamification to library services: Awareness, perception, and readiness of academic librarians in Nigeria. *The Electronic Library*, *39*(5), 767–781. Retrieved March 31, 2025, from. DOI: 10.1108/EL-05-2021-0096

Adiguzel, T., Kaya, M. H., & Cansu, F. K. (2023). Revolutionizing education with AI: Exploring the transformative potential of ChatGPT. *Contemporary Educational Technology*. Advance online publication. DOI: 10.30935/cedtech/13152

Aguilar-Ferrándiz, M. E., Toledano-Moreno, S., Casas-Barragán, A., Albornoz-Cabello, M., Tapia-Haro, R., & Correa-Rodríguez, M. (2024). Implementation of a coaching training for enhancing empathy and emotional intelligence skills in health science students: A prospective study. *BMC Medical Education*, *24*(76), 2–9. Retrieved April 01, 2025, from. DOI: 10.1186/s12909-024-05076-z

Ahmed, F. (2024). The digital divide and AI in education: Addressing equity and accessibility. *Journal of AI Integration in Education*, *1*(2), 12–23.

Ahmed, S. (2025). Integrating AI-Driven Automated Code Review in Agile Development: Benefits, Challenges, and Best Practices. *International Journal of Advanced Engineering Management Science, 11*(2), 593997.

Ahsan, K., Akbar, S., Kam, B., & Abdulrahman, M. D. A. (2023). Implementation of micro-credentials in higher education: A systematic literature review. *Education and Information Technologies*, *28*(10), 13505–13540. DOI: 10.1007/s10639-023-11739-z

Akinwalere, S. N., & Ivanov, V. (2022). Artificial intelligence in higher Education: Challenges and opportunities. *BORDER CROSSING*, *12*(1), 1–15. DOI: 10.33182/bc.v12i1.2015

Alam, M., & Hasan, M. (2024). Applications and future prospects of artificial intelligence in education. *International Journal of Humanities & Social Science Studies*, pp. 209-218. DOI: DOI: 10.29032/ijhsss.v10.i1.2024.209-218

Alam, A., & Mohanty, A. (2023). Educational technology: Exploring the convergence of technology and pedagogy through mobility, interactivity, AI, and learning tools. *Cogent Engineering*, *10*(2), 2283282. DOI: 10.1080/23311916.2023.2283282

Alam, A., & Mohanty, A. (2024). Integrated constructive robotics in education (ICRE) model: A paradigmatic framework for transformative learning in educational ecosystem. *Cogent Education*, *11*(1). Advance online publication. DOI: 10.1080/2331186X.2024.2324487

Aldeman, N. L. S., Urtiga, D. S., Aita, K. M., Machado, V. P., Mata, D., Sousa, L. C. D., & Coelho, A. G.B., Da, Silva, A. S., Silva, D., Mendes, A. P., Neres, F. J. D. O., & Monte, S. J. H. D. (2021). Smartpathk: A platform for teaching glomerulopathies using machine learning. *BMC Medical Education*, *21*, 248–248.

Aleisa, M. A., Beloff, N., & White, M. (2023). Implementing AIRM: A new AI recruiting model for the Saudi Arabia labour market. *Journal of Innovation and Entrepreneurship, 12*(1), 59. DOI: 10.1186/s13731-023-00324-w

Ali, H. ul Mustafa, A., & Aysan, A. F. (2025). Global adoption of generative AI: What matters most? *Journal of Economy and Technology, 3*, 166-176. https://www.sciencedirect.com/science/article/pii/S2949948824000520

Alier, M., García-Peñalvo, F. J., & Camba, J. D. (2024). Generative Artificial Intelligence in Education: From Deceptive to Disruptive. *International Journal of Interactive Multimedia and Artificial Intelligence, 8*(5). Advance online publication. DOI: 10.9781/ijimai.2024.02.011

Ali, U. (2022). Cognitive computing and intelligent tutoring systems in education technology. *Multidisciplinary Research in Computing Information Systems, 2*(2), 77–99.

Al-Jaf, K., Öz, C., Mahmud, H., & Rashid, T. A. (2024). *Leveraging Chatbots for Effective Educational Administration: A Systematic Review*. Can be accessed at https://www.preprints.org/frontend/manuscript/89d7afca4e6f6e3b8ac319f446f7030c/download_pub

Allen, T. J., & Mizumoto, A. (2024). ChatGPT over my friends: Japanese English-as-a-foreign-language learners' preferences for editing and proofreading strategies. *RELC Journal*. Advance online publication. DOI: 10.1177/00336882241262533

Allman, B., Kimmons, R., Rosenberg, J., & Dash, M. (2023). Trends and topics in educational technology. *TechTrends, 67*(3), 583–591. https://link.springer.com/content/pdf/10.1007/s11528-023-00840-2.pdf PMID: 37216141

Almufarreh, A. (2024). Determinants of Students' Satisfaction with AI Tools in Education: A PLS-SEM-ANN Approach. *Sustainability, 16*(13), 5354. DOI: 10.3390/su16135354

Almusharraf, I. (2023). Analyzing the role of ChatGPT as a writing assistant at higher education level: A systematic review of the literature. *Contemporary Educational Technology, 15*(4), ep464. DOI: 10.30935/cedtech/13265

Alqahtani, N., & Wafula, Z. (2024). Artificial intelligence Integration: Pedagogical strategies and policies at leading universities. *Innovative Higher Education*. Advance online publication. DOI: 10.1007/s10755-024-09749-x

Alrakhawi, H. A., Jamiat, N., & Abu-Naser, S. S. (2023). Intelligent tutoring systems in education: A systematic review of usage, tools, effects and evaluation. *Journal of Theoretical and Applied Information Technology, 101*(4), 1205–1226.

Alvarez-Icaza, I., & Huerta, O. (2024). Augmented intelligence for open education: Bridging the digital gap with inclusive design methods. *Frontiers in Education, 9*. Advance online publication. DOI: 10.3389/feduc.2024.1337932

Alwaqdani, M. (2025). Investigating teachers' perceptions of artificial intelligence tools in education: Potential and difficulties. *Education and Information Technologies, 30*, 2737–2755. DOI: 10.1007/s10639-024-12903-9

Ambani Africa. (2024). AMBANI. [Accessed 12 May, 2025] https://www.ambaniafrica.com/copy-of-about

Andrade, H. L., & Brookhart, S. M. (2020). Classroom assessment as the co-regulation of learning. *Assessment in Education: Principles, Policy & Practice, 27*(4), 350–372. https://www.tandfonline.com/doi/abs/10.1080/0969594X.2019.1571992

Andreanoff, J. (2016). The Impact of Peer Coaching on the Academic Performance of Undergraduate Students: A Mixed Methods Study. *Journal of Learning Development in Higher Education Special Edition, 1-5*(2). Advance online publication. Retrieved April 23, 2025, from. DOI: 10.47408/jldhe.v0i0.358

Ardimento, P., & Scalera, M. (2024). Enhancing Higher Education with AI: Balancing Personalized Learning and Ethical Responsibility. In *Book of Abstracts* (p. 164). Can be accessed at https://air.unimi.it/bitstream/2434/1121742/3/BOA_HELMETO2024.pdf#page=180

Arellano, F. A., Felgueroso, F., Vázquez, P., & González, E. (2008). Public-private partnerships in labour markets (IESE Business School Working Paper No. D/744). IESE Business School. https://www.iese.edu/media/research/pdfs/DI-0744-E.pdf

Asanza, T. E. P., Asanza, M. V. P., Martínez, M. A. M., & García, F. A. R. (2024). Gamification as a Didactic Motivator in Low-Resource Public English as a Foreign Language (EFL) Classrooms in Ecuador. *Ciencia Latina Education, 8*(2), 5393–5399. Retrieved May 05, 2025, from. DOI: 10.37811/cl_rcm.v8i2.10951

Ashraf, M. A., Yang, M., Zhang, Y., Denden, M., Tlili, A., Liu, J., Huang, R., & Burgos, D. (2021). A systematic review of systematic reviews on blended learning: Trends, gaps and future directions. *Psychology Research and Behavior Management*, •••, 1525–1541.

Association of Governing Boards of Universities and Colleges. (2019). Case study: Georgia State University. https://agb.org/wp-content/uploads/2019/01/case_study_innovation_georgia.pdf

Athanassopoulos, S., Manoli, P., Gouvi, M., Lavidas, K., & Komis, V. (2023). The use of ChatGPT as a learning tool to improve foreign language writing in a multilingual and multicultural classroom. *Advances in Mobile Learning Educational Research*, *3*(2), 818–824. DOI: 10.25082/AMLER.2023.02.009

Atherton, P., Topham, L., & Khan, W. (2024). AI and student feedback. *EDULEARN24 Proceedings*. Can be accessed at https://researchonline.ljmu.ac.uk/id/eprint/23757/1/AI%20AND%20STUDENT%20FEEDBACK.pdf

Atkinson, A. R., Abbott, C., Oswald, A., Boucher, A., Cavalcanti, R. B., Frank, J. R., & Snell, L. S. (2024). Strategies to Enable Transformation in Medical Education: Faculty and Trainee Development in Competence By Design. *Perspectives on Medical Education*, *13*(1). Advance online publication. DOI: 10.5334/pme.960

Austin, J. L., & Howson, A. G. (1979). Language and mathematical education. *Educational Studies in Mathematics*, *10*(2), 161–197. DOI: 10.1007/BF00230986

Awan, S., Anthony, N., & Shahbaz, K. (2023). Inclusive and Equitable Quality Education: The Context of Constitution of Pakistan and International Commitments. *Voyage Journal of Educational Studies (VJES) 3*(1), 88-89. [Accessed 23 April, 2025] https://vjes.voyageams.com/index.php/vjes/article/download/28/26

Baker, R., & Siemens, G. (2014). Educational Data Mining and Learning Analytics. In R. K. Sawyer (Ed.), *The Cambridge Handbook of the Learning Sciences* (pp. 253–272). chapter, Cambridge: Cambridge University Press.

Baker, B., Mills, K. A., McDonald, P., & Wang, L. (2023). AI, concepts of intelligence, and chatbots: The "Figure of Man," the rise of emotion, and future visions of education. *Teachers College Record*, *125*(6), 60–84. DOI: 10.1177/01614681231191291

Baker, R. S., & Inventado, P. S. (2014). Educational data mining and learning analytics. In *Learning Analytics* (pp. 61–75). Springer., DOI: 10.1007/978-1-4614-3305-7_4

Barrot, J. S. (2023). Using ChatGPT for second language writing: Pitfalls and potentials. *Assessing Writing*, *57*, 100745. DOI: 10.1016/j.asw.2023.100745

Bartlett, K. A., & Camba, J. D. (2024). Generative Artificial Intelligence in Product Design Education: Navigating Concerns of Originality and Ethics. *International Journal of Interactive Multimedia and Artificial Intelligence*, *8*(5). Advance online publication. DOI: 10.9781/ijimai.2024.02.006

Barton, B., Chan, R., King, C., Neville-Barton, P., & Sneddon, J. (2005). EAL undergraduates learning mathematics. *International Journal of Mathematical Education in Science and Technology*, *36*(7), 721–729. DOI: 10.1080/00207390500270950

Barwell, R. (2005). Ambiguity in the Mathematics Classroom. *Language and Education, 19*(2), 117–125. DOI: 10.1080/09500780508668667

Baskara, R., & Mukarto, M. (2023). Exploring the implications of ChatGPT for language learning in higher education. *Indonesian Journal of English Language Teaching and Applied Linguistics, 7*(2), 343–358. DOI: 10.21093/ijeltal.v7i2.1387

Becker, G. S. (1993). *Human capital: A theoretical and empirical analysis, with special reference to education* (3rd ed.). University of Chicago Press.

Bell, R., & Bell, H. (2023). Entrepreneurship education in the era of generative artificial intelligence. *Entrepreneurship Education, 6*(3), 229–244. DOI: 10.1007/s41959-023-00099-x

Bengesai, A. V., Amusa, L. B., & Dhunpath, R. (2023). A meta-analysis on the effect of formal peer learning approaches on course performance in higher education. *Cogent Education, 10*(1), 2203990. DOI: 10.1080/2331186X.2023.2203990

Benítez, T. M., Xu, Y., Boudreau, J. D., Kow, A. W. C., Bello, F., Van Phuoc, L., Wang, X., Sun, X., Leung, G. K. K., Lan, Y., Wang, Y., Cheng, D., Tham, Y. C., Wong, T. Y., & Chung, K. C. (2024). Harnessing the potential of large language models in medical education: Promise and pitfalls. *Journal of the American Medical Informatics Association : JAMIA, 31*(3). Advance online publication. DOI: 10.1093/jamia/ocad252

Berninger, V., & Swanson, H. (1994). Modifying Hayes and Flower's model of skilled writing to explain beginning and developing writing. In Butterfield, E. C. (Ed.), *Children's writing: toward a process of development of skilled writing* (Vol. 2, pp. 57–81). JAI Press.

Bezzina, S., & Dingli, A. (2023). Rethinking gamification through artificial intelligence. *International Conference on Human-Computer Interaction*, 252–263.

Bhatt, N., & Chakrabarti, A. (2022). Gamification of design thinking: A way to enhance effectiveness of learning. *Artificial Intelligence for Engineering Design, Analysis and Manufacturing, 36*(29). Advance online publication. Retrieved April 07, 2025, from. DOI: 10.1017/S0890060422000154

Bhise, A., Munshi, A., Rodrigues, A., & Sawant, V. (2022). Overview of AI in education. In *Artificial Intelligence in Higher Education* (pp. 31–62). CRC Press.

Bin Hady, W. R. A., Al-Kadi, A., & Alzubi, M. (2023). Exploring the dimensions of ChatGPT in English language learning: A global perspective. *Library Hi Tech.* Advance online publication. DOI: 10.1108/LHT-05-2023-0200

Binns, R. (2017). Fairness in Machine Learning: Lessons from Political Philosophy. *arXiv (Cornell University)*. https://doi.org//arxiv.1712.03586DOI: 10.48550

Bit, D., Biswas, S., & Nag, M. (2024). The impact of artificial intelligence in the educational system. *International Journal of Scientific Research in Science and Technology*. Advance online publication. DOI: 10.32628/ijsrst2411424

Bjørnerås, A. B., Witsø, A. E., Kvam, L., Eide, A. H., Jahren, L., & Horghagen, S. (2024). Identifying Key Concepts in Ambassador Interventions for Students with Disabilities in Higher Education: A Scoping Review. *International Journal of Disability Development and Education, 71*(3). Advance online publication. DOI: 10.1080/1034912X.2022.2095558

Blanuša Trošelj, D., Maričić, S., & Ćurić, A. (2024). *Growing interest in AI in education: Systematic literature review*. In Shelley, M., & Ozturk, O. T. (Eds.), *Proceedings of ICRES 2024 – International Conference on Research in Education and Science* (pp. 56–73). International Society for Technology, Education, and Science.

Böhm-Fischer, A., & Beyer, L. (2024). Blended Learning, Flipped Classroom, and Peer Teaching as a Combination to Meet the Increasing Diversity in Higher Education. *International Journal of Information and Education Technology (IJIET), 14*(2), 310–314. Retrieved April 01, 2025, from. DOI: 10.18178/ijiet.2024.14.2.2053

Bo, N. S. W. (2024). *OECD digital education outlook 2023: Towards an effective education ecosystem*. Hungarian Educational Research Journal., DOI: 10.1556/063.2024.00340

Borgonovi, F., Calvino, F., Criscuolo, C., Samek, L., Seitz, H., Nania, J., Nitschke, J., & O'Kane, L. (2023). *Emerging trends in AI skill demand across fourteen OECD countries. OECD Artificial Intelligence Papers, No. 2*. OECD Publishing., DOI: 10.1787/7c691b9a-

Borjas, G. J. (2016). *Labor economics* (7th ed.). McGraw-Hill Education.

Boscardin, C. K., Gin, B., Golde, P. B., & Hauer, K. E. (2024). ChatGPT and Generative Artificial Intelligence for Medical Education: Potential Impact and Opportunity. *Academic Medicine, 99*(1). Advance online publication. DOI: 10.1097/ACM.0000000000005439

Bradley, V. M. (2021). Learning Management System (LMS) use with online instruction. *International Journal of Technology in Education, 4*(1), 68–92.

Brogden, L., Bernie, D., Boston, M., Forster, A. M., Galbrun, L., Hepburn, L. A., & Morkel, J. (2022). A learning design framework for community resilience: International and transdisciplinary perspectives on a boundary object. *International Journal of Educational Research Open, 3*, 100200.

Brooks, C. D. (2022). Prodigy Game and Third-Grade Mathematics Achievement in an Urban Setting (Doctoral dissertation, Walden University).

Bull, C., & Kharrufa, A. (2024). Generative Artificial Intelligence Assistants in Software Development Education: A Vision for Integrating Generative Artificial Intelligence into Educational Practice, Not Instinctively Defending Against It. *IEEE Software, 41*(2). Advance online publication. DOI: 10.1109/MS.2023.3300574

Campos, K. E., Rigo, S. J., & Barbosa, J. L. V. (2025). Detecção da autoeficácia em ambientes computacionais de aprendizagem. *RECIMA21-Revista Científica Multidisciplinar, 6*(1). e616174-e616174. https://recima21.com.br/index.php/recima21/article/view/6174

Casheekar, A., Lahiri, A., Rath, K., Prabhakar, K. S., & Srinivasan, K. (2024). A contemporary review on chatbots, AI-powered virtual conversational agents, ChatGPT: Applications, open challenges and future research directions. *Computer Science Review, 52*, 100632. DOI: 10.1016/j.cosrev.2024.100632

Chai, D. S., Kim, H.-S., Kim, K.-N., Ha, Y., Shin, S. S., & Yoon, S. W. (2025). Generative artificial intelligence in instructional system design. *Human Resource Development Review*. Advance online publication. DOI: 10.1177/15344843251320256

Chandramma, R., Babu, K. S., Ranjith, K. S., Sinha, A. K., Neerugatti, V., & Reddy, D. S. (2025, January). Enhancing E-learning Accessibility through AI (Artificial Intelligence) and Inclusive Design. In *2025 6th International Conference on Mobile Computing and Sustainable Informatics (ICMCSI)* (pp. 1466-1471). IEEE. Doi: DOI: 10.1109/ICMCSI64620.2025.10883148

Chang, D. H., Lin, M. P. C., Hajian, S., & Wang, Q. Q. (2023). Educational design principles of using AI chatbot that supports self-regulated learning in education: Goal setting, feedback, and personalization. *Sustainability, 15*(17), 12921. Can be accessed at https://www.mdpi.com/2071-1050/15/17/12921

Cheng, J., Lu, C., & Xiao, Q. (2025). Effects of gamification on EFL learning: A quasi-experimental study of reading proficiency and language enjoyment among Chinese undergraduates. *Frontiers in Psychology, 16*, 1448916.

Chen, H., Chiang, R. H. L., & Storey, V. C. (2012). Business intelligence and analytics: From big data to big impact. *Management Information Systems Quarterly*, *36*(4), 1165–1188. DOI: 10.2307/41703503

Chen, L., Chen, P., & Lin, Z. (2020). Artificial intelligence in education: A review. *IEEE Access : Practical Innovations, Open Solutions*, *8*, 75264–75278. https://ieeexplore.ieee.org/stamp/stamp.jsp?arnumber=9069875

Chen, L., Ifenthaler, D., Yau, J. Y. K., & Sun, W. (2024). Artificial intelligence in entrepreneurship education: A scoping review. *Education + Training*, *66*(6), 589–608. https://www.emerald.com/insight/content/doi/10.1108/et-05-2023-0169/full/html

Chen, Y., Jensen, S., Albert, L. J., Gupta, S., & Lee, T. (2023). Artificial intelligence (AI) student assistants in the classroom: Designing chatbots to support student success. *Information Systems Frontiers*, *25*(1), 161–182. DOI: 10.1007/s10796-022-10291-4

Cheung, K. K. C., Long, Y., Liu, Q., & Chan, H. Y. (2024). Unpacking Epistemic Insights of Artificial Intelligence (AI) in Science Education: A Systematic Review. *Science and Education*. Advance online publication. DOI: 10.1007/s11191-024-00511-5

Chheang, V., Sharmin, S., Márquez-Hernández, R., Patel, M., Rajasekaran, D., Caulfield, G., . . . Barmaki, R. L. (2024, January). Towards anatomy education with generative AI-based virtual assistants in immersive virtual reality environments. In *2024 IEEE international conference on artificial intelligence and eXtended and virtual reality (AIxVR)* (pp. 21-30). IEEE. Can be accessed at https://arxiv.org/pdf/2306.17278

Chiriboga, S. P. J., Burgos, A. L. T., Avila, M. M. R., Chida, J. L. C., Macias, K. J. A., Morante, Y. E. C., & Párraga, A. P. B. (2025). Artificial Intelligence and Personalized Learning in Foreign Languages: An Analysis of Chatbots and Virtual Assistants in Education. *Revista Científica de Salud y Desarrollo Humano, 6*(1), 882-905. Can be accessed at http://revistavitalia.org/index.php/vitalia/article/download/515/1062

Choi, W. C., & Chang, C. I. (2025). *A Survey of Techniques*. Design, Applications, Challenges, and Student Perspective of Chatbot-Based Learning Tutoring System Supporting Students to Learn in Education.

Chounta, I. A., Bardone, E., Raudsep, A., & Pedaste, M. (2022). Exploring teachers' perceptions of artificial intelligence as a tool to support their practice in Estonian K-12 education. *International Journal of Artificial Intelligence in Education*, *32*, 725–755.

Christen, M., Gordijn, B., & Loi, M. (2020). *The ethics of cybersecurity*. Springer Nature. https://library.oapen.org/handle/20.500.12657/47324

Cleary, T. J., & Zimmerman, B. J. (2001). Self-Regulation Differences during Athletic Practice by Experts, Non-Experts, and Novices. *Journal of Applied Sport Psychology, 13*(2), 185–206. DOI: 10.1080/104132001753149883

Cobb, P., Nicholls, J., Wheatley, G., Trigattl, B., & Perlwitz, M. (1991). *Assessment of a problem-centered second-grade mathematics project. 22*(1), 3–29.

Cobb, P., Wood, T., Yackel, E., & Perlwitz, M. (1992). A follow-up assessment of a second-grade problem-centered mathematics project. *Educational Studies in Mathematics, 23*(5), 483–504. DOI: 10.1007/BF00571469

Collins, A., & Halverson, R. (2022). *Rethinking Education in the Age of Technology: The Digital Revolution and the Schools*. 1–10.

Collins, A., & Halverson, R. (2018). *Rethinking Education in the Age of Technology: The Digital Revolution and Schooling in America*. Teachers College Press.

Cope, B., & Kalantzis, M. (2021). A Little History of e-Learning.

Cope, B., & Kalantzis, M. (2023). A little history of e-learning: Finding new ways to learn in the PLATO computer education system, 1959–1976. *History of Education, 52*(6), 905–936.

Cope, B., Kalantzis, M., & Searsmith, D. (2020). Artificial intelligence for education: Knowledge and its assessment in AI-enabled learning ecologies. *Educational Philosophy and Theory, 52*(8), 786–800. DOI: 10.1080/00131857.2020.1728732

Corte, C., & Amrein-Beardsley, A. (2024). Faculty/Staff Training to Examine Racial Implicit Bias: Findings and Implications for Creating Inclusive Educational Spaces. *Innovative Higher Education, 49*(1). Advance online publication. DOI: 10.1007/s10755-023-09673-6

Costa, S. (2023). Artificial intelligence in education: Challenges and opportunities in learning.

Creswell, J. W. (2014). *Research design: Qualitative, quantitative, and mixed methods approaches* (4th ed.). SAGE Publications.

Criollo-C, S., Guerrero-Arias, A., Guaña-Moya, J., Samala, A. D., & Luján-Mora, S. (2024). Towards Sustainable Education with the Use of Mobile Augmented Reality in Early Childhood and Primary Education: A Systematic Mapping. In *Sustainability (Switzerland)* (Vol. 16, Issue 3). https://doi.org/DOI: 10.3390/su16031192

Csikszentmihalyi, M., & Csikzentmihaly, M. (1990). *Flow: The psychology of optimal experience* (Vol. 1990). Harper & Row.

Cullingford, C. (1984). The Battle for the Schools: Attitudes of parents and teachers towards education. *Educational Studies, 10*(2), 113–119. DOI: 10.1080/0305569840100204

Culpepper, M. K., & Gauntlett, D. (2024). The construction of everyday creative identity. *Journal of Creativity, 34*(2), 100085. Retrieved January 05, 2025, from. DOI: 10.1016/j.yjoc.2024.100085

D'Mello, S. K., & Graesser, A. (2023). Intelligent tutoring systems: How computers achieve learning gains that rival human tutors. In Schutz, P. A., & Muis, K. R. (Eds.), *Handbook of educational psychology* (pp. 603–629). Routledge., https://www.taylorfrancis.com/chapters/edit/10.4324/9780429433726-31/intelligent-tutoring-systems-sidney-mello-art-graesser

Darwish, D. (2024). Chatbots vs. AI Chatbots vs. Virtual Assistants. In *Design and Development of Emerging Chatbot Technology* (pp. 26–50). IGI Global., DOI: 10.4018/979-8-3693-1830-0.ch002

Das, S., Anowar, S., & Ghosh, B. (2024). The Rise of Artificial Intelligence in Education: Current Trends and Future Prospects (pp. 57–67). https://doi.org/DOI: 10.52756/lbsopf.2024.e01.006

Dastani, M., & Mohseni, M. (2024). Artificial intelligence chatbots in medical education: a literature review of potential benefits and challenges. *International Journal of Medical Reviews, 11*(2), 710-715. Can be accessed at https://www.ijmedrev.com/article_201393_9d2970d16312f91f0fe2c44b87ef5562.pdf

Davidoff, M. (2024). How broadening AI access can help bridge the digital divide. EDUCAUSE Review. https://er.educause.edu/articles/2024/11/how-broadening-ai-access-can-help-bridge-the-digital-divide

Davis, F. (1989). Perceived Usefulness, Perceived Ease of Use, and User Acceptance of Information Technology. *Management Information Systems Quarterly, 13*, 319–340. DOI: 10.2307/249008

Davis, F. D., Bagozzi, R. P., & Warshaw, P. R. (1989). User acceptance of computer technology: A comparison of two theoretical models. *Management Science, 35*(8), 982–1003. DOI: 10.1287/mnsc.35.8.982

De Boer, A., Pijl, S. J., & Minnaert, A. (2010). Attitudes of parents towards inclusive education: A review of the literature. *European Journal of Special Needs Education, 25*(2), 165–181. DOI: 10.1080/08856251003658694 de Caux, B. C., & Pretorius, L. (2024). Learning together through collaborative writing: The power of peer feedback and discussion in doctoral writing groups. *Studies in Educational Evaluation, 83*, 101379. DOI: 10.1016/j.stueduc.2024.101379

DeKeyser, R. M., & Prieto Botana, G. (Eds.). (2019). *Doing SLA research with implications for the classroom: Reconciling methodological demands and pedagogical applicability*. John Benjamins Publishing Company., DOI: 10.1075/lllt.52

Delello, J. A., Sung, W., Mokhtari, K., Hebert, J., Bronson, A., & De Giuseppe, T. (2025). AI in the Classroom: Insights from Educators on Usage, Challenges, and Mental Health. *Education Sciences, 15*(2), 2. Advance online publication. DOI: 10.3390/educsci15020113

Design & Intelligence Laboratory (DILab). (n.d.). *Jill Watson*. Georgia Tech. Retrieved from https://dilab.gatech.edu/jill-watson/

Dialogue and Learning in Mathematics Education (Vol. 29). (2003). Kluwer Academic Publishers. https://doi.org/DOI: 10.1007/0-306-48016-6

Diaz, A. F., & Estoque-Loñez, H. (2024). A Meta-Analysis on the Effectiveness of Gamification on Student Learning Achievement. *International Journal of Education in Mathematics. Science and Technology, 12*(5), 1236–1253.

Dichev, C., & Dicheva, D. (2017). Gamifying education: what is known, what is believed and what remains uncertain: a critical review. *International Journal of Educational Technology in Higher Education, 14*(9). Advance online publication. DOI: 10.1186/s41239-017-0042-5

Dignum, V. (2019). *Responsible artificial intelligence: how to develop and use AI in a responsible way*. Springer.

Digón-Regueiro, P., Méndez-García, R. M., Romero-Rodrigo, M. M., & Becerra-Brito, C. V. (2024). Questioning the role of technology in Early Childhood Education: Divides and false views. *Pixel-Bit. Revista de Medios y Educacion, 69*. Advance online publication. DOI: 10.12795/pixelbit.98498

Diwanji, P., Hinkelmann, K., & Witschel, H. (2018). Enhance Classroom Preparation for Flipped Classroom using AI and Analytics: *Proceedings of the 20th International Conference on Enterprise Information Systems*, 477–483. https://doi.org/DOI: 10.5220/0006807604770483

Dobslaw, F., Angelin, K., Öberg, L.-M., & Ahmad, A. (2023). The gap between higher education and the software industry: A case study on technology differences. arXiv preprint. https://arxiv.org/abs/2303.15597

Drachsler, H., Verbert, K., & Santos, O. C. (2015). Panorama of recommender systems to support learning. In *Recommender Systems Handbook* (pp. 421–451). Springer., DOI: 10.1007/978-1-4899-7637-6_14

Duterte, J. P. (2024). The Impact of Educational Gamification on Student Learning Outcomes. [IJRISS]. *International Journal of Research and Innovation in Social Science*, *8*(10), 481–482. Retrieved May 12, 2025, from. DOI: 10.47772/IJRISS.2024.8100040

Dutta, S., Ranjan, S., Mishra, S., Sharma, V., Hewage, P., & Iwendi, C. (2024). *Enhancing educational adaptability: A review and analysis of AI-driven adaptive learning platforms*. In 2024 4th International Conference on Innovative Practices in Technology and Management (ICIPTM) (pp. 1-5). IEEE. https://ieeexplore.ieee.org/abstract/document/10563448

EdTech Magazine. (2020). *Successful AI examples in higher education that can inspire our future*. EdTech Magazine. Retrieved from https://edtechmagazine.com/higher-ed/article/2020/07/successful-ai-examples-higher-education-can-inspire-our-future

EduBridge. (2022). Empowering students through AI-driven skill development and employment. EduBridge Official Website. https://www.edubridgeindia.com

Eghrefuvwoma, O. G., Agada, S. A., Ighodaro, I. H., & Olasupo, S. F. (2024). ICT in Higher Education: A Tool for Sustainable Development in West Africa. *International Journal of Research and Innovation in Applied Science*, *IX*(I). Advance online publication. DOI: 10.51584/ijrias.2024.90122

Ejjami, R. (2024). The future of learning: AI-based curriculum development. *International Journal for Multidisciplinary Research*, *6*(4), 1–31.

Elbouknify, I., Berrada, I., Mekouar, L., Iraqi, Y., Bergou, E. H., Belhabib, H., Nail, Y., & Wardi, S. (2025). AI-based identification and support of at-risk students: A case study of the Moroccan education system. arXiv.

Eling, F., & Ogwal, A. (2025). Bridging learning gaps: The role of AI-powered technologies in enhancing quality education. *International Journal of Research and Innovation in Social Science*, *9*(3), 45–52. DOI: 10.47772/IJRISS.2025.903SEDU0155

Elliott, A. (2021). *Making sense of AI: Our algorithmic world*. John Wiley & Sons.

Etomes, E. S., & Nsem, M. C. (2023). Strategies for Improving Teachers' Professional Development in Higher Education Institutions in the Southwest Region of Cameroon. *Cultivating International Connections Through Education*, *49*(2), 6–10. Retrieved April 03, 2025, from. DOI: 10.4148/0146-9282.2366

Eubanks, V. (2018). *Automating inequality: How high-tech tools profile, police, and punish the poor.* St. Martin's Press.

European Commission. (2020). White paper on artificial intelligence: A European approach to excellence and trust. Publications Office of the European Union. https://ec.europa.eu/info/sites/default/files/commission-white-paper-artificial-intelligence-feb2020_en.pdf

FABER, L. (2021). Augmenting Human Pedagogy: A Cultural History of Automation in Teaching. *Popular Culture Studies Journal*, *9*(1), 44.

Fagbohun, O., Harrison, R. M., & Dereventsov, A. (2024). An empirical categorization of prompting techniques for large language models: A practitioner's guide. *Journal of Artificial Intelligence. Machine Learning and Data Science*, *1*(4), 1–11. DOI: 10.51219/JAIMLD/Oluwole-Fagbohun/15

Faisal, S. M. (2024). *Blockchain-Enabled Security Model for VANETs: A Novel Approach to Authentication and Position.*

Faisal, S. M., Gupta, B. K., & Zaidi, T. (2022). Detection and prevention of Sybil attack in VANET using modified ACO. *Proceedings of 4th International Conference on Cybernetics, Cognition and Machine Learning Applications, ICCCMLA 2022*, 78 – 84. DOI: 10.1109/ICCCMLA56841.2022.9989157

Faisal, S. M., Ishrat, M., & Khan, W. (2025). Digital twins in healthcare: Revolutionizing patient care and medical operations. In *Digital Twins for Smart Cities and Urban Planning*. From Virtual to Reality. DOI: 10.1201/9781003510338-4

Faisal, S. M., Jadhav, S. S., Ahlawat, A., Alam, M. S., Rama Krishna, B., Ranjan, R., & Bhoopathy, V. (2025). The Future of Wastewater Treatment Plant: Integrating HCNN-BiGRU-A Model for Superior Performance. *International Research Journal of Multidisciplinary Scope*, *6*(1), 151–161. DOI: 10.47857/irjms.2025.v06i01.02213

Faisal, S. M., & Zaidi, T. (2020). Timestamp Based Detection of Sybil Attack in VANET. *International Journal of Network Security*, *22*(3), 397–408.

Ferguson, R., Coughlan, T., Egelandsdal, K., Gaved, M., Herodotou, C., Hillaire, G., Jones, D., Jowers, I., Kukulska-Hulme, A., McAndrew, P., Misiejuk, K., Ness, I. J., Rienties, B., Scanlon, E., Sharples, M., Wasson, B., Weller, M., Whitelock, D., & Open University. (2019). *Innovating Pedagogy 2019*. The Open University. https://iet.open.ac.uk/files/innovating-pedagogy-2019.pdf

Ferreira, A., & Pedrosa, D. (2024). Uso da inteligência artificial para apoiar a autor-regulação de aprendizagem: Uma revisão de literatura. *PRATICA-Revista Multimédia de Investigação em Inovação Pedagógica e Práticas de e-Learning, 7*(2), 101-111. https://parc.ipp.pt/index.php/elearning/article/view/5823

Fidan, M., & Gencel, N. (2022). Supporting the instructional videos with chatbot and peer feedback mechanisms in online learning: The effects on learning performance and intrinsic motivation. *Journal of Educational Computing Research, 60*(7), 1716–1741. DOI: 10.1177/07356331221077901

Field, A. P. (2018). *Discovering Statistics Using IBM SPSS Statistics* (5th ed.). Sage.

Fitria, T. N. (2023). Artificial intelligence (AI) technology in OpenAI ChatGPT application: A review of ChatGPT in writing English essay. *ELT Forum: Journal of English Language Teaching, 12*(1), 44-58. https://doi.org/DOI: 10.15294/elt.v12i1.64069

Flower, L., & Hayes, J. R. (1980). A cognitive process theory of writing. *College Composition and Communication, 32*(4), 365–387. DOI: 10.2307/356600

Fransiska, F. W. (2024). Game On! Teaching English with Fun and Creativity: Gamification Implementation in Remote Rural Areas (Sukaraja Village, South Lampung). *Jurnal Pengabdian Masyarakat, 1*(1), 40–46. Retrieved February 21, 2025, from. DOI: 10.62207/vwastn89

Frizell, C. A., Graham, D., DuVentre, A., & Brown, S. D. (2024). Embracing Neuro-Inclusivity Within Physician Assistant/Associate Education: Challenging Organizational Cultural Norms and Navigating Communication Challenges. *The Journal of Physician Assistant Education : the Official Journal of the Physician Assistant Education Association*. Advance online publication. DOI: 10.1097/jpa.0000000000000575

Frontier Economics & Glass. AI. (2020). A new way to read the jobs market: Using AI to map the AI skills gap. Frontier Economics. https://www.frontier-economics.com/uk/en/news-and-insights/articles/article-i21335-a-new-way-to-read-the-jobs-market-using-ai-to-map-the-ai-skills-gap/

Fui-Hoon Nah, F., Zheng, R., Cai, J., Siau, K., & Chen, L. (2023). Generative AI and ChatGPT: Applications, challenges, and AI-human collaboration. *Journal of information technology case and application research, 25*(3), 277-304. Can be accessed at https://www.tandfonline.com/doi/pdf/10.1080/15228053.2023.2233814

Gamage, K. A., & Dehideniya, S. C. (2025). Unlocking Career Potential: How Micro-Credentials Are Revolutionising Higher Education and Lifelong Learning. *Education Sciences*, *15*(5), 525.

Gan, A. W. J., Dang, Q., & Western, B. (n.d.). *AI-Mediated Group Ideation.*

Ganesalingam, M. (2013). The Language of Mathematics. In D. Hutchison, T. Kanade, J. Kittler, J. M. Kleinberg, F. Mattern, J. C. Mitchell, M. Naor, O. Nierstrasz, C. Pandu Rangan, B. Steffen, M. Sudan, D. Terzopoulos, D. Tygar, M. Y. Vardi, & G. Weikum (Eds.), *The Language of Mathematics* (Vol. 7805, pp. 17–38). Springer Berlin Heidelberg. https://doi.org/DOI: 10.1007/978-3-642-37012-0_2

García, V., Kemper, N., Bárcenas, J., & Ruiz-Velasco, E. (2023). La Inteligencia Artificial en tecnologías digitales LMS para cursos de Sistemas Digitales. In E. R. V. Sánchez & J. B. López (Coords.), *Inteligencia Artificial para la transformación de la Educación* (pp. 36-46). SMCE. https://books.google.pt/books?hl=pt-PT&lr=&id=G2LoEAAAQBAJ&oi=fnd&pg=PA36&dq=

García-Peñalvo, F. J. (2023). La percepción de la inteligencia artificial en contextos educativos tras el lanzamiento de ChatGPT: Disrupción o pánico. *Education in the Knowledge Society*, *24*, 1–9. DOI: 10.14201/eks.31279

Garg, N., Kaur, A., & Dutta, R. (2024, November). Immersive Learning: Evaluating the Effectiveness of AI Chatbots and AR in Education. In *2024 3rd Edition of IEEE Delhi Section Flagship Conference (DELCON)* (pp. 1-7). IEEE. DOI: DOI: 10.1109/DELCON64804.2024.10866724

Garvey, R., Garvey, B., & Stokes, P. (2021). *Coaching and mentoring: Theory and practice* (4th ed.). Sage.

Gautam, P. (2011). Writing skill: An instructional overview. *Journal of NELTA Gandaki*, *2*, 74–90. DOI: 10.3126/jong.v2i0.26605

Gayathri, B., Kumar, G. S., Prashanth, T., & Kumar, B. M. (2024, May). Vardhagenie: Advancing student support through ai. In *2024 International Conference on Smart Systems for applications in Electrical Sciences (ICSSES)* (pp. 1-6). IEEE. DOI: DOI: 10.1109/ICSSES62373.2024.10561262

George, A. S. (2023). Preparing students for an AI-driven world: Rethinking curriculum and pedagogy in the age of artificial intelligence. *Partners Universal Innovative Research Publication*, *1*(2), 112–136.

Ghafar, Z. N. (2023). ChatGPT: a new tool to improve teaching and evaluation of second and foreign languages. A review of ChatGPT: the future of education. *International Journal of Applied Research and Sustainable Sciences, 1*(2), 73–86. DOI: 10.59890/ijarss.v1i2.392

Gilakjani, A. P., Leong, L. M., & Ismail, H. N. (2013). Teachers'. *Use of Technology And Constructivism. Int. J. Mod. Educ. Comput. Sci., 5*, 49–63. DOI: 10.5815/ijmecs.2013.04.07

Giraffa, L., & Kohls-Santos, P. (2023). Inteligência artificial e educação: conceitos, aplicações e implicações no fazer docente. *Educação em Análise, 8*(1), 116-134. https://ojs.uel.br/revistas/uel/index.php/educanalise/article/view/48127

Goel, A. K., & Joyner, D. A. (2024). *Jill Watson: A Virtual Teaching Assistant powered by ChatGPT*. arXiv preprint arXiv:2405.11070. Retrieved from https://arxiv.org/pdf/2405.11070?

Gökçearslan, S., Tosun, C., & Erdemir, Z. G. (2024). Benefits, challenges, and methods of artificial intelligence (AI) chatbots in education: A systematic literature review. *International Journal of Technology in Education, 7*(1), 19-39. Can be accessed at https://files.eric.ed.gov/fulltext/EJ1415037.pdf

Goldie, J. G. S. (2016). Connectivism: A knowledge learning theory for the digital age? *Medical Teacher, 38*(10), 1064–1069. DOI: 10.3109/0142159x.2016.1173661

Gomes, A. J. F., Verçosa, B. F. M., Pinto, C. R. S., de Moura, C. C., dos Santos Silva, C., & dos Reis, O. B. (2024). Potencializando a aprendizagem ativa com tecnologia de IA. *Revista Ibero-Americana de Humanidades. Ciência & Educação (Bauru), 10*(8), 3625–3631. https://periodicorease.pro.br/rease/article/view/15451

Gómez Redondo, S., Rodríguez Higuera, C. J., Coca, J. R., & Olteanu, A. (2024). Transhumanism, Society and Education: An Edusemiotic Approach. *Studies in Philosophy and Education, 43*(2). Advance online publication. DOI: 10.1007/s11217-024-09927-6

Gonçalves, B. (2023). Can machines think? The controversy that led to the Turing test. *AI & Society, 38*(6), 2499–2509. DOI: 10.1007/s00146-021-01318-6

Goodfellow, I., Bengio, Y., & Courville, A. (2016). *Deep learning*. MIT Press.

Gordillo, A., López-Fernández, D., & Mayor, J. (2024). Examining and Comparing the Effectiveness of Virtual Reality Serious Games and LEGO Serious Play for Learning Scrum. *Applied Sciences (Basel, Switzerland), 14*(2), 830. Retrieved February 21, 2025, from. DOI: 10.3390/app14020830

Graefen, B., & Fazal, N. (2024). From Chat bots to Virtual Tutors: An Overview of Chat GPT's Role in the Future of Education. *Archives of pharmacy practice, 15*(2-2024), 43-52. Can be accessed at https://archivepp.com/storage/files/article/70559ce0-c956-43a3-a971-1a56e7eff80f-2by3H9rq0zQArGpf/FmZ0HtMuPZUFl4k.pdf

Green, A. (2024). *Artificial intelligence and the changing demand for skills in the labour market. OECD Artificial Intelligence Papers, No. 14*. OECD Publishing., DOI: 10.1787/88684e36-

Greene, J. C., Caracelli, V. J., & Graham, W. F. (1989). Toward a conceptual framework for mixed – method evaluation designs. *Educational Evaluation and Policy Analysis, 11*(3), 255–274. DOI: 10.3102/01623737011003255

Guerrero-Alcedo, J. M., Espina-Romero, L. C., & Nava-Chirinos, A. A. (2022). Gamification in the University Context: Bibliometric Review in Scopus (2012-2022). *International Journal of Learning. Teaching and Educational Research, 21*(5), 311–134. Retrieved May 01, 2025, from. DOI: 10.26803/ijlter.21.5.16

Guilherme, A. (2019). AI and education: The importance of teacher and student relations. *AI & Society, 34*(1), 47–54. DOI: 10.1007/s00146-017-0693-8

Guo, K., Li, Y., Li, Y., & Chu, S. K. W. (2024). Understanding EFL students' chatbot-assisted argumentative writing: An activity theory perspective. *Education and Information Technologies, 29*, 1–20. DOI: 10.1007/s10639-023-12230-5

Guo, K., Wang, J., & Chu, S. K. W. (2022). Using chatbots to scaffold EFL students' argumentative writing. *Assessing Writing, 54*, 100666. DOI: 10.1016/j.asw.2022.100666

Hall-Partee, B. (1979). Semantics—Mathematics or Psychology? In Bäuerle, R., Egli, U., & Von Stechow, A. (Eds.), *Semantics from Different Points of View* (Vol. 6, pp. 1–14). Springer Berlin Heidelberg., DOI: 10.1007/978-3-642-67458-7_1

Hamari, J., Shernoff, D. J., Rowe, E., Coller, B., Asbell-Clarke, J., & Edwards, T. (2016). Challenging games help students learn: An empirical study on engagement, flow and immersion in game-based learning. *Computers in Human Behavior, 54*, 170–179. DOI: 10.1016/j.chb.2015.07.045

Hamilton-Hinch, B. A., Stilwell, C., Manuel, C., Hutchinson, S., Woodford, K. & Ellis, A. (2023). Peer Assisted Learning: What Can Students Teach Us and Each Other?. *SCHOLE: A Journal of Leisure Studies and Recreation Education, 38*(3), 161-174. [Accessed 07 March, 2025] https://doi.org/DOI: 10.1080/1937156X.2021.1969527

Handini. B.S., Nurhasanah, & Panly. F.I., (2022). The Effect of Artificial Intelligent Technology Used (Duolingo Application) to Enhance English Learning. ELLITE. *Journal of English Language, Literature, and Teaching,1 7*(2), 86-94. Doi:.DOI: 10.32528/ellite.v7i2.8354

Hand, M. D., & Ihara, E. S. (2024). Ageism, Racism, Sexism, and Work With Older Healthcare Clients: Why an Intersectional Approach Is Needed in Practice, Policy, Education, and Research. *International Journal of Aging & Human Development, 98*(1). Advance online publication. DOI: 10.1177/00914150231171843

Han, J., Pei, J., & Kamber, M. (2011). *Data mining: Concepts and techniques* (3rd ed.). Morgan Kaufmann.

Harden, R. M. (2001). The learning environment and the curriculum. *Medical Teacher, 23*(4), 335–336. DOI: 10.1080/01421590120063321

Hasanah, R., Munawwaroh, I., Hasanah, M., & Mundiri, A. (2024). Fostering Inclusivity: Strategies for Supporting Students with Special Needs in Mainstream Classrooms. *FALASIFA: Jurnal Studi Keislaman, 15*(1), 73–85.

Hassani, H., Silva, E. S., & Unger, S., TajMazinani, M., & Mac Feely, S. (2020). Artificial Intelligence (AI) or Intelligence Augmentation (IA): What Is the Future? *AI, 1*(2), 143–155. DOI: 10.3390/ai1020008

Hay, A., Stanley-Clarke, N., Maris, R., Winder, L., & Knook, J. (2024). Building connections in health and wellbeing education: Qualitative findings of a study with New Zealand agricultural students. *Health Education Journal, 83*(2). Advance online publication. DOI: 10.1177/00178969231225089

Hayes, J. R., & Flower, L. S. (1980). Identifying the organisation of writing processes. In Gregg, L., & Steinberg, E. R. (Eds.), *Cognitive processes in writing* (1st ed., pp. 3–30). Routledge., DOI: 10.4324/9781315630274

Hébert, C., Jenson, J., & Terzopoulos, T. (2021). "Access to technology is the major challenge": Teacher perspectives on barriers to DGBL in K-12 classrooms. *E-Learning and Digital Media, 18*, 307–324. DOI: 10.1177/2042753021995315

Heffernan, N. T., & Heffernan, C. L. (2014). The ASSISTments ecosystem: Building a platform that brings scientists and teachers together for minimally invasive research on human learning and teaching. *International Journal of Artificial Intelligence in Education, 24*, 470–497. DOI: 10.1007/s40593-014-0024-x

Hennekeuser, D., Vaziri, D. D., Golchinfar, D., Schreiber, D., & Stevens, G. (2024). Enlarged education – Exploring the use of generative AI to support lecturing in higher education. *International Journal of Artificial Intelligence in Education*. Advance online publication. DOI: 10.1007/s40593-024-00424-y

Hlatshwayo, M. N., Zondi, T., & Mokoena, T. (2023). It gives me anxiety! Black Academics' experiences of teaching large classes during the Covid-19 pandemic in a South African university. *Perspectives in Education*, *41*(2). Advance online publication. Retrieved April 23, 2025, from. DOI: 10.38140/pie.v41i2.6837

Hodges, C. B., Moore, S., Lockee, B. B., Trust, T., & Bond, M. A. (2020, March 27). *The difference between emergency remote teaching and online learning*. http://hdl.handle.net/10919/104648

Holden, H., & Rada, R. (2011). Understanding the influence of perceived usability and technology self-efficacy on teachers' technology acceptance. *Journal of Research on Technology in Education*, *43*(4), 343–367. DOI: 10.1080/15391523.2011.10782576

Holmes, W., Bialik, M., & Fadel, C. (2019). *Artificial Intelligence in Education Promises and Implications for Teaching and Learning* (1st ed.). Center for Curriculum Redesign., https://discovery.ucl.ac.uk/id/eprint/10139722/

Holmes, W., Bialik, M., & Fadel, C. (2019). *Artificial intelligence in education*. Centre for Curriculum Redesign., DOI: 10.1007/978-3-319-60013-0_107-1

Holmes, W., Bialik, M., & Fadel, C. (2019). *Artificial intelligence in education: Promises and implications for teaching and learning*. Center for Curriculum Redesign.

Holmes, W., Bialik, M., & Fadel, C. (2019). *Artificial intelligence in education: Promises and Implications for Teaching and Learning*. Centre for Curriculum Redesign.

Holmes, W., & Tuomi, I. (2022). State of the art and practice in AI in education. *European Journal of Education*, *57*(4), 542–570. https://onlinelibrary.wiley.com/doi/10.1111/ejed.12533

Holzinger, A. (2021). Explainable AI and multi-modal causability in medicine. *i-com, 19*(3), 171-179. https://www.degruyterbrill.com/document/doi/10.1515/icom-2020-0024/html

Hong, W. C. H. (2023). The impact of ChatGPT on foreign language teaching and learning: Opportunities in education and research. *Journal of Educational Technology and Innovation*, *5*(1), 37–45.

Hsu, M.-H., Chen, P.-S., & Yu, C.-S. (2021). Proposing a task-oriented chatbot system for EFL learners speaking practice. *Interactive Learning Environments, 31*(7), 4297–4308. DOI: 10.1080/10494820.2021.1960864

Huang, J., & Li, S. (2023). Opportunities and challenges in the application of ChatGPT in foreign language teaching. *International Journal of Education and Social Science Research, 6*(4), 75–89. DOI: 10.37500/IJESSR.2023.6406

Huang, W., Hew, K. F., & Fryer, L. K. (2022). Chatbots for language learning—Are they really useful? A systematic review of chatbot-supported language learning. *Journal of Computer Assisted Learning, 38*(1), 237–257. DOI: 10.1111/jcal.12610

Hubona, G., & Kennick, E. (1996). The impact of external variables on information technology usage behaviour. In Sprague, R. (Ed.), *Proceedings of the 29th Annual Hawai'i International Conference on System Sciences* (Vol. 4, pp. 166–176). Washington, DC: IEEE Computing Society Press.

Hutson, J., & Plate, D. (2023). *Human-AI collaboration for smart education: Reframing applied learning to support metacognition*. IntechOpen. Can be accessed at https://digitalcommons.lindenwood.edu/cgi/viewcontent.cgi?article=1481&context=faculty-research-papers

Hu, Z., & Razlog, R. (2023). The use of game-based learning to enhance student engagement in the acupuncture programme: South African students' opinions. *Journal for the Education of Gifted Young Scientists, 11*(2), 137–152. Retrieved April 10, 2025, from. DOI: 10.17478/jegys.1277401

Ibrahim, A., & Shiring, E. (2022). The relationship between educators' attitudes, perceived usefulness, and perceived ease of use of instructional and web-based technologies: Implications from Technology Acceptance Model (TAM). *International Journal of Technology in Education, 5*(4), 535–551. DOI: 10.46328/ijte.285

Ifelebuegu, A. (2023). Rethinking online assessment strategies: Authenticity versus AI chatbot intervention. *Journal of Applied Learning and Teaching, 6*(2), 385-392. Can be accessed at https://jalt.journals.publicknowledgeproject.org/index.php/jalt/article/download/875/601

Ip, K. (2024). The rise of EdTech: Transforming education through entrepreneurial ventures. Advances in Online Education: A Peer-Reviewed Journal, 3(2), 177-193.

Irwanto, I., Wahyudiati, D., Saputro, A. D., & Laksana, S. D. (2023). Research Trends and Applications of Gamification in Higher Education: A Bibliometric Analysis Spanning 2013–2022. *International Journal of Emerging Technologies in Learning, 18*(5), 3–7. Retrieved May 01, 2025, from. DOI: 10.3991/ijet.v18i05.37021

Irzawati, I., Unamo, A. F., Agnes, A., & Angelika, V. (2024). The use of Chat GPT in ELT. *International Journal of Education, Language, Literature, Arts, Culture, and Social Humanities*, *2*(1), 32–44. DOI: 10.59024/ijellacush.v2i1.674

Ishrat, M., Khan, W., & Faisal, S. M. (2025). AI and risk forecasting: Leveraging AI for environmental, social, and governance compliance. In *Artificial Intelligence for Financial Risk Management and Analysis*. DOI: 10.4018/979-8-3373-1200-2.ch015

Islam, M. H., & Ivy, J. S. (2022). Modeling the role of efficiency for the equitable and effective distribution of donated food. *OR-Spektrum*, *44*(2), 485–534.

Jaboob, M., Hazaimeh, M., & Al-Ansi, A. (2024). Integration of Generative AI Techniques and Applications in Student Behavior and Cognitive Achievement in Arab Higher Education. *International Journal of Human-Computer Interaction*, *41*, 1–14. DOI: 10.1080/10447318.2023.2300016

Jackson, E. A. (2024). *The Evolution of Artificial Intelligence: A Theoretical Review of its Impact on Teaching and Learning in the Digital Age*. https://hdl.handle.net/10419/280893

Jaiswal, K., Kuzminykh, I., & Modgil, S. (2024). Understanding the skills gap between higher education and industry in the UK in the artificial intelligence sector. arXiv preprint. https://arxiv.org/abs/2408.10788

James, W., Oates, G., & Schonfeldt, N. (2024). Improving retention while enhancing student engagement and learning outcomes using gamified mobile technology. *Accounting Education*, •••, 1–21. Retrieved March 12, 2025, from. DOI: 10.1080/09639284.2024.2326009

Jaramillo-Mediavilla, L., Basantes-Andrade, A., Cabezas-González, M., & Casillas-Martín, S. (2024). Impact of gamification on motivation and academic performance: A systematic review. *Education Sciences*, *14*(6), 639.

Javier, D. R. C., & Moorhouse, B. L. (2023). Developing secondary school English language learners' productive and critical use of ChatGPT. *TESOL Journal*, *755*, 1–9. DOI: 10.1002/tesj.755

Jiméneza, I. A. C., Gonzálezb, J. P. C., & Ruiz, C. E. C. (2021). Developing Systemic Thinking through Gamification with Invention System Kits: Case of an Aircraft Assembly Line. *Academia y Virtualidad*, *14*(1), 27–30. Retrieved May 03, 2025, from. DOI: 10.18359/ravi.4888

Kang, S., & Yi, Y. (2023). Beyond ChatGPT: Multimodal generative AI for L2 writers. *Journal of Second Language Writing*, *62*, 101071. DOI: 10.1016/j.jslw.2023.101071

Karan, K., & Bakina, W. (2024). *Generative artificial intelligence (AI) in education: A cross-national survey on university teachers' perceptions on the use of ChatGPT*. Education and New Developments 2024 – Volume 1. https://doi.org/ DOI: 10.36315/2024v1end035

Kato, S., Gyorfi, R., & Weko, T. (2023). Micro-credentials for lifelong learning and employability: Uses and possibilities. OECD. https://www.oecd.org/content/dam/oecd/en/publications/reports/2023/03/micro-credentials-for-lifelong-learning-and-employability_13dd81a9/9c4b7b68-en.pdf

Kavitha, K., & Joshith, V. P. (2024). The Transformative Trajectory of Artificial Intelligence in Education: The Two Decades of Bibliometric Retrospect. *Journal of Educational Technology Systems*. Advance online publication. DOI: 10.1177/00472395241231815

Kayyali, M. (2024). Future possibilities and challenges of AI in education. In *Transforming education with generative AI: Prompt engineering and synthetic content creation* (pp. 118-137). IGI Global Scientific Publishing. Can be accessed at https://www.researchgate.net/profile/Mustafa-Kayyali/publication/378032423_Future_Possibilities_and_Challenges_of_AI_in_Education/links/65c397c71bed776ae337490f/Future-Possibilities-and-Challenges-of-AI-in-Education.pdf

Kayyali, M. (2025a). The Future of AI in Education: Predictions and Emerging Trends. Next-Generation AI Methodologies in Education, 367-406.

Kayyali, M. (2025b). AI in Higher Education: Revolutionizing Curriculum and Administration. In AI Adoption and Diffusion in Education (pp. 31-62). IGI Global Scientific Publishing.

Kayyali, M. (2025c). Generative AI and Education: Transforming Teaching and Learning Through Collaborative Intelligence. In Humans and Generative AI Tools for Collaborative Intelligence (pp. 25-52). IGI Global Scientific Publishing.

Kayyali, M. (2024). Future possibilities and challenges of AI in education. In *Transforming education with generative AI: Prompt engineering and synthetic content creation* (pp. 118–137). IGI Global Scientific Publishing.

Kelkar, S. (2022). Between AI and learning science: The evolution and commercialization of intelligent tutoring systems. *IEEE Annals of the History of Computing, 44*(1), 20–30.

Kelleher, J. D., Mac Carthy, M., & Korvir, R. (2015). *Fundamentals of machine learning for predictive data analytics: Algorithms, worked examples, and case studies*. MIT Press.

Khalil, M., Shakya, R., & Liu, Q. (2025). Towards Privacy-Preserving Data-Driven Education: The Potential of Federated Learning. arXiv preprint arXiv:2503.13550. https://arxiv.org/abs/2503.13550

Khapre, M., Deol, R., Sharma, A., Badyal, D., & Badyal, D. K. (2021). Near-peer tutor: A solution for quality medical education in faculty constraint setting. *Cureus, 13*(7). Advance online publication. DOI: 10.7759/cureus.16416

Khlaif, Z. N., Hamamra, B., & Hussein, E. T. (2025). *AI Paradox in Higher Education: Understanding Over-Reliance*. Its Impact, and Sustainable Integration.

Khosravi, H., Sadiq, S., & Amer-Yahia, S. (2023). Data management of AI-powered education technologies: Challenges and opportunities. *Learning Letters, 1*(2). Advance online publication. DOI: 10.59453/XLUD7002

Khurumova, V., & Pinto, J. C. (2024). Career services at HEI's: What are they offering? *Frontiers in Education, 9*, 1410628. Advance online publication. DOI: 10.3389/feduc.2024.1410628

Kim, S., Park, E., & Lee, J. (2023). A study on the utilization of OpenAI ChatGPT as a second language learning tool. *Journal of Multimedia Information System, 10*(1), 79–86. DOI: 10.33851/JMIS.2023.10.1.79

Knihová, L. (2024). *AI-Powered Immersive Learning: Transforming Tertiary Education*. Can be accessed at https://dspace.zcu.cz/bitstreams/35815e42-c43b-4315-ad30-46d238e2cdae/download

Kochmar, E., Vu, D. D., Belfer, R., Gupta, V., Serban, I. V., & Pineau, J. (2020). Automated Personalized Feedback Improves Learning Gains in An Intelligent Tutoring System. *Artificial Intelligence in Education, 12164*, 140–146. DOI: 10.1007/978-3-030-52240-7_26

Kohnke, L., Moorhouse, B. L., & Zou, D. (2023). ChatGPT for language teaching and learning. *RELC Journal*. Advance online publication. DOI: 10.1177/00336882231162868

Kolb, D. A. (1984). *Experiential learning: Experience as the source of learning and development*. Prentice Hall.

Kooli, C. (2023). Chatbots in education and research: A critical examination of ethical implications and solutions. *Sustainability, 15*(7), 5614.

Kostka, I., & Toncelli, L. (2023). Integrating AI tools into instructed second language acquisition. In Marsden, M., & Mason, S. E. (Eds.), *AI in Language Learning and Teaching* (pp. 45–67). Iowa State Digital Press., DOI: 10.31274/isudp.154

Krath, J., Schürmann, L., & Von Korflesch, H. F. (2021). Revealing the theoretical basis of gamification: A systematic review and analysis of theory in research on gamification, serious games and game-based learning. *Computers in Human Behavior*, *125*, 106963. Retrieved March 22, 2025, from. DOI: 10.1016/j.chb.2021.106963

Kristiansen, P., & Rasmussen, R. (2014). *Building a better business using the Lego serious play method*. John Wiley & Sons.

Kurti, E., Ferati, M., & Kalonaityte, V. (2024). Closing the gender gap in ICT higher education: Exploring women's motivations in pursuing ICT education. *Frontiers in Education*, *9*. Advance online publication. DOI: 10.3389/feduc.2024.1352029

Kuzmanov, I. (2024). *Reform The Ivory Tower: AI And The Democratization Of Higher Education*. Can be accessed at https://www.researchgate.net/profile/Iliyan-Kuzmanov/publication/388156030_Reform_The_Ivory_Tower_AI_And_The_Democratization_Of_Higher_Education/links/678c181195e02f182e9cb6d9/Reform-The-Ivory-Tower-AI-And-The-Democratization-Of-Higher-Education.pdf

Labadze, L., Grigolia, M., & Machaidze, L. (2023). Role of AI chatbots in education: Systematic literature review. *International Journal of Educational Technology in Higher Education*, *20*(1), 56.

Lambert, N. J., Xiaoting, L., & Akinyo, O. (2023). Knowing Me, Knowing You: Self-Reflection and Understanding Diversity for Effective Teamwork—A LEGO® Building Activity. *Management Teaching Review*, *10*(1), 24–26. Retrieved April 16, 2025, from. DOI: 10.1177/2379298123119058

Latifi, S., Noroozi, O., & Talaee, E. (2021). Peer feedback or peer feedforward? Enhancing students' argumentative peer learning processes and outcomes. *British Journal of Educational Technology*, *52*(2), 768–784. Retrieved March 22, 2025, from. DOI: 10.1111/bjet.13054

Laurillard, D. (2013). Teaching as a design science. In *Routledge eBooks*. https://doi.org/DOI: 10.4324/9780203125083

Lave, J., & Wenger, E. (1991). *Situated learning: Legitimate peripheral participation*. Cambridge University Press.

Lee, S. W. H., & Saw, P. S. (2021). The Use of Building Blocks to Teach Communication and Social Skills to First-year Pharmacy Students. *American Journal of Pharmaceutical Education*, *85*(8), 5–7. Retrieved April 20, 2025, from. DOI: 10.5688/ajpe8464

LEGO Education. (2024). MINDSTORMS. [Accessed 31 March, 2025] https://www.prnewswire.com/news-releases/lego-education-report-examines-the-state-of-classroom-engagement-302237279.html

Leppink, J. (2019). *Statistical methods for experimental research in education and psychology*. Springer.

Levine, A., & Van Pelt, S. (2021). *The great upheaval: Higher education's past, present, and uncertain future*. JHU Press.

Li, K. C., & Wong, B. T. M. (2023). Artificial intelligence in personalised learning: A bibliometric analysis. *Interactive Technology and Smart Education, 20*(3), 422–445. DOI: 10.1108/ITSE-01-2023-000

Li, L., Chen, C. P., Wang, L., Liang, K., & Bao, W. (2023). Exploring artificial intelligence in smart education: Real-time classroom behavior analysis with embedded devices. *Sustainability, 15*(10), 7940. https://www.mdpi.com/2071-1050/15/10/7940

Li, L., Hew, K. F., & Du, J. (2024). Gamification enhances student intrinsic motivation, perceptions of autonomy and relatedness, but minimal impact on competency: A meta-analysis and systematic review. *Educational Technology Research and Development, 72*(2), 765–796. DOI: 10.1007/s11423-023-10337-7

Liu, J., Wang, C., Liu, Z., Gao, M., Xu, Y., Chen, J., & Cheng, Y. (2024). A bibliometric analysis of generative AI in education: Current status and development. *Asia Pacific Journal of Education, 44*(1). Advance online publication. DOI: 10.1080/02188791.2024.2305170

Livingstone, S. (2011). Critical reflections on the benefits of ICT in education. *Oxford Review of Education, 38*(1), 9–24. DOI: 10.1080/03054985.2011.577938

Lo, C. K. (2023). What is the impact of ChatGPT on education? A rapid review of the literature. *Education Sciences, 13*(4), 1–15. DOI: 10.3390/educsci13040410

Long, D., & Magerko, B. (2020). What is AI Literacy? Competencies and Design Considerations. In *Proceedings of the 2020 CHI conference on human factors in computing systems* (pp. 1–16). ACM., https://dl.acm.org/doi/abs/10.1145/3313831.3376727

Long, H. A., French, D. P., & Brooks, J. M. (2020). Optimising the value of the critical appraisal skills programme (CASP) tool for quality appraisal in qualitative evidence synthesis. *Research Methods in Medicine & Health Sciences, 1*(1), 31–42. Retrieved March 31, 2025, from. DOI: 10.1177/2632084320947559

López, L. A. S. (2022). Inteligencia artificial y visión por computadora aplicada a la educación. *Revista Odigos, 3*(2), 61-73. https://revista.uisrael.edu.ec/index.php/ro/article/view/587

Lourenço, A. A., & Paiva, M. O. A. (2024). Globalization of Higher Education: The Internationalization from a Multifactorial Perspective. In Kayyali, M. (Ed.), *Building Resiliency in Higher Education: Globalization, Digital Skills, and Student Wellness* (pp. 285–305). IGI Global., DOI: 10.4018/979-8-3693-5483-4

Lourenço, A., Paiva, M. O., & Valente, S. (2024). Emotional Intelligence: A Catalyst for Organizational Culture and Climate in Higher Education. In Kayyali, M. (Ed.), *Building Organizational Capacity and Strategic Management in Academia* (pp. 183–212). IGI Global., DOI: 10.4018/979-8-3693-6967-8.ch007

Luckin, R., Holmes, W., & Forcier, L. B. (2016). *An argument for AI in Education.*

Luckin, R., Holmes, W., Griffiths, M., & Forcier, L. B. (2016). *Intelligence Unleashed. An argument for AI in Education.* Pearson. https://discovery.ucl.ac.uk/id/eprint/1475756/

Luckin, R., Holmes, W., Griffiths, M., & Forcier, L. B. (2016). *Intelligence Unleashed: An argument for AI in Education.* Open Ideas; Pearson Education, London.

Luckin, R. (2025). Nurturing human intelligence in the age of AI: Rethinking education for the future. *Development and Learning in Organizations*, *39*(1), 1–4.

Luckin, R., Holmes, W., Griffiths, M., & Forcier, L. B. (2016). *Intelligence Unleashed: An Argument for AI in Education.* Pearson Education.

Luckin, R., Rudolph, J., Grünert, M., & Tan, S. (2024). Exploring the future of learning and the relationship between human intelligence and AI. An interview with Professor Rose Luckin. *Journal of Applied Learning and Teaching*, *7*(1). https://journals.sfu.ca/jalt/index.php/jalt/article/view/1659

Luckyardi, S., Karin, J., Rosmaladewi, R., Hufad, A., & Haristiani, N. (2024). Chatbots as Digital Language Tutors: Revolutionizing Education Through AI. *Indonesian Journal of Science and Technology, 9*(3), 885-908. Can be accessed at https://ejournal.upi.edu/index.php/ijost/article/download/79514/30035

Lugaresi, G., Frigerio, N., & Matta, A. (2020). A New Learning Factory Experience Exploiting LEGO For Teaching Manufacturing Systems Integration. *Procedia Manufacturing*, *45*, 271–276. Retrieved May 02, 2025, from. DOI: 10.1016/j.promfg.2020.04.106

Luo, H., Luo, H., Li, Z., Li, Z., Liang, J., Li, G., & Yan, Y. (2024). Creating an immersive virtual reality game space for multiuser, synchronous co-located collaboration: Design considerations and influencing factors. *Applied Sciences (Basel, Switzerland), 14*(5), 2167. DOI: 10.3390/app14052167

Luo, X., Tong, S., Fang, Z., & Qu, Z. (2019). Machines vs. humans: The impact of artificial intelligence chatbot disclosure on customer purchases. *Marketing Science, 38*(6), 937–947. DOI: 10.1287/mksc.2019.1192

Madden, V. J. (2024). Vocal Awareness and K-12 Education: A Qualitative Research Study. *Voice & Speech Review, 18*(1). Advance online publication. DOI: 10.1080/23268263.2022.2062851

Malik, M. A., & Shah, R. (2025). *AI teachers (AI-based robots as*. Mueller, D., & Strohmeier, S. (2011). Design characteristics of virtual learning environments: State of research. *Computers & Education, 57*(4), 2505–2516.

Manda, S. (2024). Ambani takes African languages digital. [Accessed 12 May, 2025] https://www.vukuzenzele.gov.za/ambani-takes-african-languages-digital

Martínez-Requejo, S. R. D. S., & Ruiz-Lazaro, E. J. G. J. (2024). *The potential of educational chatbots for the support and formative assessment of students*. Can be accessed at https://www.researchgate.net/profile/Sara-Redondo-Duarte/publication/377299168_THE_POTENTIAL_OF_EDUCATIONAL_CHATBOTS_FOR_THE_SUPPORT_AND_FORMATIVE_ASSESSMENT_OF_STUDENTS/links/670cf1541a0a901a3e71629f/THE-POTENTIAL-OF-EDUCATIONAL-CHATBOTS-FOR-THE-SUPPORT-AND-FORMATIVE-ASSESSMENT-OF-STUDENTS.pdf

Martinez-Requejo, S., García, E. J., Duarte, S. R., Lázaro, J. R., Sanz, E. P., & Vivas, G. M. (2024). AI-driven student assistance: chatbots redefining university support. In *INTED2024 Proceedings* (pp. 617-625). IATED. Can be accessed at https://www.researchgate.net/profile/Sara-Redondo-Duarte/publication/378902826_AI-DRIVEN_STUDENT_ASSISTANCE_CHATBOTS_REDEFINING_UNIVERSITY_SUPPORT/links/65f0d4cb32321b2cff69e669/AI-DRIVEN-STUDENT-ASSISTANCE-CHATBOTS-REDEFINING-UNIVERSITY-SUPPORT.pdf?utm_source=chatgpt.com

Maryani, I., Suyatno, S., Arfiani, I., Nizaar, M., Astuti, I. A. D., & Sulisworo, D. (2025). Gamified Mobile-Based Learning Approach: Efforts to Improve Students' Engagement and Learning Quality in Remote Schools in Indonesia. *Educational Process: International Journal, 15*, e2025179. DOI: 10.22521/edupij.2025.15.179

Mavutha, W., & Mansingh, A. R. (2024). Online Education Adaptability for South African Learners with Dyscalculia and Dyslexia using Digital Learning Methods. *Chinese Sociological Review*, *19*(1), 51–80.

Mayo, E. G. M., Sarmiento, E. X. B., Ayo, M. R. S., & Llivicota, A. S. M. (2024). Implementação de inteligência artificial como estratégia de ensino para o desenvolvimento da escrita em estudantes do ensino superior: uma sequência de ensino inovadora. *Pólo do Conhecimento, 9*(10), 1649-1665. https://polodelconocimiento.com/ojs/index.php/es/article/view/8199/html

Mbukanma, I., Manganyi, M., & Vellem, B. & Neliswa Gqoli. (2024). Unlocking Potential: The Transformative Role of Gaming in Rural Higher Learning Institutions of South Africa - A Systematic Exploration. *Research in Social Sciences and Technology*, *9*(3), 141–143. Retrieved May 01, 2025, from. DOI: 10.46303/ressat.2024.52

Mezirow, J. (2000). *Learning as Transformation: Critical Perspectives on a Theory in Progress. The Jossey-Bass Higher and Adult Education Series.* Jossey-Bass Publishers, 350 Sansome Way, San Francisco, CA 94104.

Miller, A. I. (2020). *The artist in the machine: The World of AI-Powered Creativity.* MIT Press.

Mishra, P., & Koehler, M. J. (2006). Technological Pedagogical Content Knowledge: A Framework for Teacher Knowledge. *Teachers College Record, 108*(6), 1017–1054. DOI: 10.1111/j.1467-9620.2006.00684.x

Mohamed, S., Png, M. T., & Isaac, W. (2020). Decolonial AI: Decolonial theory as sociotechnical foresight in artificial intelligence. *Philosophy & Technology*, *33*, 659–684. https://link.springer.com/article/10.1007/s13347-020-00405-8

Mohammed, S. P., & Hossain, G. (2024). ChatGPT in Education, Healthcare, and Cybersecurity: Opportunities and Challenges. *2024 IEEE 14th Annual Computing and Communication Workshop and Conference, CCWC 2024*. https://doi.org/DOI: 10.1109/CCWC60891.2024.10427923

Montenegro-Rueda, M., Fernández-Cerero, J., Fernández-Batanero, J. M., & López-Meneses, E. (2023). Impact of the implementation of ChatGPT in education: A systematic review. *Computers*, *12*(8), 1–13. DOI: 10.3390/computers12080153

Moonsamy, M., Nkomo, S., & Matli, W. (2022). New Education Technologies in Higher Education: E-Leadership Perspectives on South African Student Learning During and Post-Covid Reality. *International Conference on Multidisciplinary Research 2022*(20), 241-249. [Accessed 07 May, 2025] https://doi.org/DOI: 10.26803/MyRes.2022.20

Morandini, S., Fraboni, F., De Angelis, M., Puzzo, G., Giusino, D., & Pietrantoni, L. (2023). The impact of artificial intelligence on workers' skills: Upskilling and reskilling in organisations. Informing Science. *The International Journal of an Emerging Transdiscipline*, *26*, 39–68. https://www.informingscience.org/Publications/5078

Moreno-Guerrero, A. J., López-Belmonte, J., Marín-Marín, J. A., & Soler-Costa, R. (2020). Scientific development of educational artificial intelligence in Web of Science. *Future Internet*, *12*, 124–124.

Morgan, D. L. (1996). Focus Groups. *Annual Review of Sociology*, *22*(1), 129–152. DOI: 10.1146/annurev.soc.22.1.129

Mouratoglou, N. (2018). LEGO®, Learning, And Facilitation: A Reflective Approach. *International Journal of Management and Applied Research*, *5*(4). Advance online publication. Retrieved April 07, 2025, from. DOI: 10.18646/2056.54.18-021

Muñoz, C. B., Nanclares, N. H., Zamorano, L. R. M., & Sánchez, J. A. L. (2023). *Gamification and Design Thinking in Higher Education Case Studies for Instructional Innovation in the Economics Classroom* (1st ed.). Routledge Taylor Francis Group.

Murphy, R. S., Wotley, D., & Minn, D. (2023). Integrating ChatGPT into the EFL classroom: Benefits and challenges. *Center for Fundamental Education*, *40*, 97–166.

Musa, H. G., Fatmawati, I., Nuryakin, N., & Suyanto, M. (2024). *Marketing research trends using technology acceptance model (TAM): a comprehensive review of research (2002–2022)*. https://doi.org/DOI: 10.1080/23311975.2024.2329375

Muthuswamy, P. R. (2022). *New age education models: Innovation and reform in the 21st century*. Notion Press.

Nagel, L., Karras, O., Amiri, S. M., & Schneider, K. (2024). Turning asynchronicity into an opportunity: Asynchronous communication for shared understanding with vision videos. *Requirements Engineering*, *29*(1), 49–71.

Naik, I., Naik, D., & Naik, N. (2024, July). Investigating the benefits and barriers of using AI chatbots in education. In *The International Conference on Computing, Communication, Cybersecurity & AI* (pp. 510-524). Cham: Springer Nature Switzerland. Can be accessed at https://www.techrxiv.org/doi/pdf/10.36227/techrxiv.173121417.72328214

Nami, F., Marandi, S. S., & Sotoudehnama, E. (2018). Interaction in a discussion list: An exploration of cognitive, social, and teaching presence in teachers' online collaborations. *ReCALL*, *30*(3), 375–398.

Namjildorj, O. (2025). The requirements of integrating soft skills into higher education curricula within the context of transformative education. International Journal of Learning. *Teaching and Educational Research, 24*(3), 725–739. DOI: 10.26803/ijlter.24.3.34

Narváez, P. A. H., Herrera, M. G. M., Herrera, M. R. M., & Cruz, M. E. C. (2025). Didáctica inteligente: aplicaciones de la inteligencia artificial en la enseñanza y evaluación educativa. *Polo del Conocimiento, 10*(3), 187-208. https://polodelconocimiento.com/ojs/index.php/es/article/view/9048

Nascimento-Fragoso, M. D. J., & Coutinho, D. J. G. (2025). Inteligência artificial no apoio à educação personalizada: Potencialidades e desafios. *Revista Ibero-Americana de Humanidades. Ciência & Educação (Bauru), 11*(4), 2509–2523. https://periodicorease.pro.br/rease/article/view/18748

Navarro, J. Á. M. (2024). Optimizando el aprendizaje: examinando el impacto de la inteligencia artificial en DreamBox Learning y Knewton. *Revista Electrónica Investigamos, 1*(2), 100-117. https://revistainvestigamos.com/ojs/index.php/home/article/view/16

Nemorin, S. (2024). Towards decolonising the ethics of AI in education. *Globalisation, Societies and Education*, •••, 1–13. DOI: 10.1080/14767724.2024.2333821

Nguyen, K. V. (2025). The Use of Generative AI Tools in Higher Education: Ethical and Pedagogical Principles. *Journal of Academic Ethics*. Advance online publication. DOI: 10.1007/s10805-025-09607-1

Ní Ríordáin, M., & O'Donoghue, J. (2009). The relationship between performance on mathematical word problems and language proficiency for students learning through the medium of Irish. *Educational Studies in Mathematics, 71*(1), 43–64. DOI: 10.1007/s10649-008-9158-9

Nikhil, V., Annamalai, R., & Jayapal, S. (2025). NLP-Driven Approaches to Automated Essay Grading and Feedback. In Adopting Artificial Intelligence Tools in Higher Education (pp. 99-117). CRC Press.

Nikou, S. A., Guliya, A., Van Verma, S., & Chang, M. (2024). A generative artificial intelligence empowered chatbot: System usability and student teachers' experience. In Intelligent Tutoring Systems: 20th International Conference, ITS 2024, Thessaloniki, Greece, June 10–13, 2024, Proceedings (pp. 330–340). Springer. https://doi.org/DOI: 10.1007/978-3-031-63028-6_27

Noble, S. U. (2018). *Algorithms of oppression: How Search Engines Reinforce Racism*. NYU Press.

Nofemela, F. R., & Winberg, C. (2020). The relevance of Kaizen-based work-readiness training for South African University of Technology students. *The Journal for Transdisciplinary Research in Southern Africa, 16*(1), 1–2. Retrieved April 23, 2025, from. DOI: 10.4102/td.v16i1.729

Noonia, A., Beg, R., Patidar, A., Bawaskar, B., Sharma, S., & Rawat, H. (2024). Chatbot vs Intelligent Virtual Assistance (IVA). *Conversational Artificial Intelligence*, 655-673. DOI: DOI: 10.1002/9781394200801.ch36

Novo Nordisk Foundation. (2024). Open Discovery Innovation Network (ODIN). Retrieved from https://novonordiskfonden.dk/en/projects/open-discovery-innovation-network-odin/

Nupen, D. M., & Jagernath, J. (2024). Digital Integration Insights: Exploring Highlights and Challenges of Numeracy Lecturers in Higher Education. *International Conference on Education Research 1(*1):254-262. [Accessed 23 April, 2025] https://doi.org/DOI: 10.34190/icer.1.1.2834

Nwosu, L. I., Berengb, M. C., Segotsoa, T., & Blessing, E. N. (2023). Fourth Industrial Revolution Tools to Enhance the Growth and Development of Teaching and Learning in Higher Education Institutions: A Systematic Literature Review in South Africa. *Research in Social Sciences and Technology*, *8*(1), 57–59. Retrieved May 02, 2025, from. DOI: 10.46303/ressat.2023.4

O'Brien, S., & Davenport, C. (2024). Embedding the service user voice to co-produce UK mental health nurse education—A lived experience narrative. *Journal of Psychiatric and Mental Health Nursing*, *31*(5). Advance online publication. DOI: 10.1111/jpm.13031

OECD. (2018). *The future of education and skills: Education 2030 framework.* OECD Publishing. https://www.oecd.org/education/2030-project/

OECD. (2021). The future of education and skills 2030: OECD learning compass 2030. https://www.oecd.org/education/2030-project/

OECD. (2023). *OECD digital education outlook 2023: Towards an effective education ecosystem* [White paper]. OECD Publishing. https://doi.org/DOI: 10.1787/c74f03de-en

Öncü, S. E., & Süral, İ. (2024). Leveraging AI for Enhanced Support: Satisfaction Levels of Users Utilizing Virtual Assistant in Open Education. *Asian Journal of Distance Education, 19*(1). Can be accessed at https://www.asianjde.com/ojs/index.php/AsianJDE/article/download/778/428

Oreopoulos, P., & Petronijevic, U. (2023). The Promises and Pitfalls of Using (Mostly) Low-Touch Coaching Interventions to Improve College Student Outcomes. *Economic Journal (London), 133*(656), 7–15. Retrieved April 24, 2025, from. DOI: 10.1093/ej/uead064

Ouyang, F., & Zhang, L. (2024). AI-driven learning analytics applications and tools in computer-supported collaborative learning: A systematic review. *Educational Research Review*, *44*, 100616.

Oyelere, S. S., Suhonen, J., & Sutinen, E. (2016). M-learning: A new paradigm of learning ICT in Nigeria. *International Journal of Interactive Mobile Technologies*, *10*(1). Advance online publication. DOI: 10.3991/ijim.v10i1.4872

Page, M. J., McKenzie, J. E., Bossuyt, P. M., Boutron, I., Hoffmann, T. C., Mulrow, C. D., Shamseer, L., Tetzlaff, J. M., Akl, E. A., Brennan, S. E., & Chou, R. (2021). The PRISMA 2020 statement: An updated guideline for reporting systematic reviews. *British Medical Journal*, *372*. Advance online publication. DOI: 10.1136/bmj.n71

Pandey, R., & Sharma, P. (2025). *The Effectiveness of Vedic Mathematics on Problem Solving Ability of Students at Middle Level*. https://doi.org/DOI: 10.51584/IJRIAS.2025.100600146

Panigrahi, C. M. A. (2020). Use of artificial intelligence in education. *Management Accounting (London)*, *55*, 64–67. DOI: 10.1371/journal.pone.0229596

Pappagallo, S. (2024). Chatbots in education: A dual perspective on innovation and ethics. *Journal of Digital Pedagogy, 3*(1), 3-10. Can be accessed at https://www.researchgate.net/profile/Sergio-Pappagallo/publication/379984812_Chatbots_in_Education_A_Dual_Perspective_on_Innovation_and_Ethics/links/66cdeb9764f7bf7b1944c83e/Chatbots-in-Education-A-Dual-Perspective-on-Innovation-and-Ethics.pdf

Paris, S. G., & Newman, R. S. (1990). Development Aspects of Self-Regulated Learning. *Educational Psychologist*, *25*(1), 87–102. DOI: 10.1207/s15326985ep2501_7

Park, S. (2020). The Effects of a Web-Based Tool with Reading and Cognitive Procedural Scaffolds on Algebra Learning Among Low-And-High-Achieving Readers and its Evaluation from Teachers' Perspectives (Doctoral dissertation).

Patel, R., Bajaj, P., Kumar, A., Kumari, A., Rai, V., & Kumar, S. (2023). *ChatGPT in the classroom: A comprehensive review of the impact of ChatGPT on modern education*. 2023 11th International Conference on Intelligent Systems and Embedded Design (ISED), 1–6. https://doi.org/DOI: 10.1109/ISED59382.2023.10444568

Patel, K. (2024). Ethical reflections on data-centric AI: balancing benefits and risks. *Available at SSRN* 4993089.

Perrotta, C., & Selwyn, N. (2020). Deep learning goes to school: Toward a relational understanding of AI in education. *Learning, Media and Technology*, *45*, 251–269.

Pervez, N., Mahmood, W., Akram, M., & Waqas, M. (2024). Analyzing the alignment between university curriculum and job market requirements in Pakistan: Challenges and opportunities. *Indus Journal of Social Sciences*, *2*(2), 397–410. DOI: 10.59075/ijss.v2i2.269

Pfau, A., Polio, C., & Xu, Y. (2023). Exploring the potential of ChatGPT in assessing L2 writing accuracy for research purposes. *Research Methods in Applied Linguistics*, *2*(3), 100083. DOI: 10.1016/j.rmal.2023.100083

Phillips, A., Pane, J. F., Reumann-Moore, R., & Shenbanjo, O. (2020). Implementing an adaptive intelligent tutoring system as an instructional supplement. *Educational Technology Research and Development*, *68*(3), 1409–1437.

Piaget, J. (2005). *The Psychology of Intelligence*. Routledge.

Planas, N. (2014). One speaker, two languages: Learning opportunities in the mathematics classroom. *Educational Studies in Mathematics*, *87*(1), 51–66. DOI: 10.1007/s10649-014-9553-3

Plonsky, L., & Oswald, F. L. (2014). How big is "big"? Interpreting effect sizes in L2 research. In *Language learning,* (Vol. 64, pp. 878-912). https://www.doi.org/10.1111/lang.12079

Popenici, S. A. D., & Kerr, S. (2017). Exploring the impact of artificial intelligence on teaching and learning in higher education. *Research and Practice in Technology Enhanced Learning*, *12*(1), 22. DOI: 10.1186/s41039-017-0062-8 PMID: 30595727

Potgieter, I., Coetzee, M., & Ferreira, N. (2023). University students' digital world of work readiness in relation to their employability competency. *Journal of Learning Development in Higher Education*, *27*. Advance online publication. Retrieved April 07, 2025, from. DOI: 10.47408/jldhe.vi27.922

Pradhan, M., & Panda, R. (2014). High speed multiplier using Nikhilam Sutra algorithm of Vedic mathematics. *International Journal of Electronics*, *101*(3), 300–307. DOI: 10.1080/00207217.2013.780298

Prensky, M. (2006). Listen to the natives. *Educational Leadership*, *63*(4), 8–13. https://eric.ed.gov/?id=EJ745468

Prensky, M. (2008). Backup Education? Too many teachers see education as preparing kids for the past, not the future. *Educational Technology*, *48*, 1–3.

Provost, F., & Fawcett, T. (2013). *Data science for business: What you need to know about data mining and data-analytic thinking*. O'Reilly Media.

Qian, L., Li, W., Feng, Q., & Li, L. (2024). The Effect of Generative Artificial Intelligence on Students' Academic Achievement: A Meta-analysis. *2024 International Conference on Intelligent Education and Intelligent Research (IEIR)*, 1–5. https://doi.org/DOI: 10.1109/IEIR62538.2024.10960226

Qin, F., Li, K., & Yan, J. (2020). Understanding user trust in artificial intelligence-based educational systems: Evidence from China. *British Journal of Educational Technology*, *51*, 1693–1710. DOI: 10.1111/bjet.12994

Qutieshat, A. (2025). *Artificial Intelligence in Higher Education: A Contemporary Examination of Illich's Theories*. Springer Nature.

Raheem, B. R., Anjum, F., & Ghafar, Z. N. (2023). Exploring the profound impact of artificial intelligence applications (Quillbot, Grammarly and ChatGPT) on English academic writing: A Systematic Review. [IJIR]. *International Journal of Integrative Research*, *1*(10), 599–622. DOI: 10.59890/ijir.v1i10.366

Rahim, M. A. (2023). *Managing conflict in organizations*. Routledge.

Rahman, M. K., Ismail, N. A., Hossain, M., & Hossen, M. M. (2025). Students' mindset to adopt AI chatbots for the effectiveness of online learning in higher education. *Future Business Journal*, *11*(1), 30. DOI: 10.1186/s43093-025-00459-0

Raihan, M. M. H., Subroto, S., Chowdhury, N., Koch, K., Ruttan, E., & Turin, T. C. (2024). *Dimensions and barriers for digital (in) equity and digital divide: A systematic integrative review*. Digital Transformation and Society.

Rathod, K. (2023). *A review of ChatGPT in promoting teaching and learning*. International Journal of Scientific Research in Engineering and Management., DOI: 10.55041/ijsrem24976

Ravenor, R. Y. (2023). AI-Based Facial Emotion Recognition Solutions for Education:A Study of Teacher-User and Other Categories. arXiv preprint arXiv:2308.15119. https://www.oajaiml.com/uploads/archivepdf/827742122.pdf?utm_source=chatgpt.com

Rawas, S. (2023). ChatGPT: Empowering lifelong learning in the digital age of higher education. *Education and Information Technologies*, *29*, 6895–6908. DOI: 10.1007/s10639-023-12114-8

Ray, S., & Sikdar, D. P. (2024). AI-Driven flipped classroom: Revolutionizing education through digital pedagogy. *Psychology (Irvine, Calif.)*, *7*(2), 169–179.

Razak, M. A., Kumar, M. M., Nirmala, C. R., Naseer, R., Prashanth, B. S., & Sneha, H. R. (2024, August). Enhancing Student Support with AI: A College Assistance Chatbot Using NLP and ANN. In *2024 Second International Conference on Networks, Multimedia and Information Technology (NMITCON)* (pp. 1-8). IEEE. Can be accessed at https://www.scribd.com/document/771718552/2024206868

Rennie, L. J., Stocklmayer, S., & Gilbert, J. K. (2019). *Supporting self-directed learning in science and technology beyond the school years*. Taylor & Francis.

Reyes, R. S., & Torres, S. C. S. (2024). Socratic method in the use of web tools. *American Journal of Management Science and Engineering*, *9*(4), 75–83. http://ajmgtse.org/article/10.11648/j.ajmse.20240904.11

Rezigalla, A. A. (2024). AI in medical education: Uses of AI in construction type A MCQs. *BMC Medical Education*, *24*(1). Advance online publication. DOI: 10.1186/s12909-024-05250-3

Rizvi, N. (2024). *From Chalkboards to Chatbots: The Role of Generative AI in Education*. Can be accessed at https://www.researchgate.net/profile/Nusrat-Rizvi-2/publication/382143399_From_Chalkboards_to_Chatbots_The_Role_of_Generative_AI_in_Education/links/668f1675b15ba559074f6bd0/From-Chalkboards-to-Chatbots-The-Role-of-Generative-AI-in-Education.pdf

Rizvi, I., Bose, C., & Tripathi, N. (2025). Transforming Education: Adaptive Learning, AI, and Online Platforms for Personalization. In *Technology for Societal Transformation: Exploring the Intersection of Information Technology and Societal Development* (pp. 45–62). Springer Nature Singapore.

Robinson, L., Cotten, S. R., Ono, H., Quan-Haase, A., Mesch, G., Chen, W., & Stern, M. J. (2015). Digital inequalities and why they matter. *Information Communication and Society*, *18*(5), 569–582. DOI: 10.1080/1369118X.2015.1012532

Roca, M. D. L., Chan, M. M., Garcia-Cabot, A., Garcia-Lopez, E., & Amado-Salvatierra, H. (2024). The impact of a chatbot working as an assistant in a course for supporting student learning and engagement. *Computer Applications in Engineering Education, 32*(5), e22750. Can be accessed at https://onlinelibrary.wiley.com/doi/pdf/10.1002/cae.22750

Roll, I., & Wylie, R. (2016). Evolution and revolution in artificial intelligence in education. *International Journal of Artificial Intelligence in Education*, *26*, 582–599. DOI: 10.1007/s40593-016- 0110-3

Romero, C., & Ventura, S. (2020). Educational data mining and learning analytics: An updated survey. *Wiley Interdisciplinary Reviews. Data Mining and Knowledge Discovery*, *10*(3), e1355. DOI: 10.1002/widm.1355

Rudolph, J., Tan, S., & Tan, S. (2023). ChatGPT: Bullshit spewer or the end of traditional assessments in higher education? *Journal of Applied Learning and Teaching*, *6*(1), 9. Advance online publication. DOI: 10.37074/jalt.2023.6.1.9

Ruiz-Rojas, L. I., Salvador-Ullauri, L., & Acosta-Vargas, P. (2024). Collaborative working and critical thinking: Adoption of generative artificial intelligence tools in higher education. *Sustainability*, *16*(13), 5367. https://www.mdpi.com/2071-1050/16/13/5367

Russell, S., & Norvig, P. (2020). *Artificial intelligence: A modern approach* (4th ed.). Pearson.

Rusydiana, A. S. (2024). Alternative Waqf Model for SDG-4 (Quality Education). *The Economic Review of Pesantren*, *2*(2). Advance online publication. DOI: 10.58968/erp.v2i2.370

Ryan, E., & Poole, C. (2019). Impact of virtual learning environment on students' satisfaction, engagement, recall, and retention. *Journal of Medical Imaging and Radiation Sciences*, *50*(3), 408–415.

Rym, L. (2024). *Exploring the Student s Perception on Use of Artificial Intelligence Writing Programs in Writing Essay: The Case of Third Year English foreign language students at Biskra University*. Can be accessed at http://archives.univ-biskra.dz/bitstream/123456789/29066/1/Laouni_Rym.pdf

Ryu, M., & Han, S. (2018). The educational perception of artificial intelligence by elementary school teachers. *J. Korean Assoc. Inform. Educ.*, *22*, 317–324. DOI: 10.1016/j.ridd.2019.01.002

Safkolam, R., Ahmad Zaky El Islami, R., & Sari, I. J. (2023). The Effects of Jigsaw Technique on Learning Achievement and Retention of Science Teacher Students. *Shanlax International Journal of Education*, *11*(2), 37–42.

Sajja, R., Sermet, Y., Cikmaz, M., Cwiertny, D., & Demir, I. (2024). Artificial intelligence-enabled intelligent assistant for personalized and adaptive learning in higher education. *Information, 15*(10), 596. Can be accessed at https://www.mdpi.com/2078-2489/15/10/596

Sajja, R., Sermet, Y., Cikmaz, M., Cwiertny, D., & Demir, I. (2023). Artificial intelligence-enabled intelligent assistant for personalized and adaptive learning in higher education. *Information (Basel)*, *15*, 596. DOI: 10.3390/info15100596

Sales, A. C., & Pane, J. F. (2021). Student log-data from a randomized evaluation of educational technology: A causal case study. *Journal of Research on Educational Effectiveness, 14*(1), 241–269. https://www.tandfonline.com/doi/abs/10.1080/19345747.2020.1823538

Saqr, R. R., Al-Somali, S. A., & Sarhan, M. Y. (2024). Exploring the acceptance and user satisfaction of AI-driven e-learning platforms (Blackboard, Moodle, Edmodo, Coursera and edX): An integrated technology model. *Sustainability, 16*(1), 204.

Sareen, S., & Mandal, S. (2024). Challenges of blended learning in higher education across global north-south: A systematic and integrative literature review. *Social Sciences & Humanities Open, 10*, 1–10. Retrieved March 31, 2025, from. DOI: 10.1016/j.ssaho.2024.101011

SARI, T., NAYİR, F., & BOZKURT, A. (2024). Reimagining education: Bridging artificial intelligence, transhumanism, and critical pedagogy. *Journal of Educational Technology and Online Learning*, *7*(1). Advance online publication. DOI: 10.31681/jetol.1308022

Sarker, I. H. (2021). Data Science and Analytics: An Overview from Data-Driven Smart Computing, Decision-Making and Applications Perspective. *SN Computer Science*, *2*(5). Advance online publication. DOI: 10.1007/s42979-021-00765-8

Saro, N., Muhiddin, N. I., Anwar, N. S. S., Karim, N. A., & Hisham, N. A. B. (2024). Analysis of Correlation Factors on The Effectiveness of Design Thinking Mindset Reflection. [IJRISS]. *International Journal of Research and Innovation in Social Science*, *8*(3). Advance online publication. Retrieved April 23, 2025, from. DOI: 10.47772/IJRISS.2024.803421S

Scatiggio, V. (2020). Tackling the issue of bias in artificial intelligence to design ai-driven fair and inclusive service systems. How human biases are breaching into ai algorithms, with severe impacts on individuals and societies, and what designers can do to face this phenomenon and change for the better.

Schleicher, A. (2018). Educating learners for their future, not our past. *ECNU Review of Education, 1*(1), 58-75. https://journals.sagepub.com/doi/full/10.30926/ecnuroe2018010104

Seibert, A., Aldave de las Heras, L., Boboridis, K., Colineau, E., Eloirdi, R., Fontana, C. L., Hult, M., Jenet, A., Michailidou, E., Nilsson, K. F., Paradela, C., Raison, P., Schillebeeckx, P., & Taucer, F. (2024). The nuclear research infrastructures open access scheme of the Joint Research Centre (JRC) at the European Commission – Contributions to education, training, mobility and scientific excellence. *Nuclear Engineering and Design, 420*. Advance online publication. DOI: 10.1016/j.nucengdes.2024.113000

Selwyn, N. (2019). *Should robots replace teachers? AI and the future of education.* John Wiley & Son.

Selwyn, N. (2019). *Should robots replace teachers? AI and the future of education.* Polity Press.

Selwyn, N. (2019). *Should robots replace teachers?: AI and the future of education.* John Wiley & Sons.

Senger, E., Zhang, M., van der Goot, R., & Plank, B. (2024, March). Deep learning-based computational job market analysis: A survey on skill extraction and classification from job postings. In Proceedings of the First Workshop on Natural Language Processing for Human Resources (NLP4HR 2024) (pp. 1–15). Association for Computational Linguistics.

Setati, M. (2005). Teaching Mathematics in a Primary Multilingual Classroom. *Journal for Research in Mathematics Education, 36*(5), 447–466.

Sevilla, C. G., Punsalan, T. G., Rovira, L. G., & Vendivel, F. G. (2006). *General psychology with values development lesson.* Rex Book Store, Inc.

Sezgin, S., & Fırat, M. (2024). Exploring the Digital Divide in Open Education: A Comparative Analysis of Undergraduate Students. *International Review of Research in Open and Distance Learning, 25*(1). Advance online publication. DOI: 10.19173/irrodl.v25i1.7236

Sfard, A., Nesher, P., Streefland, L., Cobb, P., & Mason, J. (1998). Learning Mathematics through Conversation: Is It as Good as They Say? *FLM Publishing Association, 18*(1), 41–51.

Sfard, A., & Kieran, C. (2001). Cognition as Communication: Rethinking Learning-by-Talking Through Multi-Faceted Analysis of Students' Mathematical Interactions. *Mind, Culture, and Activity, 8*(1), 42–76. DOI: 10.1207/S15327884MCA0801_04

Shabani, K., Khatib, M., & Ebadi, S. (2010). Vygotsky's zone of proximal development: Instructional implications and teachers' professional development. *English Language Teaching, 3*(4), 237–248.

Shafik, W. (2023). Introduction to ChatGPT. In *Advanced Applications of Generative AI and Natural Language Processing Models*. https://doi.org/DOI: 10.4018/9798369305027.ch001

Shafik, W. (2024a). Enhancing AI-Enabled Education Through Mobile Learning and Bring Your Own Device (BYOD) Integration. In *Exploring Youth Studies in the Age of AI* (pp. 140–173). IGI Global.

Shafik, W. (2024b). Generative AI for Social Good and Sustainable Development. In *Generative AI: Current Trends and Applications* (pp. 185–217). Springer.

Shafik, W. (2024c). Mobile Learning and Bring Your Own Device (BYOD): Enhancing Education in the Digital Age. In *Integrating Cutting-Edge Technology Into the Classroom* (pp. 240–267). IGI Global.

Shafik, W. (2025). Human-Computer Interaction (HCI) Technologies in Socially-Enabled Artificial Intelligence. In *Future of Digital Technology and AI in Social Sectors* (pp. 121–150). IGI Global.

Shafik, W. (2024d). *Towards Trustworthy and Explainable AI Educational Systems*., DOI: 10.1007/978-3-031-72410-7_2

Shaikh, S. (2024). Peer Teaching for Peer Learning and Sharing: A study on students' attitudes towards implementing peer teaching and learning in the ESL classroom at the University of Technology and Applied Sciences. *International Journal of English Language Teaching, 15*(5), 9–10. Retrieved April 05, 2025, from. DOI: 10.37745/ijelt.13/vol12n5117

Shalev-Shwartz, S., & Ben-David, S. (2014). *Understanding machine learning: From theory to algorithms*. Cambridge University Press.

Sharma, P. (2024). Faculty competences development components: An integrated model for the development of educational leaders in technical education institutes. *International Journal of Educational Management, 38*(2). Advance online publication. DOI: 10.1108/IJEM-07-2023-0363

Sharma, W., Lim, W. M., Kumar, S., Verma, A., & Kumra, R. (2024). Game on! A state-of-the-art overview of doing business with gamification. *Technological Forecasting and Social Change, 198*, 122988. Retrieved May 06, 2025, from. DOI: 10.1016/j.techfore.2023.122988

Sheikh, H., Prins, C., & Schrijvers, E. (2023). Artificial intelligence: definition and background. In Mission, A. I. (Ed.), *The new system technology* (pp. 15–41). Springer.

Shelton, K., & Lanier, D. (2024). The promises and perils of AI in education: Ethics and Equity Have Entered the Chat. *Lanier Learning*, 2024. ISBN 9798990840508

Shepard, L. A. (2000). The role of assessment in a learning culture. *Educational Researcher*, *29*(7), 4–14. https://journals.sagepub.com/doi/abs/10.3102/0013189x029007004

Shi, L. (2025). Global perspectives on AI competence development: Analyzing national AI strategies in education and workforce policies. *Human Resource Development Review*, *24*(1), 123–145. DOI: 10.1177/15344843251332360

Shohel, M. M. C., Ashrafuzzaman, M., Azim, F., Naomee, I., Rahman, M. S., & Siddik, M. A. B. (2022). *Blended learning space for primary and secondary education: Challenges and opportunities in resource-constrained contexts. Designing effective distance and blended learning environments in K-12*. IGI Global Scientific Publishing., DOI: 10.4018/978-1-7998-6829-3.ch012

Sikora, Y. B., Usata, O. Y., Mosiiuk, O. O., Verbivskyi, D. S., & Shmeltser, E. O. (2021). Approaches to the choice of tools for adaptive learning based on highlighted selection criteria. *CTE Workshop Proceedings*, *8*, 398–410. https://doi.org/DOI: 10.55056/cte.296

Silitonga, L. M., Hawanti, S., Aziez, F., Furqon, M., Zain, D. S. M., Anjarani, S., & Wu, T. T. (2023, August). The impact of AI chatbot-based learning on students' motivation in English writing classroom. *International Conference on Innovative Technologies and Learning* (pp. 542-549). Cham: Springer Nature Switzerland.

Simon, N. O. (2024). Participatory Design Thinking: A User-Centered Approach to Computer Science Innovation. *European Journal of Information Technologies and Computer Science*, *4*(3). Advance online publication. Retrieved May 10, 2025, from. DOI: 10.24018/compute.2024.4.3.125

Slamet, T., Brush, T., & Kwon, K. (2024). The Effects of Competition in Gamified Online Discussions on Learners' Behavioural and Cognitive Engagement. *Technology. Knowledge and Learning*, *30*, 1–27. Retrieved May 06, 2025, from. DOI: 10.1007/s10758-024-09740-7

Snekha, S., & Ayyanathan, N. (2023). An Educational CRM Chatbot for Learning Management System. *Shanlax International Journal of Education*, *11*(4), 58–62. DOI: 10.34293/education.v11i4.6360

Sohail, S. S., Farhat, F., Himeur, Y., Nadeem, M., Madsen, D. Ø., Singh, Y., Atalla, S., & Mansoor, W. (2023). Decoding ChatGPT: A taxonomy of existing research, current challenges, and possible future directions. *Journal of King Saud University. Computer and Information Sciences*, *35*(8), 101675.

Songsiengchai, S., Sereerat, B. O., & Watananimitgul, W. (2023). Leveraging artificial intelligence (AI): ChatGPT for effective English language learning among Thai students. *English Language Teaching*, *16*(11), 1–68. DOI: 10.5539/elt.v16n11p68

Sonmez Unal, D., Solovey, E., Arrington, C. M., & Walker, E. (2025). Modeling the phases of rule learning during problem solving with an interactive learning environment. *User Modeling and User-Adapted Interaction*, *35*(1), 7.

Sowa, K., Przegalinska, A., & Ciechanowski, L. (2021). Cobots in knowledge work: Human–AI collaboration in managerial professions. *Journal of Business Research*, *125*, 135–142. DOI: 10.1016/j.jbusres.2020.11.038

Stampfl, R., Ivkić, I., & Geyer, B. (2024). Role-playing simulation games using ChatGPT. *ERCIM News*, *136*, 14–15. DOI: 10.48550/arXiv.2402.09161

Stebbins, R. A. (2001). *Exploratory research in the social sciences: What is exploration? 48, 1-14*. Sage Publications., DOI: 10.4135/9781412984249

Steiss, J., Tate, T., Graham, S., Cruz, J., Hebert, M., Wang, J., Moon, Y., Tseng, W., Warschauer, M., & Olson, C. B. (2024). Comparing the quality of human and ChatGPT feedback of students' writing. *Learning and Instruction*, *91*, 101894. Advance online publication. DOI: 10.1016/j.learninstruc.2024.101894

Storey, V. A., & Wagner, A. (2024). Integrating artificial intelligence (ai) into adult education: opportunities, challenges, and future directions. *International Journal of Adult Education and Technology (IJAET)*, *15*(1), 1-15. Can be accessed at https://www.igi-global.com/viewtitle.aspx?titleid=345921

Sudirman, A., Gemilang, A. V., Kristanto, T. M. A., Robiasih, H., Hikmah, I., Nugroho, A. D., Karjono, J. C. S., Lestari, T., Widyarini, T. L., & Prastanti, A. D. (2024). Reinforcing Reflective Practice through Reflective Writing in Higher Education: A Systematic Review. *International Journal of Learning. Teaching and Educational Research*, *23*(5). Advance online publication. Retrieved April 07, 2025, from. DOI: 10.26803/ijlter.23.5.24

Suh, S., Bang, J., & Han, J. W. (2025). Developing Critical Thinking in Second Language Learners: Exploring Generative AI like ChatGPT as a tool for Argumentative Essay Writing. arXiv preprint arXiv:2503.17013. https://arxiv.org/pdf/2503.17013

Sundari, M. S., Penthala, H. R., & Nayyar, A. (2024). Transforming education through AI-enhanced content creation and personalized learning experiences. In *Impact of artificial intelligence on society* (pp. 98–118). Chapman and Hall/CRC.

Sutcliffe, R. (2024). *The Fourth Civilization, Volume Two: Technology, Ethics, and Society*. Wipf and Stock Publishers.

Su, Y., Lin, Y., & Lai, C. (2023). Collaborating with ChatGPT in argumentative writing classrooms. *Assessing Writing*, *57*, 1–11. DOI: 10.1016/j.asw.2023.100752

Swart, K., Bond-Barnard, T., & Chugh, R. (2022). Challenges and critical success factors of digital communication, collaboration and knowledge sharing in project management virtual teams: A review. *International Journal of Information Systems and Project Management*, *10*(4), 84–103.

Tallvid, M. (2016). Understanding teachers' reluctance to the pedagogical use of ICT in the 11th grade classroom. *Education and Information Technologies*, *21*, 503–519. DOI: 10.1007/s10639-014-9335-7

Tao, W. (2025). Fostering Inspirational Learning Through AI-Enhanced Formative Assessment: Strategies and Challenges in Higher Education. *Educational Assessments in the Age of Generative AI*, 207-250. Can be accessed at https://www.researchgate.net/profile/Tao-Wu-119/publication/387721559_Fostering_Inspirational_Learning_Through_AI-Enhanced_Formative_Assessment/links/67cbadeecc055043ce6f3f1f/Fostering-Inspirational-Learning-Through-AI-Enhanced-Formative-Assessment.pdf

Tasdelen, O., & Bodemer, D. (2025). Generative AI in the Classroom: Effects of Context-Personalized Learning Material and Tasks on Motivation and Performance. *International Journal of Artificial Intelligence in Education*. Advance online publication. DOI: 10.1007/s40593-025-00491-9

Taylor, E. W. (2009). Fostering transformative learning. In Mezirow, J., & Taylor, E. W. (Eds.), *Transformative learning in practice: Insights from community, workplace, and higher education* (pp. 3–17). Jossey-Bass.

Teddlie, C., & Tashakkori, A. (2009). *Foundations of mixed methods research: Integrating quantitative and qualitative approaches in the social and behavioral sciences*. Sage Publications.

Teng, M. F. (2024). A Systematic Review of ChatGPT for English as a Foreign Language Writing: Opportunities, Challenges, and Recommendations. *International Journal of TESOL Studies*, *6*(3), 36–57. DOI: 10.58304/ijts.20240304

Teräs, M. (2022). Education and technology: Key issues and debates. *International Review of Education*, *68*(4), 635–636. DOI: 10.1007/s11159-022-09971-9

Third, A., Livingstone, S., & Lansdown, G. (2025). Recognizing children's rights in relation to the digital environment: challenges of voice and evidence, principle and practice. In B. Wagner, M. C. Kettemann, K. Vieth-Ditlmann & S. Montgomery (Eds.), *Research Handbook on Human Rights and Digital Technology* (pp. 325-360). Edward Elgar Publishing.

Tibingana-Ahimbisibwe, B., Willis, S., Catherall, S., Butler, F., & Harrison, R. (2022). A systematic review of peer-assisted learning in fully online higher education distance learning programmes. *Open Learning*, *37*(3), 251–272. DOI: 10.1080/02680513.2020.1758651

Tick, A., Toktosunova, A., Fallah, H., Toutouchi, Z., & Tadzhibaeva, Z. (2023). The Impact of ChatGPT on Learning in Higher Education–Results of a Pilot Study. *Practice and Theory in Systems of Education*, *18*(1), 31–50.

Tirtha, S. B. K. Bhāratīkr̥sh atīrtha, & Agrawala, V. S. (1992). *Vedic Mathematics*. Motilal Banarsidass Publishing House.

Tolba, E. G. A., & Al-Osaimi, A. M. (2023). The effectiveness of using the model-based thinking strategy in developing first-grade high school students' physical concepts and inquiry thinking skills. *Eurasia Journal of Mathematics, Science and Technology Education*, *19*(4), 8–10. Retrieved May 10, 2025, from. DOI: 10.29333/ejmste/13111

Tomczak, M., & Tomczak, E. (2014). The need to report effect size estimates revisited. An overview of some recommended measures of effect size. *Trends in Sport Sciences*, *1*, 19–25.

Topping, K. J. (2005). Trends in peer learning. *Educational Psychology*, *25*(6), 631–645. DOI: 10.1080/01443410500345172

Trevallion, D., & Nischang, L. C. (2021). The creativity revolution and 21 st century learning. International Journal of Innovation, Creativity and Change, 15(8), 1-25. https://www.ijicc.net/images/Vol_15/Iss_8/15800_Trevallion_2021_E_R.pdf

Treve, M. (2024). Integrating Artificial Intelligence in Education: Impacts on student learning and innovation. *International Journal of Vocational Education and Training Research*, *10*(2), 61–69. DOI: 10.11648/j.ijvetr.20241002.14

U.S. Department of Education. (2025). Protecting Student Privacy: FERPA. Retrieved July 2025.

UNESCO (2023). *ChatGPT and artificial intelligence in higher education: Quick start guide*, 1-14.

UNESCO. (2019). Beijing consensus on artificial intelligence and education. In International Conference on Artificial Intelligence and Education, Planning Education in the AI Era: Lead the Leap. https://scholar.google.com/scholar_lookup?title=Beijing+Consensus+on+Artificial+Intelligence+and+Education&author=UNESCO&publication_year=2019

UNESCO. (2019). *Global education monitoring report: Migration, displacement, and education – Building bridges, not walls*. UNESCO. https://www.unesco.org/gem-report/en/migration

UNESCO. (2021). *Reimagining our futures together: A new social contract for education*. UNESCO Publishing. International Commission on the Futures of Education. https://doi.org/ https://unesdoc.unesco.org/ark:/48223/pf0000379707.locale=enDOI: 10.54675/ASRB4722

UNESCO. (2022). Reimagining our futures together: A new social contract for education. https://unesdoc.unesco.org/ark:/48223/pf0000379707

UNESCO. (2023). Digital learning holds great promise to transform education, but its benefits are not evenly distributed. https://www.unesco.org/en/articles/unesco-spotlights-how-digital-learning-can-promote-equity-low-resource-contexts

UNESCO. (2023). Ethics of Artificial Intelligence in Education. UNESCO. https://unesdoc.unesco.org/ark:/48223/pf0000380455

UNESCO. (2023). Global education monitoring report 2023: Technology in education. https://unesdoc.unesco.org/ark:/48223/pf0000385723

UNESCO. (2023). Guidance for generative AI in education and research. United Nations Educational, Scientific and Cultural Organization. https://unesdoc.unesco.org/ark:/48223/pf0000386693

UNESCO. (2023). SDG Resources for Educators: Quality Education. https://en.unesco.org/themes/education/sdgs/material/04

UNICEF. (2024). Adolescent development and participation in the Syrian Arab Republic. Retrieved from https://www.unicef.org/syria/adolescent-development-and-participation

VanLEHN, K. (2011). The Relative Effectiveness of Human Tutoring, Intelligent Tutoring Systems, and Other Tutoring Systems. *Educational Psychologist*, *46*(4), 197–221. DOI: 10.1080/00461520.2011.611369

VanLehn, K. (2011). The relative effectiveness of human tutoring, intelligent tutoring systems, and other tutoring systems. *Educational Psychologist, 46*(4), 197–221. https://www.tandfonline.com/doi/abs/10.1080/00461520.2011.611369

Vardakosta, E., Priniotakis, G., Papoutsidakis, M., Sigala, M., Tsikritsis, A., & Nikolopoulos, D. (2023). Design Thinking as a Co-Creation Methodology in Higher Education. A Perspective on the Development of Teamwork and Skill Cultivation. *European Journal of Educational Research, 12*(2), 1030–1031. Retrieved April 23, 2025, from. DOI: 10.12973/eu-jer.12.2.1029

Varlamov, O. (2021). "Brains" for Robots: Application of the Mivar expert systems for implementation of autonomous intelligent robots. *Big Data Research, 25*, 100241.

Varona Cervantes, C., & Cooper, R. (2022). Labor Market Implications of Education Mismatch. *European Economic Review, 148*, 104179. DOI: 10.1016/j.euroecorev.2022.104179

Vartanian, A. M. (2024). Fostering Environmental Responsibility in U.S. K-12 Education: A Comparative Study of Strategies Integrating STEM. *Journal of Advanced Research in Education, 3*(1). Advance online publication. DOI: 10.56397/jare.2024.01.05

Veeramachaneni, V. (2025). Large language models: A comprehensive survey on architectures, applications, and challenges. *Advanced Innovations in Computer Programming Languages, 7*(1), 20–39.

Wadsworth, L. M., Husman, J., Duggan, M. A., & Pennington, M. N. (2007). Online Mathematics Achievement: Effects of Learning Strategies and Self-Efficacy. *Journal of Developmental Education, 30*(3), 6–14.

Wahed, S., & Pitterson, N. (2024). Empowering Diverse Learners: Embracing Culturally Relevant Pedagogy (CRP) in Engineering, Higher Education, and K-12 Settings. *Lecture Notes in Networks and Systems, 901 LNNS*. https://doi.org/DOI: 10.1007/978-3-031-53022-7_20

Walton, E. (2023). Why inclusive education falters: A Bernsteinian analysis. *International Journal of Inclusive Education, 29*(4). Advance online publication. Retrieved April 23, 2025, from. DOI: 10.1080/13603116.2023.2241045

Wang, Q., Woo, H. L., Quek, C. L., Yang, Y., & Liu, M. (2011). Using the Facebook group as a learning management system: An exploratory study. *British Journal of Educational Technology, 43*(3), 428–438. DOI: 10.1111/j.1467-8535.2011.01195.x

Wardat, Y., Tashtoush, M. A., AlAli, R., & Jarrah, A. M. (2023). ChatGPT: A revolutionary tool for teaching and learning mathematics. *Eurasia Journal of Mathematics, Science and Technology Education, 19*(7), em2286. Advance online publication. DOI: 10.29333/ejmste/13272

Weber, A., Meyer, B., & Schmidt, R. (2024). Enhancing legal writing skills: The impact of formative feedback in a hybrid intelligence learning environment. *British Journal of Educational Technology, 55*(2), 215–233. DOI: 10.1111/bjet.13560

Weidener, L., & Fischer, M. (2024). Artificial Intelligence in Medicine: Cross-Sectional Study Among Medical Students on Application, Education, and Ethical Aspects. *JMIR Medical Education, 10*(1). Advance online publication. DOI: 10.2196/51247

Weinberg, A., & Wiesner, E. (2011). Understanding mathematics textbooks through reader-oriented theory. *Educational Studies in Mathematics, 76*(1), 49–63. DOI: 10.1007/s10649-010-9264-3

Wenger-Trayner, E., Wenger-Trayner, B., Reid, P., & Bruderlein, C. (2023). *Communities of practice within and across organisations: a guidebook.* Social Learning Lab. https://www.wenger-trayner.com/wp-content/uploads/2024/03/24-02-21-CoP-guidebook-second-edition-final-2.pdf

Whitaker, T. (2020). *What great teachers do differently: Nineteen things that matter most.* Routledge.

Wiliam, D., Fisher, D., & Frey, N. (2024). *Student assessment: Better evidence, better decisions, better learning*. Corwin Press.

Williamson, B. (2015). Political computational thinking: Policy networks, digital governance and 'learning to code'. *Critical Policy Studies, 10*(1), 39–58. DOI: 10.1080/19460171.2015.1052003

Williamson, B., & Eynon, R. (2020). Historical threads, missing links, and future directions in AI in education. *Learning, Media and Technology, 45*(3), 223–235.

Williamson, B., Eynon, R., Knox, J., & Davies, H. (2023). Critical perspectives on AI in education: Political economy, discrimination, commercialization, governance and ethics. In du Boulay, B., Mitrovic, A., & Yacef, K. (Eds.), *Handbook of artificial intelligence in education* (pp. 553–570). Edward Elgar Publishing., https://www.elgaronline.com/edcollchap/book/9781800375413/book-part-9781800375413-37.xml

Wilson, K. E. S., & Millar, P. (2021). Intramural sport participation: An examination of participant benefits, service quality, program satisfaction, and student retention. *Recreational Sports Journal*, *45*(2), 149–160.

Winstone, N., Bourne, J., Medland, E., Niculescu, I., & Rees, R. (2021). "Check the grade, log out": Students' engagement with feedback in learning management systems. *Assessment & Evaluation in Higher Education*, *46*(4), 631–643.

Woolf, B. P., Lane, H. C., Chaudhri, V. K., & Kolodner, J. L. (2013). AI grand challenges for education. *AI Magazine*, *34*(4), 66–84. DOI: 10.1609/aimag.v34i4.2490

World Bank. (2020). The COVID-19 pandemic: Shocks to education and policy responses. https://www.worldbank.org/en/topic/education/publication/the-covid19-pandemic-shocks-to-education-and-policy-responses

World Economic Forum. (2023). The future of jobs report 2023. https://www.weforum.org/reports/the-future-of-jobs-report-2023

Wyonch, R. (2020). Work-ready graduates: The role of co-op programs in labour market success. C.D. Howe Institute. https://cdhowe.org/publication/work-ready-graduates-role-co-op-programs-labour-market-success

Yan, L., Sha, L., Zhao, L., Li, Y., Martinez-Maldonado, R., Chen, G., Li, X., Jin, Y., & Gašević, D. (2024). Practical and ethical challenges of large language models in education: A systematic scoping review. In *British Journal of Educational Technology* (Vol. 55, Issue 1). https://doi.org/DOI: 10.1111/bjet.13370

Yan, D. (2023). Impact of ChatGPT on learners in a L2 writing practicum: An exploratory investigation. *Education and Information Technologies*, *28*(11), 13943–13967. DOI: 10.1007/s10639-023-11742-4

Yang, , LLi, , R. (2024). ChatGPT for L2 learning: Current status and implications. *System, 124*, 103351. https://doi.org/10.1016/j.system.2024.103351

Yang, Z. (2024). Revisiting Educational Issues in the Age of Generative Artificial Intelligence. *Journal of Contemporary Educational Research*, *8*(1). Advance online publication. DOI: 10.26689/jcer.v8i1.5810

Yan, J., Tian, H., Sun, X., & Song, L. (2025). Role of artificial intelligence in enhancing competency assessment and transforming curriculum in higher vocational education. *Frontiers in Education*, *10*, 1551596. DOI: 10.3389/feduc.2025.1551596

Yekollu, R. K., Bhimraj Ghuge, T., Sunil Biradar, S., Haldikar, S. V., & Farook Mohideen Abdul Kader, O. (2024, February). AI-driven personalized learning paths: Enhancing education through adaptive systems. In *International Conference on Smart data intelligence* (pp. 507-517). Singapore: Springer Nature Singapore. https://doi.org/DOI: 10.1007/978-981-97-3191-6_38

Yeo, S., Moon, J., & Kim, D.-J. (2024). Editorial: Transforming mathematics education with AI: Innovations, implementations, and insights. *The Mathematics Educator*, *63*, 387–392. DOI: 10.7468/mathedu.2024.63.2.387

Yi, H., Liu, T., & Lan, G. (2024). The key artificial intelligence technologies in early childhood education: A review. *Artificial Intelligence Review*, *57*(1). Advance online publication. DOI: 10.1007/s10462-023-10637-7

Yildiz, T. A. (2023). The impact of ChatGPT on language learners' motivation. *Journal of Teacher Education and Lifelong Learning*, *5*(2), 582–597. DOI: 10.51535/tell.1314355

Yim, I. H. Y., & Su, J. (2024). Artificial intelligence (AI) learning tools in K-12 education: A scoping review. *Journal of Computers in Education*. Advance online publication. DOI: 10.1007/s40692-023-00304-9

Zadorozhnyy, A., & Lai, W. Y. (2024). ChatGPT and L2 written communication: A game-changer or just another tool? *Languages (Basel, Switzerland)*, *9*(1), 5. DOI: 10.3390/languages9010005

Zaidi, T., & Faisal, S. (2018). An overview: Various attacks in VANET. *2018 4th International Conference on Computing Communication and Automation (ICCCA)*, 1–6.

Zawacki-Richter, O., Marín, V. I., Bond, M., & Gouverneur, F. (2019). Systematic review of research on artificial intelligence applications in higher education – where are the educators? *International Journal of Educational Technology in Higher Education*, *16*(1), 1–27. https://link.springer.com/content/pdf/10.1186/s41239-019-0171-0.pdf

Zawacki-Richter, O., Marín, V. I., Bond, M., & Gouverneur, F. (2019). Systematic review of research on artificial intelligence applications in higher education—Where are the educators? *International Journal of Educational Technology in Higher Education*, *16*(1), 39. Advance online publication. DOI: 10.1186/s41239-019-0171-0

Zayoud, M., Oueida, S., Awad, P., & Ionescu, S. (2023). *Impact of ChatGPT on education: Challenges and opportunities*. Towards Increased Business Resilience: Facing Digital Opportunities and Challenges. https://doi.org/DOI: 10.56177/11icmie2023.18

Zhan, C., Joksimović, S., Ladjal, D., Rakotoarivelo, T., Marshall, R., & Pardo, A. (2024). Preserving both privacy and utility in learning analytics. *IEEE Transactions on Learning Technologies*, *17*, 1615–1627.

Zhang, M. (2024). Computational Job Market Analysis: with Natural Language Processing.

Zhang, Z., Gao, J., Dhaliwal, R. S., & Li, T. J.-J. (2023). VISAR: A human-AI argumentative writing assistant with visual programming and rapid draft prototyping. *In Proceedings of the 36th Annual ACM Symposium on User Interface Software and Technology* (Article No. 5, pp. 1–30). Association for Computing Machinery. https://doi.org/DOI: 10.1145/3586183.3606800

Zhang, K., & Aslan, A. B. (2021). AI technologies for education: Recent research & future directions. *Computers and Education: Artificial Intelligence*, *2*, 100025–100025.

Zhang, Y., Adams, D., & Lee, K. C. S. (2024). Assessing academic staff's ICT integration in higher education: Instrument development and validation. *Journal of Computers in Education*, *11*(1). Advance online publication. DOI: 10.1007/s40692-022-00248-6

Zhang, Y., & Maconochie, M. (2022). A meta-analysis of peer-assisted learning on examination performance in clinical knowledge and skills education. *BMC Medical Education*, *22*(1), 147. DOI: 10.1186/s12909-022-03183-3

Zhao, Y., Chen, Q., Zhou, X., & Cheng, G. (2024). Integrating AI Tools into Instructed Second Language Acquisition. *Exploring Artificial Intelligence in Applied Linguistics*, 9-235.

Zhou, X. (2025). *Embodied interactions with data, algorithms, and ethics in AI learning experiences for children* [Doctoral thesis, University of Rochester]. ProQuest Dissertations Publishing. https://www.proquest.com/openview/2a66cf8379f5e4a17d25221a13f67714/1?cbl=18750&diss=y&pq-origsite=gscholar

Zickafoose, A., Ilesanmi, O., Diaz-Manrique, M., Adeyemi, A. E., Walumbe, B., Strong, R., Wingenbach, G., Rodriguez, M. T., & Dooley, K. (2024). Barriers and Challenges Affecting Quality Education (Sustainable Development Goal #4) in Sub-Saharan Africa by 2030. *Sustainability*, *16*(2657), 5–17. Retrieved April 11, 2025, from. DOI: 10.3390/su16072657

Zimmerman, B. J. (2002). Becoming a Self-Regulated Learner: An Overview. *Theory into Practice*, *41*(2), 64–70. DOI: 10.1207/s15430421tip4102_2

Zimmerman, J. (2006). Why some teachers resist change and what principals can do about it. *NASSP Bulletin*, *90*, 238–249. DOI: 10.1177/0192636506291521

Zou, M., & Huang, L. (2023). The impact of ChatGPT on L2 writing and expected responses: Voice from doctoral students. *Education and Information Technologies*, *29*, 13201 – 13219. DOI: 10.1007/s10639-023-12397-x

Zylfijaj, K., & Shaqiri, M. (2024). The Role of Vocational Education and Training in Bridging the Skills Gap in the Labor Market. Paper presented at the UBT International Conference on Management, Business and Economy. Retrieved from https://www.researchgate.net/publication/382250381_The_Role_of_Vocational_Education_and_Training_in_Bridging_the_Skills_Gap_in_the_Labor_Market

About the Contributors

Reda M. S. Abdelaal (registered member of the Egyptian Syndicate for Professional Engineers) received a B.S. in Mechanical Engineering from Helwan University, Cairo, Egypt, in 1979; an M.Eng. degree in Operations Research from the same university in 1982; and a Ph.D. degree in Industrial Engineering from the School of Industrial Technology, Bradford University, England, in 1986. Since 1986, he has worked as an Assistant Professor, Associate Professor, and Full Professor with the Department of Production Engineering, College of Engineering, Helwan University, Cairo, Egypt. His bibliography is included in Marquis Who's Who in the World (14th ed., 1997). In 2000, he joined King Abdulaziz University (KAU) as a Full Professor with the Department of Industrial Engineering, College of Engineering. He was the Director of the College Academic Accreditation Unit (AAU) from 2004 to 2007 and an active member of the College Accreditation Support Unit from May 2007 to 2021. He was the manager of the Strategic Planning Unit at the Vice-Presidency for Business and Knowledge Creativity from 2017 to 2021. He also held the position of Distinguished Adjunct Professor at King Abdulaziz University from August 2021 to December 2023. He has been recognized as an IDEAL Scholar by the Accreditation Board for Engineering and Technology (ABET, USA) and earned 21 professional development hours from ABET. Dr. Abdelaal has participated in constructing and implementing strategic planning for several public and private organizations, and he has been involved in more than 30 training programs both inside and outside Egypt, including in Arab and foreign countries. He has served as an investigator/co-investigator for more than 35 funded projects and has received over 20 appreciation certificates from different sectors. Dr. Abdelaal was a Distinguished Adjunct Professor at AlMaarefa University from July 2023 to June 2024 and currently serves as an independent researcher based in Egypt. In 2025, he contributed a book chapter titled "The Strategic Transformation Journey of AlMaarefa University: Navigating New Horizons" as part of the book "Navigating Quality Assurance and Accreditation in Global Higher Education," published by

IGI Global. His research interests and publications cover areas such as operations research, system analysis and design, strategic planning, industrial scheduling models, engineering education, multi-criteria decision-making, assessment, and accreditation subjects.

Mustafa Kayyali, Ph.D. is an ardent advocate for excellence in higher education, driven by a relentless pursuit of quality, recognition, and innovation. As the Manager of HE Higher Education Ranking, he leads initiatives that play a crucial role in shaping the landscape of academia. Having earned a Master's in Quality Management and Evaluation in Higher Education from Universitat Oberta de Catalunya, followed by a Ph.D. in Quality Management from Azteca University, his academic pursuits have laid a strong foundation for his expertise in Accreditation, Quality Assurance, and Higher Education Rankings. Dr. Kayyali has made significant contributions to academic literature, boasting more than 50 published papers and 20 book chapters. Additionally, he takes pride in his role as a translator, having translated 5 books, thus bridging language gaps and promoting knowledge exchange on a global scale. In recognition of his expertise, Dr. Kayyali holds key affiliations with esteemed institutions. He is privileged to be a part of the British Accreditation Council's Accreditation Committee, the Slovenian Quality Assurance Agency as an International Expert, and the Agency for Control and Quality Assurance of Higher Education AKOKVO as an Accreditation Expert. His international engagements also include being an expert for the Kosovo Accreditation Agency KAA and the ECBE - European Council for Business Education, as well as serving as a Lead Auditor at the Centre of Assessments for Excellence (COAE). Dr. Kayyali has also submitted a patent to USPTO about rankings entitled Holistic & Multidimensional Ranking Methodology for Universities. As an entrepreneur, researcher, translator, and publisher, Dr. Kayyali is deeply involved in various facets of the academic world. His diverse interests encompass Management, Translation, Interpretation, and Academic Consulting, contributing to a well-rounded understanding of the industry.

***

Nurul Ajleaa binti Abdul Rahman is a Head Centre of Studies at the Academy of Language Studies, Universiti Teknologi MARA (Terengganu, Malaysia). She received the Ph.D degree in TESL from Universiti Kebangsaan Malaysia (UKM), in 2017. She has more than 15 years of teaching experience. She is currently teaching several English language proficiency courses. Her interests are Technology Innovations in Education, ESL Writing Skills, ESL Oral Communication Skills, Education, Social Sciences and Innovative Teaching and Learning.

Nurul Ain Chua Binti Abdullah is a Senior Lecturer at Universiti Malaysia Terengganu (UMT), where she focuses on teaching Mandarin as a foreign language to non-native learners. She is actively involved in research related to Mandarin language acquisition and educational technology in language learning. Dr. Nurul Ain has over 30 years of experience in education and has taught at various levels, from primary to tertiary. She has presented her research at numerous national and international conferences. Her research interests include technology-enhanced language learning, language pedagogy, and differentiated instruction.

Aitor Garcés-Manzanera is an Assistant Professor (tenure-track) in the Department of Didactics of Language and Literature at the University of Murcia (UMU), teaching English language education across Education degrees. He earned a PhD in Applied Linguistics at UMU, plus an MA in Theoretical and Applied Linguistics and an MA in English Language Teaching. He previously worked at Universidad del Atlántico Medio (UNAM) as Director of the MA in Teaching Spanish as a Foreign Language (ELE), and since 2020 has taught Academic English at University of the People. He is a member of the LA_L2 research group and has participated in six nationally funded projects (SENECA, MINECO, AEI). His research examines language skills, especially writing, in face-to-face and computer-mediated settings. He has published in outlets including Espiral, SSLLT, Miscelánea, JNAER, and LTRQ, and has co-authored books with IGI Global, Dykinson, and EditUM, with forthcoming volumes with Springer and Nova Science.

Mohammad Ishrat received his PhD in Computer Science and Engineering from India. He is currently an Associate Professor in the School of Computing Science and Engineering at VIT Bhopal University, Madhya Pradesh, India. He has over 23 years of academic and research experience, including international teaching and research appointments at King Abdul-Aziz University, Saudi Arabia, and the University of Technology and Applied Sciences, Oman. His research interests include artificial intelligence, machine learning, deep learning, software security, and anomaly detection. He has published extensively in SCI/Scopus-indexed journals, holds Indian and UK patents, and actively serves as a reviewer for leading international journals, including IEEE Access and IOS Press venues.

Nilesh Kumar is an accomplished academician and professional with over 11 years of blended experience in academics and corporate sectors. He is currently serving as a Teaching Assistant and Senior Academic Coordinator at Amity University Jharkhand, where he has been contributing since 2017. He holds dual Master's degrees in Marketing Management and International Business, alongside a Master's in Data Analytics, and is presently pursuing his Ph.D. in Marketing from Sikkim Alpine University. His professional journey includes rich exposure to academic administration, curriculum coordination, classroom teaching, digital learning systems (LMS), and student development. He also has notable corporate experience in sales and logistics with organizations and has held faculty roles at institutions. Mr. Kumar has actively participated in national and international conferences, FDPs, and seminars, and has several research papers and book chapters published under reputed platforms, including Scopus and IGI Global. He is also the author of the book "Glimpse of Communication" and has certifications in Power BI and IBM Data Analytics.A certified online virtual classroom trainer (Avenu – SNHU), he combines his expertise in marketing and data analytics to create an engaging and insightful learning environment. His interests lie in digital marketing, rural entrepreneurship, retail strategy, and education technology.

Anil Kumar Nayak, an Assistant Professor of English at CHRIST (Deemed to be University), Delhi NCR, is a dedicated academic with a PhD in English Language Education from the English and Foreign Languages University (EFLU), Hyderabad. He also holds a B.Ed. (English) and M.Ed. from EFLU, and an M.Phil. in English Language Studies from the University of Hyderabad. His research interests include learner-centred pedagogy, bilingual education, multilingual classrooms, and strategies to support underperforming learners in higher education. Dr. Nayak is a prolific writer, regularly presenting papers at national and international conferences, publishing research in peer-reviewed journals, and editing volumes. His work engages with issues in language education, critical thinking, and curriculum development. As an academic, he teaches various courses, including academic and research writing, business and corporate communication, critical thinking, and language pedagogy. Beyond his academic pursuits, Dr. Nayak is deeply committed to community-based initiatives, including awareness sessions on wildlife conservation and the protection of Ramsar sites, showcasing his social responsibility and engagement.

Gareth Paul is a dedicated academic and emerging researcher with a strong focus on pedagogies, gamification, and innovative approaches to impactful education. His scholarly interests lie in exploring how creative, student-centered teaching strategies can enhance engagement, deepen understanding, and contribute to long-term employability in higher education. With experience in teaching, curriculum design, and academic leadership, Gareth bridges theory and practice by grounding research in real classroom application.

Aradhana Ramnund-Mansingh is the Manager of the Business School at MANCOSA and a Research Fellow at the University of the Free State. A prolific scholar, she has published widely in books and peer-reviewed journals, with research that critically interrogates gender, decolonisation, and the socio-historical constructs of education in South Africa. Her expertise as a human resources practitioner spans organisational transformation, talent management, and corporate culture, with a particular focus on gendered workplace dynamics, including the queen bee syndrome and the persistence of old boys' networks. Prof. Ramnund-Mansingh is frequently featured as an academic expert across print, radio, and television media.

Jessica Ruiz Quiñonero Graduate in Translation and Interpreting (English-Spanish) from the University of Murcia, with a Master's degree in English Language Teaching. Passionate about cross-cultural communication and language education.

Dania Sagheer, PhD PhD in Artificial Intelligence | Master in Artificial Intelligence | BSc in Informatics Engineering, University of Aleppo Dr. Dania Sagheer is a lecturer at Al-Shaab Private University. Her research focuses on natural language processing, especially Arabic text comprehension and summarization. She has published multiple papers in AI and NLP and has experience training and mentoring in robotics and AI applications for children and adolescents, as well as conducting professional workshops.

Wasswa Shafik (Member, IEEE) received a Bachelor of Science degree in information technology from Ndejje University, Uganda, a Master of Engineering degree in Information Technology (Computer and Communication Networks) from Yazd University, Iran, and a PhD in Computer Science with the School of Digital Science, Universiti Brunei Darussalam, Brunei Darussalam. He is also the Founder and Research Director of the Dig Connectivity Research Laboratory (DCRLab) after serving as a Research Associate at the Network Interconnectivity Research Laboratory at Yazd University. Prior to this, he worked as a Community Data Analyst at Population Services International (PSI-Uganda), a Community Data Officer at the Programme for Accessible Health Communication (PACE-Uganda), a Research Assistant at the Socio-Economic Data Centre (SEDC-Uganda), Uganda, an Assistant Data Officer at TechnoServe, Kampala, Uganda, and Asmaah Charity Organization as Cheif Executive Officer. He has hundreds of publications with renowned publishers. His research interests include Artificial Intelligence, Neural Networks, Computer Vision, Smart Agriculture, Digital Health, and Green Computing.

Panchalingam Suntharalingam is the Associate Professor for International Partnerships and Recruitment at the Birmingham School of Architecture and Design at Birmingham City University. He is also the Course Director for MA Design and Visualisation at Birmingham City University. Dr Suntharalingam has developed and taught both undergraduate and postgraduate courses in Design and Visualisation, Product Design, Interior Architecture and Design in the UK, India, Hong Kong and

China. Dr Suntharalingam's areas of expertise and interests include Design and Visualisation, Engineering Product Design, Knowledge Transfer Partnership (KTP) programmes, Software Programming, Medical Product Design, Interior Products, applied Research, Rapid Prototyping, and Computer-Aided Design (CAD). Dr Suntharalingam has extensive design and scientific knowledge in interdisciplinary fields and holds a patent for a medical product that has sold over 50,000 in the USA and over 8000 in the UK. He has published numerous international papers on medical products and is well known for opening computer-generated imagery (CGI) title sequences featured on BBC and ITV networks such as 'Top Gear'. His wealth of experience with the manufacturing industry includes 20 'Knowledge Transfer Partnerships (KTP)', with blue chip companies such as AGA Rangemaster, gaining four 'Outstanding' Innovate UK awards for achievement in innovation. In 2020, one of his KTPs was shortlisted for the Best of the Best KTPs in the United Kingdom. He is also an external examiner at various national and international universities for undergraduate, postgraduate, and PhD candidates.

Sabina Valente Adjunct Professor at Polytechnic Institute of Portalegre. Member of CARE - Research Center on Health and Social Sciences, Portalegre; and collaborator at Research Center in Education and Psychology (CIEP), University of Évora, Portugal.

Goh Ying Soon is a senior lecturer and he currently teaches Mandarin as the third language to non-native learners in MARA University of Technology, Malaysia. He is a member of the International Society for Chinese Language Teaching. He has experiences in teaching Mandarin at primary, secondary and tertiary level for more than 25 years. He has been actively presenting papers in national and international conferences. His research interests are on the use of educational technology in Mandarin teaching and learning, web-based instruction, translation, and etc. Updated resume: click here (dropbox). Google Scholar record. researchgate, academia.edu, cnki, scopus (Author ID: 25925392000), book publication,

Ayushi Zina is an Assistant Professor at CHRIST (Deemed to be) University, Delhi, NCR. She has 8 years of teaching experience. She is pursuing her PhD from Ranchi University on the topic; 'Mythology in Popular Fiction: A Study of Select Works of Amish Tripathi and Ashwin Sanghi'. She has four books, two research papers, and eight book chapters to her credit. She has done her graduation and post-graduation in English literature from St. Xavier's College, Ranchi. Her research areas include, mythological studies, feminism, popular literature, gender studies, digital narratives. She is an avid reader and a dynamic speaker. She is a soft-skills expert and has been called as a soft-skills trainer by many prestigious institutions.

Index

A

Academic Education 307, 308, 309, 310, 311, 312, 313, 314, 315, 316, 317, 332
adaptive learning 9, 10, 22, 32, 36, 41, 47, 51, 53, 54, 56, 57, 63, 64, 82, 84, 85, 91, 92, 108, 109, 141, 170, 252, 257, 283, 284, 291, 292, 294, 296, 297, 298, 305, 306
Adaptive Learning Systems 9, 22, 56, 57, 109, 170
AI Advancements 117
AI chatbots 97, 222, 253, 256, 276, 277, 279, 280, 281, 282, 283, 288, 291, 292, 293, 295, 296, 298, 299, 301, 302, 304, 305, 306
AI in Education 14, 15, 21, 24, 27, 31, 32, 39, 47, 48, 49, 50, 51, 60, 66, 75, 77, 82, 83, 84, 86, 89, 90, 91, 100, 101, 103, 104, 106, 107, 108, 109, 110, 111, 123, 146, 172, 253, 254, 255, 258, 263, 269, 271, 272, 274, 276, 280, 296, 297, 298, 303, 304, 309, 313, 339, 340
AI-powered Tools 89, 94, 95, 96, 99, 104, 107, 293
Artificial Intelligence (AI) 1, 2, 4, 5, 9, 12, 15, 25, 26, 28, 29, 31, 32, 34, 36, 47, 49, 50, 51, 53, 54, 64, 81, 82, 83, 84, 85, 86, 87, 89, 90, 91, 96, 101, 108, 116, 122, 123, 124, 126, 134, 135, 136, 137, 138, 139, 142, 143, 146, 147, 149, 150, 172, 173, 174, 209, 219, 220, 221, 244, 245, 246, 247, 248, 251, 252, 253, 254, 255, 274, 275, 276, 277, 279, 280, 300, 301, 302, 304, 305, 306, 307, 308, 309, 311, 312, 314, 316, 318, 319, 320, 321, 322, 323, 325, 329, 330, 332, 333, 335, 337, 338, 339, 340, 341
automated feedback 10, 43, 58, 75, 87, 280, 281, 282, 283, 284, 285, 286, 306

B

bespoke learning tools 177, 201

C

Chatbot-Assisted Writing Task 220, 228, 230, 232, 233, 234, 239, 240, 249
ChatGPT 26, 27, 28, 59, 73, 84, 85, 96, 136, 148, 174, 219, 220, 221, 222, 223, 224, 225, 226, 227, 228, 229, 230, 231, 232, 233, 234, 235, 236, 237, 238, 239, 240, 241, 242, 243, 244, 245, 246, 247, 248, 249, 250, 252, 256, 259, 262, 263, 268, 272, 277, 300, 301, 302, 303, 306
Coaching 133, 177, 178, 179, 180, 181, 182, 183, 184, 186, 188, 189, 191, 196, 197, 198, 200, 201, 203, 204, 205, 206, 207, 209, 211, 214, 217, 218
Collaborative Learning 108, 109, 111, 140, 150, 151, 152, 154, 155, 157, 158, 159, 163, 164, 165, 166, 168, 170, 173, 180, 184, 186, 187, 203, 280
Critical Thinking 2, 6, 18, 19, 33, 53, 55, 58, 59, 68, 70, 71, 72, 74, 78, 84, 85, 87, 89, 90, 91, 95, 98, 100, 102, 103, 104, 105, 106, 107, 108, 111, 112, 113, 115, 118, 119, 120, 127, 130, 140, 144, 153, 158, 167, 171, 178, 183, 187, 188, 192, 193, 194, 195, 197, 198, 201, 221, 224, 227, 260, 262, 268, 270, 272, 285, 293, 294, 310, 313, 317
Curriculum Design 8, 21, 22, 48, 53, 54, 56, 68, 72, 151, 202, 284, 291, 292, 297, 316, 319, 323
Curriculum Development 49, 135, 297, 312, 321, 331

D

Data Analysis 8, 57, 60, 73, 89, 95, 99, 233, 259, 260, 262, 294, 296, 309, 318, 320
Digital Skills 57, 71, 73, 83, 261, 322, 332, 336

E

Educational Chatbots 58, 252, 254, 255, 257, 259, 260, 261, 263, 264, 266, 269, 270, 271, 273, 303
Educational Innovation 56, 198
Ethical Considerations 9, 23, 24, 89, 99, 100, 101, 102, 103, 109, 111, 112, 116, 118, 141, 151, 229, 262, 280, 285, 293, 298, 299, 313, 328, 329, 330, 335
Explainable AI 28, 70, 75, 79, 80, 82, 116, 150

F

Federated Learning 116, 150, 339
Foreign Language Teaching 219, 220, 221, 231, 245
Future of Education 1, 44, 51, 84, 85, 99, 200, 244, 299, 302, 306, 339, 340

G

Gamification 9, 18, 20, 21, 40, 127, 164, 172, 177, 178, 179, 180, 181, 182, 185, 186, 187, 188, 189, 190, 191, 192, 193, 194, 196, 197, 198, 200, 201, 202, 203, 204, 205, 206, 207, 208, 209, 210, 211, 212, 213, 214, 215, 217, 218
Generative Artificial Intelligence 25, 26, 29, 53, 84, 86, 122, 136, 137, 147, 245, 276, 337

H

Human-Computer Interaction 29, 146, 172

I

Immersive Learning 89, 140, 280, 289, 290, 298, 302, 303
Intelligent Tutoring Systems 1, 9, 32, 36, 39, 49, 50, 54, 56, 60, 62, 63, 65, 81, 85, 87, 90, 92, 104, 109, 135, 138, 139, 148, 163, 172, 252, 254, 257, 276, 312
Interdisciplinary Education 1, 2, 4, 5, 7, 8, 13, 23

L

Labor Market 48, 69, 307, 308, 309, 310, 311, 312, 313, 314, 315, 316, 317, 318, 319, 320, 321, 322, 323, 325, 326, 327, 330, 331, 332, 333, 334, 335, 341
LEGO-based learning 177, 178, 179, 180, 182, 187, 188, 189, 191, 193, 195, 197, 198, 200, 201, 202, 203, 204, 205, 207, 208, 218

M

Machine Learning 16, 20, 32, 39, 40, 46, 54, 64, 70, 91, 93, 99, 109, 112, 116, 122, 131, 137, 150, 172, 244, 252, 256, 274, 280, 316, 318, 319, 320, 321, 322, 323, 324, 325, 327, 329, 331, 333, 338, 340
Mathematics Education 125, 126, 127, 128, 129, 130, 135, 136, 137, 139, 142, 143, 146, 147, 148

N

Natural Language Processing 28, 32, 54, 91, 93, 96, 109, 112, 116, 149, 150, 159, 280, 296, 298, 306, 316, 318, 325, 331, 340, 341

P

peer teaching 154, 177, 178, 179, 180, 181, 182, 183, 184, 186, 188, 189, 191, 193, 196, 198, 199, 200, 201, 202, 205, 206, 207, 208, 210, 215, 218
personalized learning 1, 8, 11, 21, 31, 51, 54, 55, 63, 64, 65, 71, 87, 126, 138, 141, 147, 280, 282, 283, 284, 292, 295, 297, 298, 300, 301, 305, 306, 312, 322, 327

R

Reinforcement Learning 118, 149, 150, 159, 162
Research 1, 2, 3, 4, 5, 6, 8, 9, 10, 11, 12, 13, 14, 15, 16, 17, 18, 19, 20, 23, 24, 26, 27, 28, 29, 32, 49, 50, 56, 64, 65, 73, 81, 84, 85, 86, 89, 90, 98, 105, 107, 110, 113, 115, 117, 118, 119, 120, 122, 124, 128, 130, 133, 134, 147, 154, 155, 161, 168, 169, 170, 171, 172, 173, 174, 177, 181, 182, 183, 185, 187, 188, 189, 190, 191, 192, 197, 199, 200, 205, 206, 208, 210, 211, 212, 213, 214, 215, 216, 219, 220, 222, 223, 224, 225, 226, 227, 228, 229, 230, 231, 234, 235, 240, 241, 242, 243, 244, 245, 246, 247, 249, 252, 253, 254, 255, 256, 257, 259, 260, 270, 272, 274, 275, 276, 277, 286, 300, 301, 302, 303, 305, 312, 320, 322, 328, 329, 330, 337, 338, 339, 340, 341

S

Skills Gap 312, 313, 314, 316, 330, 333, 338, 341
Smart Curricula 54, 55, 56, 78, 79, 80
STEM Education 89, 94
Students' Perceptions 220, 228, 238, 239
student support 8, 255, 272, 280, 282, 283, 288, 289, 294, 295, 296, 298, 302, 304

T

Teachers' Perceptions 245, 274
Teaching Pedagogy 129, 130, 132
Teamwork 18, 93, 95, 98, 103, 112, 113, 117, 149, 150, 151, 152, 154, 163, 165, 166, 170, 178, 186, 187, 188, 212, 216, 218, 293, 310, 311, 332
Transformative Skills 53, 55, 56, 68, 69, 70, 72, 74, 87

U

User Satisfaction 174, 269

V

Vedic Mathematics 126, 127, 128, 129, 133, 134, 137, 138, 139, 140, 141, 142, 143, 144, 147, 148
Virtual Assistants 10, 54, 58, 69, 97, 98, 251, 253, 255, 256, 257, 259, 261, 263, 267, 268, 270, 273, 279, 280, 281, 282, 283, 288, 291, 292, 293, 295, 296, 298, 299, 301, 306
Virtual Learning Environments 64, 149, 150, 151, 173, 293
Virtual Tutors 89, 127, 302, 306

W

Writing Process 219, 220, 222, 223, 225, 227, 228, 230, 231, 232, 238, 239, 240, 249, 250

www.ingramcontent.com/pod-product-compliance
Lightning Source LLC
LaVergne TN
LVHW080909300926
849162LV00003B/609